D0776891

French-English, English-French Dictionary

French-English, English-French Dictionary

BROCKHAMPTON PRESS
LONDON

© 1995 Geddes & Grosset Ltd,
David Dale House, New Lanark, Scotland.

This edition published 1995 by Brockhampton Press,
a member of the Hodder Headline PLC Group

4 6 8 10 9 7 5 3

ISBN 1 86019 002 2

Printed and bound in the UK

	Abbreviations	**Abréviations**
abrev	abbreviation	abréviation
adj	adjective	adjectif
adv	adverb	adverbe
art	article	articule
auto	automobile	automobile
aux	auxiliary	auxiliaire
bot	botany	botanique
chem, chim	chemistry	chimie
col	colloquial term	expression familière
com	commerce	commerce
compd	compound	compound
comput	computers	informatique
conj	conjunction	conjonction
culin	culinary term	vocabulaire culinaire
excl	exclamation	exclamation
f	feminine noun	substantif fémenin
fam	colloquial term	expression familière
fig	figurative	figuré
geol	geology	géologie
gr	grammar	grammaire
imp	impersonal	impersonnel
inform	computers	informatique
interj	interjection	interjection
invar	invariable	invariable
irr	irregular	irrégulier
jur	law term	jurisprudence
law	law term	jurisprudence
ling	linguistics	linguistique
m	masculine noun	substantif masculin
mar	marine term	vocabulaire marin
mat, math	mathematics	matémathiques
med	medicine	médicine
mil	military term	vocabulaire militaire
mus	music	musique

n	noun	substantif
orn	ornithology	ornithologie
pej	pejorative	péjoratif
pl	plural	pluriel
pn	pronoun	pronom
poet	poetical term	vocabulaire poétique
pol	political term	vocabulaire politque
prep	preposition	préposition
rad	radio	radio
rail	railway	chemin de fer
sl	slang	argot
teat	theatre	théâtre
tec	technology	technologie
TV	television	télévision
vi	intransitive verb	verbe intransitif
vr	reflexive verb	verbe réfléchi
vt	transitive verb	verbe transitif
zool	zoology	zoologie

French-English

A

A

à *prép* (in)to; at; on; by, per:—**aller ~ l'école** to go to school.

abaisser *vt* to lower.

abandon *m* abandonment, desertion.

abandonner *vt to* abandon, leave.

abattement *m* despondency; exhaustion.

abattoir *m* abattoir, slaughterhouse.

abattu *adj* despondent; exhausted.

abbaye *f* abbey.

abcès *m* abscess.

abdomen *m* abdomen.

abeille *f* bee.

aberration *f* aberration.

abîmer *vt* spoil, damage.

abolir *vt* to abolish.

abolition *f* abolition.

abondamment *adv* abundantly.

abondance *f* abundance.

abondant *adj* abundant, plentiful.

abonder *vi* to be abundant *ou* plentiful.

abonné *m*, **-ée** *f*:—*adj* subscriber.

abonnement *m* subscription.

abonner **s'~** *vr* to subscribe, take out a subscription *(à* to).

abord *m*:—**d'~** first (of all).

aborder *vt* to approach.

aboutir *vi* to succeed.

aboutissement *m* outcome; success.

abréger *vt* to shorten; abridge.

abréviation *f* abbreviation.

abri *m* shelter.

abriter *vt* to shelter:—**s'~** *vr* to shelter.

abrupt *adj* abrupt:—**~ement** *adv* abruptly.

absence *f* absence.

absent *adj* absent.

absenter (s') *vr* to leave, go out.

absolu *adj* absolute:—**~ment** *adv* absolutely:—*m* absolute.

absorbant *adj* absorbent.

absorber *vt to* absorb.

absorption *f* absorption.

abstinence *f* abstinence.

abstrait *adj* abstract.

absurde *adj* absurd:—**~ment** *adv* absurdly.

absurdité *f* absurdity.

abus *m* abuse.

abuser *vt* **~ de** to exploit; abuse.

académie *f* academy.

accélérateur *m* accelerator.

accélération *f* acceleration.

accélérer *vi* to speed up, accelerate.

accent *m* accent.

accentuer *vt* to accentuate.

acceptable *adj* acceptable.

accepter *vt* to accept.

accès *m* access.

accessible *adj* accessible.

accident *m* accident.

accidentel *adj* accidental:—**~lement** *adv* accidentally.

accommodant *adj* accommodating.

accommoder *vt* to prepare; adapt.

accompagner *vt* to accompany.

accomplir *vt* to do, accomplish.

accomplissement *m* accomplishment.

accord *m* agreement:—**d'~!** okay!, all right!:—**être d'~** to agree.

accorder *vt* to give:—**s'~** *vr* to agree.

accoucher *vi* to give birth.

accrocher *vt* to hang up (*à* on).

accroissement *m* increase.

accroître *vt* to increase.

accueil *m* welcome, reception.

accueillir *vt* to welcome.

accumuler *vt* to accumulate.

accusation *f* accusation.

accusé *m*, **-ée** *f* accused, defendant.

accuser *vt* to accuse.

achat *m* purchase.

acheter *vt* to buy.

acheteur *m* **-euse** *f* buyer.

achèvement *m* completion.

achever *vt* to finish; complete.

acide *adj* acidic:—*m* acid.

acier *m* steel.

acoustique *adj* acoustic:—*f* acoustics.

acquérir *vt* to buy, purchase.

acrobate *mf* acrobat.

acte *m* act; deed.

acteur *m* **actrice** *f* actor.

actif *adj* active.

action *f* act, action; share.

activement *adv* actively.

activer *vt* to speed up.

activité *f* activity.

actualité *f*:—**l'~** current events.

actuel *adj* current, present:— **~lement** *adv* currently.

adaptable *adj* adaptable.

adaptation *f* adaptation.

adapter *vt* to adapt (*à* to):—**s'~** *vr* to adapt (*à* to).

addition *f* addition; bill.

adéquat *adj* suitable, appropriate.

adhérer *vi* to adhere, stick.

adhésif *adj* adhesive.

adjectif *m* adjective.

admettre *vt* to admit; accept; assume.

administrer *vt* to run; administer.

admirable *adj* admirable:-**ment** *adv* admirably, brilliantly.

admiration *f* admiration.

admirer *vt* to admire.

adolescence *f* adolescence.

adolescent *m*, **-e** *f* adolescent.

adopter *vt* to adopt.

adorer *vt* to adore, worship.

adrénaline *f* adrenalin.

adresse *f* address; skill.

adresser *vt* to address; send.

adroit *adj* deft, skilful:—**ement** *adv* deftly, skilfully.

adulte *mf* adult, grown-up:—*adj* adult, full-grown.

adversité *f* adversity.

aérodrome *m* aerodrome, airfield.

aéroport *m* airport.

affable *adj* affable.

affaiblir *vt* to weaken:—**s'~** *vr* to weaken, grow weaker.

affaire *f* matter.

affamé *adj* starving.

affamer *vt* to starve.

affection *f* affection.

affectueusement *adv* affectionately.

affectueux *adj* affectionate.

affermir *vt* to strengthen.

affiche *f* poster.

affiner *vt* to refine.

affirmatif *adj* affirmative.

affirmation *f* assertion.

affirmer *vt* to assert.

affluent *m* tributary.

affoler *vt* to throw into a panic:— **s'~** *vr* to get into a panic.

affréter *vt* to charter.

affreux *adj* horrible; awful.
afin *prép*:—— **de** (in order) to:——
que in order that.
africain *adj, mf* African.
Afrique *f* Africa.
âge *m* age:—**quel ~ as-tu?** how old
are you?
âgé *adj* old:—**~ de 10 ans** 10 years
old.
agence *f* agency; branch; offices.
agenda *m* diary.
agenouiller (s') *vr* to kneel (down).
agent *m* agent; policeman.
agglomération *f* town, urban area.
aggraver *vt* to make worse; increase.
agile *adj* agile, nimble:—**~ment** *adv*
nimbly.
agilité *f* agility.
agir *vi* to act.
agitation *f* agitation.
agiter *vt* to shake; wave:—**s'~** *vr* to
move about; fidget.
agneau *m* lamb.
agrandir *vt* to make bigger; to
widen; to expand.
agrandissement *m* enlargement.
agréable *adj* agreeable, pleasant.
agressif *adj* aggressive.
agression *f* attack.
agriculteur *m* farmer.
agriculture *f* agriculture, farming.
ahuri *adj* stunned; stupefied.
aide *f* help; aid;
aider *vt* to help.
aigle *m* eagle.
aigre *adj* sour, bitter:—**~ment** *adv*
sourly.
aigu *adj* (*f* **aiguë**) shrill; acute.
aiguille *f* needle.
ail *m* garlic.
ailleurs *adv* elsewhere:—**partout ~**

everywhere else:—**nulle part ~**
nowhere else:—**d'~** moreover; by
the way.
aimable *adj* kind:—**~ment** *adv*
kindly.
aimant *m* magnet.
aimer *vt* to love.
aîné *m*, **aînée** *f* eldest child:—*adj*
elder; eldest.
ainsi *adv* so, thus.
air *m* air:—**avoir l'~ content** to
look happy.
aire *f* area.
aisé *adj* easy; well-off:—**~ment** *adv*
easily.
ajouter *vt* to add.
ajuster *vt* to adjust.
alarme *f* alarm.
alarmer *vt* to alarm:—**s'~** *vr* to get
alarmed (*de* at, about).
album *m* album.
alcool *m* alcohol.
alentours *mpl* surroundings, neighbourhood.
alerte *adj* alert; agile:—*f* alarm,
alert.
alerter *vt* to alert; notify; warn.
algue *f* seaweed.
aligner *vt* to align, line up.
aliment *m* food.
alimenter *vt* to feed:—**s'~** *vr* to eat.
alinéa *m* paragraph.
allée *f* avenue; path.
alléger *vt* to make lighter; alleviate.
aller *vi* to go:—**comment allez-
vous?** how are you?:—**allons-y**
let's go:—**s'en aller** to go away,
leave:—*m* single ticket.
allergie *f* allergy.
alliance *f* alliance; marriage; wedding ring.
allô *excl* hello!

allocation f allocation; allowance.

allouer vt to allocate.

allumer vt to light; turn ou switch on.

allumette f match.

allure f speed; look.

alors adv then:—~ **que** while; whereas.

alphabet m alphabet.

alpiniste mf mountaineer.

altérer vt to change, alter.

alternatif adj alternate.

alternative f alternative.

altitude f altitude, height.

amabilité f kindness.

amaigrir vt to make thin.

amant m lover.

amas m pile, heap.

amasser vt to amass, pile up.

amateur m amateur; connaisseur.

ambassade f embassy.

ambassadeur m, **-drice** f ambassador.

ambiance f atmosphere.

ambigu adj, f **ambiguë** ambiguous.

ambitieux adj ambitious.

ambition f ambition.

ambulance f ambulance.

âme f soul.

amélioration f improvement.

améliorer vt to improve:—**s'~** vr to improve.

aménagement m fitting out; adjustment;development.

aménager vt to fit out; adjust; develop.

amener vt to bring.

amer adj bitter.

Américain m, **-e** f American.

américain adj American.

Amérique f America.

ameublement m furniture.

ami m, **-ie** f friend.

amical adj friendly:—~**ement** adv in a friendly manner.

amitié f friendship.

amnistie f amnesty.

amoindrir vt to weaken; reduce.

amorcer vt to bait; begin.

amortir vt to soften; deaden.

amour m love.

amoureux adj in love (de with).

amovible adj detachable.

amphibie adj amphibious.

ample adj roomy; wide.

ampleur f fullness; range.

amplifier vt to increase; amplify.

amusant adj amusing.

amuser vt to amuse.

an m year:—**avoir vingt ~s** to be 20 (years old).

analogie f analogy.

analphabète adj illiterate.

analyse f analysis; test.

analyser vt to analyse.

analyste mf analyst; psychoanalyst.

ananas m pineapple.

anarchie f anarchy.

anatomie f anatomy.

ancestral adj ancestral.

ancêtre m ancestor.

ancien adj old; former:—~**nement** adv formerly.

ancre f anchor.

âne m ass, donkey.

anecdote f anecdote.

anesthésie f anaesthetic; anaesthesia.

ange m angel.

Anglais m, **-e** f Englishman; Englishwoman.

anglais adj English:—m (ling) English.

angle m angle; corner.

Angleterre f England.

anglophone *adj* English-speaking:—*mf* English speaker.

angoisse f anguish.

animal m animal.

animation f animation.

animé *adj* busy; lively.

animosité f animosity.

anneau m ring.

année f year:—**les ~s soixante** the Sixties.

annexe f annexe:—*adj* subsidiary.

annexer *vt* to annex; append.

anniversaire m birthday:—**joyeux ~!** happy birthday!

annonce f advertisement; announcement.

annoncer *vt* to announce (*à* to).

annuaire m telephone directory, phone book.

annuel *adj* annual:—**~lement** *adv* annually.

annuler *vt* to cancel; nullify.

anomalie f anomaly.

anonyme *adj* anonymous; impersonal:—**~ment** *adv* anonymously.

anorexique *adj, mf* anorexic.

anormal *adj* abnormal:—**~ement** *adv* abnormally.

antagonisme m antagonism.

antenne f (*rad, tv*) aerial; (*zool*) feeler.

antérieur *adj* earlier, previous.

anthologie f anthology.

anticancéreux *adj* cancer.

anticipation f anticipation.

anticonceptionnel *adj* contraceptive.

anticyclone m anticyclone.

antidote m antidote.

antigel m antifreeze.

antipathie f antipathy.

antipathique *adj* unpleasant.

antique *adj* ancient.

antiquité f antiquity; antique.

antirouille *adj invar* rustproof.

antisocial *adj* antisocial.

antithèse f antithesis.

antonyme m antonym.

anxiété f anxiety.

anxieux *adj* anxious.

août m August.

apaisant *adj* soothing.

apaiser *vt* to calm (down); relieve.

apathie f apathy.

apathique *adj* apathetic.

apercevoir *vt* to see; catch a glimpse of.

apéritif m aperitif.

apeuré *adj* frightened.

aphone *adj* voiceless, hoarse.

aphrodisiaque *adj, m* aphrodisiac.

apitoyer *vt* to move to pity:—**s'~** *vr* to feel pity (*sur* for).

aplanir *vt* to level (out); smooth away.

aplati *adj* flat.

apolitique *adj* apolitical; non-political.

apologie f apology.

apostrophe f apostrophe.

apparaître *vi* to appear.

appareil m device; appliance; (tele)-phone;—**~-photo** camera.

apparence f appearance.

apparent *adj* apparent.

appartement m flat, appartment.

appartenir *vi*:—**~ à** to belong to.

appauvrir *vt* to impoverish:—**s'~** *vr* to grow poorer.

appel m call; appeal.

appeler *vt* to call:—**s'~** *vr* **je m'appelle Léon** my name is Leon.

appellation f appelation; name.

appétissant *adj* appetizing.

appétit *m* appetite *(de* for).

applaudir *vt vi* to applaude.

application *f* application; use.

appliquer *vt* to apply:—**s'**~ *vr* to apply o.s.

apporter *vt* to bring.

appréciation *f* estimation, assessment

apprécier *vt* to assess; appreciate.

appréhender *vt* to apprehend; to dread.

appréhension *f* apprehension.

apprendre *vt* to learn:—~ **à lire** to learn to read:—~ **à lire à un enfant** to teach a child to read.

apprenti *m*, **-ie** *f* apprentice.

apprentissage *m* apprenticeship.

approbation *f* approval.

approche *f* approach.

approcher *vt* to move near; approach:—**s'**~ *vr* to approach.

approuver *vt* to approve of.

approvisionner *vt* to supply:—**s'**~ *vr* to stock up *(de, en* with).

approximatif *adj* approximate.

appui *m* support.

appuyer *vt* to support *vi* to press:—*vr* **s'**~ **sur** to lean on.

âpre *adj* bitter:—~**ment** *adv* bitter-ly.

après *prép* after:—**après tout** after all:—**d'**~ **elle** according to her.

après-midi *m/f invar* afternoon.

apte *adj* capable *(à* of).

aptitude *f* aptitude:—ability.

aquatique *adj* aquatic.

araignée *f* spider.

arbitraire *adj* arbitrary:—~**ment** *adv* arbitrarily.

arbitre *m* arbiter; referee.

arbitrer *vt* to arbitrate; referee.

arbre *m* tree.

arc *m* bow; arc; arch.

arc-en-ciel *m*, *pl* **arcs-en-ciel** rainbow.

arche *f* arche.

archéologie *f* archaeology.

archipel *m* archipelago.

architecte *mf* architect.

architecture *f* architecture.

archiver *vt* to file, archive.

archives *fpl* archives, records.

ardu *adj* difficult.

argent *m* silver; money.

argument *m* argument.

argumenter *vi* to argue *(sur* about).

aride *adj* arid.

aristocrate *mf* aristocrat.

aristocratie *f* aristocracy.

arithmétique *f* arithmetic:—*adj* arithmetical.

arme *f* arm, weapon.

armée *f* army.

armer *vt* to arm:—**s'**~ *vr* to arm oneself.

armoire *f* cupboard; wardrobe.

aromatique *adj* aromatic.

arôme *m* aroma; flavour.

arqué *adj* curved, arched.

arracher *vt* to pull (out); to tear off.

arrangement *m* arrangement.

arranger *vt* to arrange:—**s'**~ *vr* to come to an arrangement.

arrêt *m* stopping; stop (button).

arrêter *vt* to stop:—**s'**~ *vr* to stop.

arrière *m invar* back:—**en** ~ back(wards):—**à l'**~ at the back:—*adj invar* back, rear.

arrière-plan *m* background.

arrivant *m*, **-e** *f* newcomer.

arrivée *f* arrival, coming.

arriver *vi* to arrive, come.

arrogant *adj* arrogant.

arrondir vt to make round; to round off.

arrondissement m district.

arsenal m arsenal.

art m art.

artère f artery; road.

article m article.

articuler vt to articulate.

artificiel adj artificial:—**~lement** adv artificially.

artisan m artisan, craftsman.

artisanat m craft industry.

artiste mf artist.

artistique adj artistic:—**~ment** adv artistically.

ascenseur m lift, elevator.

ascension f ascent.

asiatique adj Asian.

asile m refuge; asylum.

aspect m appearance, look.

asphyxier vt to asphyxiate, suffocate.

aspirateur m vacuum cleaner.

aspirine f aspirin.

assaillant m assailant.

assaillir vt to assail.

assainir vt to clean up; to purify.

assaisonner vt to season.

assassin m murderer; assassin.

assassiner vt to assassinate.

assaut m assault, attack.

assemblage m assembly; assembling.

assemblée f meeting.

assembler vt to assemble:—**s'~** vr to assemble.

asseoir (s') vr to sit down.

assertion f assertion.

asservissement m enslavement; slavery.

assez adv enough; quite, rather:—**avoir ~ d'argent** to have enough money:—**~ bien** quite well.

assidu adj assiduous; regular.

assiette f plate.

assigner vt to assign.

assimiler vt to assimilate.

assis adj seated, sitting (down).

assistant(e) m(f) assistant.

assister vt to attend; to assist.

association f association.

associé(e) m(f) associate, partner.

assombrir vt to darken:—**s'~** to darken.

assommer vt to stun.

assortir vt to match:—**s'~** vr to go well together.

assoupir (s') vr to doze off.

assourdir vt to deafen; to muffle.

assourdissant adj deafening.

assouvir vt to satisfy.

assumer vt to assume.

assurance f (self-)assurance; assurance; insurance (policy).

assuré m, **-e** f assured:—adj assured.

assurer vt to assure:—**s'~** vr to insure oneself.

asthme m asthma.

astre m star.

astreignant adj demanding.

astreindre vt to force, compel.

astrologie f astrology.

astrologue m astrologer.

astronaute m astronaut.

astronome m astronomer.

astronomie f astronomy.

astuce f shrewdness; (clever) trick; pun.

astucieux adj astute.

atelier m workshop; studio.

athée mf atheist:—adj atheistic.

athlète mf athlete.

athlétisme m athletics.

atlas m atlas.

atmosphère f atmosphere.

atome *m* atom.

atomique *adj* atomic.

atout *m* trump; advantage, asset.

atroce *adj* atrocious; dreadful.

atrocité *f* atrocity.

attaché *m*, **-e** *f* attaché; assistant.

attacher *vt* to tie together; tie up; fasten; attach (*à* to).

attaque *f* attack.

attaquer *vt* to attack; tackle.

attarder (s') *vr* to linger.

atteindre *vt* to reach; affect; contact.

atteinte *f* attack (*à* on):—**hors d'~** beyond *ou* out of reach.

attendre *vt* to wait:—**s'~** *vr* :—**s'~ à qch** to expect something.

attendrir *vt* to fill with pity:—**s'~** *vr* to be moved (*sur* by).

attendrissant *adj* touching, moving.

attendu *adj* expected; long-awaited.

attentat *m* attack (*contre* on); murder attempt.

attente *f* wait; expectation.

attention *f* attention; care.

attentionné *adj* considerate, thoughtful (*pour* towards).

atténuer *vt* to alleviate; ease.

atterrir *vi* to land, touch down.

atterrissage *m* landing, touch down.

attester *vt* to testify to.

attirant *adj* attractive.

attirer *vt* to attract.

attitude *f* attitude; bearing.

attrait *m* attraction, appeal.

attraper *vt* to catch.

attribuer *vt* to attribute; award.

attribut *m* attribute.

attribution *f* attribution.

attrister *vt* to sadden.

au = à le.

aube *f* dawn, daybreak.

auberge *f* inn:—**~ de jeunesse** youth hostel.

aucun *adj* no; not any; any:— **~ement** *adv* in no way:—*pron* none; not any; any (one):— **d'entre eux** none of them.

audacieux *adj* audacious, bold; daring.

audience *f* audience; hearing.

auditeur *m*, **-trice** *f* listener; auditor.

auditoire *m* audience.

augmentation *f* increase, rise (*de* in); increasing(*de* of).

augmenter *vt* to increase, raise.

aujourd'hui *adv* today.

auparavant *adv* before, previously; before, first.

auprès *prép* **~ de** next to; compared (with).

auquel = à lequel.

aurore *f* dawn, first light.

aussi *adv* too, also; so:—**nous ~** us too:—**une ~ belle journée** such a beautiful day.

aussitôt *adv* immediately:—**~ dit, ~ fait** no sooner said than done:— **~ que** as soon as.

autant *adv* as much; as many; so much; such; so many; such a lot of; the same:—**~ que je sache** as far as I know:—**~ que possible** as much as possible.

autel *m* altar.

auteur *m* author.

authentique *adj* authentic:—**~ment** *adv* authentically.

auto-école *f* driving school.

auto-stop *m* hitchhiking:—**faire de l'~** to hitchhike.

auto-stoppeur *m*, **-euse** *f* hitchhiker.

autobiographie *f* autobiography.

autocar *m* coach.

autodéfense *f* self-defence.

autodidacte *mf* self-taught.

automatique *adj* automatic:— ~**ment** *adv* automatically.

automne *m* autumn.

automobile *f* motor car.

automobiliste *mf* motorist.

autonome *adj* autonomous.

autopsie *f* autopsy, post-mortem (examination).

autorisation *f* authorization, permission; permit.

autoriser *vt* to authorize, give permission for.

autorité *f* authority.

autoroute *f* motorway.

autour *prép* ~ **de** (a)round:—*adv* (a)round.

autre *adj* other:—~ **chose** something else *ou* different:—~ **part** somewhere else:—**d'**~ **part** on the other hand:—*pn* another.

autrefois *adv* in the past, in days gone by.

autrement *adv* differently; otherwise:—**je n'ai pas pu faire ~** I couldn't do differently *ou* otherwise.

aux = à les.

auxiliaire *adj* auxiliary:—*m* auxiliary:—*mf* assistant.

avalanche *f* avalanche.

avaler *vt* to swallow.

avance *f* advance; lead:—**arriver en ~** to arrive early:—**payer d'~** to pay in advance.

avancer *vt* to move forward:—**s'**~ *vr* to advance, move forward:—*vi* move forward, advance; make progress.

avant *prép* before:—~ **peu** shortly:—~ **tout** above all:—*adv* before:—**en ~** in front, ahead:—*m* front; bow; forward.

avant-bras *m invar* forearm.

avant-hier *adv* the day before yesterday.

avantage *m* advantage.

avantageux *adj* profitable, worthwhile; attractive; flattering.

avarie *f* damage.

avec *prép* with; to.

avenir *m* future.

aventure *f* adventure; venture; experience.

avenue *f* avenue.

avérer (s') *vr* to turn out, prove to be.

aversion *f* aversion.

avertir *vt* to warn; inform.

avertissement *m* warning.

aveugle *adj* blind:—*mf* blind person.

aveuglement *m* blindness.

aveugler *vt* to blind.

aviation *f* flying; aviation.

avide *adj* greedy; eager.

avion *m* (air)plane, aircraft.

avis *m* opinion.

avisé *adj* wise, sensible.

aviser *vt* to advise:—**s'**~ *vr* **s'aviser de** to realize suddenly.

avoir *vt* to have:—**il y a** there is/ are:—**il y a deux mois** two months ago:—**qu'as-tu?** what's the matter?:—*m* resources; credit.

avortement *m* abortion.

avoué *m* solicitor.

avril *m* April.

axe *m* axis; axle; main road.

B

babiole f trinket, trifle.
bac m ferry.
badge m badge.
bagage m luggage.
bagarre f fight, brawl.
bagatelle f trinket; trifling sum.
bague f ring.
baguette f stick; loaf of French bread.
baie f (geog) bay.
baigner vt vi to bathe:—**se ~** vr to have a bathe, swim.
baignoire f bathtub.
bâiller vi to yawn.
bain m bath; bathe, swim.
baiser m kiss:—vt to kiss.
baisse f fall, drop.
baisser vi to fall, drop vt to lower.
bal m dance.
balai m broom, brush.
balance f balance; scales.
balançoire f swing; seesaw.
balayer vt to sweep, brush.
balbutier vt to stammer, mumble.
balcon m balcony.
baleine f whale.
balle f bullet; ball.
ballon m ball; balloon.
balustrade f balustrade; handrail.
bambou m bamboo.
banal adj banal, trite:—**~ement** adv tritely.
banane f banana.
bancaire adj banking, bank.
bandage m bandage.
bande f band; tape.

bandeau m headband; blindfold.
bander vt to bandage; stretch.
bandit m bandit.
banlieue f suburbs.
bannière f banner.
bannir vt to banish.
banque f bank; banking.
banquette f seat, stool.
banquier m banker.
baptiser vt to baptise.
bar m bar.
barbare adj barbarian; barbaric.
barbe f beard.
barème m list, schedule.
baril m barrel, cask.
baromètre m barometer.
barque f small boat.
barre f bar, rod.
barrer vt to bar, block.
barricader vt to barricade:—**se ~** vr to barricade o.s.
barrière f barrier; fence.
bas adj low, base:—n stocking; sock.
bascule f weighing machine, scales.
base f base; basis.
baser vt to base:—**se baser sur** vr to depend on, rely on.
basse f (mus) bass; shoal, reef.
bassesse f meanness; vulgarity.
bassin m pond, pool; dock.
bataille f battle.
batailler vi to battle.
bateau m boat, ship.
bâtiment m building.
bâtir vt to build.

bâton *m* stick, staff.

batte *f* bat; beating.

batterie *f* battery.

battre *vt* to beat, defeat.

baume *m* balm, balsam.

bavard *m*, **-e** *f* chatterbox:—*adj* talkative, loquacious.

bavardage *m* chatting, gossiping.

bavarder *vi* to chat, gossip.

bazar *m* bazaar; general store.

béat *adj* blessed; complacent.

béatitude *f* beatitude; bliss.

beau, *f* **belle** *adj* beautiful, lovely.

beaucoup *adv* a lot, a great deal:—~ **de monde** a lot of people.

beauté *f* beauty, loveliness.

beaux-arts *m pl* fine art.

bébé *m* baby.

bec *m* beak, bill.

bégayer *vi* to stammer, stutter.

beige *adj* beige:—*m* beige.

bêler *vi* to bleat.

Belge *mf* Belgian.

belge *adj* Belgian.

Belgique *f* Belgium.

belligérant *m*, **-ante** *f* belligerent:—*adj* belligerent.

bénédiction *f* benediction, blessing.

bénéfice *m* profit; benefit.

bénéficier *vi* to benefit; enjoy.

bénin, *f* **bénigne** *adj* benign; harmless.

bénir *vt* to bless.

bénit *adj* consecrated, holy.

béquille *f* crutch; prop.

berceau *m* cradle.

bercer *vt* to rock, cradle.

béret *m* beret.

berge *f* riverbank; barge.

berger *m* shepherd:**-ère** *f* shepherdess.

besogne *f* work; job.

besoin *m* need; want:—**avoir ~ de** to need.

bête *adj* stupid, silly:—**~ment** *adv* stupidly, foolishly:—*f* animal.

bêtise *f* stupidity, foolishness.

béton *m* concrete.

beurre *m* butter.

biberon *m* baby's bottle.

bible *f* bible.

bibliographie *f* bibliography.

bibliothécaire *mf* librarian.

bibliothèque *f* library; bookcase.

bicyclette *f* bicycle.

bidon *m* tin, can; flask.

bien *adv* well; properly; very:—*n* property, estate.

bien-être *m* well-being.

bienfaiteur *m* benefactor, **-trice** *f* benefactress.

bienheureux *adj* blessed; lucky; happy.

bientôt *adv* soon.

bienvenu *adj* welcome.

bière *f* beer; coffin.

bifteck *m* steak.

bigot *adj* bigoted.

bijou *m* jewel.

bijouterie *f* jewellery.

bilan *m* balance sheet; assessment.

bilingue *adj* bilingual.

billet *m* ticket; note.

billetterie *f* cash dispenser.

billion *m* billion.

binaire *adj* binary.

biodégradable *adj* biodegradable.

biographie *f* biography.

biologie *f* biology.

biologiste *mf* biologist.

bipède *m* biped.

biscuit *m* cake; biscuit.

bisexuel *adj* bisexual.

bissextile *adj* bissextile, leap (year).

bitumer vt to asphalt, tarmac.

bizarre adj bizarre, strange:— **~ment** adv strangely, oddly.

blague f joke, trick.

blaguer vi to joke.

blagueur m, **-euse** f joker, wag:— adj jokey, teasing.

blaireau m badger.

blâme m blame, rebuke.

blâmer vt to blame, rebuke.

blanc adj, f **blanche** white:—m white; blank:—mf white person:— f minim.

blancheur f whiteness.

blanchir vi to turn white:—vt to whiten.

blanchisserie f laundry.

blasphème m blasphemy.

blé m wheat.

blêmir vi to turn pale.

blessé adj injured, wounded.

blesser vt to injure, wound.

bleu adj blue:—n blue; bruise.

bleuir vi to turn blue:—vt to make blue.

bloc m block, group, unit.

blond adj blond, fair.

blondir vi to turn blond, turn golden:—vt to bleach.

bloquer vt to block, blockade.

blouse f blouse; overall.

bœuf m ox, bullock.

boire vt to drink:—vi to drink, tipple.

bois m wood.

boisson f drink.

boîte f box.

boiter vi to limp.

boiteux adj lame.

bol m bowl.

bombarder vt to bombard, bomb.

bombe f bomb.

bon adj, f **bonne** good:—m slip, coupon, bond.

bonbon m sweet, candy.

bond m leap; bounce.

bondir vi to jump, leap; to bounce.

bonheur m happiness; luck.

bonhomme m, pl **bonshommes** chap, fellow.

bonifier vt to improve:—**se ~** vr to improve.

bonjour m hello, good morning.

bonsoir m good evening.

bonté f goodness, kindness.

bord m side, edge.

border vt to edge, border.

borner vt to restrict, limit.

botanique f botany:—adj botanical.

botaniste f botanist.

botte f boot.

bouche f mouth.

bouché adj cloudy, overcast.

bouche-à-bouche m kiss of life.

bouchée f mouthful.

boucher vt to butcher:—m, **-ère** f butcher.

boucherie f butcher's; butchery.

bouchon m cork.

boudeur adj sullen, sulky.

boudin m pudding.

boue f mud.

bouée f buoy.

bouger vi to move:—vt to move, shift.

bougie f candle.

bouillir vi to boil.

bouilloire f kettle.

boulanger m, **-ère** f baker.

boulangerie f bakery.

boule f ball, bowl.

boulevard m boulevard.

bouleversement m confusion, disruption.

bouleverser *vt* to confuse, disrupt.
boulon *m* bolt.
bourdon *m* bumblebee.
bourdonner *vi* to buzz, hum.
bourg *m* market-town.
bourgeois *m*, **-e** *f* bourgeois, middle-class person:—*adj* bourgeois, middle-class.
bourse *f* purse; stock exchange.
boursier *m*, **-ière** *f* broker; speculator.
bousculer *vt* to jostle, hustle.
bout *m* end; piece, scrap.
bouteille *f* bottle.
boutique *f* shop, store.
bouton *m* button.
boutonner *vt* to button.
boxe *f* boxing.
boxer *vi* to box.
boycotter *vt* to boycott.
bracelet *m* bracelet.
braguette *f* fly (trousers).
brancher *vt* to connect, link.
bras *m* arm.
brasse *f* breaststroke.
brasser *vt* to brew; to mix.
brasserie *f* bar; brewery.
brave *adj* brave, courageous.
braver *vt* to brave, defy.
brèche *f* breach, gap.
bredouiller *vi* to stammer, mumble.
bref *adj*, *f* **brève** brief, concise:—**en ~** *adv* in short.
brevet *m* licence, patent.
bric-à-brac *m* bric-a-brac.
bricolage *m* DIY, odd jobs.
bricoler *vi* to do odd jobs.
bride *f* bridle.
brider *vt* to restrain, restrict.
brièveté *f* brevity.
brillant *adj* brilliant, shining.
briller *vi* to shine.

brique *f* brick, slab.
brise *f* breeze.
briser *vt* to smash, shatter.
broche *f* brooch.
brochure *f* brochure, pamphlet.
bronze *m* bronze.
bronzer *vi* to get a tan.
brosse *f* brush.
brosser *vt* to brush.
brouette *f* wheelbarrow.
brouillard *m* fog, mist.
brouter *vt vi* to graze.
bruine *f* drizzle.
bruit *m* noise, sound.
bruitage *m* sound-effects.
brûler *vt vi* to burn.
brûlure *f* burn.
brume *f* haze, mist.
brun *m* dark-haired man, **brune** *f* brunette:—*adj* brown.
brusque *adj* brusque, abrupt.
brut *adj* crude, raw.
brutal *adj* brutal, rough.
brutalité *f* brutality.
brute *f* brute; animal.
bruyant *adj* noisy.
bûche *f* log.
bûcheron(ne) *m(f)* woodcutter, lumberjack.
budget *m* budget.
buée *f* condensation; steam.
buffet *m* sideboard, buffet.
bulbe *m* bulb.
bulletin *m* bulletin.
bureau *m* office; desk.
bureaucrate *mf* bureaucrat.
bus *m* bus.
buste *m* bust, chest.
but *m* objective, goal.
buvable *adj* drinkable.
buvette *f* refreshment-room.
buveur *m*, **-euse** *f* drinker.

C

ça *pron* that; it:—**~ va?** How goes it?:—**~ alors!** you don't say!

cabaret *m* cabaret; tavern.

cabine *f* cabin, cab; cockpit.

cabinet *m* surgery; office, study.

câble *m* cable.

cacahouète *f* peanut.

cacao *m* cocoa.

caché *adj* hidden, secluded.

cacher *vt* to hide, conceal.

cadavre *m* corpse.

cadeau *m* present.

cadenasser *vt* to padlock.

cadet *m*, **-ette** *f* youngest child.

cadre *m* frame; context; scope.

caduc *adj f* **caduque** null and void; obsolete.

café *m* coffee.

cafétéria *f* cafeteria.

cafetière *f* coffeepot.

cage *f* cage.

cahier *m* notebook.

caillou *m* stone; pebble.

caisse *f* box; till; fund.

caissier *m*, **-ière** *f* cashier.

calcul *m* sum, calculation.

calculatrice, calculette *f* calculator.

calculer *vt* to calculate, reckon:—*vi* to budget carefully.

caleçon *m* shorts, pants.

calendrier *m* calendar.

calibre *m* calibre, bore.

calmant *m* tranquilliser, sedative:—*adj* tranquillising.

calme *m* calm, stillness:—*adj* calm, still.

calmer *vt* calm, soothe, pacify.

calorie *f* calorie.

camarade *mf* companion, friend.

camaraderie *f* camaraderie, friendship.

cambrioler *vt* to burgle.

caméra *f* camera.

camion *m* lorry.

camionneur *m* lorry driver, trucker.

camouflage *m* camouflage.

camp *m* camp.

campagnard *m* countryman, **-e** *f* countrywoman:—*adj* country, rustic.

campagne *f* country, countryside.

camper *vi* to camp.

canal *m* canal, channel.

canapé *m* sofa, settee.

cancer *m* cancer.

cancéreux *adj* cancerous.

candidat *m*, **-e** *f* candidate.

candide *adj* frank, ingenuous.

canne *f* cane, rod.

canoë *m* canoe.

canon *m* cannon, gun.

cantatrice *f* singer.

cantine *f* canteen.

caoutchouc *m* rubber.

cap *f* cape; course.

capable *adj* capable, competent.

capacité *f* capacity.

capitaine *m* captain.

capital *adj* capital, cardinal, major:—*m* capital, stock.

capitale *f* capital (letter, city).

capitaliste *mf* capitalist.

capituler *vt* to capitulate.

capoter *vt* to capsize, overturn.

caprice *m* caprice, whim.

capricieux *adj* capricious.

capsule *f* capsule.

captif *m*:—**ve** *f* captive:—*adj* captive.

captiver *vt* to captivate, enthrall.

captivité *f* captivity.

capture *f* capture.

capturer *vt* to capture.

car *conj* for; because:—*m* bus; van.

caractère *m* character, disposition.

caractériser *vt* to characterise.

caractérisque *f* characteristic, feature:—*adj* characteristic.

carat *m* carat.

caravane *f* caravan.

carbone *m* carbon.

carburant *m* motor-fuel.

cardiaque *adj* cardiac.

carence *f* deficiency; insolvency.

caressant *adj* affectionate.

caresse *f* caress.

caresser *vt* to caress, fondle.

cargaison *f* cargo, freight.

caricature *f* caricature.

caricaturer *vt* to caricature.

caritatif *adj* charitable.

carnaval *m* carnival.

carnet *m* notebook; logbook.

carnivore *mf* carnivore:—*adj* carnivorous.

carotte *f* carrot.

carreau *m* tile; pane.

carrefour *m* crossroads.

carrière *f* career.

carrosserie *f* bodywork, coachwork.

carte *f* card; map.

cartilage *m* cartilage.

carton *m* cardboard.

cartonner *vt* to bind (book).

cas *m* case; circumstance.

cascade *f* waterfall.

case *f* square; box.

casier *m* compartment; filing cabinet.

casino *m* casino.

casque *m* helmet.

cassant *adj* brittle.

casse-croûte *m invar* snack.

casser *vt* to break:—**se ~** *vr* to break.

casserole *f* saucepan.

cassette *f* cassette; cash-box.

catalogue *m* catalogue.

cataloguer *vt* to catalogue.

catastrophe *f* catastrophe.

catastrophique *adj* catastrophic.

catégorie *f* category.

catégorique *adj* categorical.

cathédrale *f* cathedral.

catholique *adj* Catholic.

cauchemar *m* nightmare.

cause *f* cause, reason.

causer *vt* to cause; to chat:—*vi* to talk, chat.

cavalerie *f* cavalry.

cavalier *m*, **-ière** *f* rider.

cave *f* cellar.

caverne *f* cave, cavern.

cavité *f* cavity.

ce *adj* **cet** (*bef. vowel and mute h*), *f* **cette**, *pl* **ces** this, these:—**cet homme-là** that man:—*pron*:—**c'est le facteur** it's the postman:—**~ sont mes lunettes** these are my glasses.

ceci *pron* this.

céder *vi* to give in:—*vt* to give up, transfer.

ceinture *f* belt, girdle.

cela *pron* that:—*emphasis* **qui ~?** who? (do you mean)?:—**comment ~?** how? (do you mean?).

célèbre *adj* famous.

célébrer *vt* to celebrate.

célébrité *f* fame, celebrity.

célibataire *mf* single person:—*adj* single, unmarried.

cellule *f* cell, unit.

celluloïde *m* celluloid.

celui *pron, f* **celle** this one, *pl* **ceux** these ones.

cendre *f* ash.

censure *f* censorship.

cent *adj* a hundred:—**tu as ~ fois raison** you are absolutely right:—*m* a hundred:—**~ pour ~** per cent.

centenaire *m* centenarian:—*adj* a hundred years old.

centigrade *m* centigrade.

centigramme *m* centigram.

centime *m* centime.

centimètre *m* centimetre.

central *adj* central.

centre *m* centre.

cependant *conj* however.

cercle *m* circle, ring.

céréale *f* cereal.

cérébral *adj* cerebral.

cérémonie *f* ceremony.

certain *adj* certain, sure:—**~s** *pn* some, certain.

certificat *m* certificate.

certifier *vt* to certify; to guarantee.

certitude *f* certainty, certitude.

cervelle *f* brain.

cesser *f* to cease, stop.

cessez-le-feu *m* cease-fire.

cet *adj f* **cette** *see* **ce**.

ceux *see* **ce**.

chacun *pron* each one:—**~e d'entre elles** each of them.

chagrin *m* sorrow, chagrin.

chaîne *f* chain.

chair *f* flesh.

chaise *f* chair.

châlet *m* chalet.

chaleur *f* heat.

chaleureux *adj* warm, cordial.

chambre *f* room.

chameau *m* camel.

champ *m* field.

champignon *m* mushroom.

champion *m*, **-onne** *f* champion.

championnat *m* championship.

chance *f* luck.

chanceler *vi* to stagger, totter.

chanceux *adj* lucky, fortunate.

changement *m* change, changing.

changer *vi* to change:—*vt* to change.

chanson *f* song.

chantage *m* blackmail.

chanter *vi*, *vt* to sing.

chanteur *m*, **-euse** *f* singer.

chantier *m* building site.

chaos *m* chaos.

chapeau *m* hat.

chapelle *f* chapel.

chapitre *m* chapter.

chaque *adj* each.

charbon *m* coal.

charge *f* load; responsibility.

charger *vt* to load:—**se ~ de** to take responsibility for, attend to.

charisme *m* charisma.

charitable *adj* charitable, kind.

charité *f* charity.

charme *m* charm.

charmer *vt* to charm, beguile.

charpente *f* structure, framework.

charpentier *m* carpenter.

charrue *f* plough.

chasse-neige *m invar* snowplough.

chasser *vt* to hunt, chase.

châssis *m* chassis.

chat *m*, **chatte** *f* cat.

château m castle, château.

châtiment m chastisement, punishment.

chaud adj warm, hot.

chaudière f boiler.

chauffage m heating.

chauffer vi to heat:—vt to heat up.

chauffeur m driver.

chaumière f cottage.

chaussée f road, street.

chaussette f sock.

chaussure f shoe.

chauve-souris f bat.

chef m head, boss; chef.

chef-d'œuvre m masterpiece.

chemin m way, road:—~ de fer railway.

cheminée f chimney.

chemise f shirt.

chêne m oak.

chèque m cheque.

chéquier m chequebook.

cher adj f **chère** dear, expensive.

chercher vt to look for.

chéri m, **-ie** f darling:—adj cherished.

cheval m horse.

cheveu m hair.

cheville f ankle.

chèvre f goat.

chez prép at home:—**je rentre ~ moi** I'm going home.

chic m style, stylishness.

chien m, **chienne** f dog.

chiffre m figure.

chimie f chemistry.

chimiste mf chemist.

chimpanzé m chimpanzee.

chirurgie f surgery.

chirurgien m surgeon.

choc m shock, crash.

chocolat m chocolate.

choir vi to fall.

choisir vt to choose.

choix m choice.

chômage m unemployment.

chômeur m, **-euse** f unemployed person.

choquer vt to shock.

chose f thing, matter, object.

chou m cabbage.

chouette f owl.

chrétien m, **-ienne** f Christian, adj christian.

christianisme m Christianity.

chronologie f chronology.

chuchoter vi to whisper.

chuinter vi to hiss.

chute f fall, drop.

chuter vi to fall.

ci adv:—**ces fleurs-ci** these flowers:—**ci-joint** enclosed.

cible f target.

cicatrice f scar.

cidre m cider.

ciel m, pl **cieux, ciels** sky.

cierge m candle.

cigare m cigar.

cigarette f cigarette.

cil m eyelash.

ciment m cement.

cimetière m cemetery.

cinéma m cinema.

cingler vt to lash, sting.

cinq m five.

cinquante m fifty.

cinquième mf fifth, adj fifth.

cirage m polish.

circonférence f circumference.

circonspect adj circumspect.

circonstance f circumstance.

circuit m circuit, tour.

circulaire adj circular.

circulation f circulation; traffic.

circuler *vi* to circulate, move.

cirer *vt* to polish.

cirque *m* circus.

ciseau *m* chisel; scissor(s).

citadelle *f* citadel.

citadin(e) *m(f)* city dweller:—*adj* town, urban.

citation *f* citation, summons.

cité *f* city.

citer *vt* to quote, cite.

citoyen *m*, **-enne** *f* citizen.

citron *m* lemon.

civil *adj* civil:—**-ement** *adv* civilly.

civilisation *f* civilisation.

civiliser *vt* to civilise.

clair *adj* clear, bright:—**-ement** *adv* clearly.

clameur *f* clamour.

clandestin *adj* clandestine.

claque *f* slap, smack.

claquer *vi* to bang, slam.

clarifier *vt* to clarify:—**se ~** *vr* to become clear.

clarté *f* light, brightness.

classe *f* class, standing.

classer *vt* to file, classify.

classification *f* classification.

classique *adj* classical, standard.

clause *f* clause.

claustrophobie *f* claustrophobia.

clavier *m* keyboard.

clé, clef *f* key.

cliché *m* cliché; negative.

client *m*, **-e** *f* client.

cligner *vi* to blink.

clignoter *vi* to blink, flicker.

climat *m* climate.

climatisation *f* air conditioning.

clinique *f* clinic.

clochard *m*, **-e** *f* down-and-out.

cloche *f* bell.

cloison *f* partition.

clore *vt* to close, conclude.

clou *m* nail.

clouer *vt* to nail.

coalition *f* coalition.

cocaïne *f* cocaine.

cochon *m*, **-onne** *f* pig.

code *m* code.

cœur *m* heart.

coffre *m* chest:—**-~-fort** safe.

cohabitation *f* cohabitation.

cohérent *adj* coherent.

cohésion *f* cohesion.

coiffer *vt* to arrange so's hair:—**se ~** *vr* to do one's hair.

coiffeur *m*, **-euse** *f* hairdresser.

coin *m* corner.

coïncidence *f* coincidence.

col *m* neck.

colère *f* anger.

colis *m* parcel.

collaborateur *m*, **-trice** *f* collaborator, colleague.

collaborer *vi* to collaborate.

collection *f* collection.

collectionner *vt* to collect.

collège *m* college, school.

collègue *mf* colleague.

coller *vt* to stick, glue:—*vi* to stick, be sticky.

colline *f* hill.

collision *f* collision.

colonie *f* colony.

coloniser *vt* to colonise.

coloration *f* colouring, staining.

colorier *vt* to colour in.

coma *m* coma.

comateux *adj* comatose.

combat *m* combat, fight.

combattre *vt* to fight, combat:—*vi* to fight.

combien *adv* how much, how many:— **-~ de temps** how much time.

combiner *vt* to combine.

combustible *m* fuel.

combustion *f* combustion.

comédie *f* comedy.

comédien *m*:-**ienne** *f* actor.

comète *f* comet.

comique *adj* comic:—~**ment** *adv* comically.

comité *m* committee.

commande *f* command, order.

commander *vt vi* to order, command.

comme *conj* as, like:—~ ci ~ ça so-so:—*adv* how.

commémorer *vt* to commemorate.

commencer *vt* to begin:-*vi* to begin, start.

comment *adv* how:—~ **dire?** how shall we say?

commentaire *m* comment; commentary.

commenter *vt* to comment.

commerçant *m*, -**e** *f* merchant, trader.

commerce *m* business, commerce.

commercial *adj* commercial:—~**ement** *adv* commercially.

commercialiser *vt* to market.

commettre *vt* to commit.

commission *f* commission, committee.

commodité *f* convenience.

commun *adj* common, joint.

communal *adj* common, communal.

commune *f* town, district.

communication *f* communication.

communiquer *vt* to communicate, transmit:—*vi* to communicate.

communiste *mf* communist.

compact *adj* compact, dense.

compagne *f* companion.

compagnon *m* companion.

comparable *adj* comparable.

comparaison *f* comparison.

comparer *vt* to compare.

compartiment *m* compartment.

compas *m* compass.

compassion *f* compassion.

compatible *adj* compatible.

compatriote *mf* compatriot.

compensation *f* compensation.

compenser *vt* to compensate; offset.

compétence *f* competence.

compétitif *adj* competitive.

compétitivité *f* competitiveness.

complaisant *adj* kind; complacent.

complément *m* complement; extension.

complet *adj* complete, full.

compléter *vt* to complete.

complexe *adj* complex, complicated.

complication *f* complication.

complice *mf* accomplice.

compliment *m* compliment.

compliquer *vt* to complicate.

comportement *m* behaviour; performance.

comporter *vt* to consist of:—**se** ~ *vr* to behave.

composer *vt* to compose, make up:—**se** ~ *vr*:—**se** ~ **de** to be made up of.

compréhensible *adj* comprehensible.

compréhensif *adj* comprehensive, understanding.

comprendre *vt* to understand; consist of.

compression *f* compression; reduction.

comprimer *vt* to compress; to restrain.

compromettre *vt* to compromise.

comptable *mf* accountant.

compter *vt vi* to count.

comptoir *m* counter, bar.

concentration *f* concentration.

concept *m* concept.

conception *f* conception, design.

concerner *vt* to concern, regard.

concert *m* concert.

concession *f* concession; privilege.

concevoir *vt* to imagine, conceive.

concierge *mf* caretaker, concierge.

conciliation *f* conciliation; reconciliation.

concilier *vt* to reconcile; to attract.

concision *f* conciseness, brevity.

conclure *vt* to conclude; to decide.

conclusion *f* conclusion.

concours *m* competition; conjuncture.

concret *adj* concrete, solid.

concubin *m*, **-e** *f* concubine; cohabitant.

concurrence *f* competition.

condamnation *f* condemnation; sentencing.

condamner *vt* to condemn; to sentence.

condensation *f* condensation.

condenser *vt* to condense, compress.

condition *f* condition, term.

conditionner *vt* to condition; to package.

conducteur *m*, **-trice** *f* driver; operator.

conduire *vt vi* to lead; to drive.

conduite *f* conduct; driving; running.

cône *m* cone.

conférence *f* conference.

confession *f* confession.

confiance *f* confidence, trust.

confidence *f* confidence; disclosure.

confidentiel *adj* confidential.

confier *vt* to confide, entrust:—**se ~** *vr* to confide in.

confiner *vt* to confine:—**se ~** to be confined.

confirmer *vt* to confirm:—**se ~** *vr* to be confirmed.

confiserie *f* confectionery.

confiture *f* jam.

conflit *m* conflict, contention.

confondre *vt* to confuse, mingle.

conforme *adj* consistent; true.

conformer *vt* to model:—**se ~** *vr* to conform.

confort *m* comfort.

confortable *adj* comfortable, cosy.

confronter *vt* to confront.

confus *adj* confused, indistinct.

confusion *f* confusion, disorder.

congédier *vt* to dismiss.

congeler *vt* to freeze.

congratuler *vt* to congratulate.

congrégation *f* congregation.

congrès *m* congress, conference.

conjurer *vt* to conspire; to implore.

connaissance *f* knowledge; consciousness.

connaisseur *m*, **-euse** *f* connoisseur; expert.

connaître *vt* to know, be acquainted with.

connecter *vt* to connect.

connexion *f* connection, link.

connu *adj* known; famous.

conquérir *vt* to conquer.

conquête *f* conquest.

conscience *f* consciousness; conscience.

consciencieux *adv* conscientious.

conscient *adj* conscious, aware.

consécutif *adj* consecutive.

conseil *m* advice, counsel.

conseiller *vt* to advise, counsel.

consentir *vi* to consent, acquiesce.

conséquence *f* consequence, result.

conséquent *adj* consequent, logical.

conservateur *m*, **-trice** *f* conservative; curator.

conservation *f* conservation.

conserver *vt* to keep, preserve:—**se ~** *vr* to keep.

considérable *adj* considerable; notable.

considération *f* consideration, respect.

considérer *vt* to consider, regard.

consistance *f* consistency; strength.

consister *vi*:—**~ en** to consist of.

consolation *f* consolation, solace.

consoler *vt* to console, comfort.

consolider *vt* to consolidate, reinforce.

consommateur *m*, **-trice** *f* consumer.

consommation *f* consumption; accomplishment.

consommer *vt* to consume, use.

conspirer *vi* to conspire, plot.

constant *adj* constant, continuous.

constat *m* report; acknowledgement.

constater *vt* to record; to verify.

constellation *f* constellation, galaxy.

consterner *vt* to dismay.

constipation *f* constipation.

constituer *vt* to constitute, form.

constitution *f* constitution, formation.

constructeur *m*, **-trice** *f* builder, maker.

construction *f* building, construction.

construire *vt* to construct, build.

consulat *m* consulate.

consultant *m*, **-e** *f* consultant.

consulter *vt* to consult, take advice from.

consumer *vt* to consume, spend.

contact *m* contact, touch.

contagieux *adj* contagious, infectious.

contaminer *vt* to contaminate, pollute.

conte *m* story, tale.

contempler *vt* to contemplate, meditate.

contemporain *adj* contemporary.

contenir *vt* to contain.

contentement *m* contentment, satisfaction.

contenter *vt* to please, satisfy.

contenu *m* contents, enclosure.

contester *vt* to contest, dispute.

contexte *m* context.

continent *m* continent.

continental *adj* continental.

continuation *f* continuation.

continuel *adj* continual, continuous.

continuer *vt* to continue, proceed with:—*vi* to continue, go on.

contour *m* contour, outline.

contraceptif *adj* contraceptive.

contracter *vt* to contract, acquire:—**se ~** *vr* to contract, shrink.

contradiction *f* contradiction, discrepancy.

contraindre *vt* to constrain, compel.

contraire *m* opposite, contrary:—*adj* opposite, contrary.

contrarier *vt* to annoy; to oppose.

contraste *m* contrast.

contrat *m* contract, agreement.

contre *prép* against:—**par ~** on the other hand.

contre-attaquer *vi* to counter-attack.

contrebande *f* contraband, smuggling.

contrecœur:—**à ~** reluctantly.

contredire *vt* to contradict, refute.

contrefaire *vt* to counterfeit, forge.

contrepartie *f* compensation; consideration.

contresens *m* nonsense; misunderstanding; mistranslation.

contribuer *vt vi* to contribute.

contribution *f* contribution; tax.

contrôler *vt* to control, check.

contrôleur *m*, **-euse** *f* inspector; auditor.

controverse *f* controversy.

convaincre *vt* to convince, persuade.

convalescence *f* convalescence.

convenable *adj* fitting, suitable:— **~ment** *adv* suitably, fitly.

convenir *vi* to agree, accord.

convention *f* convention, agreement.

conventionnel *adj* conventional; contractual.

conversation *f* conversation, talk.

conversion *f* conversion.

convertir *vt* to convert:—**se ~** *vr* to be converted.

conviction *f* conviction.

convoi *m* convoy; train.

convoquer *vt* to convoke, convene.

coopération *f* cooperation.

coopérative *f* cooperative.

coopérer *vi* to cooperate, collaborate.

coordination *f* coordination; committee.

copain *m* friend, pal.

copie *f* copy, reproduction.

copier *vt* to copy, reproduce.

copilote *m* co-pilot.

coq *m* cock, rooster.

coquet *adj* stylish, smart.

coquin *m*, **-e** *f* naughty, mischievous.

corail *m* coral.

coran *m* Koran.

corbeille *f* basket.

corde *f* rope; string.

cordial *adj* cordial, warm.

cordialité *f* cordiality, warmth.

cordon *m* cord, string; cordon.

corne *f* horn, antler.

corneille *f* crow.

cornet *m* cornet, cone.

corporatif *adj* corporative, corporate.

corporation *f* corporation, guild.

corps *m* body, corpse.

corpulent *adj* corpulent.

correct *adj* correct, accurate.

correcteur *m*, **-trice** *f* examiner; proofreader.

correction *f* correction; proofreading.

correspondance *f* correspondence, communication.

correspondre *vi* to correspond, communicate.

corridor *m* corridor, passage.

corriger *vt* to correct.

corroder *vt* to corrode.

corrompre *vt* to corrupt, debase.

corrosion *f* corrosion.

corruption *f* corruption, debasement.

corset *m* corset.

cortège *m* cortège, procession.

cosmétique *m* cosmetic.

cosmique *adj* cosmic.

cosmopolite *adj* cosmopolitan.

cosmos *m* cosmos.

costume *m* costume, dress.

côte *f* coast; rib; slope.

côté *m* side; point.

coteau *m* hill.

coter *vt* to quote; to classify.

coton *m* cotton.

cou *m* neck.

couche *f* layer, coat.

coucher *vt* to put to bed:—**se ~** *vr* to go to bed.

coucou *m* cuckoo.

coude *m* elbow.

coudre *vt vi* to sew.

couler *vi* to flow, run.

couleur *f* colour, shade.

coulisser *vi* to slide, run.

couloir *m* corridor, passage.

coup *m* blow; shot:—**tout à ~** suddenly:—**après ~** afterwards, after the event:—**~ de feu** shot:—**jeter un ~ d'œil** to glance.

coupable *mf* culprit:—*adj* guilty.

coupe *f* cut; cutting.

couper *vt* to cut, slice.

couple *m* couple, pair.

coupon *m* coupon, voucher, ticket.

cour *f* court, yard, courtyard.

courage *m* courage, daring.

courageux *adj* courageous.

courant *adj* current; present:—*m* stream, current.

courbe *f* curve; contour.

courber *vt* to curve, bend.

coureur *m*, **-euse** *f* runner.

courir *vi* to run, race.

couronne *f* crown, wreath.

courrier *m* mail, post.

cours *m* course; flow; path.

course *f* running; race; flight; journey.

coursier *m*, **-ière** *f* courier, messenger.

court *adj* short, brief.

court-circuiter *vt* to short-circuit.

courtier *m*, **-ière** *f* broker, agent.

courtois *adj* courteous.

cousin *m*, **-e** *f* cousin.

coussin *m* cushion, pillow.

coût *m* cost, charge.

couteau *m* knife.

coûter *vi, vt* to cost.

coûteux *adj* costly, expensive.

coutume *f* custom, habit.

couvent *m* convent.

couvercle *m* lid, cap.

couvert *m* shelter; cover; pretext:—*adj* covered; secret.

couverture *f* blanket; cover; roofing.

couvrir *vt* to cover.

crabe *m* crab.

cracher *vt* to spit.

craie *f* chalk.

craindre *vt* to fear.

crampe *f* cramp.

crâne *m* cranium, skull.

crapaud *m* toad.

craquement *m* crack, creaking, snap.

craquer *vi* to creak, squeak, crack.

cratère *m* crater.

cravate *f* tie.

créateur *m*, **-trice** *f* creator, author.

création *f* creation.

créature *f* creature.

crèche *f* creche; crib.

crédible *adj* credible.

crédit *m* credit, trust.

crédule *adj* credulous, gullible.

créer *vt* to create, produce.

crème *f* cream.

crémerie *f* dairy.

crêpe *f* pancake:—*m* crepe.

crépiter *vi* to crackle; to rattle.

crépuscule *m* twilight, dusk.

crête *f* crest, comb.

crétin m, **-e** f cretin, idiot.

creuser vi to dig, burrow:—vt to dig, hollow.

crevaison f puncture, flat.

crever vt to burst; to gouge:—vi to burst; to split.

cri m cry, howl, yell.

crible m riddle, sieve.

crier vi to cry, shout.

crime m crime, offence.

criminel m, **elle** f criminal:—adj criminal.

crise f crisis, attack.

cristal m crystal, glassware.

cristalliser vt to crystallise.

critère m criterion, standard.

critique adj critical, censorious:—f criticism; critique.

critiquer vt to criticise, censure.

crochet m hook, clip.

crocodile m crocodile.

croire vt to believe, think.

croiser vt to cross; to fold:—se ~ vr to cross, intersect.

croisière f cruise.

croissance f growth, increase.

croître vi to grow, rise.

croix f cross.

croquer vt to crunch, munch.

croquette f croquette.

croquis m sketch, outline.

croustiller vi to be crusty, crispy.

croûte f crust.

croyance f belief.

croyant adj believing.

cru adj raw, uncooked:—m vineyard; wine.

cruauté f cruelty, inhumanity.

crucial adj crucial, decisive.

crucifix m crucifix.

crudité f crudity, coarseness.

cruel adj cruel.

crypter vt to encode, scramble.

cube m cube, block.

cueillir vt to pick, gather.

cuiller, cuillère f spoon, spoonful.

cuir m leather, hide.

cuire vi to cook.

cuisine f kitchen; cookery.

cuisiner vt vi to cook.

cuisinier m, **-ière** f cook.

cuisse f thigh.

cuisson f cooking, baking.

cuit adj cooked.

cul-de-sac m blind alley, cul-de-sac.

culminer vi to culminate, tower.

culotte f knickers; underpants; shorts.

culpabiliser vt to make someone feel guilty.

culte m cult, veneration.

cultivateur m, **-trice** f farmer.

cultiver vt to cultivate:—se ~ vr to improve oneself

culture f culture; cultivation.

culturel adj cultural.

cumuler vt to accumulate.

cupide adj greedy.

cure f cure; treatment.

curé m parish priest, parson.

curieux adj curious, inquisitive.

cuvette f basin, bowl.

cycle m cycle; stage.

cyclique adj cyclical.

cyclisme m cycling.

cycliste mf cyclist.

cyclone m cyclone.

cygne m swan.

cylindre m cylinder.

cynique adj cynical:—~ment adv cynically.

cynisme m cynicism.

D

dactylographe *mf* typist.
dactylographier *vt* to type.
dame *f* lady.
damier *m* draughtboard.
danger *m* danger, risk.
dangereux *adj* dangerous, risky.
dans *prép* in; into.
danse *f* dance; dancing.
danser *vi* to dance.
danseur *m* -euse *f* dancer.
dard *m* dart; sting.
date *f* date.
dater *vt* to date.
dauphin *m* dolphin.
davantage *adv* more.
de *prép* of; from:—deux ~ plus two
  more:—*art* some, any.
dé *m* die; thimble.
débâcle *f* disaster; collapse.
débarquer *vt* to land, unship:—*vi* to
  disembark, land.
débarrasser *vt* to clear, rid.
débat *m* debate; dispute, contest.
débattre *vi* to debate, discuss.
débile *adj* weak, feeble.
débilitant *adj* debilitating, weaken-
  ing.
débiteur *m*, -trice *f* debtor.
débloquer *vt* to release, unlock.
déboiser *vt* to deforest.
débordant *adj* exuberant, overflow-
  ing.
déborder *vi* to overflow; to out-
  flank.
debout *adv* upright, standing:—être
  ~ to stand.

débris *m* debris, waste.
début *m* beginning, outset.
débuter *vi* to start, begin:—*vt* to
  lead, start.
décadence *f* decadence, decline.
décadent *adj* decadent.
décaféiné *adj* decaffeinated.
décaler *vt* to stagger; to shift.
décathlon *m* decathlon.
décéder *vi* to die.
déceler *vt* to detect; to disclose.
décembre *m* December.
décence *f* decency.
décennie *f* decade.
décent *adj* decent, proper.
décentraliser *vt* to decentralise.
déception *f* disappointment; deceit.
décès *m* death, decease.
décevoir *vt* to disappoint; to deceive.
déchaîner *vt* to unleash.
décharge *f* discharge; receipt.
décharger *vt* to unload, discharge.
déchet *m* loss, waste.
déchiffrer *vt* to decipher, decode.
déchirer *vt* to tear, rip.
décibel *m* decibel.
décidé *adj* decided; determined.
décimal *adj* decimal.
décision *f* decision.
déclarer *vt* to declare, announce.
déclencher *vt* to release, set off.
décliner *vi* to decline, refuse.
décollage *m* take-off, lift-off.
décoller *vi* to unpaste.
décolleté *adj* low-cut.

décomposer *vt* to decompose; to break up.

décompte *m* discount; deduction.

décongeler *vt* to thaw, defrost.

déconnecter *vt* to disconnect.

décontenancé *adj* embarrassed; disconcerted.

décor *m* scenery; setting.

décorateur *m*, **-trice** *f* decorator; set designer.

décoration *f* decoration, embellishment.

décorer *vt* to decorate, adorn.

découper *vt* to carve, cut up.

décourageant *adj* discouraging, disheartening.

décourager *vt* discourage, dishearten.

découvert *adj* uncovered; open.

découverte *f* discovery.

découvrir *vt* to discover.

décréter *vt* to decree, enact.

décrire *vt* to describe.

décroître *vi* to decrease, diminish.

déçu *adj* disappointed.

dédaigner *vt* to disdain, scorn.

dédaigneux *adj* disdainful, scornful.

dedans *adv* inside, indoors:—*m* inside:—**au ~ inside.**

dédier *vt* to consecrate, dedicate to.

dédommager *vt* to compensate, indemnify.

déduction *f* deduction.

déduire *vt* to deduct; to deduce.

défaire *vt* to undo, dismantle.

défaite *m* defeat, overthrow.

défaut *m* defect, fault.

défavorable *adj* unfavourable.

défection *f* defection.

défectueux *adj* defective, faulty.

défendeur *m*, **-deresse** *f* defendant.

défendre *vt* to defend, protect; to prohibit.

défense *f* defence; prohibition.

défi *m* defiance; challenge.

déficience *f* deficiency.

déficit *m* deficit, shortfall.

défier *vt* to challenge, defy.

défiler *vi* to parade, march.

définir *vt* to define, specify.

définitif *adj* definitive, final.

définition *f* definition.

déformation *f* deformation, distortion.

déformer *vt* to deform.

défouler *vt* to unwind, relax.

défunt *m*, **-e** *f* deceased:—*adj* late, deceased.

dégagement *m* freeing, clearance.

dégager *vt* to free, clear:—**se ~** *vr* to free oneself.

dégât *m* havoc, damage.

dégel *m* thaw.

dégénérer *vi* to degenerate, decline.

dégoût *m* disgust, distaste.

dégradation *f* degradation, debasement.

dégrader *vt* to degrade, debase.

degré *m* degree; grade.

déguiser *vt* to disguise:—**se ~** *vr* to disguise oneself.

dégustation *f* tasting, sampling.

dehors *adv* outside, outdoors:—**en ~ de** outside; apart from:—*m* outside, exterior.

déjà *adv* already.

déjeuner *vi* to lunch:—*m* lunch.

delà *adv*:—**au ~ de** beyond:—**par ~** beyond.

délai *m* delay; respite; time limit.

délaisser *vt* to abandon, quit.

délasser *vt* to refresh, relax:—**se ~** *vr* to rest, relax.

délayer vt to thin; to drag out.

délectation f delectation, delight.

délégation f delegation.

délégué m, **-e** f delegate:—adj delegated.

déléguer vt to delegate.

délibéré adj deliberate; resolute.

délicat adj delicate, dainty.

délicieux adj delicious, delightful.

délimiter vt to delimit, demarcate.

délinquant m, **-e** f delinquent, offender:—adj delinquent.

délire m delirium, frenzy.

délirer vi to be delirious.

délit m offence, misdemeanour.

délivrer vt to deliver; to release.

déloyal adj disloyal, unfaithful.

delta m delta.

demain adv tomorrow.

demande f request, petition; question.

demander vt to ask, request:—se ~ vr to wonder.

démaquiller vt to remove make-up.

démarche f bearing; gait, walk.

déménager vi to move house.

dément adj mad, insane, crazy.

démentir vt to deny, refute.

demeure f residence, dwelling place.

demeurer vi to live at, reside, stay.

demi adj half:—**à** ~ halfway:—m half.

demi-cercle m semicircle.

demi-douzaine f half-dozen.

demi-heure f half hour.

demi-lune f half-moon.

démilitariser vt to demilitarise.

démission f resignation.

démissionner vi to resign.

démocrate mf democrat.

démocratie f democracy.

démocratique adj democratic.

démodé adj old-fashioned, out-of-date.

demoiselle f young lady.

démolir vt to demolish, knock down.

démolition f demolition.

démonstration f demonstration; proof.

démonter vt to dismantle, take down, dismount.

démontrer vt demonstrate; to prove.

démoraliser vt to demoralise.

déni m denial, refusal.

dénier vt to deny, disclaim.

dénigrer vt to denigrate, disparage.

dénombrer vt to number, enumerate.

dénomination f denomination, designation.

dénoncer vt to denounce; to inform against.

dénonciation f denunciation.

dénoyauter vt to stone (fruit).

dense adj dense, thick.

densité f density, denseness.

dent f tooth.

dentelle f lace.

dentifrice m toothpaste.

dentiste mf dentist.

dénuder vt to bare, denude.

dépanner vt to repair, fix.

dépanneur m, **-euse** f breakdown mechanic.

départ m departure; start.

département m department.

dépasser vt to exceed; to go past.

dépêcher vt to dispatch, send:—se ~ vr to hurry, rush.

dépendant adj dependent.

dépendre vi to depend on, be dependent on.

dépenser vt to expend, spend:—se ~ vr to exert oneself.

dépérir vi to decline, waste away.

dépit m spite; grudge:—**en ~ de** in spite of.

déplacement m displacement; removal.

déplacer vt to displace; to move:—**se ~** vr to change residence.

déplaire vi to displease; to offend.

déplaisant adj disagreeable, unpleasant.

déplorable adj deplorable, disgraceful.

déployer vt to deploy; to display.

déportation f deportation, transportation.

déporter vt to deport, transport.

déposer vt to lodge, deposit.

dépôt m deposit; warehouse.

dépouillement m scrutiny, perusal; despoiling.

dépréciation f depreciation.

déprécier vt to depreciate.

dépression f depression, slump; dejection.

déprimant adj depressing.

déprimer vt to depress; to discourage.

depuis prép since, from; after.

déraillement m derailment.

dérangement m derangement; inconvenience.

déranger vt to upset, unsettle.

déraper vi to skid, slip.

dérision f derision, mockery.

dérisoire adj derisory; pathetic.

dériver vi to drift.

dernier adj last; latest; back:—m, -**ière** f last one; latter.

dernièrement adv recently; lately.

dérober vt to steal; to hide:—**se ~** vr to steal away, escape.

déroger vi to derogate; to detract.

déroulement m unfolding; progress, development.

dérouler vt to unwind, uncoil:—**se ~** vr to develop; to unfold.

dérouter vt to rout, overthrow.

derrière prép behind:—adv:—**par ~** by the back:—m bottom; back:—**de ~** back, rear.

des art = de les:—see **un, une**.

dès prép from, since:—**~ que** when; as soon as.

désaccord m disagreement, discord.

désaffecté adj disused.

désagréable adj disagreeable, unpleasant.

désagréger vt to separate:—**se ~** vr to become separated.

désagrément m displeasure, annoyance.

désapprobation f disapproval.

désapprouver vt to disapprove, object.

désarmement m disarmament.

désarroi m disarray, confusion.

désastre m disaster.

désavantage m disadvantage; prejudice.

désavantager vt to disadvantage, handicap.

descendant m, -**e** f descendant.

descendre vi to descend, go down:—vt to take down.

descente f descent, way down.

descriptif adj descriptive, explanatory.

description f description.

désenchantement m disenchantment; disillusion.

déséquilibré adj unbalanced, unhinged.

désert m desert, wilderness:—adj deserted.

déserter vt to desert.

désespéré adj desperate, hopeless.

désespérer vi to despair, give up hope.

désespoir m despair, despondency.

déshabiller vt to undress:—**se ~** vr to undress.

déshériter vt to disinherit.

désignation f designation, nomination; name.

désigner vt to designate, indicate.

désillusionner vt to disillusion; to disappoint.

désinfectant m disinfectant:—adj disinfectant.

désintégration f disintegration.

désintégrer vt to split, break up:—**se ~** vr to disintegrate.

désintéressé adj disinterested, unselfish.

désir m desire, wish, longing.

désirable adj desirable.

désirer vt to desire, wish, long.

désobéir vi to disobey.

désolation f desolation; ruin; grief.

désolé adj desolate; disconsolate, grieved.

désordonné adj untidy; inordinate; reckless.

désordre m disorder, confusion, disturbance.

désorienté adj disorientated.

désormais adv from now on, henceforth.

dessécher vt to dry, parch:—**se ~** vr to dry out.

dessein m design, plan, scheme:—**à ~** intentionally.

desserrer vt to unscrew:—**se ~** vr to work loose.

dessert m dessert, sweet.

dessin m drawing, sketch; draft.

dessiner vt to draw, sketch; to design.

dessous adv under, beneath:—m underside, bottom.

dessus adv over, above:—m ~ top.

destin m destiny, fate, doom.

destinataire mf addressee, consignee.

destination f destination; purpose.

destiner vt to determine; to intend, destine, aim.

destruction f destruction.

détachable adj detachable.

détachement m detachment, indifference.

détacher vt to detach, unfasten.

détail m detail, particular.

détaillant m, **-e** f retailer.

détailler vt to detail; to sell retail.

détecter vt to detect.

détecteur m detector.

détection f detection.

détective m detective.

détendre vt to release, loosen.

détenir vt to detain; to hold.

détente f relaxation, easing.

détérioration f deterioration.

détériorer vt to damage, impair:—**se ~** vr to deteriorate, worsen.

détermination f determination; resolution.

déterminer vt to determine, decide.

détestable adj detestable, odious.

détester vt to detest, hate.

détonation f detonation, explosion.

détour m detour; curve; evasion.

détournement m diversion, rerouting.

détourner vt to divert, reroute.

détresse f distress, trouble.

détruire vt to destroy, demolish.

dette f debt.

deuil m mourning, bereavement, grief.

deux *adj* two:—*m* two:—**en moins de ~** in a jiffy.

deuxième *adj* second:—*mf* second.

dévaliser *vt* to burgle; to rifle.

dévaloriser *vt* to depreciate, reduce the value of.

dévaluation *f* devaluation.

devancer *vt* to outstrip, outrun; to precede.

devant *prép* in front of, before:—*adv* in front:—*m* front.

devanture *f* display; shop-front.

développement *m* development; growth; progress.

développer *vt* to develop, expand:—**se ~** *vr* to develop, grow.

devenir *vi* to become, grow.

dévêtir *vt* to undress:—**se ~** *vr* to get undressed.

déviation *f* deviation; diversion.

deviner *vt* to guess; to solve; to foretell.

devise *f* currency.

dévisser *vt* to unscrew, undo.

devoir *m* duty; homework:—*vt* to owe; to have to.

dévorer *vt* to devour, consume.

dévotion *f* devotion, piety.

dextérité *f* dexterity, adroitness.

diabétique *adj* diabetic.

diable *m* devil.

diagnostic *m* diagnosis.

diagnostiquer *vt* to diagnose.

diagonale *f* diagonal.

diagramme *m* diagram; graph.

dialecte *m* dialect.

dialogue *m* dialogue, conversation.

diamant *m* diamond.

diamètre *m* diameter.

dictateur *m*, **-trice** *f* dictator.

dictée *f* dictating; dictation.

dictionnaire *m* dictionary.

diesel *m* diesel.

diète *f* diet.

diététicien *m*, **-ienne** *f* dietician.

dieu *m* god.

diffamer *vt* to defame, slander.

différence *f* difference.

différencier *vt* to differentiate.

différent *adj* different; various.

différer *vt* to differ; to vary.

difficile *adj* difficult; awkward, tricky.

difficulté *f* difficulty; problem.

diffuser *vt* to diffuse, circulate, broadcast.

digérer *vt* to digest.

digestion *f* digestion.

digne *adj* worthy; dignified.

dignité *f* dignity.

dilapider *vt* to squander; to embezzle.

dilemme *m* dilemma.

diluer *vt* to dilute.

dimanche *m* Sunday.

dimension *f* dimension, size.

diminuer *vt* to diminish, reduce:—*vi* to diminish, lessen.

diminutif *m* diminutive.

diminution *f* reduction, lessening.

dîner *vi* to dine:—*m* dinner.

diocèse *m* diocese.

diplomate *m* diplomat.

diplomatie *f* diplomacy.

diplomatique *adj* diplomatic.

diplôme *m* diploma, certificate.

dire *vt* to say; to tell:—**se ~** to say to oneself; to call oneself:—*vr* **se ~ que** to be said that.

direct *adj* direct:—*m* express.

directeur *m*, **-trice** *f* director.

direction *f* direction, management.

diriger *vt* to run, direct:—**se ~** *vr*:—**se ~ vers** to head for, make for.

discerner *vt* to discern, distinguish.

disciple *m* disciple.

discipline *f* discipline.

discorde *f* discord, dissension.

discothèque *f* discotheque.

discours *m* speech, talking.

discréditer *vt* to discredit.

discret *adj* discreet.

discrétion *f* discretion, prudence.

discrimination *f* discrimination.

discriminer *vt* to distinguish; to discriminate.

disculper *vt* to excuse, exonerate.

discussion *f* discussion, debate.

discuter *vi, vt* to discuss, debate.

disgrâce *f* disgrace.

disparaître *vi* to disappear, vanish.

disparité *f* disparity, incongruity.

disparition *f* disappearance; death; extinction.

dispenser *vt* to dispense, exempt.

dispersion *f* dispersal, scattering.

disponible *adj* available; transferable.

disposer *vt* to arrange, dispose.

dispositif *m* device, mechanism.

disposition *f* arrangement, layout.

dispute *f* dispute, argument.

disque *m* disk; record.

disquette *f* diskette.

dissertation *f* dissertation.

dissidence *f* dissidence, dissent.

dissident *adj* dissident.

dissimuler *vt* to dissemble, conceal.

dissipation *f* dissipation, waste.

dissiper *vt* to dispel; to dissipate.

dissolution *f* dissolution.

dissoudre *vt* to dissolve.

dissuader *vt* to dissuade.

distance *f* distance, interval.

distant *adj* distant.

distiller *vt* to distil.

distillerie *f* distillery.

distinct *adj* distinct, different.

distinction *f* distinction.

distingué *adj* distinguished.

distinguer *vt* to distinguish; to discern.

distraire *vt* to distract; to amuse:—**se ~** *vr* to enjoy oneself.

distrait *adj* inattentive, absentminded.

distribuer *vt* to distribute.

distribution *f* distribution.

district *m* district.

divaguer *vi* to ramble, rave.

divergence *f* divergence.

diverger *vi* to diverge, differ.

divers *adj* diverse, varied.

diversification *f* diversification.

diversifier *vt* to vary, diversify:—**se ~** *vr* to diversify.

diversité *f* diversity, variety.

divertir *vt* to amuse, entertain:—**se ~** *vr* to amuse oneself.

divertissant *adj* amusing, entertaining.

divin *adj* divine, exquisite.

divinité *f* divinity.

diviser *vt* to divide, split.

division *f* division.

divorce *m* divorce.

divorcer *vi* to get divorced.

dix *adj, m* ten.

dix-huit *adj, m* eighteen.

dix-huitième *adj, mf* eighteenth.

dix-neuf *adj, m* nineteen.

dix-neuvième *adj, mf* nineteenth.

dix-sept *adj, m* seventeen.

dix-septième *adj, mf* seventeenth.

dixième *adj, mf* tenth.

docile *adj* docile, submissive.

docteur *m* doctor.

doctrine *f* doctrine.

document *m* document.

documentaire *adj* documentary.

documentation *f* documentation; information.

documenter *vt* to document.

dogmatique *adj* dogmatic.

doigt *m* finger.

doigté *m* touch; fingering technique.

domaine *m* domain, estate; sphere.

domestique *adj* domestic, household.

domestiquer *vt* to domesticate, tame.

domicile *m* domicile, address.

dominant *adj* dominant, prevailing.

domination *f* domination; to dominion.

dominer *vt* to dominate; to prevail:—**se ~** to control oneself.

dommage *m* damage; harm:—**c'est ~** it's a pity.

dompter *vt* to tame, train.

don *m* gift; talent.

donation *f* donation.

donc *conj* so, therefore, thus:—**pourquoi ~?** why was that?.

donné *adj* given; fixed:—**étant ~** seeing that, in view of.

donnée *f* datum.

donner *vt* to give:—*vi* to knock, beat.

donneur *m*, **-euse** *f* giver, donor; dealer.

dont *pron* whose, of which.

dormir *vi* to sleep, be asleep; to be still.

dortoir *m* dormitory.

dos *m* back; top; ridge.

dose *f* dose; amount; quantity.

dossier *m* dossier, file; case.

douane *f* customs.

douanier *adj* custom(s).

double *adj* double, duplicate, dual:—*m* copy, double.

doubler *vt vi* to double, duplicate.

douceur *f* softness, gentleness.

douche *f* shower.

doucher (se) *vr* to take a shower.

doué *adj* gifted, endowed with.

douleur *f* pain, ache; anguish.

douloureux *adj* painful, grievous.

doute *m* doubt, misgiving:—**sans ~** without doubt.

douter *vi* to doubt, question:—**se ~ que** to suspect that, expect that.

douteux *adj* doubtful, dubious.

doux *adj* (*f* **douce**) soft; sweet; mild.

douzaine *f* dozen.

douze *adj m* twelve.

douzième *adj* twelfth:—*mf* twelfth.

dragon *m* dragon.

dramatique *adj* dramatic.

dramaturge *mf* playwright.

drame *m* drama.

drap *m* sheet.

drapeau *m* flag.

drogue *f* drug.

drogué(e) *m(f)* drug addict:—*adj* drugged.

droguer *vt* to drug, administer drugs.

droit *adj* right; straight; sound; honest:—*adv* straight, straight ahead:—*m* right; law; tax.

droite *f* right side; right (wing); straight line.

droitier *adj* right-handed.

drôle *adj* funny, amusing; peculiar.

du *art* of the.

dû *adj* owed; due:—**~ment** *adv* duly.

dubitatif *adj* doubtful, dubious.

duc *m* duke, **duchesse** *f* duchess.

dune *f* dune.

duo *m* duo; duet.

duper *vt* to dupe, take in.

dupliquer *vt* to duplicate.

dur *adj* hard, tough; difficult.

durable *adj* durable, lasting.

durant *prép* during, for.

durcir *vt vi* to harden:—**se ~** *vr* to become hardened.

durée *f* duration, length.

durer *vi* to last.

duvet *m* down.

dynamique *f* dynamic; dynamics:— *adj* dynamic.

dynamite *f* dynamite.

dynamo *f* dynamo.

dynastie *f* dynasty.

dyslexie *f* dyslexia.

dyslexique *adj* dyslexic.

E

eau *f* water; rain.

eau-de-vie *f* brandy.

éblouir *vt* to dazzle; to fascinate.

ébriété *f* intoxication.

écart *m* distance; interval; discrepancy.

écarter *vt* to separate; to avert; to dismiss.

ecclésiastique *adj* ecclesiastical:— *m* ecclesiastic, clergyman.

échafaud *m* scaffold.

échange *m* exchange, barter, trade.

échanger *vt* to exchange.

échantillon *m* sample.

échappement *m* exhaust; release.

échapper *vi* to escape, avoid, elude.

écharpe *f* scarf; arm-sling.

échauffer *vt* to heat, overheat; to excite.

échec *m* failure, defeat.

échelle *f* ladder; scale.

échelonner *vt* to grade; to stagger, set at intervals.

échine *f* backbone, spine.

écho *m* echo; rumour.

échoir *vi* to fall due; to befall.

éclair *m* flash; lightning flash; spark.

éclairage *m* lighting, light.

éclaircir *vt* to lighten, brighten up.

éclairer *vt* to light; clarify, explain.

éclat *m* brightness; splendour.

éclatement *m* explosion, bursting, rupture.

éclipse *f* eclipse.

éclipser *vt* to eclipse, overshadow.

écœurer *vt* to nauseate, disgust.

école *f* school, schooling; sect, doctrine.

écolier *m* schoolgirl, **-ière** *f* schoolgirl.

écologie *f* ecology.

écologiste *mf* ecologist.

économe *adj* thrifty.

économie *f* economy, thrift; economics.

économique *adj* economic.

économiser *vt* to economise, save.

Écossais *m* Scotsman, **-e** *f* Scotswoman.

écossais *adj* Scottish.

Écosse *f* Scotland.

écoulement *m* flow, discharge, outlet.

écouler *vt* to flow, discharge; to sell.

écouter *vt* to listen to, hear.

écran *m* screen.

écraser *vt* to crush; to run over:—**s'~** *vr* to crash.

écrire *vt* to write; to spell.

écriture *f* writing; handwriting; script.

écrivain *m* writer.

écrouler (s') *vr* to collapse, crumble.

écume *f* foam, froth; scum.

écureuil *m* squirrel.

édifice *m* edifice, building.

édifier *vt* to build, construct; to edify.

éditer *vt* to publish, produce; to edit.

éditeur *m* **-trice** *f* publisher; editor.

éducation *f* education; upbringing.

éduquer *vt* to educate; to bring up, raise.

effacer *vt* to efface, erase, wipe off.

effaroucher *vt* to frighten; to shock.

effectif *m* staff; size, complement:—*adj* effective, positive.

effectuer *vt* to effect, execute, carry out.

effet *m* effect; bill, note.

efficace *adj* effective; efficient.

efficacité *f* effectiveness, efficiency.

efforcer (s') *vr* to endeavour, do one's best.

effort *m* effort, exertion; stress, strain.

effrayer *vt* to frighten, scare.

effroi *m* terror, dismay.

effronté *adj* shameless, impudent, cheeky.

effroyable *adj* horrifying, appalling.

égal *adj* equal; even, level; equable.

égaler *vt* to equal, match.

égaliser *vt* to equalise; to level out.

égalité *f* equality; equableness; evenness.

égard *m* consideration, respect:—**à l'~ de** concerning, regarding.

égarer *vt* to mislead, lead astray:—**s'~** *vr* to get lost.

église *f* church.

égoïsme *m* selfishness, egoism.

égoïste *mf* egotist:—*adj* egotistic.

éjecter *vt* to eject, throw out.

élaborer *vt* to elaborate, develop.

élan *m* surge, momentum, speed; spirit, elan.

élargir *vt* to widen, stretch:—**s'~** *vr* to get wider.

élastique *adj* elastic; flexible:—*m* elastic, elastic band.

élection *f* election; choice.

électorat *m* electorate; constituency; franchise.

électricité *f* electricity.

électrique *adj* electric.

électroménager *m* household appliance.

élégance *f* elegance, stylishness.

élégant *adj* elegant, stylish.

élémentaire *adj* elementary; basic.

éléphant *m* elephant.

élève *mf* pupil, student.

élever *vt* to bring up, raise:—**s'~** *vr* to rise, go up.

éligible *adj* eligible.

élimination *f* elimination.

éliminer *vt* to eliminate, discard.

élire *vt* to elect.

élite *f* elite.

elle *pron* she; it; her:—**~-même** herself.

élocution *f* elocution, diction.

éloigné *adj* distant, remote.

éloigner vt to move away:—**s'~** vr to go away.

éloquent adj eloquent.

émancipation f emancipation, liberation.

émanciper vt to emancipate:—**s'~** vr to become emancipated.

emballer vt to pack up, wrap up.

embarcation f boat, craft.

embargo m embargo.

embarquer vt to embark:—vi to embark.

embarras m embarrassment, confusion; trouble.

embarrasser vt to embarrass; to hamper.

embaucher vt to take on, hire.

embellir vt to beautify, make more attractive.

emblème m symbol, emblem.

embouteillage m traffic jam; bottling.

embrasser vt to kiss, embrace.

embrayage m clutch.

embryon m embryo.

embuscade f ambush.

émerger vi to emerge; to stand out.

émerveiller vt to astonish, amaze:—**s'~** vr to marvel at.

émettre vt to send out, emit, transmit.

émeute f riot.

émigration f emigration.

émigrer vi to emigrate.

éminent adj eminent, distinguished.

émission f sending out; transmission; broadcast; emission.

emménager vi to move in.

emmener vt to take away; to lead.

émoi m agitation, emotion.

émotion f emotion; commotion.

émouvoir vt to move, upset:—**s'~** vr to be moved.

empaqueter vt to parcel up, pack.

emparer (s') vr to seize, grab; to take possession of.

empêcher vt to prevent, stop.

empereur m emperor.

empiler vt to pile up, stack.

empire m empire; influence, ascendancy.

empirer vi to get worse, deteriorate.

emplacement m site, location.

emploi m use; job, employment.

employé m, **-e** f employee.

employer vt to use, spend; to employ.

employeur m, **euse** f employer.

empoisonner vt to poison.

emporter vt to take; to carry off.

emprisonner vt to imprison, trap.

emprunter vt to borrow; to assume; to derive.

ému adj moved, touched, excited.

en prép in; to; by; on:—**~ tant que** as:—pn from there; of it, of them:—**je n'~ veux plus** I don't want any more.

encadrer vt to frame; to train; to surround.

encaisser vt to collect, receive; to cash.

enceinte f pregnant.

encercler vt to encircle, surround.

enchaînement m linking; link; sequence.

enchaîner vt to chain.

enchanté adj enchanted, delighted.

enchanter vt to enchant, delight.

enclave f enclave.

encombrer vt to clutter, obstruct.

encore adv still; only; again; more:—**~ que** even though.

encouragement *m* encouragement.

encourager *vt* to encourage; to incite.

encre *f* ink.

encyclopédie *f* encyclopaedia.

endetter (s') *vr* to get into debt.

endommager *vt* to damage.

endormir *vt* to put to sleep:—**s'~** *vr* to fall asleep.

endosser *vt* to put on; to shoulder; to endorse.

endroit *m* place.

enduit *m* coating.

endurance *f* endurance, stamina.

endurcir *vt* to harden:—**s'~** *vr* to become hardened.

endurer *vt* to endure, bear.

énergie *f* energy; spirit, vigour.

énergique *adj* energetic, vigorous.

énerver *vt* to irritate, annoy:—**s'~** *vr* to get worked up.

enfance *f* childhood; infancy.

enfant *mf* child; native.

enfer *m* hell.

enfermer *vt* to lock up; to confine.

enfin *adv* at last; in short; after all.

enflammer *vt* to set on fire:—**s'~** *vr* to ignite.

enfler *vi* to swell up, inflate.

enfuir (s') *vr* to run away, flee.

engagement *m* agreement, commitment.

engager *vt* to bind; to involve:—**s'~** *vr* to undertake to.

engin *m* machine; instrument; contraption.

engouffrer *vt* to engulf.

engourdi *adj* numb; dull.

engraisser *vi* to get fatter.

énigme *f* enigma, riddle.

enivrer *vt* to intoxicate, make drunk:—**s'~** *vr* to get drunk.

enlever *vt* to remove; to abduct.

enneigé *adj* snowy, snowbound.

ennemi(e) *m(f)* enemy.

ennui *m* boredom, tedium, weariness.

ennuyer *vt* to bore, bother:—**s'~** *vr* to get bored.

énorme *adj* enormous, huge.

enquête *f* inquiry, investigation; survey.

enquêter *vi* to hold an inquiry; to investigate.

enraciner *vt* to implant, root.

enregistrer *vt* to record; to register.

enrichir *vt* to enrich, expand:—**s'~** *vr* to get rich.

enrober *vt* to wrap, cover, coat.

enrôler *vt* to enlist, enrol.

enrouler *vt* to roll up, wind up.

enseignant(e) *m(f)* teacher.

enseignement *m* education, training, instruction.

enseigner *vt* to teach.

ensemble *adv* together, at the same time:—*m* unity; whole.

ensoleillé *adj* sunny.

ensuite *adv* then, next, afterwards.

entasser *vt* to pile up, heap up.

entendement *m* understanding, comprehension.

entendre *vt* to hear; to intend, mean; to understand:—**s'~** *vr* to agree; to know how to.

entendu *adj* agreed:—**bien ~** of course.

enterrer *vt* to bury, inter.

entêté *adj* stubborn, obstinate.

enthousiasme *m* enthusiasm.

enthousiaste *adj* enthusiastic:—*mf* enthusiast.

entier *adj* entire, whole; intact.

entité *f* entity.

entourer *vt* to surround, frame, encircle:—*vr:*—**s'~ de** to surround oneself with.

entraider (s') *vr* to help one another.

entrain *m* spirit, liveliness.

entraîner *vt* to drag; to lead; to train:—**s'~** *vr* to train oneself.

entraîneur *m* trainer, coach.

entre *prép* between, among, into.

entrée *f* entry, entrance; insertion:—**d'~ de jeu** from the outset.

entremêler *vt* to intermingle, intermix.

entrepôt *m* warehouse, bonded warehouse.

entreprendre *vt* to embark upon, undertake.

entrepreneur *m* **-euse** *f* contractor; entrepreneur.

entreprise *f* company; venture, business.

entrer *vi* to enter, go in.

entretemps *adv* meanwhile.

entretenir *vt* to maintain, look after; to speak with.

entretien *m* upkeep, maintenance; conversation.

entrevue *f* meeting, interview.

énumérer *vt* to enumerate, list.

envahir *vt* to invade, overrun.

enveloppe *f* envelope; covering; exterior.

envelopper *vt* to envelop; to wrap up; to veil.

envers *prép* towards, to:—*m:*—**à l'~** inside out, upside down.

envie *f* desire, longing, inclination; envy.

envier *vt* to envy.

environ *adv* about, around:—**~s** *mpl* vicinity, neighbourhood.

environnement *m* environment.

environnemental *adj* environmental.

environner *vt* to surround, encircle.

envisager *vt* to view, envisage.

envoi *m* dispatch, remittance; kick-off.

envoyer *vt* to send, dispatch; hurl, fire.

épais *adj* thick; deep.

épaissir *vi* to thicken:—*vt*; **s'~** *vr* to get thicker.

épanouir *vt* to brighten; to open out:—**s'~** *vr* to bloom.

épargner *vt* to save; to spare.

épaule *f* shoulder.

épeler *vt* to spell.

éperdu *adj* distraught, overcome.

épice *m* spice.

épicier *m*, **-ière** *f* grocer.

épidémie *f* epidemic.

épier *vt* to spy on.

épine *f* spine; thorn; quill.

épingle *f* pin.

épiscopal *adj* episcopal.

épisode *m* episode.

épitaphe *f* epitaph.

éponge *f* sponge.

éponger *vt* to sponge, mop.

époque *f* time, epoch, age, period.

épouser *vt* to marry, wed; espouse.

épouvanter *vt* to terrify, appall.

époux *m*, **épouse** *f* spouse.

éprendre(s') *vr* to fall in love with.

épreuve *f* test; ordeal, trial; proof.

éprouver *vt* to feel, experience.

épuisement *m* exhaustion.

épuiser *vt* to exhaust, wear out.

épurer *vt* to purify, refine.

équateur *m* equator.

équation *f* equation.

équilibre *m* balance, equilibrium; harmony.

équilibrer *vt* to balance.

équipe *f* team, crew, gang, staff.

équipement *m* equipment; fitting out, fittings.

équiper *vt* to equip, fit out.

équitable *adj* equitable, fair.

équivalence *f* equivalence.

équivalent *adj* equivalent, same:— *m* equivalent.

équivoque *adj* equivocal, questionable.

ère *f* era.

érection *f* erection; establishment.

ergot *m* spur; lug.

ermite *m* hermit.

éroder *vt* to erode.

érotique *adj* erotic.

errer *vi* to wander, roam.

erreur *f* error, mistake, fault.

érudition *f* erudition, learning.

éruption *f* eruption.

escalade *f* climbing; escalation.

escalader *vt* to climb, scale.

escalier *m* stairs, steps.

escargot *m* snail.

esclavage *m* slavery, bondage.

esclave *mf* slave.

escompte *m* discount.

escompter *vt* to discount.

escorte *f* escort; retinue.

escorter *vt* to escort.

espace *m* space, interval.

espacer *vt* to space out.

espèce *f* sort, kind; species.

espérance *f* hope, expectation.

espérer *vt* to hope.

espion *m*, **-onne** *f* spy.

espionner *vt* to spy.

espoir *m* hope.

esprit *m* mind, intellect; spirit; wit.

esquisse *f* sketch, outline.

esquisser *vt* to sketch, outline.

esquiver *vt* to dodge; to shirk.

essai *m* test, trial; attempt; essay.

essayer *vt* to test, try, try on.

essence *f* petrol; essential oil.

essentiel *adj* essential, basic.

essieu *m* axle.

essuyer *vt* to wipe, mop:—**s'~** *vr* to wipe oneself.

est *m* east.

esthéticien(ne) *m(f)* beautician.

estimation *f* valuation; estimation, reckoning.

estimer *vt* to value, assess, estimate.

estival *adj* summer.

estivant *m*, **-e** *f* holidaymaker, summer visitor.

estomac *m* stomach.

et *conj* and.

établi *adj* established:—*m* workbench.

établir *vt* to establish **s'~** *vr* to become established.

établissement *m* establishing, building; establishment.

étage *m* floor, storey; stage, level.

étanche *adj* waterproof.

étang *m* pond.

étape *f* stage, leg; staging point.

état *m* state, condition; statement.

étayer *vt* to prop up, support.

été *m* summer.

éteindre *vt* to put out, extinguish.

étendre *vt* to spread, extend:—**s'~** *vr* to spread; to stretch out.

étendue *f* expanse, area; duration.

éternel *adj* eternal, everlasting.

éternité *f* eternity; ages.

éternuer *vi* to sneeze.

éthnique *adj* ethnic.

ethnologie *f* ethnology.

étinceler *vi* to sparkle, gleam.

étincelle *f* spark; gleam, glimmer.

étiquette *f* label, ticket; etiquette.

étoffe *f* material, fabric; stuff.

étoile *f* star.

étonnement *m* surprise, astonishment.

étonner *vt* to astonish, surprise:—**s'~** *vr* to be astonished.

étouffer *vt* to suffocate:—**s'~** *vr* to be suffocated, to swelter.

étourdi *adj* absentminded.

étourdir *vt* to stun, daze; to deafen.

étourdissement *m* blackout, dizzy spell.

étrange *adj* strange, funny.

étranger *m*, **-ère** *f* foreigner, stranger, alien:—*adj* foreign, strange, unknown.

étrangeté *f* strangeness, oddness.

étrangler *vt* to strangle, stifle:—**s'~** *vr* to strangle oneself, choke.

être *vi* to be:—**c'est-à-dire** namely, that is to say:—*m* being, person, soul.

étreindre *vt* to embrace, hug; to seize.

étroit *adj* narrow; strict.

étude *f* study; survey; office.

étudier *vt* to study, examine.

étymologie *f* etymology.

eu = *p.p.* avoir had.

eucalyptus *m* eucharist.

eucharistie *f* euphoria.

européen *m*, **-enne** *f* European:— *adj* European.

euthanasie *f* euthanasia.

eux *pron* they, them:—**c'est à ~** it's up to them; it's theirs:—**~-mêmes** themselves.

évacuer *vt* to evacuate, clear.

évader (s') *vr* to escape.

évaluation *f* evaluation, appraisal.

évaluer *vt* to evaluate, appraise.

évanouir (s') *vr* to faint, pass out.

évanouissement *m* faint, blackout.

évaporation *f* evaporation.

évaporer (s') *vr* to evaporate.

évasion *f* escape; escapism.

éveiller *vt* to waken, arouse:—**s'~** *vr* to wake up.

événement *m* event, incident.

éventualité *f* eventuality, possibility.

éventuel *adj* possible.

évêque *m* bishop.

évidence *f* evidence, proof.

évident *adj* obvious, evident.

évier *m* sink.

éviter *vt* to avoid; to spare.

évoluer *vi* to evolve, develop.

évolution *f* evolution, development.

évoquer *vt* to evoke, recall.

exacerber *vt* to exacerbate, aggravate.

exact *adj* exact, accurate.

exagération *f* exaggeration.

exagéré *adj* exaggerated, excessive.

exagérer *vt* to exaggerate.

examen *m* examination, survey, investigation.

examiner *vt* to examine, survey.

exaspérer *vt* to exasperate.

excellent *adj* excellent.

exceller *vi* to excel.

excentrique *adj* eccentric.

excepté *adj* apart, aside:—*prép* except, but for.

exception *f* exception, derogation.

exceptionnel *adj* exceptional.

excès *m* excess, surplus.

excitant *m* stimulant:—*adj* exciting, stimulating.

exciter *vt* to excite, stimulate:—**s'~** *vr* to get excited.

exclamation *f* exclamation.

exclamer (s') *vr* to exclaim.

exclure *vt* to exclude, oust, expel.

exclusif *adj* exclusive.

exclusion *f* exclusion, suspension.

excursion *f* excursion, trip.

excuse *f* excuse, pretext.

excuser *vt* to excuse, forgive:—**s'~** *vr* to apologise for.

exécuter *vt* to execute, carry out, perform; to produce.

exécution *f* execution, carrying out, performance.

exemple *m* example, model, instance.

exercer *vt* to exercise, perform, fulfil:—**s'~** *vr* to practise.

exercice *m* exercise, practice, use; financial year.

exhaustif *adj* exhaustive.

exhiber *vt* to exhibit, show.

exhibition *f* exhibition, show; display.

exhorter *vt* to exhort, urge.

exiger *vt* to demand, require.

exiler *vt* to exile, banish:—**s'~** *vr* to go into exile.

existence *f* existence, life.

exister *vi* to exist; to be.

exonérer *vt* to exempt.

exotique *adj* exotic.

expansion *f* expansion, development.

expectative *f* expectation, hope.

expédier *vt* to send, dispatch; to dispose of.

expédition *f* dispatch; consignment.

expérience *f* experience; experiment.

expérimental *adj* experimental.

expérimentation *f* experimentation.

expérimenter *vt* to test; to experiment with.

expert *adj* expert, skilled in:—*m* expert; connoisseur; assessor.

expertise *f* expertise; expert appraisal.

explicatif *adj* explanatory.

explication *f* explanation, analysis.

explicite *adj* explicit.

expliquer *vt* to explain, account for; to analyse.

exploitation *f* working; exploitation; concern.

exploiter *vt* to work, exploit; run, operate.

explorer *vt* to explore.

exploser *vi* to explode.

explosion *f* explosion.

exportation *f* export, exportation.

exporter *vt* to export.

exposer *vt* to display; to expose.

exposition *f* display; exposition; exposure.

express *adj* fast:—*m* fast train.

expression *f* expression.

exprimer *vt* to express, voice:—**s'~** *vr* to express oneself.

expropriation *f* expropriation.

expulser *vt* to expel; to evict.

exquis *adj* exquisite.

extase *f* ecstacy; rapture.

extension *f* extension; stretching; expansion.

exténuer *vt* to exhaust:—**s'~** *vr* to exhaust oneself.

extérieur *m* exterior, outside:—*adj* outer, external, exterior.

exterminer *vt* exterminate.

externe *adj* external, outer.

extinction *f* extinction, extinguishing.

extradition *f* extradition.

extraire *vt* to extract; to mine.

extraordinaire *adj* extraordinary.

extravagant *adj* extravagant, wild.

extraverti *m*, **-e** *f* extrovert:—*adj* extrovert.

extrême *adj* extreme.

extrémiste *mf*, *adj* extremist.

exubérance *f* exuberance.

exubérant *adj* exuberant.

F

fable *f* fable, story, tale.

fabricant *m*, **-ante** *f* manufacturer, maker.

fabrique *f* factory.

fabriquer *vt* to manufacture; to forge; to fabricate.

façade *f* façade, front.

face *f* face, side, surface, aspect:—**en ~** opposite:—**~ à** facing.

fâcher *vt* to anger; to grieve:—**se ~** *vr* to get angry.

fâcheux *adj* deplorable, regrettable.

facile *adj* easy; facile.

facilité *f* easiness, ease; ability; facility.

faciliter *vt* to make easier, facilitate.

façon *f* way, fashion; make; imitation:—**de toute ~** at any rate.

façonner *vt* to shape, fashion.

facteur *m* postman.

facture *f* bill, invoice; construction, technique.

facturer *vt* to invoice, charge for.

faculté *f* faculty; power, ability; right.

fade *adj* insipid, bland, dull.

faible *adj* weak, feeble; slight, poor.

faiblesse *f* weakness, feebleness, faintness.

faillir *vi* to come close to; to fail:—**j'ai failli tomber** I almost fell.

faim *f* hunger; appetite; famine.

faire *vt* to do; to make:—**rien à ~!** nothing doing!:—**s'en ~** to worry.

faisable *adj* feasible.

fait *m* event; fact; act.

falaise *f* cliff.

falloir *vi* to be necessary:—**il faut que tu partes** you must leave.

falsifier *vt* to falsify, alter.

familial *adj* family, domestic.

familiariser *vt* to familiarise:—**se ~** *vr* to familiarise oneself.

familiarité *f* familiarity.

familier *adj* familiar; colloquial; informal.

famille *f* family.

famine *f* famine.

fanatique *adj* fanatic:—*mf* fanatic.

faner *vt* to fade:—**se ~** *vr* to wither, fade.

fantaisie *f* whim, extravagance; imagination.

fantastique *adj* fantastic.

fantôme *m* ghost, phantom.

farce *f* joke, prank; farce.

farcir *vt* to stuff, cram.

fardeau *m* load, burden.

farine *f* flour.

farouche *adj* shy, timid; unsociable.

fascination *f* fascination.

fasciner *vt* to fascinate, bewitch.

fasciste *mf*, *adj* fascist.

fastidieux *adj* tedious, boring.

fatal *adj* fatal, deadly; fateful.

fatalité *f* fatality; inevitability.

fatigue *f* fatigue, tiredness.

fatiguer *vt* to tire; to overwork, strain:—**se ~** *vr* to get tired.

faubourg *m* suburb.

faune *f* wildlife, fauna.

faussaire *mf* forger.

fausser *vt* to distort, alter; to warp.

faute *f* mistake, foul, fault:—**~ de mieux** for lack of anything better.

fauteuil *m* armchair.

fautif *m*, **-ive** *f* culprit:—*adj* at fault.

faux *adj* false, forged, fake; wrong; bogus.

faux-semblant *m* sham, pretence.

faveur *f* favour.

favorable *adj* favourable, sympathetic.

favori *m*, **-ite** *f* favourite:—*adj* favourite.

favoriser *vt* to favour, further.

fécond *adj* fertile; prolific, fruitful; creative.

féconder *vt* to impregnate; to fertilise, pollinate.

fédéral *adj* federal.

fédération *f* federation.

feindre *vt* to feign, pretend.

fêlé *adj* cracked, hare-brained.

félicitation *f* congratulation.

féliciter *vt* to congratulate.

femelle *f* female.

féminin *adj* feminine, female.

féministe *mf adj* feminist.

féminité *f* femininity.

femme *f* woman; wife.

fendre *vt* to split, cleave, crack:—**se ~** *vr* to crack.

fenêtre *f* window.

fente *f* crack, fissure; slot.

fer *m* iron, point, blade:—**~ à cheval** horseshoe.

férié *adj* holiday.

ferme *adj* firm, steady; definite:—*f* farm.

ferment *m* ferment, leaven.

fermentation *f* fermentation, fermenting.

fermer *vt* to close; block; turn off:—

se ~ *vr* to close, shut up; to close one's mind to.

fermeté *f* firmness, steadiness.

fermier *m*, **-ière** *f* farmer.

féroce *adj* ferocious, savage.

férocité *f* ferocity, fierceness.

ferroviaire *adj* railway.

fertile *adj* fertile, productive.

fertilité *f* fertility.

fervent *adj* fervent, ardent.

festin *m* feast.

festival *m* festival.

fête *f* feast, holiday.

fêter *vt* to celebrate, fête.

feu *m* fire; light; hearth:—**en ~** on fire.

feuille *f* leaf.

feuilleter *vt* to leaf through.

fiable *adj* reliable; dependable.

fiancer (se) *vr* to become engaged.

fiasco *m* fiasco.

fibre *f* fibre.

ficelle *f* string; stick (bread).

fiche *f* card; sheet; certificate.

ficher *vt* to file, put on file.

fictif *adj* fictitious; imaginary.

fiction *f* imagination, fiction.

fidèle *adj* faithful, loyal.

fidélité *f* fidelity, loyalty.

fier *adj* proud, haughty; noble.

fier (se) *vr* to trust, rely on.

fierté *f* pride; arrogance.

fièvre *f* fever, temperature; excitement.

figuratif *adj* figurative, representational.

figure *f* face; figure; illustration, diagram.

figurer *vt* to represent:—*vi* to appear, feature:—**se ~** *vr* to imagine.

fil *m* thread; wire; cord:—**~ de fer** wire.

file f line, queue:—**à la ~** in line, in succession.

filer vt to spin.

filière f path; procedures; network.

fille f daughter, girl.

fillette f (small) girl.

film m film, picture.

filmer vt to film.

fils m son.

filtre m filter.

fin f end, finish:—adj thin, fine; delicate.

final adj final.

finance f finance.

financer vt to finance.

financier m, **-ière** f financier.

finesse f fineness; neatness.

fini adj finished, over, complete.

finir vt to finish, complete:—vi to finish, end; to die.

fissure f crack, fissure.

fixe adj fixed, permanent, set:—**~ment** adv fixedly, steadily.

fixer vt to fix; to arrange.

flacon m bottle, flask.

flagrant adj flagrant, blatant.

flair m sense of smell, nose; intuition.

flambeau m torch; candlestick.

flamme f flame; fervour; ardour.

flanc m flank, side.

flâner vi to stroll; to lounge about.

flatter vt to flatter, gratify.

flatterie f flattery.

flèche f arrow.

fléchir vi to bend, yield, weaken:—vt to bend, sway.

fleur f flower.

fleurir vi to blossom, flower:—vt to decorate with flowers.

fleuve m river.

flexibilité f flexibility.

flexible adj flexible, pliant.

flocon m fleck, flake.

flore f flora.

flot m stream, flood; floodtide; wave.

flotte f fleet; rain.

flotter vi to float; to drift; to wander; to waver.

fluctuation f fluctuation.

fluide adj fluid, flowing.

flux m flood; flow; flux.

foi f faith, trust.

foie m liver.

foin m hay.

foire f fair, trade fair.

fois f time, occasion.

folie f madness, insanity; extravagance.

foncé adj dark, deep (colours).

fonction f post, duty; function.

fonctionnaire mf civil servant.

fonctionner vi to work, function, operate.

fond m bottom, back:—**au ~** basically, in fact:—**à ~** thoroughly, in depth.

fondamental adj fundamental, basic.

fondamentaliste mf:—adj fundamentalist.

fondateur m, **-trice** f founder.

fondation f foundation.

fonder vt to found; to base.

fondre vi to melt:—vt to melt; to cast.

fonds m business; fund; money; stock.

fontaine f fountain, spring.

football m football, soccer.

force f strength, force, violence, energy.

forcé adj forced; emergency:—**~ment** adv inevitably.

forcer vt to force:—vi to overdo:—**se ~** vr to force oneself to.

forêt f forest.

forger vt to forge, form, mould.

formalité f formality.

formation f formation; training.

forme f form, shape; mould, fitness.

formel adj definite; positive; formal.

former vt to form; to train:—**se ~** vr to form; to train oneself

formidable adj tremendous:—**~ment** adv tremendously.

formulaire m form.

formule f formula; phrase; system.

formuler vt to formulate; express.

fort adj strong; high; loud; pronounced:—adv loudly; greatly; most:—m fort; strong point, forte.

fortifier vt to fortify, strengthen:—**se ~** vr to grow stronger.

fortuit adj fortuitous, chance.

fortune f fortune, luck.

fosse f pit; grave.

fou adj, f **folle** mad, wild; tremendous; erratic.

foudre f lightning, thunderbolt.

foudroyer vt to strike (lightning).

fouiller vt to search, scour.

foulard m scarf.

foule f crowd; masses, heaps.

four m oven; furnace; fiasco.

fourgon m coach, wagon, van.

fourmi f ant.

fourmiller vi to swarm, teem.

fournir vt to supply, provide.

fournisseur m, **-euse** f purveyor, supplier.

fourrer vt to stuff; to line.

fourrure f coat, fur.

foyer m home; fireplace; focus.

fracas m crash; roar, din.

fraction f fraction, part.

fracture f fracture.

fragile adj fragile, delicate.

fragment m fragment.

fragmenter vt to break up:—**se ~** vr to fragment.

fraîcheur f freshness, coolness.

frais mpl expenses:—adj, f **fraîche** fresh, cool.

franc adj, f **franche** frank, open.

Français m Frenchman, **-e** f Frenchwoman.

français adj French:—m French.

France f France.

franchir vt to clear, get over, cross.

francophone mf French-speaker, adj French-speaking.

frange f fringe; threshold.

frapper vt to hit; to strike down:—vi to strike, knock.

fraternel adj fraternal.

fraternité f fraternity.

fraude f fraud, cheating.

frein m brake; check.

freiner vi to brake, slow down:—vt to slow down; to curb, check.

frémir vi to quiver, tremble.

frénétique adj frenetic.

fréquence f frequency.

fréquent adj frequent.

frère m brother.

friand adj partial to, fond of.

frigidaire m refrigerator.

frire vt to fry.

frisé adj curly, curly-haired.

frisson m shiver, shudder.

frissonner vi to shudder, tremble, shiver.

frite f chip.

frivole adj frivolous, shallow.

frivolité f frivolity.

froid adj cold, cool:—m cold; coolness; refrigeration.

froideur f coldness, chilliness.

fromage *m* cheese.
front *m* forehead; face; front.
frontière *f* border, frontier.
frotter *vt* to rub, scrape.
fructueux *adj* fruitful, profitable.
frugal *adj* frugal.
frugalité *f* frugality.
fruit *m* fruit, result.
frustration *f* frustration.
frustrer *vt* to frustrate, deprive.
fugitif *m*, **-ive** *f* fugitive:—*adj* fugitive, runaway.
fuir *vi* to avoid; to flee; to leak.
fuite *f* flight, escape; leak.
fumé *adj* smoked.
fumée *f* smoke; vapour.
fumer *vi* to smoke, steam, give off smoke:—*vt* to smoke.

fumeur *m*, **-euse** *f* smoker.
funérailles *fpl* funeral.
funéraire *adj* funeral, funerary.
fureur *f* fury; violence.
furieux *adj* furious, violent.
furtif *adj* furtive; stealthy.
fusée *f* rocket, missile.
fusil *m* rifle, gun.
fusiller *vt* to shoot.
fusion *f* fusion; melting; merger; blending.
fusionner *vt* to merge, combine.
futile *adj* futile.
futilité *f* futility.
futur *adj* future:—*m* intended, fiancé; future.
fuyard *m*, **-e** *f*:—*adj* runaway.

G

gâcher *vt* to mix; to waste.
gachette *f* trigger.
gadget *m* gadget; gimmick.
gage *m* security; pledge; proof.
gagnant *m*, **-e** *f* winner:—*adj* winning.
gagner *vt* to earn, to win:—*vi* to win.
gai *adj* cheerful, happy, gay.
gain *m* earnings; gain, profit, benefit; saving.
gala *m* official reception; gala.
galant *adj* gallant, courteous.
galaxie *f* galaxy.
galerie *f* gallery; tunnel.
galet *m* pebble.

Gallois *m* Welshman, **-e** *f* Welshwoman.
gallois *adj* Welsh:—*m* Welsh (language).
galop *m* gallop; canter.
galoper *vi* to gallop; to run wild.
gamin *m*, **-e** *f* kid, street urchin.
gamme *f* range; scale.
gant *m* glove.
gap *m* gap; difference, discrepancy.
garage *m* garage.
garagiste *mf* garage owner.
garantie *f* guarantee, surety.
garantir *vt* to guarantee, secure.
garçon *m* boy; assistant; waiter.

garde *f* custody; guard; surveillance:—*m* guard, warder.

garde-boue *m* mudguard.

garde-robe *f* wardrobe.

garder *vt* to look after; to stay in; to keep on.

gardien *m*, **-ienne** *f* guard, guardian, warden; protector.

gare *f* rail station; basin; depot.

gargouiller *vi* to gurgle; to rumble.

garnir *vt* to fit with; to trim, decorate.

garnison *f* (*mil*) garrison.

gaspiller *vt* to waste, squander.

gastronomie *f* gastronomy.

gâté *adj* ruined; spoiled.

gâteau *m* cake.

gâter *vt* to ruin; to spoil:—**se ~** *vr* to go bad, go off.

gauche *adj* left; awkward, clumsy:—*f* left; left wing.

gaucher *adj* left-handed.

gaz *m invar* gas; fizz; wind.

gazeux *adj* gaseous; fizzy.

gazon *m* lawn; turf.

géant *m* giant, **-e** *f* giantess.

gel *m* frost; gel.

geler *vi* to freeze, be frozen:—*vt* to freeze.

gémir *vi* to groan, moan.

gendarme *m* policeman; gendarme.

gendarmerie *f* police force, constabulary.

gêne *f* discomfort; trouble:—**être sans ~** to be inconsiderate.

généalogie *f* genealogy.

gêner *vt* to bother; to hinder; to make uneasy.

général *adj* general, broad; common:—*m* general.

généralisation *f* generalisation.

généraliser *vt* to generalise:—**se ~** *vr* to become widespread.

générateur *m* generator.

génération *f* generation.

générer *vt* to generate

généreux *adj* generous; noble; magnanimous.

générosité *f* generosity; nobility; magnanimity.

génétique *adj* genetic.

génie *m* genius; spirit; genie.

genou *m* knee.

genre *m* kind, type; gender; genre.

gens *mpl* people, folk.

gentil *adj*, *f* **gentille** kind; good; pleasant.

géographie *f* geography.

géographique *adj* geographic.

géologie *f* geology.

géométrie *f* geometry.

géométrique *adj* geometric.

gérant *m*, **-e** *f* manager.

gérer *vt* to manage, administer.

germe *m* germ; seed.

geste *m* gesture; act, deed.

gesticuler *vi* to gesticulate.

gestion *f* management, administration.

ghetto *m* ghetto.

gicler *vi* to spurt, squirt.

gifler *vt* to slap, smack.

gilet *m* waistcoat.

girafe *f* giraffe.

gisement *m* deposit; mine; pool.

gîte *m* shelter; home; gîte.

givre *m* frost, rime.

glace *f* ice; ice cream; mirror.

glacer *vt* to freeze; to chill; to glaze.

glaçon *m* icicle; ice cube.

glande *f* gland.

glaner *vt* to glean.

glissement *m* sliding; gliding; downturn, downswing.

glisser *vi* to slide, slip, skid.

global *adj* global, overall:—**ement** *adv* globally.

globe *m* globe, sphere; earth.

gloire *f* glory; distinction; celebrity.

glorieux *adj* glorious.

glorifier *vt* to glory, honour:—**se ~** *vr* to glory in; to boast.

glossaire *m* glossary.

gluant *adj* sticky, gummy.

gobelet *m* beaker, tumbler.

golf *m* golf.

golfeur *m*, **-euse** *f* golfer.

gomme *f* gum; rubber, eraser.

gommer *vt* to rub out; to gum.

gonflable *adj* inflatable.

gonfler *vt* to pump up, inflate:—**se ~** *vr* to swell; to be puffed up.

gorge *f* throat.

gothique *m*, *adj* Gothic.

goudronner *vt* to tar.

goulu *adj* greedy, gluttonous.

goupille *f* pin.

gourde *f* gourd; flask.

gourmand *adj* greedy.

gourmet *m* gourmet.

goût *m* taste; liking; style.

goûter *vt* to taste; to appreciate:—*vi* to have a snack; to taste good:—*m* snack.

goutte *f* drop; gout.

gouvernail *m* rudder; helm.

gouvernement *m* government.

gouverner *vt* to govern, rule; to control; to steer.

grâce *f* grace; favour; mercy; pardon:—**~ à** thanks to.

gracieux *adj* gracious.

grade *m* rank; grade; degree.

graduel *adj* gradual; progressive.

graduer *vt* to step up; to graduate.

grain *m* grain, seed; bead.

graisse *f* grease, fat.

grammaire *f* grammar.

grammatical *adj* grammatical.

gramme *m* gram.

grand *adj* big; tall; great; leading:—**pas ~-chose** not up to much.

grand-mère *f* grandmother.

grand-parents *mpl* grandparents

grand-père *m* grandfather.

grandeur *f* size; greatness; magnitude.

grandir *vi* to grow bigger, increase:—*vt* to magnify; to exaggerate.

graphique *m* graph:—*adj* graphic.

gras *adj f* **grasse** fatty; fat; greasy; crude.

gratification *f* gratuity; bonus.

gratis *adv* free, gratis.

gratitude *f* gratitude, gratefulness.

gratuit *adj* free, gratuitous.

grave *adj* grave, solemn.

graver *vt* to engrave, imprint.

gravitation *f* gravitation.

gravité *f* gravity.

gravure *f* engraving, carving.

gré *m* liking, taste:—**au ~ de** depending on, at the mercy of:—**savoir ~** to be grateful.

greffer *vt* to transplant, graft.

grêle *f* hail.

grelotter *vi* to shiver.

grenier *m* attic, garret.

grenouille *f* frog.

grève *f* strike; shore.

griffe *f* claw.

griffer *vt* to scratch.

griffonner *vt* to scribble, jot down.

grillade *f* grill.

grille *f* railings; gate; grill.

grille-pain *m invar* toaster.

griller *vt* to toast, scorch; to put bars on:—*vi* to toast, grill.

grimace *f* grimace

grimper *vi* to climb up.

grippe *f* flu, influenza.

gris *adj* grey.

griser *vt* to intoxicate:—**se ~** *vr* to get drunk.

grogner *vi* to grumble, moan.

grommeler *vi* to mutter; to grumble:—*vt* to mutter.

gronder *vt* to scold:—*vi* to rumble, growl.

gros *adj*, *f* **grosse** big; fat; serious; coarse:—**en ~** in bulk:—*m* bulk; wholesale; fat man.

grossesse *f* pregnancy.

grosseur *f* thickness; weight; fatness.

grossir *vi* to get fatter; to swell, grow:—*vt* to magnify; to exaggerate.

grossiste *mf* wholesaler.

grotesque *adj* grotesque, ludicrous

groupe *m* group; party; cluster.

grouper *vt* to group together; to bulk:—**se ~** *vr* to gather.

grue *f* crane.

guépard *m* cheetah.

guêpe *f* wasp.

guère *adv* hardly, scarcely.

guérir *vi* to get better; to heal:—*vt* to cure, heal:—**se ~** *vr* to get better; to recover from.

guérison *f* recovery; curing.

guerre *f* war; warfare.

guerrier *m*, **-ière** *f* warrior.

guetter *vt* to watch; to lie in wait for.

gueule *f* mouth; face; muzzle.

guichet *m* counter; ticket office, booking office.

guichetier *m*, **-ière** *f* counter clerk.

guide *m* guide.

guider *vt* to guide:—**se ~** *vr* to be guided by.

guidon *m* handlebars.

guillotine *f* guillotine.

guise *f* manner, way:—**en ~ de** by way of:—**à ta ~** as you please.

guitare *f* guitar.

guitariste *mf* guitarist.

gymnastique *f* gymnastics.

gynécologue, gynécologiste *mf* gynaecologist.

H

habile *adj* skilful, skilled.

habiliter *vt* to qualify; to authorise.

habiller *vt* to dress, clothe:—**s'~** *vr* to get dressed.

habitant(e) *m(f)* inhabitant; occupant; dweller.

habitation *f* dwelling; residence; house.

habiter *vi* to live:—*vt* to live in; to occupy.

habitude *f* habit, custom, routine.

habituel *adj* usual, customary.

habituer *vt* to accustom; to teach:—**s'~** *vr* to get used to.

hache *f* axe, hatchet.

haie *f* hedge.

haine f hatred.

haïr vt to hate, detest.

hâle m tan, sunburn.

haleine f breath, breathing.

haleter vi to pant, gasp for breath.

hall m hall, foyer.

halle f covered market; hall.

hallucination f hallucination.

halte f stop, break; stopping place.

hameçon m fish-hook.

hanche f hip; haunch.

handicap m handicap.

hanter vt to haunt.

harceler vt to harass; to pester; to plague.

hardi adj bold, daring; brazen.

hargne f spite.

haricot m bean.

harmonie f harmony; wind section.

harmoniser vt to harmonise:—**s'~** vr to be in harmony.

harpe f harp.

hasard m chance; accident; hazard; risk.

hasardeux adj hazardous, risky.

hâte f haste; impatience.

hâter vt to hasten; to quicken:—**se ~** vr to hurry.

hâtif adj precocious; early; hasty.

hausse f rise, increase.

hausser vt to raise; to heighten.

haut adj high, tall; upper; superior.

haut-parleur m loudspeaker.

hauteur f height; elevation; haughtiness; bearing.

hebdomadaire adj:—m weekly.

hélice f propeller; helix.

hélicoptère m helicopter.

hémisphère m hemisphere.

hémophile adj haemophiliac.

herbe f grass:—**en ~** under grass.

herboriste mf herbalist.

héréditaire adj hereditary.

hérédité f heredity; heritage; right of inheritance.

hérisser vt to bristle; to spike.

hérisson m hedgehog.

héritage m inheritance; heritage, legacy.

hériter vi to inherit.

héritier m heir, **-ière** f heiress.

hermétique adj hermetic.

hernie f hernia, rupture.

héroïne f heroine; heroin.

héroïque adj heroic.

héroïsme m heroism.

héros m hero.

hésitation f hesitation.

hésiter vi to hesitate.

hétérosexuel adj heterosexual.

heure f hour; time of day:—**de bonne ~** early.

heureux adv lucky; happy.

heurter vt to strike, hit; to jostle.

hibernation f hibernation.

hibou m owl.

hier adv yesterday.

hilarité f hilarity, laughter.

hippopotame m hippopotamus.

hirondelle f swallow.

hisser vt to hoist, haul up.

histoire f history; story; business:— **~ de dire** just to say.

historien m, **-ienne** f historian.

historique adj historic; historical.

hiver m winter.

hivernal adj winter; wintry.

hocher vt to nod; to shake one's head.

homard m lobster.

homicide m homicide

homme m man.

homogène adj homogeneous.

homologuer vt to ratify; to approve.

homosexuel(le) *m(f)* homosexual.

honnête *adj* honest; decent; honourable.

honnêteté *f* honesty, decency.

honneur *m* honour; integrity; credit:—**en l'~ de** in honour of.

honorable *adj* honourable; reputable.

honorer *vt* to honour; to esteem.

honte *f* shame, disgrace.

honteux *adj* shameful; disgraceful.

hôpital *m* hospital.

horaire *m* timetable:—*adj* hourly.

horizon *m* horizon.

horizontal *adj* horizontal.

horloge *f* clock.

hormone *f* hormone.

horreur *f* horror.

horrible *adj* horrible; dreadful.

horrifier *vt* to horrify.

hors *prép* outside; beyond; save; except.

hors-d'œuvre *m invar* hors d'œuvre, starter.

hospice *m* home, asylum; hospice.

hospitalier *adj* hospital; hospitable.

hospitaliser *vt* to hospitalise.

hospitalité *f* hospitality.

hostile *adj* hostile.

hostilité *f* hostility.

hôte *m*, **hôtesse** *f* host; landlord.

hôtel *m* hotel.

hôtelier *m*, **-ière** *f* hotelier:—*adj* hotel.

houle *f* swell.

huer *vt* to boo.

huile *f* oil; petroleum.

huit *adj*, *m* eight.

huitième *adj* eighth:—*mf* eighth.

huître *f* oyster.

humain *adj* human; humane:—*m* human.

humanitaire *adj* humanitarian.

humanité *f* humanity.

humble *adj* humble; modest.

humeur *f* mood, humour; temper.

humide *adj* humid.

humidité *f* humidity.

humilier *vt* to humiliate.

humilité *f* humility.

humour *m* humour.

hurler *vi*:—*vt* to roar, yell.

hutte *f* hut.

hybride *adj m* hybrid.

hydraulique *adj* hydraulic.

hygiène *f* hygienics; hygiene.

hygiénique *adj* hygienic.

hymne *m* hymn.

hypermarché *m* hypermarket.

hypnose *f* hypnosis

hypnotiser *vt* to hypnotise.

hypocondriaque *mf adj* hypochondriac.

hypocrisie *f* hypocrisy.

hypocrite *mf* hypocrite:—*adj* hypocritical.

hypothèque *f* mortgage.

hypothéquer *vt* to mortgage.

hypothèse *f* hypothesis; assumption.

hypothétique *adj* hypothetical.

hystérie *f* hysteria.

hystérique *mf* hysterical:—*adj* hysteric.

I

iceberg *m* iceberg.
idéal *adj:—m* ideal.
idée *f* idea.
identifier *vt* to identify:—s'~ *vr* to identify with.
identique *adj* identical.
identité *f* identity; similarity.
idiot *m*, **-e** *f* idiot, fool:—*adj* idiotic, stupid.
ignorance *f* ignorance.
ignorant *adj* ignorant; unacquainted; uninformed.
ignorer *vt* to be ignorant of; to be unaware of; to ignore.
il *pron* he, it.
île *f* island, isle.
illégal *adj* illegal; unlawful.
illégitime *adj* illegitimate; unwarranted.
illicite *adj* illicit.
illogique *adj* illogical.
illusion *f* illusion
illustration *f* illustration.
illustrer *vt* to illustrate.
image *f* image, picture; reflection.
imagination *f* imagination.
imaginer *vt* to imagine; to suppose.
imbécile *mf* idiot, imbecile:—*adj* stupid, idiotic.
imitation *f* imitation; mimicry; forgery.
imiter *vt* to imitate.
immatriculation *f* registration.
immédiat *adj* immediate; instant.
immense *adj* immense, boundless.
immeuble *m* building; block of flats; real estate.

immigrant *m*, **-e** *f* immigrant.
immigration *f* immigration.
imminent *adj* imminent, impending.
immobilier *adj* property:—*m* property business.
immobiliser *vt* to immobilise; to bring to a standstill.
immoral *adj* immoral.
immortel *adj* immortal.
immunité *f* immunity.
impair *adj* odd, uneven.
imparfait *adj* imperfect.
impartial *adj* impartial.
impartialité *f* impartiality.
impassible *adj* impassive.
impatience *f* impatience.
impatient *adj* impatient.
imperceptible *adj* imperceptible.
impersonnel *adj* impersonal.
impertinence *f* impertinence.
impertinent *adj* impertinent.
imperturbable *adj* unshakeable; imperturbable.
impétueux *adj* impetuous.
impitoyable *adj* merciless, pitiless.
implacable *adj* implacable.
implantation *f* implantation; establishment; introduction.
implanter *vt* to introduce; to establish; to implant.
implication *f* implication; involvement.
implicite *adj* implicit.
impliquer *vt* to imply; to necessitate; to implicate.
impoli *adj* impolite, rude.

impolitesse *f* impoliteness, rudeness.

importance *f* importance, significance; size.

important *adj* important, significant; sizeable.

importation *f* import, importation.

importer *vt* to import:—*vi* to matter:—**n'importe qui** anybody:—**n'importe quoi** anything.

imposer *vt* to impose, lay down.

impossibilité *f* impossibility.

impossible *adj* impossible.

impôt *m* tax, duty.

$imprégner *vt* impregnate; to permeate; to imbue.

impression *f* feeling, impression.

$impressioniste *mf*:—*adj* impressionist.

impressionner *vt* to impress; to upset.

imprévisible *adj* unforeseeable; unpredictable.

$imprévu *adj* unforeseen, unexpected.

imprimer *vt* to print.

imprimeur *m* printer.

improbable *adj* improbable, unlikely.

improviser *vt* to improvise.

imprudent *adj* careless, imprudent.

impudence *f* impudence; shamelessness.

impuissant *adj* powerless, helpless.

impulsif *adj* impulsive.

inacceptable *adj* unacceptable.

inaccessible *adj* inaccessible.

inactif *adj* inactive, idle.

inactivité *f* inactivity.

inadmissible *adj* inadmissible.

inanimé *adj* inanimate; unconscious.

inaperçu *adj* unnoticed.

inattendu *adj* unexpected, unforeseen.

incapable *adj* incapable; incompetent.

incapacité *f* incompetence; disability.

incarcérer *vt* to incarcerate.

incendie *m* fire, blaze.

incertain *adj* uncertain, unsure.

incessant *adj* incessant, ceaseless.

incident *m* incident, point of law.

inciter *vt* to incite, urge.

inclure *vt* to include; to insert.

incommoder *vt* to disturb, bother.

incomparable *adj* incomparable.

incompatible *adj* incompatible.

incompréhensible *adj* incomprehensible.

inconfortable *adj* uncomfortable; awkward.

incongru *adj* unseemly; incongruous.

inconnu *m*, **-e** *f* stranger, unknown person:—*m* unknown:—*adj* unknown.

inconscience *f* unconsciousness; thoughtlessness.

inconscient *adj* unconscious; thoughtless, reckless:—*m* subconscious, unconscious.

inconsidéré *adj* inconsiderate; thoughtless.

incontestable *adj* incontestable, unquestionable.

inconvénient *m* drawback, inconvenience.

incorporer *vt* to incorporate, integrate.

incorrect *adj* faulty, incorrect.

incroyable *adj* incredible; unbelievable.

indécis *adj* indecisive; unsettled; undefined.

indéfini *adj* undefined; indefinite:—**~ment** *adv* indefinitely.

indemne *adj* unharmed, unhurt.

indemnité *f* compensation; indemnity.

indéniable *adj* undeniable, indisputable.

indépendant *adj* independent.

indéterminé *adj* undetermined; unspecified.

index *m* index; index finger.

indication *f* indication; piece of information; instruction.

indice *m* indication; clue; sign.

indifférent *adj* indifferent; immaterial.

indigène *mf* native; local:—*adj* indigenous, native.

indigestion *f* indigestion.

indigne *adj* unworthy; undeserving.

indiquer *vt* to indicate, point out; to tell.

indirect *adj* indirect; circumstantial; collateral.

indiscret *adj* indiscreet; inquisitive.

indispensable *adj* indispensable; essential.

indisponible *adj* unavailable.

individu *m* individual.

individuel *adj* individual.

indulgent *adj* indulgent; lenient.

industrie *f* industry; dexterity, ingenuity.

industriel *m*, **-elle** *f* industrialist, manufacturer:—*adj* industrial.

inédit *adj* unpublished; original.

inefficace *adj* ineffective; inefficient.

inégal *adj* unequal; uneven; irregular.

inépuisable *adj* inexhaustible.

inertie *f* inertia, apathy.

inévitable *adj* inevitable, unavoidable.

inexact *adj* inexact, inaccurate.

inexplicable *adj* inexplicable.

infaillible *adj* infallible.

infantile *adj* infantile, childish.

infecter *vt* to infect; to contaminate:—**s'~** *vr* to become infected.

infection *f* infection.

inférieur *adj* inferior; lower.

infériorité *f* inferiority.

infester *vt* to infest; overrun.

infidèle *adj* unfaithful, disloyal.

infini *adj* infinite; interminable.

infirme *adj* feeble; crippled, disabled.

infirmier *m*, **-ière** *f* nurse.

infirmité *f* disability; infirmity.

inflation *f* inflation.

inflexible *adj* inflexible, rigid.

influence *f* influence.

influencer *vt* to influence, sway.

information *f* piece of information; information; inquiry.

informatique *f* computing; data processing:—*adj* computer.

informer *vt* to inform, tell.

ingénieur *m* engineer.

ingénieux *adj* ingenious, clever.

ingénu *adj* ingenuous, naive.

ingrédient *m* ingredient; component.

initial *adj* initial.

initiative *f* initiative; enterprise.

initier *vt* to initiate.

injecter *vt* to inject.

injure *f* injury; insult.

injuste *adj* unjust, unfair.

injustice *f* injustice.

inné *adj* innate, inborn.

innocence f innocence.

innocent m, **-e** f innocent person; simpleton:—adj innocent.

innovation f innovation.

inondation f inundation.

inouï adj unprecedented, unheard of.

inquiet adj worried, anxious, uneasy.

inscription f inscription; registration; matriculation.

inscrire vt to inscribe; to register:—s'~ vr to join.

insecte m insect.

insensible adj insensible, insensitive.

insérer vt to insert.

insinuer vt to insinuate, imply.

insipide adj insipid, tasteless.

insister vi to insist, be insistent; to stress.

insolent adj insolent; brazen.

insomnie f insomnia.

insoutenable adj unbearable; untenable.

inspecter vt to inspect, examine.

inspection f inspection.

inspiration f inspiration; suggestion.

inspirer vt to inspire; to breathe in.

instable adj unstable; unsettled.

installation f installation; installing.

installer vt to install; to fit out.

instant m moment, instant.

instinct m instinct.

instinctif adj instinctive.

institut m institute; school.

institution f institution; establishment.

instruction f instruction; education; inquiry.

instruire vt to instruct; to teach; to conduct an inquiry.

instrument m instrument, implement.

insuffisant adj insufficient, inadequate.

insulte f insult.

insulter vt to insult, affront.

insupportable adj unbearable, intolerable.

intact adj intact.

intégral adj integral, complete.

intégrer vt to integrate:—s'~ vr to become integrated; to fit in.

intégrité f integrity.

intellectuel m, **-uelle** f intellectual:—adj intellectual, mental.

intelligence f intelligence; understanding.

intelligent adj intelligent.

intelligible adj intelligible.

intense adj intense; severe.

intensifier vt to intensify:—s'~ vr to intensify.

intensité f intensity; severity.

intention f intention; purpose, intent.

intercepter vt to intercept.

interdire vt to forbid, ban, prohibit.

intéressant adj interesting; attractive, worthwhile.

intéresser vt to interest; to affect:—s'~ vr:—s'~ à to be interested in.

intérêt m interest; significance, importance.

interférence f interference; conjunction.

intérieur adj interior, internal, inland.

interlocuteur m, **-trice** f interlocutor, speaker.

intermittent adj intermittent, sporadic.

international adj international.

interne *adj* internal:—*mf* boarder; house doctor.

interprète *mf* interpreter.

interpréter *vt* to interpret; to perform.

interrogation *f* interrogation, questioning; question.

interroger *vt* to question; to interrogate:—**s'~** *vr* to wonder.

interrompre *vt* to interrupt, break.

interruption *f* interruption, break.

intervalle *m* interval; space, distance.

intervenir *vi* to intervene; to take part in.

intervention *f* intervention; operation.

intime *adj* intimate; private:—*mf* close friend.

intimider *vt* to intimidate.

intimité *f* intimacy; privacy.

intolérance *f* intolerance.

intolérant *adj* intolerant.

intrépide *adj* intrepid, fearless.

introduction *f* introduction; launching; institution.

introduire *vt* to introduce, insert; to present.

introverti *m*, **-e** *f* introvert:—*adj* introverted.

intuitif *adj* intuitive.

intuition *f* intuition.

inutile *adj* useless; unavailing; pointless.

invalide *adj* disabled; invalid.

invariable *adj* invariable; unvarying.

invasion *f* invasion.

inventer *vt* to invent; to devise; to make up.

invention *f* invention; inventiveness.

inverse *adj* opposite:—*m* opposite, reverse.

inversion *f* inversion; reversal.

investissement *m* investment; investing.

invincible *adj* invincible, indomitable.

invisible *adj* invisible; unseen.

invitation *f* invitation.

inviter *vt* to invite, ask.

involontaire *adj* involuntary; unintentional.

invoquer *vt* to invoke; to call up; to plead.

invraisemblable *adj* unlikely, improbable.

invulnérable *adj* invulnerable.

Irlandais *m* Irishman, **-e** *f* Irishwoman

irlandais *adj* Irish.

Irlande *f* Ireland.

ironique *adj* ironic:—**~ment** *adv* ironically.

irrationnel *adj* irrational.

irréel *adj* unreal.

irrégularité *f* irregularity; variation; unevenness.

irrégulier *adj* irregular; varying; uneven.

irremplaçable *adj* irreplaceable.

irrésistible *adj* irresistible:—**~ment** *adv* irresistibly.

irresponsable *adj* irresponsible

irrigation *f* irrigation.

irriter *vt* to irritate; to provoke.

isoler *vt* to isolate; to insulate.

issue *f* outlet; solution; outcome.

ivre *adj* drunk, inebriated.

ivrogne *mf* drunkard.

J

jadis *adv* formerly, long ago.

jalousie *f* jealousy, envy.

jaloux *adj* jealous, envious.

jamais *adv* never, not ever:—**à ~** for ever.

jambe *f* leg.

jambon *m* ham.

janvier *m* January.

jardin *m* garden.

jardinier *m*, **-ière** *f* gardener.

jargon *m* jargon, slang; gibberish.

jaune *adj* yellow:—*m* yellow.

jaunir *vi* to yellow, turn yellow:—*vt* to make yellow.

jazz *m* jazz.

je, j' *pron* I.

jetable *adj* disposable.

jetée *f* pier.

jeter *vt* to throw.

jeton *m* token; counter.

jeu *m* play; game; gambling:—**~ de mots** pun.

jeudi *m* Thursday.

jeune *adj* young:—*m* youth, young man:—*f* young girl.

jeûne *m* fast.

jeunesse *f* youth, youthfulness.

joaillerie *f* jewelling; jewellery.

joie *f* joy, happiness; pleasure.

joindre *vt* to join, link.

jointure *f* joint *(anat)*.

joli *adj* pretty; good, handsome.

jonction *f* junction.

joue *f* cheek.

jouer *vi* to play; to gamble; to act.

jouet *m* toy.

joueur *m*, **-euse** *f* player; gambler.

jouir *vi* to enjoy; to delight in.

jouissance *f* enjoyment; use.

jour *m* day; daylight:—**tous les ~s** every day:—**à ~** up to date:—**~ férié** public holiday:—**mise à ~** updating; update.

journal *m* newspaper; bulletin:—**~ télévisé** television news.

journaliste *mf* journalist.

journée *f* day; day's work.

jovial *adj* jovial, jolly.

joyau *m* jewel, gem.

joyeux *adj* joyful.

judaïsme *m* Judaism.

judiciaire *adj* judicial, legal.

judicieux *adj* judicious.

juge *m* judge.

jugement *m* judgment.

juger *vt* to judge; to decide; to consider.

juif *m* Jew; Jewish:—**juive** *f* Jewess; Jewish.

juillet *m* July.

juin *m* June.

jumeau *m*, **-elle** *f* twin:—*adj* twin; double.

jumelle(s) *f(pl)* binoculars.

jungle *f* jungle.

jupe *f* skirt.

jurer *vt* to swear, pledge.

juridiction *f* jurisdiction; court of law.

juridique *adj* legal, juridical.

jury *m* jury; board of examiners.

jus *m* juice.

jusque, jusqu' *prép* to, as far as; until.

juste *adj* just, fair; exact; sound.

justesse *f* accuracy; aptness; soundness.

justice *f* justice, fairness.

justification *f* justification; proof.

justifier *vt* to justify, prove.

juteux *adj* juicy; lucrative.

juvénile *adj* young, youthful.

K

kaléidoscope *m* kaleidoscope.

kangourou *m* kangaroo.

karaté *m* karate.

képi *m* kepi.

kermesse *f* fair; bazaar.

kidnapper *vt* to kidnap, abduct.

kidnappeur *m*, **-euse** *f* kidnapper.

kilogramme *m* kilogramme.

kilomètre *m* kilometre.

kiosque *m* kiosk, stall.

klaxon *m* horn.

klaxonner *vi* to sound one's horn.

koala *m* koala.

L

la *art pn see* **le**.

là *adv* there; over there; then:—**par ~** that way;**~-dedans** inside, in there:—**~-dessous**, under there:—**~-dessus** on that; thereupon:—**~-haut** up there:—**celui-~** that one.

label *m* label; seal.

labeur *m* labour, toil.

laboratoire *m* laboratory.

lac *m* lake.

lacer *vt* to lace up; to tie up.

lâche *adj* slack; lax; cowardly.

lâcher *vt* to loosen; to release.

laid *adj* ugly, unsightly.

laideur *f* ugliness, unsightliness.

laine *f* wool.

laisser *vt* to leave; to let:—**~ tomber** to drop.

laisser-passer *m invar* pass, permit.

lait *m* milk.

laitue *f* lettuce.

lame *f* blade; strip; metal plate.

lamentable *adj* lamentable, distressing.

lamenter (se) *vr* to lament, bewail.

lampe *f* lamp, light; bulb.

lance *f* lance, spear.

lancement *m* launching; starting up; throwing.

lancer *vt* to throw; to launch.

langage *m* language, speech.

langoureux *adj* languid, languorous.

langouste *f* spiny lobster.

langue *f* tongue; language.

langueur *f* languor.

lanterne *f* lantern; lamp.

lapin *m*, **-e** *f* rabbit.

large *adj* wide; generous; lax; great.

largeur *f* width, breadth.

larme *f* tear.

las *adj*, *f* **lasse** weary, tired.

lasser *vt* to tire:—**se ~** *vr* to grow tired of.

latéral *adj* lateral, side.

latin *adj* Latin:—*m* Latin.

latitude *f* latitude; margin.

lavabo *m* washbasin.

lavage *m* washing; bathing.

laver *vt* to wash; to cleanse:—**se ~** *vr* to wash oneself.

laxatif *adj* laxative:—*m* laxative.

le *art*, *f* **la**, *devant voyelle* **l'**, *pl* **les** the:—*pron* him, her, them.

leçon *f* lesson; reading; class.

lecteur *m*, **-trice** *f* reader.

lecture *f* reading; perusal.

légal *adj* legal, lawful.

légalité *f* legality, lawfulness.

légendaire *adj* legendary.

légende *f* legend; inscription.

léger *adj* light; inconsiderate.

légèreté *f* lightness; thoughtlessness.

législatif *adj* legislative:—*m* legislature.

législation *f* legislation, laws.

légitime *adj* legitimate, lawful.

légitimité *f* legitimacy.

légume *m* vegetable.

lendemain *m* next day, day after.

lent *adj* slow; tardy; sluggish.

lenteur *f* slowness.

lequel *pron*, *f* **laquelle**, *pl* **lesquels**, **lesquelles** who, whom, which.

leste *adj* nimble, agile:—**~ment** *adv* nimbly.

léthargie *f* lethargy.

léthargique *adj* lethargic.

lettre *f* letter, note; literature:— **suivre à la ~** to carry out to the letter.

leur *pron* them:—**le ~, la ~, les ~s** theirs.

lever *vt* to lift, raise; to levy:—**se ~** *vr* to get up.

levier *m* lever.

lèvre *f* lip.

lexique *m* vocabulary, lexis.

lézard *m* lizard.

liaison *f* connection; liaison, link.

libéral *adj* liberal:—*m* liberal.

libération *f* release, liberation.

libérer *vt* to release; to liberate.

liberté *f* liberty, freedom.

libraire *mf* bookseller.

librairie *f* bookshop; bookselling.

libre *adj* free; independent.

licence *f* degree; permit; licentiousness.

licenciement *m* redundancy; dismissal.

licencier *vt* to make redundant; to dismiss.

lien *m* bond; link, connection; tie.

lier *vt* to bind; to link:—**se ~** *vr*:—**se ~ avec** to make friends.

lieu *m* place; occasion:—**avoir ~** to take place:—**au ~ de** instead of.

lièvre *m* hare.

ligne *f* line; row; range.

lignée *f* lineage; offspring.

ligue *f* league.

lime *f* file.

limitation *f* limitation, restriction.

limite *f* boundary, limit:—**à la ~** ultimately.

limiter *vt* to limit, restrict.

limonade *f* lemonade.

limpide *adj* limpid, clear.

linéaire *adj* linear.

linge *m* linen; washing.

lingerie *f* linen room; underwear, lingerie.

linguiste *mf* linguist.

lion *m* lion, **lionne** *f* lioness.

liquéfier *vt* to liquefy:—**se ~** *vr* to liquefy.

liqueur *f* liqueur; liquid.

liquide *m* liquid.

liquider *vt* to wind up; to eliminate

lire *vt* to read.

lisible *adj* legible; readable.

lisse *adj* smooth, glossy.

lisser *vt* to smooth, gloss.

liste *f* list; schedule.

lit *m* bed; layer.

litige *m* lawsuit; dispute.

litre *m* litre.

littéral *adj* literal.

littérature *f* literature; writing.

littoral *m* coast:—*adj* coastal.

livraison *f* delivery; number, issue.

livre *m* book:—*f* pound (weight, currency).

livrer *vt* to deliver, hand over; to give away.

livreur *m* delivery man, **-euse** *f* delivery woman.

local *adj* local.

localité *f* locality; town.

locataire *mf* tenant; lodger.

location *f* renting; lease, leasing.

loge *f* lodge; dressing room; box.

logement *m* housing; accommodation.

loger *vt* to accommodate; to billet:—*vi* to live in.

logiciel *m* software.

logique *f* logic:—*adj* logical.

logo *m* logo.

loi *f* law; act, statute; rule.

loin *adv* far, a long way:—*m* distance; background:—**au ~** in the distance:—**de ~** from a distance.

lointain *adj* distant, remote:—*m* distance; background

loisir *m* leisure, spare time.

long *adj*, *f* **longue** long, lengthy.

longévité *f* longevity.

longitude *f* longitude.

longtemps *adv* for a long time.

longueur *f* length.

loquace *adj* loquacious, talkative.

lors *adv* then **~ de** at the time of:—**dès ~** from that time.

lorsque *conj* when.

lot *m* prize; lot; portion.

loterie *f* lottery; raffle.

lotion *f* lotion.

louange *f* praise, commendation.

louer *vt* to rent, lease; to book.

loup *m* wolf.

lourd *adj* heavy; sultry.

lourdeur *f* heaviness.

loyal *adj* loyal, faithful.

loyauté *f* loyalty

loyer *m* rent.

lucide *adj* lucid, clear.

lucidité *f* lucidity, clearness.

lueur *f* glimmer, gleam; glimpse.

lugubre *adj* lugubrious, gloomy.

lui *pron* him, her, it:—**c'est à ~** It is his:—**~-même** himself, herself, itself.

luire *vt* to shine, gleam.

lumière *f* light; daylight; lamp; insight.

lumineux *adj* luminous; illuminated.

lunaire *adj* lunar, moon.
lundi *m* Monday.
lune *f* moon.
lunette *f* telescope; sight:—s glasses.
lutte *f* struggle; contest; strife.
lutter *vi* to struggle, fight.

luxe *m* luxury, excess.
luxueux *adj* luxurious.
lycée *m* secondary school.
lyncher *vt* to lynch.
lyre *f* lyre.
lyrique *adj* lyric.
lyrisme *m* lyricism.

M

mâcher *vt* to chew.
machinal *adj* mechanical, automatic.
machine *f* machine; engine; apparatus.
machinerie *f* machinery, plant.
mâchoire *f* jaw.
maçon *m* builder, mason.
madame *f* Madam; Mrs; lady.
mademoiselle *f* Miss; young lady.
magasin *m* shop, store; warehouse.
magazine *m* magazine.
magicien(ne) *m(f)* magician.
magie *f* magic
magistrat *m* magistrate.
magnanime *adj* magnanimous.
magnétique *adj* magnetic.
magnétophone *m* tape recorder.
magnifique *adj* magnificent; sumptuous.
mai *m* May.
maigre *adj* thin; meagre, scarce.
maigrir *vi* to get thinner; to waste away.
maillot *m* jersey; leotard.
main *f* hand:—**avoir la ~** to have the lead.

main-d'œuvre *f* workforce.
maintenance *f* maintenance, servicing.
maintenant *adv* now:—**à partir de ~** from now on.
maintenir *vt* to keep.
maintien *m* maintenance; preservation; keeping up.
maire *m* mayor, **-esse** *f* mayoress.
mais *conj* but.
maison *f* house; home; building; premises.
maître *m* **-esse** *f* master; ruler; lord; proprietor.
maîtresse *f* mistress; teacher
maîtrise *f* mastery; control; expertise.
majoritaire *adj* majority.
majorité *f* majority.
mal *adv* wrong, badly:—*m* evil, wrong; harm; pain.
malade *adj* sick, ill; diseased:—*mf* invalid, sick person.
maladie *f* illness; malady, complaint; disorder.
maladroit *adj* clumsy, awkward.
malchanceux *adj* unlucky, unfortunate.

mâle *m* male:—*adj* male; manly, virile.

malentendu *m* misunderstanding.

malgré *prép* in spite of; despite.

malheur *m* misfortune; calamity.

malheureux *adj* unfortunate; unlucky; unhappy.

malhonnête *adj* dishonest, crooked; uncivil.

malicieux *adj* malicious, spiteful; mischievous.

malnutrition *f* malnutrition.

malsain *adj* unhealthy, unwholesome; immoral.

maltraiter *vt* to abuse; to handle roughly.

malveillant *adj* malevolent, spiteful.

maman *f* mother, mummy, mum.

mammifère *m* mammal.

manche *f* sleeve; game, round:—*m* handle, shaft.

mangeable *adj* edible.

manger *vt* to eat; to consume, squander

maniable *adj* handy, workable.

manier *vt* to handle; to manipulate.

manière *f* manner, way, style.

manifeste *adj* manifest, evident, obvious:—*m* manifesto.

manifester *vt* to display, make known; to demonstrate.

manipulation *f* handling; manipulation.

manipuler *vt* to handle; to manipulate

manœuvre *f* manoeuvre, operation; scheme:—*m* labourer.

manœuvrer *vt* to manoeuvre:—*vi* to manoeuvre, move.

manque *m* lack, shortage; shortcoming, deficiency.

manquer *vt* to miss; to fail; to be absent.

manteau *m* coat; mantle, blanket; cloak.

manuel *m* manual, handbook:—*adj* manual.

manufacture *f* factory; manufacture.

manufacturier *m* **-ière** *f* factory owner; manufacturer:—*adj* manufacturing.

manuscrit *m* manuscript; typescript:—*adj* handwritten.

maquillage *m* make-up.

marathon *m* marathon.

marbre *m* marble; marble statue.

marchand(e) *m(f)* merchant:—*adj* market, trade.

marchandise *f* merchandise, commodity; goods.

marche *f* walk; journey; progress; movement:—**mettre en ~** to start up; to turn on.

marché *m* market; transaction, contract.

marcher *vi* to walk, march; to progress; to work.

mardi *m* Tuesday.

marée *f* tide.

marge *f* margin; latitude, freedom; mark-up.

marginal *adj* marginal.

mari *m* husband.

mariage *m* marriage.

marié *m* bridegroom:—*adj* married.

marier *vt* to marry; blend, harmonise:—**se ~** *vr* to get married.

marin *m* sailor.

marine *f* navy; seascape; marine.

maritime *adj* maritime; seaboard.

marque *f* mark, sign; brand; make.

marquer *vt* to mark; to note down; to score.

mars *m* March.

marteau *m* hammer; knocker.

masculin *adj* masculine.

masque *m* mask; facade, front.

massage *m* massage.

masse *f* mass, heap; bulk; mob.

masser *vt* to mass, assemble; to massage.

masseur *m* masseur, **euse** *f* masseuse.

massif *adj* massive, solid, heavy:— *m* massif; clump.

match *m* match; game.

matelas *m* mattress.

matérialiser (se) ~ *vr* to materialise.

matériaux *mpl* material, materials.

matériel *adj* material, physical; practical.

maternel *adj* maternal, motherly.

maternité *f* motherhood; pregnancy; maternity hospital.

mathématicien(ne) *m(f)* mathematician.

mathématique *adj* mathematical:— *f* mathematics.

matière *f* material, matter; subject:—~ **première** raw material.

matin *m* morning; dawn.

matrice *f* womb; mould; matrix.

maturité *f* maturity; prime.

maussade *adj* sulky, sullen.

mauvais *adj* bad; wicked; faulty; hurtful; poor.

maximum *m* maximum.

me, m' *pn* me; myself.

mécanicien(ne) *m(f)* mechanic; engineer.

mécanique *f* mechanics:—*adj* mechanical.

méchant *adj* spiteful; wicked; mischievous.

méconnu *adj* unrecognised; misunderstood.

mécontentement *m* discontent; displeasure.

médecin *m* doctor, physician.

médecine *f* medicine

médical *adj* medical.

médiocre *adj* mediocre; indifferent.

méditation *f* meditation.

méditer *vi* to meditate:—*vt* to contemplate, have in mind.

méfier (se) *vr* to mistrust, distrust; to be suspicious.

meilleur *adj* better, preferable:—**le ~, la ~e** the best.

mélancolique *adj* melancholy; melancholic.

mélange *m* mixture.

mélanger *vt* to mix, blend; to muddle.

mêler *vt* to mix; to combine:—**se ~** *vr* to mix, mingle

mélodie *f* melody, tune.

membre *m* member; limb.

même *adv* even:—**tout de ~** nevertheless, all the same:—*adj* same, identical:—*pn*:—**le/la ~, les ~s** the same one(s).

mémoire *f* memory:—*m* memorandum, report.

mémorable *adj* memorable.

menace *f* threat; intimidation; danger.

menacer *vt* to threaten, menace; to impend.

ménage *m* housework, housekeeping; household.

ménager *vt* to treat with caution; to manage; to arrange:—*adj* household, domestic.

ménagère *f* housewife.

mendiant(e) *m(f)* beggar, mendicant.

mener *vt* to lead, guide; to steer; to manage.

ménopause f menopause.

mensonge m lie, falsehood; error, illusion.

menstruation f menstruation.

mental adj mental.

menteur m **-euse** f liar:—adj lying, deceitful.

mention f mention; comment; grade.

mentionner vt to mention.

mentir vi to lie, tell lies; to be deceptive.

menton m chin.

menu m menu; meal:—adj slender, thin; petty, minor.

mépriser vt to scorn, despise.

mer f sea; tide.

merci m thank you:—f mercy:—**sans ~** merciless.

mercredi m Wednesday.

mère f mother.

méridien m meridian; midday.

mériter vt to deserve, merit.

merveilleux adj marvellous, wonderful.

message m message.

messager m **-ère** f messenger.

messe f mass

mesure f measure; gauge; measurement:—**au fur et à ~** as; one by one:—**dans la mesure où** insofar as:—**en ~** in time.

mesurer vt to measure; to assess; to limit:—**se ~** vr to try one's strength.

métal m metal.

métaphore f metaphor.

météore m meteor.

météoroloque, météorologiste mf meteorologist.

méthode f method, way.

méthodique adj methodical.

métier m job; occupation:—**~ à tisser** weaving loom.

mètre m metre.

métro m underground, metro.

métropole f metropolis.

mettre vt to put, place; to put on:—**~ en marche** to start up:—**se ~ à** to begin to:—**se ~ en route** to start off.

meuble m piece of furniture.

meurtrier m murderer, **-ière** f murderess.

mi- adj half:—**à ~chemin** halfway:—**~clos** half-closed:—**à ~jambe** up to the knees:—**à ~voix** in a low voice.

miauler vi to mew.

micro-onde f microwave:—m **micro-ondes** microwave oven.

micro-ordinateur m microcomputer.

microbe m germ, microbe.

microfilm m microfilm.

microphone m microphone.

microscope m microscope.

midi m midday, noon.

miel m honey.

mien pron, f **mienne**:—**le ~, la mienne, les ~s, les miennes** mine, my own.

mieux m improvement:—**le ~** the best:—**de ~ en ~** better and better.

migraine f headache; migraine.

migrateur m migrant.

migration f migration.

milieu m middle, centre; medium; environment.

militaire m serviceman:—adj military, army.

militant(e) m(f) adj militant.

militer vi to militate; to be a militant.

mille m adj one thousand.

milliard m thousand million; milliard.

millième *m adj* thousandth.

millier *m* thousand.

million *m* million.

millionnaire *adj* millionaire; worth millions:—*mf* millionaire.

mime *m* mime:—*mf* mimic.

mimer *vt* to mime; to mimic, imitate.

mince *adj* thin, slender; meagre, trivial.

mincir *vi* to get slimmer, get thinner.

mine *f* expression; appearance; mine:—**avoir bonne ~** to look good.

minéral *adj* mineral; inorganic:—*m* mineral.

mineur(e) *m(f)* minor:—*adj* minor:—*m* miner.

mini-jupe *f* miniskirt.

miniature *f* miniature.

minimal *adj* minimal, minimum.

minimum *m* minimum.

ministère *m* ministry; agency.

ministre *m* minister; clergyman.

minorité *f* minority.

minuit *m* midnight.

minute *f* minute, moment.

minutieux *adj* meticulous; minute.

miracle *m* miracle, wonder.

miraculeux *adj* miraculous.

mirage *m* mirage.

miroir *m* mirror, reflection.

mise *f* putting, placing; stake; deposit; investment:—~ **en scène** production, staging:—~ **en liberté** release:—~ **en ordre** ordering, arrangement:—~ **en œuvre** implementation.

misérable *adj* miserable; destitute; pitiable.

misère *f* misery; poverty; destitution.

mission *f* mission, assignment.

missionnaire *m* missionary.

mitigé *adj* mitigated; lukewarm.

mitoyen *adj* common; semi-detached.

mixer *vt* to mix; to blend.

mixte *adj* mixed; joint; combined.

mobile *adj* moving; movable:—*m* motive; moving body.

mobilier *m* furniture.

mobilité *f* mobility.

mode *f* fashion; custom:—*m* form, mode; way.

modèle *m* model; pattern; design; example.

modeler *vt* to model; to shape.

modem *m* modem.

modération *f* moderation; diminution.

modéré *adj* moderate.

modérer *vt* to moderate.

moderne *adj* modern, up-to-date.

moderniser *vt* to modernise.

modeste *adj* modest, simple; unassuming.

modestie *f* modesty.

modification *f* modification, alteration.

modifier *vt* to modify, alter.

moelle *f* marrow; core.

mœurs *fpl* morals; customs.

moi *pn* me, I:—**c'est à ~** it is mine, it is my turn:—~-**même** myself.

mois *m* month.

moisson *f* harvest.

moissonner *vt* to reap, mow.

moite *adj* moist, damp.

moitié *f* half.

molécule *f* molecule.

moment *m* moment, instant, while; time; opportunity.

momentané *adj* momentary; brief.

mon *pron*, *f* **ma**, *pl* **mes** my.

monastère *m* monastery.

mondain *adj* worldly, mundane; society, fashionable.

monde *m* world, earth; society, company.

mondial *adj* world, worldwide.

moniteur *m* **-trice** *f* instructor, coach; supervisor.

monnaie *f* currency; coin; change.

monopole *f* monopoly.

monopoliser *vt* to monopolise.

monotone *adj* monotonous.

monsieur *m* sir, gentleman, Mr, *pl* **messieurs** gentlemen, Messrs.

monstre *m* monster.

mont *m* mountain; mount.

montage *m* assembly; setting up; editing.

montagne *f* mountain.

montagneux *adj* mountainous.

montée *f* climb, climbing; ascent; rise.

monter *vi* to go up, ascend; get into (vehicle):—*vt* to go up; to carry/ bring up.

montre *f* watch.

montrer *vt* to show, point to; prove.

monument *m* monument, memorial.

moquer (se) *vr* to make fun, jeer, laugh at.

moqueur *m* **-euse** *f* mocker, scoffer:—*adj* mocking.

moral *adj* moral, ethical; intellectual.

moralité *f* morals, morality.

morceau *m* piece, morsel, fragment; extract.

mordre *vt* to bite, gnaw; to grip.

morose *adj* sullen, morose.

mort *m* dead man, **-e** *f* dead woman:—*adj* dead:—*f* death.

mortalité *f* mortality; death rate.

mortel *adj* mortal; fatal.

mortuaire *adj* mortuary; funeral.

mosquée *f* mosque

mot *m* word; saying:—**~s croisés** crossword.

moteur *m* engine, motor:—*adj* motor, driving.

motif *m* motive, grounds; motif, design.

motivation *f* motivation.

motiver *vt* to justify; to motivate.

moto *f* motorbike.

mou *adj* (*f* **molle**) soft; gentle; muffled.

mouche *f* fly.

moucher (se) *vr* to blow one's nose.

mouchoir *m* handkerchief.

moudre *vt* to mill, grind.

mouiller *vt* to wet; to water down:— **se ~** *vr* to get wet.

moule *m* mould:—*f* mussel.

mouler *vt* to mould; to model.

moulin *m* mill.

mourir *vi* to die.

mousser *vi* to froth, foam

mousseux *adj* sparkling; frothy:—*m* sparkling wine.

moustache *f* moustache; whiskers.

moustique *m* mosquito.

mouton *m* sheep; mutton.

mouvement *m* movement, motion; animation.

mouvoir *vt* to drive, power:—**se ~** *vr* to move.

moyen *m* means; way:—*adj* average, medium, moderate:—**~ âge** Middle Ages.

moyenne *f* average.

muet(te) *m(f)* mute:—*adj* dumb; silent, mute.

multicolore *adj* multicoloured.

multiple *adj* numerous, multiple:—
m multiple.

multiplication *f* multiplication.

multiplier (se) *vr* to multiply, increase.

municipal *adj* municipal; local.

municipalité *f* town, municipality.

munir *vt* to provide, equip with:—
se ~ *vr* to equip oneself.

mur *m* wall.

mûr *adj* ripe, mature; worn out.

mûrir *vi* to ripen, mature.

murmure *m* murmur; muttering;
grumbling.

murmurer *vi* to murmur.

muscle *m* muscle.

musculaire *adj* muscular.

musée *m* art gallery, museum.

musicien(ne) *m(f)* musician:—*adj*
musical.

musique *f* music.

musulman(e) *m(f) adj* Moslem.

muter *vt* to transfer, move.

myope *mf* short-sighted person:—
adj short-sighted.

myopie *f* short-sightedness, myopia.

mystère *m* mystery.

mystérieux *adj* mysterious.

mystifier *vt* to mystify; to hoax.

mystique *adj* mystical:—*mf* mystic.

mythe *m* myth.

mythique *adj* mythical.

mythologie *f* mythology.

N

nager *vi* to swim.

nageur *m*, **-euse** *f* swimmer; rower.

naissance *f* birth, extraction; dawn,
beginning.

naître *vi* to be born; to arise, spring
up.

naïveté *f* naïvety, artlessness, gullibility.

narcotique *m* drug, narcotic:—*adj*
narcotic.

narrateur *m*, **-trice** *f* narrator.

nasal *adj* nasal.

natalité *f* birth rate.

nation *f* nation.

national *adj* national; domestic.

nationaliste *mf* nationalist:—*adj*
nationalist.

nationalité *f* nationality.

nature *f* nature; kind, sort; temperament.

naturel *adj* natural; bodily; native;
unsophisticated:—**~lement** *adv*
naturally; of course.

nautique *adj* nautical.

navigation *f* sailing, navigation.

navire *m* ship, vessel.

ne *adv* no, not.

né *adj* born

néanmoins *adv* nevertheless.

nécessaire *adj* necessary; requisite;
indispensable.

nécessité *f* necessity; need; inevitability.

nécessiter *vt* to require, necessitate.

négatif *adj* negative.

négligent *adj* negligent, careless; nonchalant.

négliger *vt* to neglect; to be negligent about.

négociation *f* negotiation.

négocier *vi* to negotiate; to trade:— *vt* to negotiate.

neige *f* snow.

neiger *vi* to snow, be snowing.

nerf *m* nerve.

nerveux *adj* nervous; vigorous; excitable.

net *adj*, *f* **nette** clean; clear; plain; sharp; net.

nettoyage *m* cleaning; clearing up.

nettoyer *vt* to clean; to ruin, clean out.

neuf *adj* nine:—*m* nine.

neutre *adj* neutral; neuter.

neuvième *adj* ninth:—*mf* ninth.

neveu *m* nephew.

nez *m* nose; flair:—**avoir du ~** to have flair.

niais *adj* silly, simple, inane.

nid *m* nest; den; berth.

nièce *f* niece.

nier *vt* to deny; to repudiate.

niveau *m* level; standard; par; gauge.

noble *adj* noble, dignified.

noce *f* wedding, wedding feast; marriage ceremony.

nocif *adj* noxious, harmful.

nocturne *adj* nocturnal, night.

Noël *m* Christmas.

nœud *m* knot, bow; crux.

noir *adj* black; dark:—*m* black; darkness; black man

noircir *vt* to blacken; to dirty:—**se ~** *vr* to darken, grow black.

noix *f* walnut

nom *m* name; fame; noun

nombre *m* number, quantity.

nombreux *adj* numerous, frequent.

nommer *vt* to appoint; nominate.

non *adv* no; not.

non-sens *m* nonsense.

nonchalant *adj* nonchalant.

nord *m* north, northerly (wind)

normal *adj* normal, usual; standard-sized.

norme *f* norm; standard.

nostalgique *adj* nostalgic.

notable *adj* notable; noteworthy.

note *f* note; minute; mark; bill.

noter *vt* to note down; to notice; to mark.

notice *f* note; directions; instructions.

notion *f* notion, idea.

notoire *adj* notorious; well-known, acknowledged.

notre *adj* (*pl* **nos**) ours, our own.

nôtre *poss pn*:—**le ~, la ~, les ~s** ours, our own.

nouer *vt* to tie, knot.

nourrir *vt* to feed, provide for; to stoke:—**se ~** *vr* to feed o.s.

nourriture *f* food; sustenance.

nous *pron* we; us:—**c'est à ~** it's ours; it's our turn:—**~-mêmes** ourselves.

nouveau *adj* new; recent; additional.

nouvelle *f* piece of news; short story.

novembre *m* November.

novice *mf* novice, beginner.

noyer *vt* to drown; to flood:—**se ~** *vr* to drown.

nu *adj* naked, nude; plain, unadorned.

nuage *m* cloud.

nucléaire *adj* nuclear:—*m* nuclear energy.

nudité *f* nakedness, nudity.

nuire *vi* to harm, injure; to prejudice.

nuisible *adj* harmful; noxious.

nuit *f* night, darkness.

nul *adj* no; nil; null and void:—

~lement *adv* not at all.

numérique *adj* numerical; digital.

numéro *m* number; issue.

numéroter *vt* to number.

nylon *m* nylon.

O

obéir *vt* to obey, be obedient; to comply.

obéissant *adj* obedient.

obèse *adj* obese.

objecter *vt* to object.

objectif *adj* objective, unbiased:— *m* objective, target.

objection *f* objection.

objet *m* object, thing; purpose; matter.

obligation *f* obligation, duty; bond.

obligatoire *adj* obligatory, compulsory.

obliger *vt* to oblige, require; to bind.

oblitérer *vt* to obliterate; to cancel (stamp)

obscène *adj* obscene.

obscur *adj* obscure, dark, gloomy.

obscurcir *vt* to darken; to obscure:—**s'~** *vr* to get dark.

obscurité *f* obscurity; darkness.

observation *f* observation; remark.

observatoire *m* observatory.

observer *vt* to observe.

obsession *f* obsession.

obstacle *m* obstacle, hindrance.

obstination *f* obstinacy, stubbornness.

obstiné *adj* obstinate, stubborn.

obstiner (s') *vr* to insist, persist.

obtenir *vt* to obtain.

occasion *f* occasion, opportunity; bargain.

occidental *adj* western.

occupant *m*, **-e** *f* occupant, occupier.

occupation *f* occupation; occupancy.

occuper *vt* to occupy:—**s'~** *vr* to keep busy.

océan *m* ocean.

octobre *m* October.

odeur *f* smell, odour.

odieux *adj* hateful, obnoxious.

odorat *m* smell (sense).

œil *m* (*pl* **yeux**) eye; look; bud.

œuf *m* egg.

œuvre *f* work; action, deed; production.

offense *f* offence; injury.

offenser *vt* to offend:—**s'~** *vr* to take offence.

offensif *adj* offensive.

office *m* office; duty; function.

officiel *adj* official.

officier *m* officer.

officieux *adj* officious; unofficial.

offre *f* offer, tender, bid.

offrir *vt* to offer.

oie *f* goose.

oignon *m* onion; bulb.

oiseau *m* bird.

oisif *adj* idle.

oisiveté *f* idleness.

olive *f* olive.

olivier *m* olive tree.

olympique *adj* Olympic.

ombre *f* shade, shadow.

omelette *f* omelette.

omettre *vt* to omit.

omission *f* omission.

omniprésent *adj* omnipresent.

on *pn* one; someone, anyone.

once *f* ounce.

oncle *m* uncle.

onde *f* wave.

onduler *vi* to undulate; to ripple.

onéreux *adj* onerous; costly.

ongle *m* nail; claw, talon; hoof.

onze *adj* eleven:—*m* eleven.

onzième *adj* eleventh:—*mf* eleventh.

opaque *adj* opaque; impenetrable.

opéra *m* opera.

opération *f* operation, performance.

opérationnel *adj* operational.

opérer *vt* to operate.

opiniâtre *adj* stubborn; persistent.

opinion *f* opinion, view.

opportun *adj* timely, opportune.

opposant *m*, **-e** *f* opponent:—*adj* opposing.

opposé *adj* opposite:—*m* opposite:—**à l'~** contrary to.

opposer *vt* to oppose.

opposition *f* opposition; conflict.

oppresser *vt* to oppress, weigh down.

oppressif *adj* oppressive.

optimiste *mf* optimist:—*adj* optimistic.

option *f* option, choice.

optionnel *adj* optional.

opulent *adj* opulent, wealthy.

or *m* gold:—*conj* now.

orage *m* storm.

orageux *adj* stormy.

oral *adj* oral, verbal.

orange *f* orange:—*adj* orange.

orateur *m*, **-trice** *f* orator.

orbite *f* orbit; socket; sphere.

orchestre *m* orchestra.

ordinaire *adj* ordinary:—*m* usual routine:—**d'~**, **à l'~** ordinarily, usually.

ordinateur *m* computer.

ordonner *vt* to order.

ordre *m* order, command; class.

ordure *f* filth; rubbish.

oreille *f* ear; hearing.

oreiller *m* pillow.

organe *m* organ; instrument; medium.

organique *adj* organic.

organisateur *m*, **-trice** *f* organiser.

organisation *f* organisation.

organiser *vt* to organise, arrange.

orgueil *m* pride, arrogance.

orgueilleux *adj* proud, arrogant.

orient *m* orient, east.

oriental *adj* eastern, oriental.

orienter *vt* to orientate.

original *adj* original, novel:—*m* original.

originalité *f* originality.

origine *f* origin:—**à l'~** originally.

originel *adj* original, primitive.

orner *vt* to adorn, decorate.

orphelin *m*, **-e** *f* orphan.

orteil *m* toe.

orthodoxe *adj* orthodox:—*mf* orthodox.

os *m* bone

oser *vt* to dare.

ossature *f* skeleton; framework.

ostensible *adj* open, conspicuous.
otage *m* hostage.
ôter *vt* to take away.
ou *conj* or
où *adv* where, in which; *pron* where.
oubli *m* forgetfulness; oblivion.
oublier *vt* to forget.
ouest *m* west; *adj* west.
oui *adv* yes.
ouïe *f* hearing.
ouragan *m* hurricane, whirlwind.
ours *m*, **-e** *f* bear.
outil *m* tool, implement.
outillage *m* (set of) tools; equipment.

outiller *vt* to equip; to provide with tools.
outrage *m* outrage, insult, wrong.
outre *prép* as well as, besides:—**en ~** moreover.
ouvert *adj* open; exposed; frank.
ouverture *f* opening.
ouvrable *adj* working, business.
ouvrage *m* work; piece of work.
ouvrier *m*, **-ière** *f* worker:—*adj* labour.
ouvrir *vt* to open; to unlock; to broach.
oxygène *m* oxygen.
ozone *f* ozone.

P

pacifier *vt* to pacify.
pacifique *adj* peaceful.
pacte *m* pact, treaty.
page *f* page; passage.
paiement *m* payment
païen(ne) *m(f)* pagan:—*adj* pagan.
paille *f* straw.
pain *m* bread; loaf; bar
pair *adj* even:—*m* peer; par.
paire *f* pair
paisible *adj* peaceful; calm.
paix *f* peace; stillness.
palais *m* palace.
pâle *adj* pale, pallid.
pâleur *f* paleness, pallor.
pâlir *vi* to turn pale; to dim; to fade.
pallier *vt* to palliate; to offset.
palme *f* palm leaf; palm.

palmier *m* palm tree.
palpable *adj* palpable.
palper *vt* to feel, touch; to palpate.
palpiter *vi* to palpitate; to beat; to race.
panache *m* panache; gallantry
pancarte *f* sign, notice; placard.
panda *m* panda.
panique *f* panic.
paniquer *vi* to panic.
panne *f* breakdown; fault.
panneau *m* panel; sign, notice.
pansement *m* dressing, bandage.
panser *vt* to dress, bandage.
pantalon *m* trousers.
pantomime *f* pantomime; mime.
pantoufle *f* slipper.
papa *m* dad; daddy.

pape *m* pope.

papeterie *f* stationery.

papier *m* paper.

papillon *m* butterfly.

Pâques *fpl* Easter.

paquet *m* packet, pack.

par *prép* by, with, through; from; along:—**~-ci**, **~-là** here and there.

parachever *vt* to perfect; to complete.

parachute *m* parachute.

parade *f* parade, show; parry.

paradis *m* paradise; gallery.

paradoxal *adj* paradoxical.

paradoxe *m* paradox.

paragraphe *m* paragraph.

paraître *vi* to appear; to seem.

parallèle *adj* parallel.

paralyser *vt* to paralyse.

paralysie *f* paralysis.

paranoïaque *adj* paranoid.

parapluie *m* umbrella.

parasite *m* parasite, sponger.

parasol *m* parasol; sunshade.

parc *m* park; grounds; depot.

parce que *conj* because.

parcelle *f* particle; parcel.

parcourir *vt* to travel through.

pardon *m* pardon, forgiveness.

pardonner *vt* to pardon.

pare-brise *m invar* windscreen.

pare-chocs *m invar* bumper.

pareil(le) *m(f)* equal; match:—*adj* like, similar; identical.

parent(e) *m(f)* relative, relation; (*pl*) parents.

parental *adj* parental.

parenté *f* relationship, kinship.

paresse *f* laziness.

paresseux *adj* lazy.

parfaire *vt* to perfect.

parfait *adj* perfect, flawless.

parfois *adv* sometimes.

parfumer *vt* to perfume.

pari *m* bet, wager.

parier *vt* to bet, wager.

parking *m* car park; parking.

parlement *m* Parliament.

parlementaire *adj* parliamentary:— *mf* MP.

parler *vi* to talk, speak:—*vt* to speak.

parmi *prép* among.

paroi *f* wall; surface.

parole *f* word; speech; voice; lyrics.

parquer *vt* to park.

parrain *m* godfather; patron.

parrainer *vt* to sponsor, propose.

part *f* part; share; portion:—**prendre ~ à** to participate in:—**autre ~** elsewhere:—**nulle ~** nowhere.

partage *m* sharing, distribution.

partager *vt* to divide up.

partenaire *mf* partner.

parti *m* party; match.

partial *adj* partial, biased.

participant(e) *m(f)* participant, member.

participation *f* participation.

participer *vi* to participate.

particulier *adj* particular, specific:— *m* person, private individual.

partie *f* part; subject; party.

partiel *adj* part, partial.

partir *vi* to leave.

partisan(e) *m(f)* partisan.

partout *adv* everywhere.

parvenir *vi*:—**~ à** to reach.

pas *m* step; pace:—*adv* no, not.

passable *adj* passable, tolerable.

passage *m* passage; transit.

passager *m* **-ère** *f* passenger:—*adj* passing, transitory.

passant(e) *m(f)* passer-by.

passe *f* pass; permit; channel.

passé *m* past.

passe-temps *m invar* pastime

passeport *m* passport.

passer *vi* to pass:—**se ~** *vr* to take place.

passion *f* passion.

passionné *adj* passionate.

passionner (se) *vr* to be fascinated by, have a passion for.

passivité *f* passivity.

paternel *adj* paternal, fatherly.

paternité *f* paternity; fatherhood.

pathétique *adj* pathetic.

patience *f* patience.

patient *adj* patient.

patin *m* skate.

patiner *vi* to skate; to slip; to spin.

patineur *m* **-euse** *f* skater.

pâtisserie *f* cake shop, confectioner's.

pâtissier *m* **-ière** *f* pastry cook, confectioner.

patrie *f* homeland, country.

patriotisme *m* patriotism.

patron(ne) *m(f)* owner, boss.

patronner *vt* to patronise.

patte *f* leg, paw, foot.

paume *f* palm.

paupière *f* eyelid.

pause *f* pause; half-time.

pauvre *adj* poor; indigent:—*mf* pauper.

paye *f* pay, wages.

payer *vt* to pay.

pays *m* country; region.

paysage *m* landscape; scenery.

paysan *m* countryman **-anne** *f* countrywoman.

péage *m* toll; tollgate.

peau *f* skin; hide, pelt.

pêche *f* peach; fishing.

pêcher *vi* to sin.

pêcher *vt* to fish; to catch.

pécheur *m* **-eresse** *f* sinner

pêcheur *m* fisherman.

pédale *f* pedal; treadle.

pédaler *vi* to pedal.

pédestre *adj* pedestrian.

peigne *m* comb.

peigner (se) *vr* to comb one's hair.

peindre *vt* to paint.

peine *f* effort; pain; punishment.

peiner *vi* to toil; to struggle.

peintre *m* painter.

peinture *f* painting; paintwork.

peler *vi* to peel.

pèlerinage *m* pilgrimage.

peloton *m* pack; platoon.

pelouse *f* lawn.

pénaliser *vt* to penalise.

pencher *vi* to lean:—**se ~** *vr* to bend down.

pendant *prép* during; for:—**~ que** while.

pendre *vi* to hang.

pendule *f* clock:—*m* pendulum.

pénétrer *vi* to enter, penetrate:—*vt* to penetrate.

pénible *adj* hard, tiresome.

péninsule *f* peninsula.

pénis *m* penis.

pénitencier *m* prison, penitentiary.

pensée *f* thought.

penser *vt* to think, suppose, believe:—*vi* to think.

pension *f* pension; boarding house.

pensionnaire *mf* boarder; lodger.

pente *f* slope; gradient.

Pentecôte *f* Pentecost.

pépère *m* granddad, grandpa.

percée *f* opening, breach.

perception *f* perception.

percer *vt* to pierce.

percevoir *vt* to perceive; to collect.

percussion f percussion.

percuter vt to strike.

perdant(e) m(f) loser.

perdre vt to lose.

père m father; sire.

perfection f perfection.

perfectionnement m perfection.

perfectionner vt to perfect.

perfectionniste mf perfectionist:—adj perfectionist.

performance f performance.

performant adj high-performance

péril m peril, danger.

périmètre m perimeter.

période f period; epoch, era.

périodique adj periodic.

péripétie f event, episode.

périphérie f periphery.

périphérique adj peripheral

périple m voyage; journey.

périr vi to perish, die.

permanence f permanence.

permanent adj permanent.

perméable adj permeable.

permettre vt to allow, permit.

permis adj permitted:—m permit, licence.

permission f permission; leave.

permuter vt to permutate.

perpendiculaire adj perpendicular.

perpétuel adj perpetual.

perpétuité f perpetuity.

perplexe adj perplexed, confused.

perplexité f perplexity, confusion.

perquisition f search.

perroquet m parrot.

persécuter vt to persecute.

persécution f persecution.

persévérance f perseverance.

persévérer vi to persevere; to persist in.

persil m parsley.

persistance f persistence.

persister vi to persist, keep up.

personnage m character, individual.

personnalité f personality.

personne f person; self; appearance:—**en ~** in person:—pron anyone, anybody; nobody.

personnel adj personal.

perspective f perspective; view; angle.

perspicace adj perspicacious.

persuader vt to persuade; to convince.

persuasion f persuasion; conviction.

perte f loss, losing; ruin.

pertinent adj pertinent.

perturber vt to disrupt, disturb.

pervers adj perverse; perverted.

perversité f perversity.

pesanteur f gravity; heaviness.

peser vt to weigh.

pessimisme m pessimism.

pessismiste mf pessimist:—adj pessimistic.

peste f pest, nuisance; plague.

petit adj small, tiny; slim; young.

petit-fils m grandson.

petite-fille f granddaughter.

petitesse f smallness; meanness.

pétition f petition.

petits-enfants mpl grandchildren.

pétrifié adj petrified.

pétrole m oil, petroleum.

peu adv little, not much, few:—**un petit ~** a little bit:—**quelque ~** a little:—**pour ~ que** however little:—**~ de** little, few.

peuple m people, nation; crowd.

peupler vt to populate, stock; to plant.

peur f fear, terror, apprehension:—**avoir ~** to be afraid.

peut-être *adv* perhaps.

phare *m* lighthouse; headlight.

pharmaceutique *adj* pharmaceutical.

pharmacie *f* pharmacy; pharmacology.

pharmacien(ne) *m(f)* pharmacist.

phase *f* phase, stage.

phénoménal *adj* phenomenal.

phénomène *m* phenomenon.

philosophe *mf* philosopher.

philosophie *f* philosophy.

philosophique *adj* philosophical.

phobie *f* phobia.

phonétique *f* phonetics:—*adj* phonetic.

photo *f* photo.

photocopie *f* photocopy.

photogénique *adj* photogenic.

photographe *mf* photograph.

photographie *f* photography.

photographier *vt* to photograph.

phrase *f* sentence; phrase.

physicien(ne) *m(f)* physicist.

physiologique *adj* physiological.

physionomie *f* countenance, physiognomy.

physiothérapie *f* physiotherapy.

physique *f* physics:—*adj* physical.

pianiste *mf* pianist.

piano *m* piano.

pic *m* peak.

pictural *adj* pictorial.

pièce *f* piece; room; document.

pied *m* foot; à ~ on foot.

piège *m* trap; pit; snare.

piéger *vt* to trap, set a trap.

pierre *f* stone.

piété *f* piety.

piéton *m* pedestrian.

pieu *m* post, stake, pile.

pieux *adj* pious, devout.

pigment *m* pigment.

pile *f* pile; battery.

piler *vt* to crush, pound.

pilier *m* pillar.

pilote *m* pilot; driver.

piloter *vt* to pilot, fly; to drive.

pilule *f* pill.

piment *m* pepper.

pin *m* pine.

pinceau *m* brush, paintbrush.

pincer *vt* to pinch.

pingouin *m* penguin.

pinte *f* pint.

piolet *m* ice axe.

pionnier *m* pioneer.

pipe *f* pipe.

pique-nique *m* picnic.

pique-niquer *vi* to picnic.

piquer *vt* to sting.

piqûre *f* prick; sting; bite.

pirate *m* pirate.

pire *adj* worse:—**le ~** the worst.

pis-aller *m invar* last resort, stopgap.

piscine *f* swimming pool.

piste *f* track; clue.

pistolet *m* pistol, gun.

piteux *adj* pitiful, pathetic.

pitié *f* pity, mercy.

pittoresque *adj* picturesque.

pivoter *vi* to revolve, pivot.

placard *m* poster, notice.

place *f* place; square; seat:—**à la ~ de** instead of.

placer *vt* to place; to invest.

placide *adj* placid, calm.

plafond *m* ceiling; roof.

plage *f* beach.

plaider *vt* to plead.

plaie *f* wound, cut.

plaignant(e) *m(f)* plaintiff.

plaindre *vt* to pity:—**se ~** *vr* to complain.

plaine f plain.

plainte f complaint.

plaire vi to please:—**se ~** vr to enjoy.

plaisant adj pleasant, agreeable.

plaisanter vi to joke, jest.

plaisir m pleasure.

plan m plan; plane, level.

planche f plank, board.

plancher m floor.

planer vi to glide, soar.

planète f planet.

planeur m glider.

planifier vt to plan.

plante f plant.

planter vt to plant.

plaque f sheet, plate; plaque.

plastique m plastic:—adj plastic.

plat adj flat; straight; dull:—m plate; course.

plateau m tray; turntable; plateau.

plâtre m plaster.

plâtrer vt to plaster.

plébiscite m plebiscite.

plein adj full; entire.

pleur m tear, sob:—**en ~s** in tears.

pleurer vi to cry, weep.

pleuvoir vi to rain.

pli m fold; crease; envelope.

pliant adj collapsible, folding.

plier vt to fold; to bend.

plissement m creasing, folding.

plisser vt to pleat, fold.

plomb m lead; sinker; fuse.

plomber vt to weight; to fill.

plomberie f plumbing.

plongée f diving, dive.

plongeon m dive.

plonger vi to dive; to plunge.

plongeur m **-euse** f diver.

pluie f rain; shower.

plume f feather.

plupart f most; majority.

pluriel m plural:—adj plural.

plus adv more, most:—**~ grand que** bigger than:—**de ~ en ~** more and more:—**de ~** moreover:—**non ~** neither, not either.

plusieurs adj several.

plutôt adv rather, quite, fairly.

pluvieux adj rainy, wet.

pneu m tyre.

pneumonie f pneumonia.

poche f pocket; pouch; bag.

poêle m stove:—f frying pan.

poème m poem.

poète m poet.

poids m weight, influence.

poignée f handful:—**~ de mains** handshake.

poil m hair; bristle.

poinçon m hallmark.

poinçonner vt to hallmark.

poing m fist:—**coup de ~** punch.

point m point; full stop:—**mettre au ~** to finalise; to perfect:—**être sur le ~ de** to be about to:—**à~** medium, just right:—**~ de vue** point of view.

pointe f point, head; spike:—**sur la ~ des pieds** on tiptoe.

pointu adj pointed, sharp.

poire f pear.

poireau m leek.

pois m pea.

poison m poison.

poisson m fish.

poitrine f chest, breast; bosom.

poivre m pepper.

poivrer vt to pepper.

polaire adj polar.

pôle m pole; centre.

polémique f controversy:—adj controversial.

poli *adj* polite; polished, smooth.

police *f* police.

policier *m* policeman, **-ière** *f* police-woman.

polir *vt* to polish; to refine.

politesse *f* politeness, courtesy.

politicien(ne) *m(f)* politician.

politique *f* politics; policy:—*adj* political.

politiser *vt* to politicise.

polluer *vt* to pollute.

pollution *f* pollution.

polyglotte *adj* polyglot:—*mf* polyglot.

pomme de terre *f* potato.

pomme *f* apple.

pompe *f* pump.

pomper *vt* to pump.

pompeux *adj* pompous; pretentious.

pompier *m* fireman.

poncer *vt* to sand down, rub down.

ponctualité *f* punctuality.

ponctuel *adj* punctual.

ponctuer *vt* to punctuate.

pondre *vt* to lay; to produce.

pont *m* bridge; deck; axle.

ponton *m* pontoon; landing stage.

populaire *adj* popular.

popularité *f* popularity.

population *f* population.

porc *m* pig; pork.

porche *m* porch.

pore *m* pore.

poreux *adj* porous.

port *m* port; pass; wearing.

portatif *adj* portable.

porte *f* door; gate; threshold.

porte-avions *m invar* aircraft carrier.

porte-clefs, porte-clés *m invar* key ring.

porte-parole *m invar* spokesperson.

portée *f* reach, range; significance:—**à la ~ de** within reach:—**hors de ~** out of reach.

portefeuille *m* wallet; portfolio.

porter *vt* to carry; to take; to wear.

porteur *m* **-euse** *f* porter; carrier:—*adj* booster; strong, buoyant.

portière *f* door.

portion *f* portion, share.

portrait *m* portrait.

pose *f* pose, posture; setting.

poser *vt* to put; to install:—**se ~** *vr* to land, settle.

positif *adj* positive, definite.

position *f* position; situation; state; stance.

positionner *vt* to position, locate.

posséder *vt* to possess.

possesseur *m* possessor, owner.

possession *f* possession.

possibilité *f* possibility; potential.

possible *adj* possible; potential:—*m* **faire son ~** to do one's best.

postal *adj* postal, mail.

poste *f* post office, post:—*m* position; job.

poster *vt* to post, mail; to position.

postérieur *adj* subsequent.

postérité *f* posterity; descendants.

postier *m* **-ière** *f* post office worker.

postuler *vt* to apply for; to postulate.

posture *f* posture, position.

pot *m* jar; pot; can.

pot-de-vin *m* bribe.

potable *adj* drinkable; passable.

potage *m* soup.

poteau *m* post, stake.

potentiel *adj* potential:—*m* potential

poterie *f* pottery.

potier *m* potter.

poubelle *f* dustbin.

pouce *m* thumb; big toe; inch.

poudre *f* powder, dust.

poudrer *vt* to powder.

poule *f* hen, fowl.

poulet *m* chicken.

pouls *m* pulse.

poumon *m* lung.

poupon *m* baby.

pouponnière *f* creche

pour *prép* for; to; in favour of; in order:—~ **que** in order that.

pourboire *m* tip.

pourcentage *m* percentage.

pourparlers *mpl* talks, negotiations.

pourquoi *adv* why:—~ **pas?** why not?:—*m* reason, question.

pourri *adj* rotten.

pourrir *vi* to rot.

pourriture *f* rot, rottenness.

poursuite *f* pursuit; prosecution.

poursuivre *vt* to pursue; to prosecute.

pourtant *adv* however, yet, nevertheless.

pourvoir *vt* to provide, equip.

pourvu *conj*:—~ **que** provided that.

poussée *f* pressure; thrust.

pousser *vt* to push:—*vi* to push; to grow.

poussière *f* dust.

poussiéreux *adj* dusty.

pouvoir *vi* can, be able; may:—*m* power; authority.

pragmatique *adj* pragmatic.

prairie *f* meadow, prairie.

praticable *adj* practicable; passable.

pratique *f* practice; exercise; observance:—*adj* practical.

pratiquer *vt* to practise, exercise; to carry out.

pré *m* meadow.

préalable *adj* preliminary.

préavis *m* notice, advance warning.

précaire *adj* precarious.

précaution *f* precaution; care.

précédent *adj* previous:—*m* precedent.

précéder *vt* to precede.

prêcher *vt* to preach.

précieux *adj* precious.

précipice *m* precipice.

précipitation *f* haste, violent hurry.

précipiter *vt* to hasten, precipitate.

précis *adj* precise, exact.

préciser *vt* to specify:—**se** ~ *vr* to become clear.

précision *f* precision.

précoce *adj* precocious.

précurseur *m* precursor.

prédateur *m* predator.

prédécesseur *m* predecessor.

prédiction *f* prediction.

prédire *vt* to predict, foretell.

prédominance *f* predominance.

prédominer *vi* to predominate.

préfabriqué *adj* prefabricated.

préférable *adj* preferable.

préféré(e) *m(f)* favourite.

préférence *f* preference.

préférer *vt* to prefer.

préjudice *m* loss; damage.

préjudiciable *adj* prejudicial.

préjudicier *vt* to be prejudicial.

préjugé *m* prejudice.

préliminaire *m* preliminary:—*adj* preliminary.

prématuré *adj* premature.

préméditation *f* premeditation.

premier *m* first:—*adj* first; primary

prémonition *f* premonition.

prénatal *adj* prenatal.

prendre *vt* to take:—**se** ~ *vr* to consider oneself.

prénom *m* first name, forename.

préoccuper *vt* to preoccupy:—**se ~**
vr to concern oneself.

préparation *f* preparation.

préparer *vt* to prepare.

prérogative *f* prerogative.

près *adv* near; almost:—**de ~**
closely:—**à peu ~** just about.

prescrire *vt* to prescribe.

présence *f* presence.

présent *m* present:—*adj* present:—
m present:—**à ~** just now.

présentation *f* presentation; introduction.

présenter *vt* to introduce; to present.

préservatif *m* condom.

préserver *vt* to preserve.

présidence *f* presidency.

président(e) *m(f)* president.

présider *vt* to preside, chair.

présomption *f* presumption.

présomptueux *adj* presumptuous.

presque *adv* almost.

presse *f* press.

pressentiment *m* presentiment.

pressentir *vt* to have a presentiment
of.

presser *vt* to press; to hurry up:—**se
~** *vr* to hurry.

pression *f* pressure.

pressoir *m* press (wine, cider)

prestation *f* benefit; payment.

prestige *m* prestige.

présumer *vt* to presume.

prêt *adj* ready; prepared:—*m* loan.

prêt-à-porter *m* ready-to-wear.

prétendant(e) *m(f)* candidate.

prétendre *vt* to claim; to want; to intend.

prétendu *adj* so-called, supposed.

prétentieux *adj* pretentious.

prétention *f* pretension, claim.

prêter *vt* to lend; to attribute.

prétexte *m* pretext, excuse.

prêtre *m* priest.

preuve *f* proof, evidence.

prévaloir *vi* to prevail.

prévenant *adj* considerate.

prévenir *vt* to prevent; to warn.

prévention *f* prevention.

prévisible *adj* foreseeable.

prévision *f* prediction; forecast.

prévoir *vt* to anticipate; to plan.

prévoyance *f* foresight.

prévoyant *adj* provident.

prévu *adj* provided for.

prier *vi* to pray.

prière *f* prayer; entreaty.

primaire *adj* primary.

primate *m* primate.

prime *f* premium, subsidy.

primer *vi* to dominate:—*vt* to outdo.

primitif *adj* primitive.

primordial *adj* primordial.

prince *m* prince.

princesse *f* princess.

principal *m* principal:—*adj* main,
principal.

principe *m* principle; origin.

printanier *adj* spring.

printemps *m* spring.

prioritaire *adj* priority.

priorité *f* priority.

prise *f* hold, grip; catch; plug; dose
—**~ de sang** blood sample:—**~ de
courant** plug, power point:—**~ de
conscience** awareness, realisation.

prison *f* prison; jail.

prisonnier *m* **-ière** *f* prisoner:—*adj*
captive.

privation *f* deprivation.

privatiser *vt* to privatise.

privé *adj* private; unofficial.

priver *vt* to deprive.

privilège *m* privilege.

privilégié *adj* privileged, favoured.
privilégier *vt* to favour.
prix *m* price, cost; prize.
probabilité *f* probability.
probable *adj* probable, likely.
problématique *adj* problematical.
problème *m* problem, issue.
procédé *m* process; behaviour.
procéder *vi* to proceed.
procédure *f* procedure; proceedings.
procès *m* proceedings; lawsuit.
procès-verbal *m* minutes; report.
procession *f* procession.
prochain *adj* next; imminent:—*m* neighbour.
proche *adj* nearby; close.
proclamation *f* proclamation.
proclamer *vt* to proclaim, declare.
procurer *vt* to procure.
procureur *m* prosecutor.
prodigieux *adj* prodigious.
producteur *m* **-trice** *f* producer.
productif *adj* productive.
production *f* production.
productivité *f* productivity.
produire *vt* to produce.
produit *m* product; yield.
profane *adj* secular, profane.
professeur *m* teacher, professor.
profession *f* profession; occupation.
professionnel(le) *m(f)* professional; skilled worker:—*adj* professional.
profil *m* profile, outline.
profiler *vt* to profile.
profit *m* profit; advantage.
profitable *adj* profitable.
profiter *vi* to profit.
profond *adj* deep, profound.
profondeur *f* depth; profundity.
profusion *f* profusion.
programme *m* programme.

programmer *vt* to programme; to schedule.
progrès *m* progress; improvement; advance.
progresser *vi* to progress; to advance.
progression *f* progress.
prohiber *vt* to prohibit, ban.
proie *f* prey, victim.
projection *f* projection, casting.
projet *m* plan; draft.
projeter *vt* to plan; to cast, project.
prolétaire *mf* proletarian.
prolifération *f* proliferation.
proliférer *vi* to proliferate.
prolongement *m* continuation, extension.
prolonger *vt* to prolong.
promenade *f* walk, stroll.
promener (se) *vr* to go for a walk.
promeneur *m* **-euse** *f* walker.
promesse *f* promise.
promettre *vt* to promise.
promotion *f* promotion.
promouvoir *vt* to promote.
prompt *adj* prompt.
prononcer *vt* to pronounce.
prononciation *f* pronunciation.
pronostic *m* forecast; prognosis.
pronostiquer *vt* to forecast, prognosticate.
propagande *f* propaganda.
propagation *f* propagation.
propager *vt* to propagate.
prophète *m* prophet.
prophétique *adj* prophetic.
prophétiser *vt* to prophesy.
propice *adj* propitious.
proportion *f* proportion, ratio.
proportionnel *adj* proportional.
propos *m* talk, remarks; intention:—
à ~ de about, on the subject of.

proposer *vt* to propose.
proposition *f* proposition.
propre *adj* clean; own; suitable.
propreté *f* cleanliness; tidiness.
propriétaire *mf* owner; landlord.
propriété *f* ownership; suitability.
propulser *vt* to propel, power.
propulsion *f* propulsion.
prorogation *f* prorogation.
proroger *vt* to prorogue.
proscrire *vt* to proscribe.
prose *f* prose.
prospecter *vt* to prospect.
prospecteur *m* **-trice** *f* prospector.
prospectus *m* leaflet; prospectus.
prospère *adj* prosperous.
prospérer *vi* to prosper, flourish.
prospérité *f* prosperity.
prostituée *f* prostitute.
prostitution *f* prostitution.
protagoniste *m* protagonist
protection *f* protection.
protéger *vt* to protect.
protestant(e) *m(f)* Protestant:—*adj* Protestant.
protestation *f* protest.
protester *vi* to protest; to affirm.
prototype *m* prototype.
prouesse *f* prowess.
prouver *vt* to prove; to demonstrate.
provenir *vi* to come from.
proverbe *m* proverb.
province *f* province.
provincial *adj* provincial
provision *f* provision; supply.
provisoire *adj* provisional, temporary.
provocation *f* provocation.
provoquer *vt* to provoke; to cause.
proximité *f* proximity.
prudence *f* prudence, care.
prudent *adj* prudent, careful.
pseudonyme *m* pseudonym.

psychanalyser *vt* to psychoanalyse
psychanalyste *mf* psychoanalyst.
psychiatre *mf* psychiatrist
psychiatrie *f* psychiatry.
psychique *adj* psychic.
psychisme *m* psyche, mind.
psychologie *f* psychology.
psychologique *adj* psychological.
psychologue *mf* psychologist:—*adj* psychological.
psychosomatique *adj* psychosomatic.
puberté *f* puberty.
public *adj*, *f* **publique** public:—*m* public, audience.
publicité *f* publicity.
publier *vt* to publish.
puce *f* flea.
pudique *adj* modest; chaste.
puer *vi* to stink:—*vt* to stink.
puéril *adj* puerile, childish.
puérilité *f* puerility, childishness.
puis *adv* then, next.
puisque *conj* since; as.
puissance *f* power, strength.
puissant *adj* powerful.
puits *m* well; shaft.
pulmonaire *adj* pulmonary, lung.
pulsation *f* pulsation.
pulvériser *vt* to pulverise; to powder.
punir *vt* to punish.
punition *f* punishment.
pupille *f* pupil; ward.
pupitre *m* desk; console.
pur *adj* pure; neat.
pureté *f* purity, pureness.
purifier *vt* to purify, cleanse.
puritain(e) *m(f) adj* puritan.
pur-sang *m invar* thoroughbred.
putréfier *vt* to putrefy, rot.
pyjama *m* pyjamas.
pylône *m* pylon.
pyramide *f* pyramid.

Q

quai *m* quay, wharf; platform.
qualificatif *adj* qualifying.
qualification *f* qualification.
qualifier *vt* to describe; to qualify.
qualitatif *adj* qualitative.
qualité *f* quality; skill; position.
quand *conj* when, while.
quant *prép*:—~ **à lui** as for him/it.
quantifier *vt* to quantify.
quantitatif *adj* quantitative.
quantité *f* quantity, amount.
quarante *adj, m inv* forty.
quarantième *adj, mf* fortieth.
quart *m* quarter; watch.
quartier *m* district; quarter.
quasi *adv* almost, nearly.
quatorze *adj m* fourteen.
quatorzième *adj mf* fourteenth.
quatre *adj m* four.
quatre-vingt(s) *adj m* eighty.
quatre-vingt-dix *adj m* ninety.
quatre-vingtième *adj mf* eightieth.
quatrième *adj mf* fourth.
que *conj* that; than:—*pron* that; whom; what; which.
quel, *f* **quelle** *adj* who, what, which.
quelconque *adj* some, any; least, indifferent.

quelqu'un, *f* **-une** someone *pl* **quelques-uns, -unes** *pron* some.
quelque *adj* some:—~ **part** somewhere.
quelque chose *pron* something.
quelquefois *adv* sometimes
querelle *f* quarrel; row; debate.
quereller (se) *vr* to quarrel.
question *f* question; issue.
questionnaire *m* questionnaire.
questionner *vt* to question.
quête *m* quest, search.
queue *f* tail; stalk; queue.
qui *pn* who, whom; which.
quiconque *pn* whoever, whosoever.
quiétude *f* quiet; peace.
quincaillerie *f* hardware, ironmongery.
quintuple *adj* quintuple:—*m* quintuple.
quintupler *vi* to quintuple.
quinzaine *f* about fifteen; fortnight.
quinze *adj, m* fifteen.
quinzième *adj, mf* fifteenth.
quitter *vt* to leave.
quoi *pn* what:—~ **que** whatever.
quoique *conj* although, though.
quotidien *adj* daily:—*m* everyday life.

R

rabais *m* reduction, discount.

rabaisser *vt* to humble.

rabattre *vt* to close; to reduce.

rabbin *m* rabbi.

raccommoder *vt* to mend, repair.

raccord *m* join; link; pointing.

raccorder *vt* to link up.

raccourci *m* shortcut.

raccourcir *vt* to shorten.

raccrocher *vt* to ring off, hang up.

race *f* race; stock; breed.

rachat *m* repurchase, purchase.

racheter *vt* to repurchase.

racial *adj* racial.

racine *f* root:—~ **carrée** square root.

raciste *mf* racist:—*adj* racist.

raconter *vt* to tell, recount.

radar *m* radar.

rade *f* harbour, roads.

radiateur *m* radiator; heater.

radiation *f* radiation.

radical *adj* radical.

radieux *adj* radiant, dazzling.

radio *f* radio; X-ray.

radio-taxi *m* radio taxi.

radioactif *adj* radioactive.

radiodiffuser *vt* to broadcast (radio).

radiographie *f* radiography; X-ray photography.

radiologue *mf* radiologist.

radis *m* radish.

radoucir *vt* to soften.

rafale *f* gust, blast; flurry.

raffermir *vt* to harden.

raffinage *m* refining.

raffiné *adj* refined, sophisticated.

raffiner *vt* to refine.

raffoler *vi*:—~ **de** to be crazy about.

rafraîchir *vt* to cool, freshen.

rafraîchissant *adj* refreshing, cooling.

rage *f* rage, fury; mania; rabies.

raid *m* raid; trek.

raide *adj* stiff; steep; broke.

raideur *f* stiffness; steepness.

raidir *vt* to stiffen.

raie *f* line; furrow; scratch.

rail *m* rail; railway.

railler *vt* to scoff at, mock.

raillerie *f* mockery, scoffing.

raisin *m* grape.

raison *f* reason; motive; ratio:— **avoir** ~ to be right:—**en** ~ **de** because of.

raisonnable *adj* reasonable, sensible.

raisonnement *m* reasoning.

raisonner *vi* to reason; to argue.

rajeunir *vt* to rejuvenate.

rajuster *vt* to readjust.

ralenti *adj* slow:—*m* slow motion:—**au** ~ ticking over, idling.

ralentir *vi* to slow down.

ralentissement *m* slowing down.

râler *vi* to groan, moan.

rallier *vt* to rally; to win over.

rallumer *vt* to relight.

ramadan *m* Ramadan.

ramassage *m* gathering.

ramasser *vt* to collect, gather.

rame *f* oar; underground train.

rameau *m* branch.

ramener *vt* to bring back, restore.

ramer *vi* to row.

rameur *m*, **euse** *f* rower.

ramollir (se) *vr* to soften.

ramoner *vt* to sweep.

rampe *f* ramp, slope; gradient.

ramper *vi* to crawl, slither.

rance *adj* rancid, rank.

rançon *f* ransom.

rancune *f* grudge, rancour.

randonnée *f* drive; ride; ramble.

randonneur *m*, **-euse** *f* hiker, rambler.

rang *m* row, line; rank; class.

rangée *f* row, range, tier.

ranger *vt* to arrange.

ranimer *vt* to reanimate.

rapatriement *m* repatriation.

rapatrier *vt* to repatriate.

rapide *adj* rapid, quick.

rapidité *f* rapidity, quickness.

rapiécer *vt* to patch up.

rappel *m* recall; reminder

rappeler *vt* to recall; to remind:—**se ~** *vr* to remember.

rapport *m* report; relation; reference.

rapporter *vt* to report; to bring back.

rapporteur *m*, **-euse** *f* reporter.

rapprochement *m* reconciliation.

rapprocher (se) *vr* to approach; to be reconciled.

raquette *f* racket.

rare *adj* rare; odd.

raréfier (se) *vr* to rarefy.

rareté *f* rarity; scarcity.

ras *adj* close-shaven, shorn.

raser *vt* to shave off; to raze:—**se ~** *vr* to shave.

rasoir *m* razor.

rassemblement *m* assembling; crowd.

rassembler *vt* to rally:—**se ~** *vr* to gather, assemble.

rasseoir (se) *vr* to sit down again.

rassurant *adj* reassuring, comforting.

rassurer *vt* to reassure.

rat *m* rat.

raté *m* **-e** *f* failure:—*m* misfire.

rater *vt* to miss; to fail:—*vi* to misfire.

ratification *f* ratification.

ratifier *vt* to ratify, confirm.

ration *f* ration, allowance.

rationnel *adj* rational.

rationner *vt* to ration.

rattacher *vt* to refasten; to attach; to link.

rattraper *vt* to catch again; to recover.

rature *f* deletion, erasure.

raturer *vt* to delete, erase.

rauque *adj* hoarse, raucous.

ravage *m* havoc; devestation.

ravager *vt* to ravage; devastate.

ravin *m* ravine, gully.

ravir *vt* to delight.

raviser (se) *vr* to change one's mind.

ravissant *adj* ravishing, delightful.

ravitaillement *m* revictualling.

ravitailler *vt* to revictual.

raviver *vt* to revive.

rayer *vt* to scratch; to cross out.

rayon *m* ray, beam; spoke; shelf.

rayonnement *m* radiance.

rayonner *vi* to radiate, shine.

rayure *f* stripe; streak; groove.

réaccoutumer (se) *vr* to become reaccustomed.

réacteur *m* reactor; jet-engine.

réaction *f* reaction.

réactionnaire *adj* reactionary:—*mf* reactionary.

réagir *vi* to react.

réalisateur *m*, **-trice** *f* director, film-maker.

réalisation *f* realisation.

réaliser *vt* to realise:—**se ~** *vr* to be realised, come true.

réalisme *m* realism.

réalité *f* reality.

réanimation *f* resuscitation.

réanimer *vt* to reanimate.

réapparaître *vi* to reappear.

rebelle *mf* rebel:—*adj* rebel, rebellious.

rebeller (se) *vr* to rebel.

rébellion *f* rebellion.

reboiser *vt* to reafforest.

rebondir *vi* to rebound.

rebondissement *m* rebound.

rebut *m* scrap; repulse, rebuff.

receler *vt* to harbour.

récent *adj* recent; new.

réceptif *adj* receptive.

réception *f* reception, welcome.

réceptionniste *mf* receptionist.

récession *f* recession.

recette *f* recipe; formula; receipt.

receveur *m*, **-euse** *f* recipient; collector.

recevoir *vt* to receive.

rechange *m* spare.

recharge *f* reloading.

rechargeable *adj* reloadable.

recharger *vt* to reload.

réchauffer *vt* to reheat.

rêche *adj* rough, harsh.

recherche *f* search; research.

rechercher *vt* to seek; to investigate.

rechute *f* relapse; lapse.

récidiver *vi* to reoffend; to recur.

récif *m* reef.

récipient *m* container, receptacle.

réciproque *adj* reciprocal, mutual.

récit *m* account, story.

récitation *f* recitation.

réciter *vt* to recite.

réclamation *f* complaint; claim.

réclamer *vt* to claim.

réclusion *f* reclusion.

récolte *f* harvest; collection.

récolter *vt* to harvest; to collect.

recommandation *f* recommendation.

recommander *vt* to recommend; to register (letter).

recommencement *m* renewal.

recommencer *vi* to begin again.

récompense *f* reward; award.

réconciliation *f* reconciliation.

réconcilier *vt* to reconcile.

réconfort *m* comfort.

réconfortant *adj* comforting; tonic.

réconforter *vt* to comfort.

reconnaissance *f* recognition.

reconnaissant *adj* grateful.

reconnaître *vt* to recognise; to acknowledge; to be grateful.

reconsidérer *vt* to reconsider.

reconstituer *vt* to reconstitute.

reconstitution *f* reconstitution.

reconstruire *vt* to rebuild.

record *m* record.

recourbé *adj* curved, hooked.

recourir *vi* to run again.

recours *m* recourse; appeal.

récréatif *adj* recreative.

récréation *f* recreation.

récrimination *f* recrimination.

récriminer *vi* to recriminate.

recrue *f* recruit.

recrutement *m* recruitment.

recruter *vt* to recruit.

rectangle *m* rectangle.

rectangulaire *adj* rectangular.

rectification *f* rectification.

rectifier *vt* to rectify.

rectiligne *adj* rectilinear.

reçu *p.p.* **recevoir** accepted, successful:—*m* receipt.

recueil *m* collection, miscellany.

recueillir *vt* to gather:—**se ~** *vr* to collect one's thoughts.

reculer *vi* to fall back.

récupération *f* recovery.

récupérer *vt* to recover.

recycler *vt* to recycle.

rédacteur *m*, **-trice** *f* editor.

rédaction *f* drafting, drawing up.

rédemption *f* redemption.

redevance *f* rent; tax; fees.

rédiger *vt* to compile; to draft.

redire *vt* to repeat.

redoutable *adj* redoubtable, formidable.

redouter *vt* to dread, fear.

redresser *vt* to rectify; to true.

réduction *f* reduction.

réduire *vt* to reduce.

réduit *adj* reduced:—*m* retreat; recess.

rééducation *f* re-education.

rééduquer *vt* to re-educate.

réel *adj* real, genuine.

réélire *vt* to re-elect.

refaire *vt* to redo; to remake.

réfectoire *m* refectory.

référence *f* reference.

référendum *m* referendum.

réfléchir *vi* to think, reflect.

reflet *m* reflection.

refléter *vt* to reflect, mirror.

réflexe *m* reflex.

réflexion *f* thought, reflection:—**~ faite** all things considered.

réforme *f* reform.

réformer *vt* to reform.

réfraction *f* refraction.

réfréner *vt* to curb.

réfrigérateur *m* refrigerator.

réfrigérer *vt* to refrigerate.

refroidir *vt* to cool:—*vi* to get cold.

refuge *m* refuge.

réfugié(e) *m(f)* refugee:—*adj* refugee.

réfugier (se) *vr* to take refuge.

refus *m* refusal.

refuser *vt* to refuse.

réfuter *vt* to refute.

regagner *vt* to regain.

régaler *vt* to regale.

regard *m* look; glance.

regarder *vt* to look at.

régénération *f* regeneration.

régénérer *vt* to regenerate, revive.

régie *f* administration.

régime *m* system, régime.

région *f* region, area.

régional *adj* regional.

régir *vt* to govern, rule.

registre *m* register, record.

règle *f* rule; order.

règlement *m* regulation, rules.

réglementation *f* regulations; control.

réglementer *vt* to regulate.

régler *vt* to pay; to regulate.

règne *m* reign.

régner *vi* to reign.

régresser *vi* to regress.

régression *f* regression.

regret *m* regret.

regretter *vt* to regret, be sorry; to miss.

regroupement *m* reassembly

regrouper *vt* to reassemble:—**se ~** *vr* to assemble.

régulariser *vt* to regularise.

régularité *f* regularity.

régulier *adj* regular; consistent.

réhabilitation *f* rehabilitation.

réhabiliter *vt* to rehabilitate.

réhabituer (se) *vr* to reaccustom oneself.

rein *m* kidney.

réincarnation *f* reincarnation.

reine *f* queen.

réinsertion *f* reinsertion.

réintégrer *vt* to reinstate.

réitérer *vt* to reiterate.

rejet *m* rejection.

rejeter *vt* to reject.

rejoindre *vt* to rejoin.

rejouer *vt* to replay.

réjouir *vt* to delight:—**se ~** *vr* to rejoice.

réjouissance *f* rejoicing.

relâche *f* intermission, respite.

relâchement *m* relaxation.

relâcher (se) *vr* to relax; to become lax.

relais *m* relay.

relatif *adj* relative.

relation *f* relation; reference.

relaxation *f* relaxation.

relaxer (se) *vr* to relax.

relayer *vt* to relieve; to relay.

relecture *f* rereading.

reléguer *vt* to relegate.

relève *f* relief.

relevé *m* statement; bill.

relever *vt* to raise again; to rebuild.

relief *m* relief; contours; depth.

relier *vt* to link up; to bind.

religieux *m* monk, **-euse** *f* nun:—*adj* religious.

religion *f* religion.

relire *vt* to reread.

reluire *vi* to gleam, shine.

remaniement *m* recasting; revision.

remanier *vt* to recast; to amend.

remarquable *adj* remarkable.

remarque *f* remark, comment.

remarquer *vt* to remark; to notice.

remboursement *m* reimbursement.

rembourser *vt* to reimburse.

remède *m* remedy, cure.

remédier *vi* ~ **à** to remedy, cure.

remerciement *m* thanks; thanking.

remercier *vt* to thank.

remettre *vt* to replace:—**se ~** *vr* to recover.

réminiscence *f* reminiscence.

remise *f* delivery; remittance:—**~ en état** repairing:—**~ à neuf** restoration:—**~ en question** calling into question:—**~ en cause** calling into question.

remmener *vt* to take back.

remonter *vi* to go up again:—*vt* to take up.

remorque *f* trailer; towrope.

remorquer *vt* to tow.

remorqueur *m* tug.

rempart *m* rampart; defence.

remplaçant *m*, **-e** *f* replacement.

remplacer *vt* to replace.

remplir *vt* to fill.

remporter *vt* to take away.

remue-ménage *m invar* commotion; hullabaloo.

remuer *vi* to move; to fidget.

rémunération *f* remuneration.

rémunérer *vt* to remunerate, pay.

renaissance *f* rebirth, Renaissance.

renaître *vi* to be reborn.

renard *m* fox.

rencontre *f* meeting, encounter.

rencontrer *vt* to meet; to find.

rendement *m* yield; output.

rendez-vous *m* appointment; date; meeting place.

rendormir (se) *vr* to go back to sleep.

rendre *vt* to render; to give back:—**se ~** *vr* to surrender.

renfermer *vt* to contain, hold.
renflouer *vt* to refloat.
renforcer *vt* to strengthen.
renfort *m* reinforcement.
renifler *vt* to sniff.
renom *m* renown, fame.
renommée *f* renowned.
renoncement *m* renouncement.
renoncer *vi* to renounce.
renonciation *f* renunciation.
renouer *vt* to tie again.
renouveau *m* spring.
renouveler *vt* to renew.
renouvellement *m* renewal.
rénovation *f* renovation.
rénover *vt* to renovate.
renseignement *m* information.
renseigner *vt* to inform.
rentable *adj* profitable.
rente *f* rent; profit.
rentrer *vi* to re-enter; to return home.
renversement *m* reversal.
renverser *vt* to reverse; to overturn.
renvoi *m* sending back; dismissal.
renvoyer *vt* to send back; to dismiss.
réorganisation *f* reorganisation.
réorganiser *vt* to reorganise.
répandre *vt* to pour out.
répandu *adj* widespread.
réparation *f* repairing; restoration.
réparer *vt* to repair; to restore.
repartir *vi* to set off again.
répartir *vt* to share out.
répartition *f* sharing out.
repas *m* meal.
repeindre *vt* to repaint.
repentir (se) *vr* to repent, rue.
répercussion *f* repercussion.
répercuter (se) *vr* to reverberate; to echo.
repère *m* line, mark.
repérer *vt* to spot, pick out.

répertorier *vt* to itemise; to index.
répéter *vt* to repeat.
répétitif *adj* repetitive.
répétition *f* repetition; rehearsal.
répit *m* respite, rest.
repli *m* fold, coil, meander.
replier *vt* to fold up.
réplique *f* reply, retort.
répliquer *vt* to reply.
répondeur *m* answering machine.
répondre *vt* to answer, reply.
réponse *f* response, reply.
report *m* postponement, deferment.
reporter *vt* to take back:—*m* reporter.
repos *m* rest; landing.
reposer *vt* to put back:—**se ~** *vr* to rest oneself.
repoussant *adj* repulsive; repellent.
repousser *vt* to repel.
reprendre *vt* to retake, recapture.
représentant *m* representative.
représentation *f* representation; performance.
représenter *vt* to represent.
répressif *adj* repressive.
répression *f* repression.
réprimander *vt* to reprimand.
réprimer *vt* to repress.
reprise *f* resumption:—**à plusieurs ~s** several times.
reproche *m* reproach.
reprocher *vt* to reproach, blame.
reproduction *f* reproduction.
reproduire *vt* to reproduce.
reptile *m* reptile.
républicain *m*, **-e** *f* republican:—*adj* republican.
république *f* republic.
répudier *vt* to repudiate.
répugnance *f* repugnance.
répugnant *adj* repugnant.

réputation *f* reputation; character; fame.
réputé *adj* reputable, renowned.
requérir *vt* to request.
requête *f* request.
réquisition *f* requisition.
réseau *m* network, net.
réservation *f* reservation.
réserve *f* reserve; reservation.
réservé *f* reserved.
réserver *vt* to reserve.
réservoir *m* tank; reservoir.
résidence *f* residence.
résidentiel *adj* residential
résider *vi* to reside.
résignation *f* resignation.
résistance *f* resistance.
résistant *adj* resistant.
résister *vi* to resist, withstand.
résolu *adj* resolved, determined.
résolution *f* resolution; solution.
résonner *vi* to resonate.
résoudre *vt* to solve; to resolve.
respect *m* respect, regard.
respectable *adj* respectable.
respecter *vt* to respect.
respectif *adj* respective.
respectueux *adj* respectful.
respiration *f* respiration.
respiratoire *adj* respiratory.
respirer *vi* to breathe, respire.
responsabilité *f* responsibility.
responsable *adj* responsible; liable:—*mf* official, manager.
ressemblance *f* resemblance.
ressembler *vi* to resemble.
ressentiment *m* resentment.
ressentir *vt* to feel, experience.
resserrement *m* contraction.
resserrer *vt* to tighten.
ressort *m* spring.
ressortissant *m*, **-e** *f* national.

ressource *f* resource; resort.
ressusciter *vi* to reawaken.
restant *m* rest, remainder.
restaurant *m* restaurant.
restauration *f* restoration; catering.
restaurer *vt* to restore:—**se ~** *vr* to take refreshment.
reste *m* rest, remainder:—**du ~** besides.
rester *vi* to stay; to be left.
restituer *vt* to return; to refund.
restitution *f* restitution.
restreindre *vt* to restrict.
restrictif *adj* restrictive.
restriction *f* restriction, limitation.
résultat *m* result; profit.
résulter *vi*:—**~ de** to result from.
résumé *m* summary.
résumer *vt* to sum up.
résurrection *f* resurrection.
rétablir *vt* to re-establish, restore.
rétablissement *m* re-establishment, restoring.
retard *m* lateness; delay.
retardé *adj* backward, slow.
retarder *vt* to delay.
retenir *vt* to hold back, retain.
réticence *f* reticence.
réticent *adj* reticent.
retirer (se) *vr* to retire, withdraw.
rétorquer *vt* to retort.
retour *m* return; recurrence.
retourner *vi* to return, go back.
rétracter *vt* to retract.
retrait *m* retreat; withdrawal.
retraite *f* retreat; retirement.
retraité(e) *m(f)* pensioner:—*adj* retired.
rétrécissement *m* narrowing; shrinking.
rétribuer *vt* to remunerate.
rétribution *f* retribution.

rétroactif *adj* retroactive.

rétroaction *f* retroaction.

rétrograde *adj* reactionary.

rétrograder *vi* to go backward.

rétrospectif *adj* retrospective.

retrouver *vt* to find again; to recover:—**se ~** *vr* to meet up.

réunifier *vt* to reunify.

réunir (se) *vr* to meet; to assemble.

réussir *vi* to succeed.

réussite *f* success.

revanche *f* revenge:—**en ~** on the other hand.

rêve *m* dream, dreaming; illusion.

réveil *m* awaking; alarm clock.

réveiller *vt* to wake:—**se ~** *vr* to awaken.

révélation *f* revelation.

révéler *vt* to reveal.

revendeur *m*, **-euse** *f* retailer.

revendiquer *vt* to claim; to demand.

revendre *vt* to resell

revenir *vi* to come back, reappear.

revenu *m* income, revenue.

rêver *vi* to dream; to muse.

réverbère *m* street lamp.

révérer *vt* to revere.

rêverie *f* reverie, musing.

revers *m* back, reverse.

réversible *adj* reversible.

rêveur *m*, **-euse** *f* dreamer:—*adj* dreamy

revigorer *vt* to invigorate.

revirement *m* reversal; turnaround.

réviser *vt* to review; to revise.

révision *f* revision.

revivre *vt* to relive.

révocation *f* removal; revocation.

revoir *vt* to see again.

révolte *f* revolt, rebellion.

révolter (se) *vr* to rebel, revolt.

révolu *adj* past, bygone.

révolution *f* revolution.

révolutionnaire *mf* revolutionary:—*adj* revolutionary.

révoquer *vt* to revoke.

revue *f* review.

rez-de-chaussée *m invar* ground floor.

rhabiller (se) *vr* to dress again.

rhétorique *f* rhetoric:—*adj* rhetorical.

rhinocéros *m* rhinoceros.

rhum *m* rum.

rhume *m* cold.

riant *adj* smiling; cheerful.

riche *adj* rich, wealthy.

richesse *f* richness; wealth.

ride *f* wrinkle; ripple; ridge.

rideau *m* curtain.

ridicule *adj* ridiculous.

ridiculiser *vt* to ridicule.

rien *pron* nothing:—**de ~** don't mention it:—*m* nothingness; mere nothing.

rieur *adj* cheerful; laughing.

rigide *adj* rigid.

rigidité *f* rigidity.

rigoureux *adj* rigorous, harsh.

rigueur *f* rigour; harshness.

rime *f* rhyme.

rimer *vi* to rhyme (with)

rincer *vt* to rinse out; to rinse.

riposter *vi* to answer back, retaliate.

rire *vi* to laugh; to smile:—*m* laughter, laugh.

risée *f* laugh; ridicule.

risible *adj* laughable.

risque *m* risk, hazard.

risquer *vt* to risk; to venture.

rivage *m* shore

rival *m*, **-e** *f* rival:—*adj* rival.

rivaliser *vi* to rival.

rivalité *f* rivalry.

rive f shore, bank.

riverain adj riverside, lakeside.

rivière f river.

riz m rice.

robe f dress; gown:—~ de chambre dressing gown.

robinet m tap.

robot m robot.

robuste adj robust.

roc m rock.

rocher m rock, boulder.

roder vt to grind.

rôder vi to roam; to prowl.

rôdeur m, **-euse** f prowler.

rognon m kidney.

roi m king

rôle m role, character; roll, catalogue.

roman m novel; romance.

romancier m, **-ière** f novelist.

romantique adj romantic.

rompre vt to break:—vi to break; to burst.

rond m circle, ring; round:—adj round; chubby.

rond-point m roundabout.

ronde f patrol; round; beat.

ronflement m snore, snoring.

ronfler vi to snore.

ronronner vi to purr; to hum.

rose f rose:—adj pink:—m pink.

rosée f dew.

rossignol m nightingale.

rotation f rotation; turnover.

rôti m joint, roast.

rôtir vt to roast.

rôtisserie f rotisserie, steakhouse.

roue f wheel.

rouge adj red:—m red.

rouge-gorge m robin.

rougeur f redness, blushing.

rougir vi to blush, go red:—vt to redden.

rouille f rust.

rouiller vi to rust.

roulement m rotation; movement.

rouler vt to wheel:—vi to drive.

roulotte f caravan.

route f road; way; direction.

routier adj road:—m lorry driver; transport cafe.

routine f routine.

routinier adj humdrum, routine.

roux m, **rousse** f redhead:—adj red, auburn.

royal adj royal, regal.

royaume m kingdom.

ruban m ribbon; tape.

rubis m ruby.

rubrique f column; rubric.

rude adj rough; hard; unrefined.

rudesse f roughness; harshness.

rudiment m rudiment; principle.

rudimentaire adj rudimentary.

rue f street.

ruelle f alley.

rugir vi to roar.

rugissement m roar, roaring.

ruine f ruin; wreck.

ruiner vt to ruin.

ruineux adj ruinous; extravagant.

ruisseau m stream, brook.

ruisseler vi to stream, flow.

rumeur f rumour; murmur.

rupture f break, rupture.

rural adj rural, country.

ruse f cunning, slyness.

rusé adj cunning, crafty.

rustique adj rustic.

rythme m rhythm; rate, speed.

rythmique adj rhythmic.

S

sable *m* sand.

sablé *adj* sandy, sanded.

sabotage *m* sabotage.

saboter *vt* to sabotage.

saboteur *m* -euse *f* saboteur.

sac *m* bag:—~ à main handbag.

saccade *f* jerk, jolt.

saccharine *f* saccharin.

sachet *m* bag; sachet; packet.

sacré *adj* sacred.

sacrifice *m* sacrifice.

sacrifier *vt* to sacrifice.

sacrilège *m* sacrilege.

sadique *adj* sadistic:—*mf* sadist.

safran *m* saffron.

saga *f* saga.

sagace *adj* sagacious, shrewd.

sage *adj* wise; well-behaved:—*m* sage, wise man.

sage-femme *f* midwife.

sagesse *f* wisdom, sense; good behaviour.

saignant *adj* bleeding.

saigner *vi* to bleed.

saillant *adj* protruding.

saillir *vi* to gush out; to project.

sain *adj* healthy; sound; sane.

saint(e) *m(f)* saint:—*adj* holy, saintly.

sainteté *f* saintliness; holiness.

saisie *f* seizure.

saisir *vt* to seize.

saison *f* season.

saisonnier *adj* seasonal.

salade *f* salad.

salaire *m* salary, pay; reward.

salarié(e) *m(f)* salaried employee:—*adj* salaried.

sale *adj* dirty, filthy; obscene.

salé *adj* salty, salted.

saler *vt* to salt, add salt.

saleté *f* dirt; rubbish; obscenity.

salière *f* saltcellar.

salir *vt* to make dirty:—se ~ *vr* to get dirty.

salive *f* saliva.

salle *f* room; hall:—~ de séjour living room:—~ à manger dining room:—~ de bain bathroom.

salon *m* lounge; exhibition.

salubre *adj* healthy, salubrious.

saluer *vt* to greet; to salute.

salut *m* safety; welfare; salute.

salutation *f* salutation, greeting.

samedi *m* Saturday.

sanctifier *vt* to sanctify, bless.

sanction *f* sanction; approval.

sanctionner *vt* to punish; to sanction.

sanctuaire *m* sanctuary.

sandale *f* sandal.

sang *m* blood; race; kindred.

sanglant *adj* bloody, gory.

sanglot *m* sob.

sangloter *vi* to sob.

sanguinaire *adj* sanguinary, bloodthirsty.

sanitaire *adj* health, sanitary.

sans-abris *mf invar* homeless person.

santé *f* health, healthiness.

saper *vt* to undermine, sap.

sapeur-pompier *m* fireman.

sapin *m* fir tree, fir.

sarcasme *m* sarcasm.

sarcastique *adj* sarcastic.

sardine *f* sardine.

sardonique *adj* sardonic

satellite *m* satellite.

satiété *f* satiety:—**à ~** ad nauseam.

satin *m* satin.

satire *f* satire, lampoon.

satirique *adj* satirical.

satisfaction *f* satisfaction.

satisfaire *vt* to satisfy.

satisfaisant *adj* satisfying.

saturation *f* saturation.

saturé *adj* saturated.

saturer *vt* to saturate.

sauce *f* sauce, dressing.

saucisse *f* sausage.

sauf *prép* save, except; unless:—*adj* safe, unhurt.

saumon *m* salmon.

saut *m* jump, bound; waterfall.

sauter *vi* to jump; to blow up.

sauvage *adj* savage; unsociable.

sauvegarde *f* safeguard; backup.

sauvegarder *vt* to safeguard.

sauver *vt* to save.

sauvetage *m* rescue; salvage.

sauveteur *m* rescuer.

savant *adj* learned; expert:—*m* scientist, scholar.

saveur *f* flavour; savour.

savoir *vt* to know; to be able:—*m* learning, knowledge.

savoir-faire *m* know-how.

savon *m* soap.

savonner *vt* to soap, lather.

savoureux *adj* tasty, savoury.

scandale *m* scandal.

scandaleux *adj* scandalous.

scandaliser *vt* to scandalise.

scaphandre *m* diving suit.

sceau *m* seal.

sceller *vt* to seal.

scénario *m* scenario; screenplay.

scénariste *mf* scriptwriter.

scène *f* stage; scenery, scene.

scepticisme *m* scepticism.

sceptique *adj* sceptical:—*mf* sceptic.

schéma *m* diagram, sketch; outline.

schizophrène *mf* schizophrenic:—*adj* schizophrenic.

schizophrénie *f* schizophrenia.

scie *f* saw; bore.

sciemment *adv* knowingly, on purpose.

science *f* science; skill; knowledge.

science-fiction *f* science fiction.

scientifique *adj* scientific.

scintillant *adj* sparkling, glistening.

scintiller *vi* to sparkle, glisten.

scolaire *adj* school; academic.

scolarité *f* schooling.

scooter *m* scooter.

score *m* score.

scout *m* scout, boy scout.

script *m* printing; script.

scrupule *m* scruple, doubt.

scrupuleux *adj* scrupulous.

sculpter *vt* to sculpt; to carve.

sculpteur *m* sculptor.

sculpture *f* sculpture.

se *pron* oneself, himself, herself, itself, themselves.

séance *f* meeting, session; seat.

seau *m* bucket, pail.

sec *adj, f* **sèche** dry, arid.

séchage *m* drying; seasoning.

sèche-cheveux *m invar* hair-drier.

sécher *vi* to dry.

sécheresse *f* drought.

second *adj* second.

secondaire *adj* secondary.

seconde *f* second.

secouer *vt* to shake, toss.

secourir *vt* to help, assist.

secouriste *mf* first-aid worker.

secours *m* help, assistance; relief; rescue.

secousse *f* jolt, bump.

secret *m* secret:—*adj* secret; discreet.

secrétaire *mf* secretary:—*m* writing desk.

sécrétion *f* secretion.

secte *f* sect.

secteur *m* sector, section.

section *f* section, division; branch.

séculaire *adj* secular.

sécuritaire *adj* security.

sécurité *f* security; safety.

sédatif *m* sedative:—*adj* sedative.

sédiment *m* sediment.

séduction *f* seduction; captivation

séduire *vt* to seduce; to charm, captivate.

segment *m* segment.

segmenter *vt* to segment.

ségrégation *f* segregation.

seigneur *m* lord, nobleman.

sein *m* breast, bosom; womb:—**au ~ de** within.

séisme *m* earthquake, seism.

seize *adj*, *m* sixteen.

seizième *adj*, *mf* sixteenth.

séjour *m* stay, sojourn.

séjourner *vi* to stay, sojourn.

sel *m* salt; wit.

sélectif *adj* selective.

sélection *f* choosing, selection.

sélectionner *vt* to select, pick.

selle *f* saddle.

selon *prép* according to.

semaine *f* week.

semblable *adj* like, similar.

semblant *m* appearance, look.

sembler *vi* to seem, appear.

semence *f* seed.

semer *vt* to sow.

semestre *m* half-year; semester.

semestriel *adj* half-yearly; semestral.

séminaire *m* seminary; seminar.

sénat *m* senate.

sénateur *m* senator.

sénile *adj* senile.

sénilité *f* senility.

sens *m* sense; judgement; meaning; direction.

sensation *f* sensation, feeling.

sensationnel *adj* sensational.

sensé *adj* sensible.

sensibiliser *vt* to make sensitive to.

sensibilité *f* sensitivity.

sensible *adj* sensitive; perceptive.

sensualité *f* sensuality.

sensuel *adj* sensual.

sentence *f* sentence.

sentier *m* path, track.

sentiment *m* sentiment; feeling.

sentimental *adj* sentimental.

sentir *vt* to feel; to perceive.

séparation *f* separation.

séparatiste *mf* separatist.

séparer *vt* to separate:—**se ~** *vr* to separate.

sept *adj*, *m* seven.

septembre *m* September

septième *adj*, *mf* seventh.

sépulture *f* sepulture, burial.

séquence *f* sequence.

serein *adj* serene, calm.

sérénité *f* serenity, calmness.

sergent *m* sergeant.

série *f* series.

sérieux *adj* serious.

seringue *f* syringe.

serment *m* oath.

séropositif *adj* HIV positive, seropositive.

serpent *m* serpent, snake.

serpenter *vi* to meander, wind.

serre *f* greenhouse; claw.

serrer *vt* to tighten.

serrure *f* lock.

sérum *m* serum.

servante *f* servant.

serveur *m* waiter, **-euse** *f* waitress.

service *m* service; function.

serviette *f* towel; serviette.

servile *adj* servile, slavish.

servilité *f* servility.

servir *vi* to be of use:—*vt* to serve:—**se ~ de** to make use of.

servitude *f* servitude.

session *f* session, sitting.

seuil *m* threshold.

seul *adj* alone; single.

sévère *adj* severe, austere.

sévérité *f* severity; strictness

sexe *m* sex.

sexiste *mf* sexist:—*adj* sexist.

sexualité *f* sexuality.

sexuel *adj* sexual.

sexy *adj* sexy.

short *m* shorts.

si *adv* so, so much; yes:—*conj* if; whether.

SIDA *m* AIDS.

sidérurgiste *mf* steel worker.

siècle *m* century.

siège *m* seat; head office.

siéger *vi* to sit; to be located.

sien *pron, f* **sienne**:—**le ~ his**, its, his own, its own, **la sienne** her, its, her own, its own, **les ~s, les siennes** their, their own.

siffler *vi* to whistle; to hiss.

sigle *m* abbreviation; acronym.

signal *m* signal, sign.

signaler *vt* to signal, indicate.

signature *f* signature; signing.

signe *m* sign; mark.

signer *vt* to sign.

signet *m* bookmark.

significatif *adj* significant.

signification *f* significance.

signifier *vt* to mean, signify.

silence *m* silence.

silencieux *adj* silent; still.

silhouette *f* silhouette.

similaire *adj* similar.

similarité *f* similarity.

simple *adj* simple; mere; single.

simplicité *f* simplicity.

simplification *f* simplification.

simplifier *vt* to simplify.

simulation *f* simulation.

simuler *vt* to simulate.

simultané *adj* simultaneous.

sincère *adj* sincere, honest.

sincérité *f* sincerity, honesty.

singe *m* monkey.

singularité *f* singularity.

singulier *adj* singular, peculiar.

sinistre *m* disaster; accident:—*adj* sinister.

sinistré(e) *m(f)* disaster victim.

sinon *conj* otherwise, if not; except.

sinueux *adj* sinuous, winding.

site *m* setting, beauty spot.

sitôt *adv* as soon:—**~ que** as soon as.

situation *f* situation, position.

situer *vt* to site, situate.

six *adj, m* six.

sixième *adj, mf* sixth.

ski *m* ski, skiing.

skier *vi* to ski.

skieur *m* **-euse** *f* skier.

slip *m* briefs; panties.

snob *adj* snobbish.

snobisme *m* snobbishness.

sobre *adj* sober, temperate.

sobriété *f* sobriety, temperance.

sociable *adj* sociable; social.

social *adj* social.

socialiste *mf* socialist:—*adj* socialist.

société *f* society; company.

sociologique *adj* sociological.

sociologue *mf* sociologist.

sœur *f* sister; nun.

sofa *m* sofa.

soi *pn* one(self); self:—~-**même** oneself, himself, herself, itself.

soie *f* silk.

soif *f* thirst.

soigner *vt* to look after.

soigneux *adj* neat; careful.

soin *m* care.

soir *m* evening; night.

soit *conj* either; or; whether:—*adv* granted; that is to say.

soixante *adj*, *m* sixty.

soixantième *adj*, *mf* sixtieth.

sol *m* ground; floor; soil.

soldat *m* soldier

solde *f* pay:—*m* balance.

solder *vt* to pay; to settle.

soleil *m* sun, sunshine; sunflower.

solennel *adj* solemn.

solidarité *f* solidarity.

solide *adj* solid; sound.

solidifier *vt* to solidify.

solitaire *mf* recluse:—*adj* solitary, lone.

solitude *f* solitude; loneliness.

solution *f* solution.

solvable *adj* solvent.

sombre *f* dark; gloomy.

sommaire *m* summary:—*adj* basic, summary.

sommeil *m* sleep; sleepiness.

sommeiller *vi* to slumber.

sommet *m* summit; crest.

somnambule *mf* sleepwalker:—*adj* sleepwalking.

somnifère *m* sleeping pill.

somnoler *vi* to doze.

somptueux *adj* sumptuous, lavish.

son *m* sound:—*adj*, *f* **sa**; *pl* **ses** his, her, its.

songe *m* dream.

songer *vt* to dream.

sonner *vi* to ring.

sonore *adj* resonant, deep-toned.

sophistiqué *adj* sophisticated.

sordide *adj* sordid, squalid.

sort *m* fate, destiny, lot.

sorte *f* sort, kind.

sortie *f* exit, way out; trip; sortie.

sortir *vi* to go out.

sot *adj* (*f* **sotte**) silly, foolish.

sottise *f* stupidity; stupid remark.

souci *m* worry; concern.

soucier *vr*:—**se ~ de** to care about.

soucieux *adj* concerned, worried.

soudain *adj* sudden, unexpected.

souder *vt* to solder; to weld.

souffle *m* blow, puff; breath.

souffler *vi* to blow; to breathe.

souffrance *f* suffering; pain.

souffrir *vi* to suffer.

souhait *m* wish.

souhaiter *vt* to wish for, desire.

soulagement *m* relief.

soulager *vt* to relieve, soothe.

soulever *vt* to lift:—**se ~** *vr* to rise; to revolt.

soulier *m* shoe.

souligner *vt* to underline.

soumettre *vt* to subdue.

soumission *f* submission.

soupape *f* valve.

soupçon m suspicion.
soupçonner vt to suspect.
soupçonneux adj suspicious.
soupe f soup.
soupir m sigh; gasp.
soupirer vi to sigh; to gasp.
souple adj supple; pliable.
souplesse f suppleness.
source f source.
sourcil m eyebrow.
sourd(e) m(f) deaf person:—adj deaf; muted.
sourd(e)-muet(te) m(f) deaf-mute:—adj deaf and dumb.
souriant adj smiling, cheerful.
sourire m smile, grin.
souris f mouse.
sournois adj deceitful.
sous prép under, beneath, below.
sous-alimenté adj undernourished.
sous-développé adj underdeveloped.
sous-entendre vt to imply.
sous-estimer vt to underestimate.
sous-marin m submarine:—adj underwater.
sous-titre m subtitle.
sous-titrer vt to subtitle.
sous-traitant m subcontractor.
sous-traiter vt to subcontract.
souscrire vi to subscribe.
soustraction f subtraction.
soustraire vt to subtract.
soute f hold; baggage hold.
soutenir vt to sustain.
souterrain adj underground.
soutien m support.
soutien-gorge m bra.
souvenir m memory; recollection.
souvenir (se) vr to remember
souvent adv often, frequently.
souverain(e) m(f) sovereign:—adj sovereign.

spacieux adj spacious, roomy.
spaghettis mpl spaghetti.
spasme m spasm.
spécial adj special.
spécialiser vt to specialise.
spécieux adj specious.
spécification f specification.
spécifier vt to specify.
spécifique adj specific.
spécimen m specimen.
spectacle m spectacle, scene.
spectaculaire adj spectacular.
spectateur m -trice f spectator.
spectre m ghost.
spéculateur m -trice f speculator.
spéculer vi to speculate.
sphère f sphere.
spiritualité f spirituality.
spirituel adj witty; spiritual.
splendeur f splendour, brilliance.
splendide adj splendid.
spontané adj spontaneous.
sport m sport.
sportif m sportsman, -ive f sportswoman:—adj sports.
square m square.
squelette m skeleton.
stabiliser vt to stabilise.
stabilité f stability.
stable adj stable.
stade m stadium; stage.
stage m training course.
stagiaire mf trainee.
standard adj standard.
star f star.
starter m choke.
station f station; stage.
stationnaire adj stationary.
stationnement m parking.
stationner vi to park.
station-service f service station.
statique adj static.

statistique f statistics:—*adj* statistical.

statue f statue.

statuer vt to rule.

statut m statute.

statutaire *adj* statutory.

stencil m stencil.

sténodactylo mf shorthand typist.

sténographie f shorthand.

stéréotype m stereotype.

stérile *adj* sterile, infertile.

stériliser vt to sterilise.

stérilité f sterility.

stimulant *adj* stimulating:—m stimulant.

stimulation f stimulation.

stimuler vt to stimulate.

stipuler vt to stipulate.

stock m stock, supply.

stocker vt to stock, stockpile.

stoïque *adj* stoical.

stop m stop; stop sign.

stopper vt to stop.

store m blind, shade.

stratégie f strategy.

stratégique *adj* strategic.

stress m stress.

stressant *adj* stessful.

strict *adj* strict, severe.

strident *adj* strident, shrill.

structural *adj* structural.

structure f structure.

studieux *adj* studious.

studio m studio; film theatre.

stupéfier vt to stupefy; to astound.

stupeur f amazement; stupor.

stupide *adj* stupid, foolish.

stupidité f stupidity.

style m style; stylus.

styliste mf designer; stylist.

stylo m pen.

suave *adj* suave, smooth.

subconscient m subconscious:—*adj* subconscious.

subir vt to sustain; to undergo.

subit *adj* sudden.

subjectif *adj* subjective.

subjectivité f subjectivity.

subjuguer vt to subjugate.

sublime *adj* sublime.

submerger vt to submerge.

subséquent *adj* subsequent.

subside m grant.

subsistance f subsistence.

subsister vi to subsist.

substance f substance.

substantiel *adj* substantial.

substantif m noun, substantive.

substituer vt to substitute.

substitut m substitute.

substitution f substitution.

subtil *adj* subtle.

subtilité f subtlety.

subvention f grant, subsidy.

subventionner vt to subsidise.

subversif *adj* subversive.

succéder vi:—~ à to succeed, follow.

succès m success; hit.

successeur m successor.

succession f succession.

succinct *adj* succinct.

succomber vi to succumb.

succulent *adj* succulent, delicious.

sucursale f branch.

sucer vt to suck.

sucre m sugar.

sud m south.

suer vi to sweat, perspire.

sueur f sweat.

suffire vi to suffice.

suffisant *adj* sufficient, adequate.

suffoquer vi to choke, suffocate.

suffrage m suffrage; vote.

suggérer vt to suggest.

suggestion f suggestion.

suicide m suicide.

suicider (se) vr to commit suicide.

suite f continuation; series:—**tout de ~ at once:—et ainsi de ~** and so on.

suivant adj following, next:—*prép* according to.

suivi m follow-up.

suivre vt to follow:—**~ son cours** to take its course:—**à suivre** to be continued.

sujet m subject, topic:—*adj* subject.

super adj ultra, super.

superbe adj superb.

superficie f area, surface.

superficiel adj superficial.

superflu adj superfluous.

supérieur adj upper; superior.

supériorité f superiority.

superlatif m superlative:—*adj* superlative.

superstitieux adj superstitious.

superstition f superstition.

superviser vt to supervise.

supplanter vt to supplant.

supplément m supplement.

supplémentaire adj supplementary.

support m support, prop; stand.

supporter vt to support; to endure.

supposer vt to suppose.

suppression f suppression.

supprimer vt to suppress.

suprématie f supremacy.

suprême adj supreme.

sur prép on; over, above; into; out of, from.

sûr adj sure, certain; secure:—**~ de soi** self-assured:—**bien ~** of course.

surabondance f overabundance.

suranné adj outmoded, outdated.

surcharge f surcharge.

surcroît m surplus:—**de ~** in addition.

surdité f deafness.

surélever vt to raise, heighten.

surestimer vt to overestimate.

sûreté f safety; guarantee.

surface f surface.

surgeler vt to deep-freeze.

surgir vi to appear; to arise.

surlendemain m day after tomorrow.

surmonter vt to surmount.

surnaturel adj supernatural.

surnom m nickname.

surnommer vt to nickname.

surpasser vt to surpass, outdo.

surplomber vt to overhang.

surplus m surplus.

surpopulation f overpopulation.

surprenant adj surprising.

surprendre vt to surprise.

surprise f surprise.

sursaut m start, jump.

sursauter vi to start, jump.

surtaxe f surcharge.

surtout adv especially; above all.

surveillance f surveillance.

surveiller vt to watch; to supervise.

survenir vi to take place, occur.

survie f survival.

survivant(e) m(f) survivor:—*adj* surviving.

survivre vi to survive.

survoler vt to fly over.

susceptible adj susceptible:—**être ~ de** to be likely to.

susciter vt to arouse, incite.

suspect(e) m(f) suspect.

suspecter vt to suspect.

suspendre vt to hang up; to suspend.

suspension f suspension.

suspicieux adj suspicious.

suspicion f suspicion.

susurrer vt to whisper.

svelte adj svelte, slim.

syllabe f syllable.
symbole m symbol
symbolique adj symbolic; token.
symboliser vt to symbolise.
symétrie f symmetry.
symétrique adj symmetrical.
sympathie f liking; sympathy.
sympathique adj likeable, nice; friendly.
symphonie f symphony.
symptôme m symptom.
synagogue f synagogue.

synchroniser vt to synchronise.
syndical adj trade-union.
syndicaliste mf trade unionist:—adj trade union.
syndicat m trade union; association.
synonyme m synonym:—adj synonymous.
synthèse f synthesis.
synthétique adj synthetic.
systématique adj systematic.
système m system.

T

tabac m tobacco.
table f table:—~ **ronde** round-table conference.
tableau m table; chart.
tablette f bar; tablet.
tablier m apron; overall.
tabouret m stool.
tache f mark; stain; spot.
tâche f task, assignment; work.
tacite adj tacit.
taciturne adj taciturn, silent.
tact m tact.
tactile adj tactile.
tactique f tactics:—adj tactical.
taille f height, stature, size.
tailler vt to cut; to carve.
taire(se) vr to be quiet.
talent m talent, ability.
talentueux adj talented.
talon m heel; crust; spur.
tambour m drum; barrel.
tamis m sieve; riddle.

tamiser vt to sieve; to sift.
tampon m stopper, plug; tampon.
tandem m tandem; duo.
tandis conj:—~ **que** while; whereas.
tangible adj tangible.
tank m tank.
tanner vt to tan, weather.
tant adv so much:—~ **que** as long as:—~ **mieux** that's a good job:— ~ **pis** too bad.
tante f aunt.
tantôt adv sometimes; this afternoon; shortly.
tapage m din, uproar, racket.
tape f slap.
taper vt to beat; to slap; to type.
tapis m carpet; rug; cloth.
tapisser vt to wallpaper; to cover.
tapisserie f tapestry.
taquin adj teasing.
taquiner vt to tease; to plague.
tard adv late.

tarder *vi* to delay, put off; to dally.

tardif *adj* late; tardy.

tarif *m* tariff; price-list.

tarir (se) *vr* to dry up.

tarte *f* tart, flan.

tartre *m* tartar; fur, scale.

tas *m* heap, pile; lot, set.

tasse *f* cup; coffee cup.

tassement *m* settling, sinking.

tasser *vt* to heap up:—**se ~** *vr* to sink; subside.

tâter *vt* to feel, try.

tatonner *vi* to feel one's way.

tatouer *vt* to tattoo.

taudis *m* hovel, slum.

taureau *m* bull.

taux *m* rate; ratio:—**~ de change** exchange rate.

taverne *f* tavern.

taxation *f* taxation, taxing.

taxe *f* tax; duty; rate.

taxer *vt* to tax.

taxi *m* taxi.

te *pn* you, yourself.

technicien(ne) *m(f)* technician.

technique *f* technique:—*adj* technical.

technologie *f* technology.

technologique *adj* technological.

teindre *vt* to dye.

teint *m* complexion, colouring.

teinter *vt* to tint; to stain.

teinture *f* dye; dyeing.

tel *adj* such; like, similar:—**~ quel** such as it is:—**en tant que ~** as such.

télé *f* TV, telly.

télécommande *f* remote control.

télécopie *f* facsimile transmission; fax.

télégramme *m* telegram; cable.

télégraphier *vt* to telegraph, cable.

télépathie *f* telepathy.

téléphérique *m* cableway; cable-car.

téléphone *m* telephone.

téléphoner *vi* to telephone.

télescope *m* telescope.

télescopique *adj* telescopic.

téléviseur *m* television set.

télévision *f* television.

télex *m* telex.

tellement *adj* so, so much:—**~ de** so many, so much.

téméraire *adj* rash, reckless.

témoignage *m* testimony.

témoigner *vi* to testify.

témoin *m* witness.

tempérament *m* temperament.

température *f* temperature

tempête *f* tempest.

temple *m* temple.

temporaire *adj* temporary.

temps *m* time; while; tense; beat; weather:—**de ~ en ~** from time to time.

tenace *adj* tenacious, stubborn.

ténacité *f* tenacity; stubbornness.

tenaille *f* pincers; tongs.

tendance *f* tendency; trend.

tendancieux *adj* tendentious.

tendon *m* tendon, sinew.

tendre *adj* tender, soft; delicate.

tendresse *f* tenderness; fondness.

tendu *adj* tight; stretched; delicate

ténébreux *adj* dark, gloomy.

teneur *f* terms; content; grade.

tenir *vt* to hold, keep:—**~ à** to value, care about.

tennis *m* tennis:—**~ de table** table tennis.

tentation *f* temptation.

tentative *f* attempt, bid.

tente *f* tent.

tenter *vt* to tempt.

tenue f holding; deportment; dress, appearance.

terme m term; termination, end; word.

terminaison f ending.

terminal adj terminal:—m terminal.

terminer vt to finish off:—**se ~** vr to terminate.

terminologie f terminology.

terne adj colourless; drab.

terrain m ground, earth; site; field.

terrasse f terrace.

terre f earth; ground, land:—**mettre pied à ~** to land, alight.

terrestre adj land; terrestrial.

terreur f terror, dread.

terrible adj terrible, dreadful; terrific, great.

terrier m burrow; earth; terrier.

terrifiant adj terrifying, fearsome.

terrifier vt to terrify.

territoire m territory, area.

territorial adj land, territorial.

terroir m soil.

terroriser vt to terrorise.

terroriste mf terrorist:—adj terrorist.

test m test.

testament m will, testament.

tester vt to test; to make out one's will.

tête à tête m private conversation.

tête f head; top; sense:—**tenir ~** to cope:—**être en ~** to head.

tétine f teat; udder; dummy.

téton m breast.

têtu adj headstrong, stubborn.

texte m text; theme; passage.

textile adj textile.

textuel adj textual, literal.

texture f texture.

thé m tea.

théâtral adj theatrical, dramatic.

théâtre m theatre; drama.

thème m theme.

théologie f theology.

théorie f theory.

théorique adj theoretical.

thérapeute mf therapist.

thérapie f therapy.

thermique adj thermal; thermic.

thermomètre m thermometer.

thermos f/m thermos.

thèse f thesis.

thym m thyme.

ticket m ticket.

tiède adj lukewarm, tepid.

tien poss pn:—**le ~, la ~ne, les ~(ne)s** yours.

tiers adj third:—**~-monde** Third World:—m third; third party.

tigre m tiger.

timbre m stamp; postmark; bell.

timbrer vt to stamp; to postmark.

timide adj timid, shy.

timidité f timidity, shyness.

tintement m ringing toll.

tinter vi to ring, toll; to chime.

tir m shooting; shot:—**~ à l'arc** archery.

tirailler vt to tug; to pester.

tire-bouchon m corkscrew.

tirelire f moneybox.

tirer vt to pull; to draw.

tiret m dash; hyphen.

tireur m **-euse** f gunner; drawer (cheque).

tiroir m drawer.

tisser vt to weave.

tissu m texture, fabric; tissue.

titre m title; heading; right; deed:—**à ~ de** by right of.

tituber vi to stagger.

titulaire mf incumbent, holder:—adj titular.

toi pn you:—**~-même** yourself:—

c'est à ~ it's your's; it's your turn.

toile *f* cloth; canvas; sheet.

toilette *f* cleaning, grooming:— **faire sa ~** to wash oneself.

toit *m* roof; home.

tolérable *adj* tolerable, bearable.

tolérant *adj* tolerant.

tolérer *vt* to tolerate.

tomate *f* tomato.

tombe *f* tomb; grave.

tomber *vi* to fall:—**laisser ~** to drop.

tome *m* book; volume.

ton *adj*, *f* **ta**, *pl* **tes** your:—*m* tone; pitch; shade.

tondre *vt* to shear; mow.

tonifiant *m* tonic.

tonifier *vt* to tone up.

tonique *adj* tonic; fortifying:—*m* tonic.

tonne *f* ton, tonne.

tonneau *m* barrel, cask.

tonnerre *m* thunder.

topographie *f* topography.

toquade *f* infatuation; fad, craze.

toquer *vi* to tap, rap.

torche *f* torch.

torcher *vt* to wipe, mop up.

torchon *m* cloth; duster.

tordre *vt* to twist, contort.

tordu *adj* twisted, crooked.

torpeur *f* torpor.

torrent *m* torrent.

torrentiel *adj* torrential.

torride *adj* torrid; scorching.

torse *m* chest; torso.

torsion *f* twisting; torsion.

tort *m* fault; wrong; prejudice:— **avoir ~** to be wrong:—**faire du ~** to harm.

tortiller *vt* to twist:—**se ~** *vr* to wriggle.

tortionnaire *mf* torturer.

tortue *f* tortoise.

tortueux *adj* tortuous, winding.

torture *f* torture.

torturer *vt* to torture.

tôt *adv* early; soon:—**au plus ~** as soon as possible:—**plus ~** sooner.

total *adj* total.

totalitaire *adj* totalitarian.

totalité *f* totality.

touche *f* touch.

toucher *vt* to touch.

touffe *f* tuft, clump.

toujours *adv* always; still.

tour *f* tower:—*m* turn, round; circuit; tour; trick:—**~ à ~** by turns.

tourbillon *m* whirlwind.

tourbillonner *vi* to whirl, eddy.

tourisme *m* tourism.

touriste *mf* tourist.

touristique *adj* tourist.

tourment *m* torment, agony.

tourmenter *vt* to torment.

tournant *m* bend; turning point:— *adj* revolving.

tournée *f* tour; round.

tourner *vi* to turn:—**se ~** *vr* to turn round.

tournesol *m* sunflower.

tournevis *m* screwdriver.

tournoi *m* tournament.

tournure *f* turn; turn of phrase.

tousser *vi* to cough.

tout *adj* (*pl* **tous**, **toutes**) all; whole; every:—**~ le monde** everybody:— *pn* everything; all:—*m* whole:— *adv* entirely, quite.

toutefois *adv* however.

toux *f* cough.

toxicomane *mf* drug addict.

toxique *adj* toxic.

trac *m* nerves, stage fright.

tracasser *vt* to worry; to harass.

trace f track; outline, trace.
tracer vt to trace.
tract m leaflet, tract.
tractation f transaction.
tracteur m tractor.
tradition f tradition.
traditionnel adj traditional; usual.
traducteur m **-trice** f translator.
traduction f translation.
traduire vt to translate.
trafic m traffic; trading.
trafiquer vi to traffic, trade.
tragédie f tragedy.
tragique adj tragic.
trahir vt to betray.
trahison f betrayal, treason.
train m train; pace, rate.
traîneau m sleigh, sledge.
traînée f trail, track; drag.
traîner vi to drag on, lag.
traire vt to milk.
trait m trait, feature; relation.
traite f trade; draft, bill; milking.
traité m treaty; treatise, tract.
traitement m treatment; salary.
traiter vt to treat; to process.
traiteur m caterer.
traître m traitor.
traîtrise f treachery.
trajet m distance; course.
tramer vt to plot; to weave.
trampoline m trampoline.
tranche f slice; edge; section.
trancher vt to cut, sever.
tranquille adj quiet, tranquil.
tranquilliser vt to reassure.
tranquillité f tranquillity.
transaction f transaction.
transatlantique adj transatlantic.
transcription f transcription.
transcrire vt to transcribe.
transe f trance.

tranférer vt to transfer.
transfert m transfer.
transformateur m transformer.
transformation f transformation.
transformer vt to transform.
transfusion f transfusion.
transgresser vt to transgress.
transgression f transgression.
transistor m transistor.
transiter vi to pass in transit.
transition f transition.
transitoire adj transitory.
transmettre vt to transmit.
transmissible adj transmissible.
transmission f transmission.
transparence f transparency.
transparent adj transparent.
transpercer vt to pierce.
transplanter vt to transplant.
transport m carrying; transport.
transporter vt to transport
transporteur m haulier; carrier.
transposer vt to transpose.
transversal adj transverse.
trapèze m trapeze.
trapéziste mf trapeze artist.
trappe f trap door.
trappeur m trapper.
traquer vt to track; to hunt down.
traumatiser vt to traumatise.
travail m pl **travaux** work, labour.
travailler vi to work.
travailleur m, **-euse** f worker:—adj
    diligent; hard-working.
travers m breadth:—à ~ through,
    across.
traversée f crossing; traverse.
traverser vt to cross, traverse.
trébucher vi to stumble.
trèfle m clover.
treillis m trellis; wire mesh.
treize adj, m thirteen.

treizième *adj, mf* thirteenth.

tremblement *m* trembling ~ **de terre** earthquake.

trembler *vi* to tremble, shake.

trémousser (se) *vr* to wriggle.

tremper *vt* to soak.

tremplin *m* springboard.

trentaine *f* about thirty.

trente *adj, m* thirty.

trentième *adj mf* thirtieth.

trépidant *adj* pulsating, quivering.

trépigner *vi* to stamp one's feet.

très *adv* very; most; very much.

trésor *m* treasure.

trésorier *m* **-ière** *f* treasurer.

tressaillir *vi* to thrill; to shudder.

tresse *f* plait, braid.

tresser *vt* to plait, braid.

trêve *f* truce; respite.

tri *m* sorting out; grading.

triangle *m* triangle.

triangulaire *adj* triangular.

tribal *adj* tribal.

tribu *f* tribe.

tribunal *m* court, tribunal.

tribune *f* gallery; rostrum.

tribut *m* tribute.

tricher *vi* to cheat.

tricheur *m*, **-euse** *f* cheater.

tricolore *adj* three-coloured, tricolour.

tricoter *vt* to knit.

tridimensionnel *adj* three-dimensional.

trier *vt* to sort out.

trilingue *adj* trilingual.

trimestre *m* quarter; term.

trimestriel *adj* quarterly; three-monthly.

trinquer *vi* to toast; to booze.

trio *m* trio.

triomphal *adj* triumphal.

triomphe *m* triumph, victory.

triompher *vi* to triumph.

triple *adj* triple, treble.

tripler *vi* to triple.

triste *adj* sad, melancholy.

tristesse *f* sadness.

trivial *adj* trivial; crude.

trivialité *f* triviality; crudeness.

troc *m* exchange; barter.

trois *adj, m* three.

troisième *adj, mf* third.

trombe *f*:— **d'eau** cloudburst.

trompe *f* trumpet; trunk.

tromper *vt* to deceive, trick:—**se ~** *vr* to be mistaken.

tromperie *f* deception, deceit.

trompette *f* trumpet.

trompeur *adj* deceitful; deceptive.

tronc *m* trunk, shaft.

trône *m* throne.

tronquer *vt* to truncate, curtail.

trop *adv* too; too much:—*m* ~ excess.

trophée *m* trophy.

tropical *adj* tropical.

tropique *m* tropic.

troquer *vt* to barter, swap.

trotter *vi* to trot; to toddle.

trottinette *f* scooter.

trottoir *m* pavement.

trou *m* hole; gap; cavity.

troublant *adj* disturbing.

trouble *adj* unclear, murky:—*m* trouble, disturbance.

troubler *vt* to trouble, disturb.

trouer *vt* to make a hole in.

troupe *f* troupe; troop.

troupeau *m* herd, drove.

trousse *f* case, kit; wallet.

trouver *vt* to find.

truc *m* (*fam*) trick; gadget.

truite *f* trout.

truquage *m* rigging, fiddling.

truquer *vt* to rig, fiddle.

tu *pn* you.

tube *m* tube, pipe; duct.

tuer *vt* to kill.

tuerie *f* slaughter.

tueur *m* **-euse** *f* killer.

tuile *f* tile.

tulipe *f* tulip.

tumeur *f* tumour.

tumulte *m* tumult, commotion.

tumultueux *adj* tumultuous.

tunnel *m* tunnel.

turbine *f* turbine.

turbulence *f* turbulence.

turbulent *adj* turbulent.

tutelle *f* guardianship.

tuteur *m* **tutrice** *f* guardian:—*m* stake, prop.

tutoyer *vt* to address s.o. as *tu*.

tuyau *m* pipe.

type *m* type; model; bloke, chap.

typhon *m* typhoon.

typique *adj* typical.

tyran *m* tyrant.

tyrannique *adj* tyrannical.

U

ulcère *m* ulcer.

ultérieur *adj* subsequent:—**~ement** *adv* later.

ultimatum *m* ultimatum.

ultime *adj* ultimate, final.

un, une *art* a, an; one—l'~ l'autre, **les ~s les autres** one another.

unanime *adj* unanimous.

unification *f* unification.

unifier *vt* to unify.

uniforme *adj* uniform.

uniformité *f* uniformity; regularity.

unilatéral *adj* unilateral.

union *f* union.

unique *adj* only, single; unique:— **~ment** *adv* only, solely, exclusively.

unir *vt* to unite.

unisson *m* unison.

unité *f* unity; unit.

univers *m* universe; world.

universel *adj* universal.

universitaire *adj* university:—*mf* academic.

université *f* university.

urbain *adj* urban, city.

urbanisme *m* town planning.

urgence *f* urgency.

urgent *adj* urgent.

urne *f* ballot box; urn.

usage *m* use; custom.

usager *m* **ère** *f* user.

usé *adj* worn; banal, trite.

user *vt* to use.

usine *f* factory.

ustensile *m* implement; utensil.

usuel *adj* ordinary; everyday:— **~lement** *adv* ordinarily.

usurper *vt* to usurp.

utérus *m* womb, uterus.

utile *adj* useful.

utilisateur *m*, **-trice** *f* user.

utiliser *vt* to use, utilise.

utilité *f* usefulness; use; profit.

utopie *f* utopia.

utopique *adj* utopian.

V

vacance *f* vacancy:——**s** holiday,
vacation.
vacancier *m*, **-ière** *f* holidaymaker.
vacant *adj* vacant.
vacarme *m* racket, row.
vaccin *m* vaccine.
vache *f* cow.
vagabond *m*, **-e** *f* tramp, vagabond.
vagin *f* vagina.
vague *adj* vague:——*m* vagueness:——*f*
wave.
vaguer *vi* to wander, roam.
vaillant *adj* brave, courageous.
vain *adj* vain; shallow.
vaincre *vt* to defeat, overcome.
vainqueur *m* conqueror, victor.
vaisseau *m* vessel; ship.
vaisselle *f* crockery; dishes.
valable *adj* valid; worthwhile.
valeur *f* value, worth; security.
valider *vt* to validate.
valise *f* suitcase.
vallée *f* valley.
valoir *vt* to be worth.
valser *vi* to waltz.
vandale *mf* vandal.
vanité *f* vanity, conceit.
vaniteux *adj* vain, conceited.
vantard *adj* boastful, bragging.
vanter *vt* to praise, vaunt:——**se ~** *vr*
to boast.
vapeur *f* haze, vapour.
vaporiser *vt* to spray.
variable *adj* variable, changeable.
variation *f* variation, change.
varié *adj* varied; variegated.

varier *vi* to vary.
variété *f* variety, diversity.
vaste *adj* vast, huge.
vaurien(ne) *m(f)* good-for-nothing.
vautrer (se) *vr* to wallow in.
veau *m* calf; veal.
vedette *f* star; leading light.
végétal *adj* vegetable.
végétarien(ne) *m(f)* vegetarian:——
adj vegetarian.
végétatif *adj* vegetative.
véhémence *f* vehemence.
véhément *adj* vehement.
véhicule *m* vehicle.
veille *f* wakefulness; watch; eve.
veiller *vi* to stay up, sit up.
veine *f* vein; inspiration; luck.
vélo *m* cycle.
vélodrome *m* velodrome.
velours *m* velvet.
vendange *f* wine harvest; vintage.
vendangeur *m* **-euse** *f* grape-picker.
vendeur *m* **-euse** *f* seller, salesper-
son.
vendre *vt* to sell.
vendredi *m* Friday.
vénéneux *adj* poisonous.
vénérable *adj* venerable.
vénérer *vt* to venerate.
vengeance *f* vengeance.
venger *vt* to avenge.
venin *m* venom.
venir *vi* to come.
vent *m* wind; breath; vanity.
vente *f* sale; selling.
ventre *m* stomach, belly; womb.

ventriloque *mf* ventriloquist.

venue *f* coming.

ver *m* worm; grub.

véracité *f* veracity; truthfulness.

verbal *adj* verbal.

verbe *m* verb; word.

verdict *m* verdict.

verdure *f* greenery, verdure.

verge *f* stick, cane.

verger *m* orchard.

vérification *f* check; verification.

vérifier *vt* to verify; to audit.

véritable *adj* real, genuine.

vérité *f* truth; truthfulness.

vermine *f* vermin.

verni *adj* varnished.

vernis *m* varnish; glaze.

verre *m* glass; lens; drink.

verrou *m* bolt.

verrouiller *vt* to bolt; to lock.

vers *prép* towards; around:—*m* line, verse.

versatile *adj* versatile.

verser *vt* to pour.

version *f* version.

vert *m* green:—*adj* green.

vertèbre *f* vertebra.

vertical *adj* vertical.

vertu *f* virtue.

vertueux *adj* virtuous.

verve *f* verve, vigour.

veste *f* jacket.

vestiaire *m* cloakroom.

vestibule *m* hall, vestibule.

veston *m* jacket.

vêtement *m* garment.

vêtir (se) *vr* to dress oneself.

veto *m* veto.

veuf *m* widower:—*adj* widowed.

veuve *f* widow:—*adj* widowed.

vexer *vt* to annoy; to hurt.

viable *adj* viable.

viande *f* meat.

vice *m* vice; fault, defect.

victime *f* victim, casualty.

victoire *f* victory.

victorieux *adj* victorious.

vide *adj* empty, vacant:—*m* vacuum.

vidéo *f* video:—*adj invar* video.

vidéocassette *f* videocassette.

vider *vt* to empty.

vie *f* life:—**être en ~** to be alive.

vieillard *m* old man.

vieillesse *f* old age.

vieillir *vi* to get old.

vierge *f* virgin:—*adj* virgin; blank; unexposed.

vieux *adj*, *f* **vieille** old; obsolete.

vif *adj* lively; quick; eager.

vigilant *adj* vigilant.

vigne *f* vine; vineyard.

vigneron *m*, **-onne** *f* wine grower.

vignoble *m* vineyard.

vigoureux *adj* vigorous.

vigueur *f* vigour, strength.

vil *adj* vile; lowly.

villa *f* villa, detached house.

village *m* village.

villageois *m*, **-e** *f* village, rustic.

ville *f* town, city.

vin *m* wine.

vinaigre *m* vinegar.

vindicatif *adj* vindictive.

vingt *adj*, *m* twenty.

vingtaine *f* about twenty.

vingtième *adj*, *mf* twentieth.

vinicole *adj* wine, wine-growing.

viol *m* rape.

violation *f* violation.

violence *f* violence; force.

violent *adj* violent.

violer *vt* to violate; to rape.

violet *adj* violet:—*m* violet.

violeur *m* rapist.

violon *m* violin.

violoniste *mf* violinist.

vipère *f* viper, adder.

virage *m* turn, bend.

virer *vt* to transfer:—*vi* to turn.

virginité *f* virginity; purity.

viril *adj* virile; male, masculine.

virilité *f* virility; masculinity.

virtuel *adj* virtual.

virulence *f* virulence.

virulent *adj* virulent.

virus *m* virus.

vis *f* screw.

visa *m* stamp, visa.

visage *m* face; expression.

vis-à-vis *prép* opposite:—*m* encounter:—**en ~** opposite each other.

viser *vt* to aim, target; to visa.

viseur *m* sights; viewfinder.

visibilité *f* visibility.

visible *adj* visible; evident.

vision *f* eyesight; vision.

visionnaire *mf* visionary:—*adj* visionary.

visite *f* visit; inspection; visitor.

visiter *vt* to visit.

visiteur *m*, **-euse** *f* visitor.

visqueux *adj* viscous, thick.

visser *vt* to screw on.

visuel *adj* visual.

vital *adj* vital.

vitalité *f* energy, vitality.

vitamine *f* vitamin.

vite *adv* quickly, fast.

vitesse *f* speed, swiftness; gear.

viticulteur *m* wine grower.

vitrail *m* stained-glass window.

vitre *f* pane, window.

vitreux *adj* glassy, vitreous.

vitrier *m* glazier.

vitrine *f* shop window.

vitupérer *vi* to vituperate.

vivace *adj* hardy, perennial.

vivacité *f* vivacity, liveliness.

vivant *adj* alive, living; lively.

vivement *adv* quickly; keenly.

vivifiant *adj* refreshing.

vivifier *vt* to enliven.

vivre *vi* to live.

vivres *mpl* victuals, supplies.

vocabulaire *m* vocabulary.

vocal *adj* vocal.

vocation *f* vocation, calling.

vœu *m* vow; wish.

vogue *f* fashion:—**en ~** in fashion.

voici *prép* here is, here are; ago, past.

voie *f* way, road; means:—**~ ferrée** railway.

voilà *prép* there is, there are; ago.

voile *f* sail:—*m* veil.

voiler *vt* to veil.

voir *vt* to see:—**avoir à ~ avec** to have to do with.

voisin *m*, **-e** *f* neighbour:—*adj* neighbouring.

voisinage *m* neighbourhood.

voiture *f* car; carriage; cart.

voix *f* voice; vote.

vol *m* flight:—**à ~ d'oiseau** as the crow flies.

volant *m* steering wheel:—*adj* flying.

volatile *adj* volatile.

volcan *m* volcano.

volcanique *adj* volcanic.

volée *f* flight; volley.

voler *vi* to fly:—*vt* to steal; to rob.

volet *m* shutter; flap, paddle.

voleur *m*, **-euse** *f* thief.

volontaire *adj* voluntary.

volonté *f* will; willpower.

volontiers *adv* willingly.

volubile *adj* voluble.

volume *m* volume.
volumineux *adj* voluminous.
volupté *f* voluptuousness.
voluptueux *adj* voluptuous.
vomir *vi* to vomit.
vorace *adj* voracious.
voracité *f* voracity.
vos = *pl* votre.
votant *m*, **-e** *f* voter.
vote *m* vote; voting.
voter *vi* to vote.
votre *adj*, *pl* **vos** your, your own.
vôtre *poss pn*:—**le/la ~, les ~s** yours.
vouer *vt* to vow.
vouloir *vt* to want, wish.
voulu *adj* required; deliberate.
vous *pn* you, yourself.

voûte *f* vault.
vouvoyer *vt* to address someone as *vous*.
voyage *m* journey, trip; travelling.
voyager *vi* to travel, journey.
voyageur *m* **-euse** *f* traveller, passenger.
voyelle *f* vowel.
vrac *adv*:—**en ~** in bulk.
vrai *adj* true, genuine.
vraisemblable *adj* likely, probable.
vrille *f* tendril; spiral.
vu *adj* seen:—*prép* in view of.
vue *f* sight, eyesight.
vulgaire *adj* vulgar.
vulgarité *f* vulgarity, coarseness.
vulnérable *adj* vulnerable.

W

wagon *m* wagon, truck.
wagon-restaurant *m* restaurant car.
W.-C. (water-closet) *mpl* lavatory.

week-end *m* weekend.
whisky *m* whisky.

XYZ

xénophobe *mf* xenophobe:—*adj* xenophobic.
xénophobie *f* xenophobia.
xylophone *m* xylophone.
yacht *m* yacht.
yaourt *m* yoghurt.

yeux = *pl* œil.
yoga *m* yoga.
yoghurt *m* = yaourt.
yogi *m* yogi.
yucca *m* yucca.
zèle *m* zeal.

zélé *adj* zealous.

zénith *m* zenith.

zéro *m* zero, nought, nothing.

zézayer *vi* to lisp.

zigzag *m* zigzag.

zigzaguer *vi* to zigzag.

zodiaque *m* zodiac.

zone *f* zone, area.

zoo *m* zoo.

zoologie *f* zoology.

zoologiste *mf* zoologist.

zut *interj* damn!, rubbish!

English-French

A

a *art* un, une.
abacus *n* abaque, boulier *m*.
abandon *vt* abandonner, laisser.
abash *vt* couvrir de honte.
abate *vt* baisser:—*vi* baisser; se calmer.
abbey *n* abbaye *f*.
abbreviate *vt* abréger.
abbreviation *n* abréviation *f*.
abdicate *vt* abdiquer; renoncer à.
abdomen *n* abdomen *m*.
abduct *vt* kidnapper, enlever.
abeyance *n* suspension *f*.
abhor *vt* abhorrer, exécrer.
abhorrent *adj* exécrable.
abide *vt* supporter, souffrir.
ability *n* capacité, aptitude *f*.
abject *adj* misérable; abject.
able *adj* capable:—**to be ~** pouvoir.
abnegation *n* renoncement *m*.
abnormal *adj* anormal.
abnormality *n* anomalie *f*.
aboard *adv* à bord.
abode *n* domicile *m*.
abolish *vt* abolir, supprimer.
abolition *n* abolition *f*.
abominable *adj* abominable.
aboriginal *adj* aborigène.
abort *vi* avorter.
abortion *n* avortement *m*.
abound *vi* abonder.
about *prep* au sujet de; vers:—*adv* çà et là:—**to be ~ to** être sur le point de.
above *prep* au-dessus de:—*adv* au-dessus:—**~ all** surtout, principalement.

abrasion *n* écorchure *f*.
abrasive *adj* abrasif.
abroad *adv* à l'étranger.
abrupt *adj* abrupt; brusque.
abscess *n* abcès *m*.
absence *n* absence *f*.
absent *adj* absent:—*vi* s'absenter.
absent-minded *adj* distrait.
absolute *adj* absolu.
absolve *vt* absoudre.
absorb *vt* absorber.
absorption *n* absorption *f*.
abstain *vi* s'abstenir.
abstinence *n* abstinence *f*.
abstinent *adj* abstinent.
abstract *adj* abstrait:—*n* abrégé *m*.
abstraction *n* abstraction *f*.
absurd *adj* absurde.
absurdity *n* absurdité *f*.
abundance *n* abondance *f*.
abundant *adj* abondant.
abuse *vt* abuser de:—*n* abus *m*.
abyss *n* abîme *m*.
academic *adj* universitaire; scolaire; théorique.
academy *n* académie *f*.
accelerate *vt* accélérer.
acceleration *n* accélération *f*.
accelerator *n* accélérateur *m*.
accent *n* accent *m*:—*vt* accentuer.
accept *vt* accepter.
acceptable *adj* acceptable.
acceptance *n* acceptation *f*.
access *n* accès *m*.
accessible *adj* accessible.
accident *n* accident *m*.

accidental *adj* accidentel.

acclaim *vt* acclamer.

accommodate *vt* loger; accommoder.

accommodation *n* logement *m*.

accompany *vt* accompagner.

accomplice *n* complice *mf*.

accomplish *vt* accomplir.

accomplishment *n* accomplissement *m*.

accord *n* accord *m*:—**of one's own ~** de son propre chef.

accordance *n*:—**in ~ with** conformément à.

according *prep* selon:—**~ as** selon que:—**~ly** *adv* en conséquence.

accost *vt* accoster.

account *n* compte *m*:—**on no ~** en aucun cas:—**on ~ of** en raison de:—*vt* **to ~ for** expliquer.

accountability *n* responsabilité *f*.

accountancy *n* comptabilité *f*.

accountant *n* comptable *mf*.

accumulate *vt* accumuler:—*vi* s'accumuler.

accumulation *n* accumulation *f*.

accuracy *n* exactitude *f*.

accurate *adj* exact.

accusation *n* accusation *f*.

accuse *vt* accuser.

accused *n* accusé(e) *m(f)*.

accustom *vt* accoutumer.

ace *n* as *m*.

ache *n* douleur *f*:—*vi* faire mal.

achieve *vt* réaliser; obtenir.

achievement *n* réalisation *f*.

acid *adj* acide:—*n* acide *m*.

acknowledge *vt* reconnaître.

acknowledgment *n* reconnaissance *f*.

acoustics *n* acoustique *f*.

acquaint *vt* informer, aviser.

acquaintance *n* connaissance *f*.

acquiesce *vi* acquiescer, consentir.

acquiescent *adj* consentant.

acquire *vt* acquérir.

acquisition *n* acquisition *f*.

acquit *vt* acquitter.

acrimonious *adj* acrimonieux.

across *adv* en travers:—*prep* à travers.

act *vt* jouer:—*vi* agir; jouer la comédie:—*n* acte *m*.

action *n* action *f*.

activate *vt* activer.

active *adj* actif.

activity *n* activité *f*.

actor *n* acteur *m*.

actress *n* actrice *f*.

actual *adj* réel; concret.

acute *adj* aigu; perspicace

ad lib *vt* improviser.

ad nauseam *adv* à satiété.

adamant *adj* inflexible.

adapt *vt* adapter, ajuster.

adaptable *adj* adaptable.

adaptation *n* adaptation *f*.

add *vt* ajouter.

addict *n* intoxiqué *m*, -e *f*.

addiction *n* dépendance *f*.

addition *n* addition *f*.

additional *adj* additionnel.

address *vt* adresser.

adept *adj* adroit.

adequate *adj* adéquat; suffisant.

adhere *vi* adhérer.

adhesion *n* adhésion *f*.

adhesive *adj* adhésif.

adjacent *adj* adjacent, contigu.

adjective *n* adjectif *m*.

adjoin *vi* être contigu.

adjourn *vt* reporter, remettre.

adjournment *n* ajournement *m*.

adjust *vt* ajuster, adapter.

adjustable *adj* ajustable.

adjustment *n* ajustement *m*; réglage *m*.

administer *vt* administrer.

administration *n* administration *f.*

administrative *adj* administratif.

admirable *adj* admirable.

admiral *n* amiral *m.*

admiration *n* admiration *f.*

admire *vt* admirer.

admirer *n* admirateur *m*, -trice *f.*

admission *n* admission, entrée *f.*

admit *vt* admettre:—**to ~ to** reconnaître.

admonish *vt* admonester.

admonition *n* admonestation.

adolescence *n* adolescence *f.*

adopt *vt* adopter.

adoption *n* adoption *f.*

adoptive *adj* adoptif.

adorable *adj* adorable.

adore *vt* adorer.

adorn *vt* orner.

adrift *adv* à la dérive.

adroit *adj* adroit, habile.

adulation *n* adulation *f.*

adult *adj* adulte:—*n* adulte *mf.*

adultery *n* adultère *m.*

advance *vt* avancer:—*vi* avancer:—*n* avance *f.*

advantage *n* avantage *m*:—**to take ~ of** profiter de.

advantageous *adj* avantageux.

a.m. *adv* du matin.

adventure *n* aventure *f.*

adventurous *adj* aventureux.

adversary *n* adversaire *mf.*

adverse *adj* défavorable.

adversity *n* adversité *f.*

advertise *vt* faire de la publicité pour.

advertisement *n* publicité *f*; annonce *f.*

advice *n* conseil *m*; avis *m.*

advise *vt* conseiller; aviser.

advisory *adj* consultatif.

advocacy *n* plaidoyer *m.*

advocate *n* avocat *m*:—*vt* plaider pour.

aerial *n* antenne *f.*

aerobics *npl* aérobic *m.*

aeroplane *n* avion *m.*

aeroplane *n* avion *m.*

aerosol *n* aérosol *m.*

affability *n* affabilité *f.*

affable *adj* affable.

affair *n* affaire *f.*

affect *vt* toucher; affecter.

affection *n* affection *f.*

affectionate *adj* affectueux.

affiliate *vt* affilier.

affinity *n* affinité *f.*

affirm *vt* affirmer, déclarer.

affirmative *adj* affirmatif.

afflict *vt* affliger.

affluent *adj* riche; abondant.

afford *vt* fournir:—**to be able to ~** avoir les moyens d'acheter.

affront *n* affront *m*, injure *f*:—*vt* affronter; insulter.

afloat *adv* à flot.

afraid *adj* apeuré:—**I am ~** j'ai peur.

after *prep* après:—*adv* après:—**~ all** après tout.

afterbirth *n* placenta *m.*

aftermath *n* conséquences *fpl.*

afternoon *n* après-midi *mf.*

afterward(s) *adv* ensuite.

again *adv* à nouveau.

against *prep* contre.

age *n* âge *m*:—*vt* vieillir.

agency *n* agence *f.*

agenda *n* ordre du jour *m.*

agent *n* agent *m.*

aggravate *vt* aggraver; énerver.

aggravation *n* aggravation *f.*

aggression *n* agression *f.*

aggressive *adj* agressif.

aggressor *n* agresseur *m*.

agile *adj* agile; adroit.

agility *n* agilité *f*; adresse *f*.

agitate *vt* agiter.

agitation *n* agitation *f*.

ago *adv*:—**how long ~?** il y a combien de temps?

agony *n* agonie *f*.

agree *vt* convenir:—*vi* être d'accord.

agreeable *adj* agréable.

agreed *adj* convenu:—~! *adv* d'accord!

agreement *n* accord *m*.

agricultural *adj* agricole.

agriculture *n* agriculture *f*.

ahead *adv* en avant.

aid *vt* aider, secourir:—*n* aide *f*.

AIDS *n* SIDA *m*.

ailment *n* maladie *f*.

aim *vt* pointer; viser.

air *n* air *m*.

air terminal *n* aérogare *f*.

air-conditioned *adj* climatisé.

air-conditioning *n* climatisation *f*.

aircraft *n* avion *m*.

airiness *n* aération, ventilation *f*.

airlift *n* pont aérien *m*.

airline *n* ligne aérienne *f*.

airmail *n*:—**by ~** par avion.

airport *n* aéroport *m*.

airsick *adj*:—**to be ~** avoir le mal de l'air.

airtight *adj* hermétique.

aisle *n* nef d'église *f*.

ajar *adj* entrouvert.

akin *adj* ressemblant.

alarm bell *n* sonnette d'alarme *f*.

alarm *n* alarme *f*:—*vt* alarmer; inquiéter.

alarmist *n* alarmiste *mf*.

albeit *conj* bien que.

album *n* album *m*.

alcohol *n* alcool *m*.

alcoholic *adj* alcoolisé:—*n* alcoolique *mf*.

ale *n* bière *f*.

alert *adj* vigilant:—*n* alerte *f*.

alertness *n* vigilance *f*.

alien *adj* étranger:—*n* étranger *m*, -ère *f*; extra-terrestre *mf*.

alienate *vt* aliéner.

alight *vi* mettre pied à terre:—*adj* en feu.

alike *adj* semblable, égal:—*adv* de la même façon.

alimentation *n* alimentation *f*.

alive *adj* en vie, vivant; actif.

all *adj* tout:—*adv* totalement:—~ **the same** cependant:—~ **the better** tant mieux:—**not at ~!** pas du tout!:—*n* tout *m*.

allege *vt* alléguer.

allegiance *n* loyauté, fidélité *f*.

allergy *n* allergie *f*.

alley *n* ruelle *f*.

alliance *n* alliance *f*.

allocate *vt* allouer.

allocation *n* allocation *f*.

allot *vt* assigner.

allow *vt* permettre; accorder.

allowance *n* allocation *f*; concession *f*.

allude *vi* faire allusion à.

allure *n* charme, attrait *m*.

allusion *n* allusion *f*.

allusive *adj* allusif.

ally *n* allié *m*, -e *f*:—*vt* allier.

almost *adv* presque.

alone *adj* seul:—*adv* seul.

along *adv* le long (de):—~**side** à côté.

aloud *adj* à voix haute.

alphabet *n* alphabet *m*.
alphabetical *adj* alphabétique.
already *adv* déjà.
also *adv* aussi.
altar *n* autel *m*.
alter *vt* modifier.
alteration *n* modification *f*.
alternate *adj* alterné:—*vt* alterner.
alternation *n* alternance *f*.
alternative *n* alternative *f*:—*adj* alternatif:—**ly** *adv* sinon.
although *conj* bien que, malgré.
altitude *n* altitude *f*.
always *adv* toujours.
amalgamate *vt* amalgamer; *vi* s'amalgamer.
amalgamation *n* amalgamation *f*.
amass *vt* accumuler, amasser.
amateur *n* amateur *m*.
amaze *vt* stupéfier.
amazement *n* stupéfaction *f*.
ambassador *n* ambassadeur *m*.
ambidextrous *adj* ambidextre.
ambiguity *n* ambiguïté *f*.
ambiguous *adj* ambigu.
ambition *n* ambition *f*.
ambitious *adj* ambitieux.
ambulance *n* ambulance *f*.
ambush *n* embuscade *f*:—*vt* tendre une embuscade à.
ameliorate *vt* améliorer.
amelioration *n* amélioration *f*.
amend *vt* modifier; amender.
amendment *n* amendement *m*.
amenities *npl* commodités *fpl*.
America *n* Amérique *f*.
American *adj* américain.
amiability *n* amabilité *f*.
amiable *adj* aimable.
amicable *adj* amical.
amid(st) *prep* entre, parmi.
ammunition *n* munitions *fpl*.

amnesia *n* amnésie *f*.
amnesty *n* amnistie *f*.
among(st) *prep* entre, parmi.
amorous *adj* amoureux
amount *n* montant *m*:—*vi* se monter.
amphibian *n* amphibie *m*.
amplify *vt* amplifier.
amplitude *n* amplitude *f*.
amputate *vt* amputer.
amputation *n* amputation *f*.
amuse *vt* distraire, divertir.
amusement *n* distraction *f*.
amusing *adj* divertissant.
an *art* un, une.
anachronism *n* anachronisme *m*.
anaemic *adj* (*med*) anémique.
anaesthetic *n* anesthésique *m*.
analogy *n* analogie *f*.
analysis *n* analyse *f*.
analytical *adj* analytique.
analyze *vt* analyser.
anarchic *adj* anarchique.
anarchy *n* anarchie *f*.
anatomical *adj* anatomique
anatomy *n* anatomie *f*.
ancestor *n* ancêtre *mf*.
anchor *n* ancre *f*.
ancient *adj* ancien, antique
and *conj* et.
anecdote *n* anecdote *f*.
angel *n* ange *m*.
anger *n* colère *f*:—*vt* irriter.
angle *n* angle *m*:—*vi* pêcher à la ligne.
angler *n* pêcheur à la ligne *m*.
angry *adj* en colère, irrité.
anguish *n* angoisse *f*.
angular *adj* angulaire.
animal *n* adj animal *m*.
animate *vt* animer:—*adj* vivant.
animation *n* animation *f*.

animosity n animosité f.
ankle n cheville f.
annex vt annexer:—n annexe f.
annihilate vt annihiler, anéantir.
anniversary n anniversaire m.
annotate vt annoter.
annotation n annotation f.
announce vt annoncer.
announcement n annonce f.
annoy vt ennuyer.
annoyance n ennui m.
annual adj annuel
annul vt annuler.
anomaly n anomalie.
anonymity n anonymat m.
anonymous adj anonyme.
another adj un autre:—**one** ~ l'un
l'autre.
answer vt répondre à:—n réponse f.
ant n fourmi f.
antagonism n antagonisme m.
antagonize vt provoquer.
antarctic adj antarctique.
antenna n antenne f.
anterior adj antérieur.
anthem n hymne m.
anthology n anthologie f.
anthropology n anthropologie f.
antibiotic n antibiotique m.
anticipate vt prévoir.
anticipation n attente f.
antidote n antidote m.
antipathy n antipathie f.
antiquarian n antiquaire mf.
antique n antiquité f.
antiquity n antiquité f.
antithesis n antithèse f.
antler n corne f.
anxiety n anxiété f; désir m.
anxious adj anxieux.
any adj pn n'importe quel, n'importe quelle; un, une; tout:—

~**body** quelqu'un; n'importe qui;
personne:—~**thing** quelque chose;
n'importe quoi; rien.
apart adv séparément.
apartment n appartement m.
apathetic adj apathique.
apathy n apathie f.
aperture n ouverture f.
apex n sommet m; apex m.
apologize vt excuser.
apology n apologie, défense f.
apostle n apôtre m.
appall vt horrifier, atterrer.
apparatus n appareil m.
apparent adj évident, apparent.
apparition n apparition, vision f.
appeal vi faire appel:—n (law) appel m.
appear vi paraître.
appearance n apparence f.
appellant n (law) appelant m.
append vt annexer.
appetite n appétit m.
appetizing adj appétissant.
applaud vt vi applaudir.
applause n applaudissements mpl.
apple n pomme f.
apple tree n pommier m.
appliance n appareil m.
applicable adj applicable.
applicant n candidat m, -e f.
application n application f.
apply vt appliquer:—vi s'adresser.
appoint vt nommer.
appointment n rendez-vous m; nomination f.
apportion vt répartir.
apposite adj adapté.
appraisal n estimation f.
appraise vt évaluer.
appreciate vt apprécier.
appreciation n appréciation f.

appreciative *adj* reconnaissant.
apprehend *vt* appréhender.
apprehension *n* appréhension *f*.
apprentice *n* apprenti *m*.
approach *vi* approcher (s'):—*n* approche *f*.
appropriate *adj* approprié, adéquat.
approval *n* approbation *f*.
approve (of) *vt* approuver.
approximate *adj* approximatif.
approximation *n* approximation *f*.
April *n* avril *m*.
apron *n* tablier *m*.
apt *adj* idéal.
aqualung *n* scaphandre autonome *m*.
aquarium *n* aquarium *m*.
aquatic *adj* aquatique.
arable *adj* arable.
arbiter *n* arbitre *m*.
arbitrary *adj* arbitraire.
arbitrate *vt* arbitrer.
arbitration *n* arbitrage *m*.
arcade *n* galerie *f*.
arch *n* arc *m*.
archbishopric *n* archevêché *m*.
archeological *adj* archéologique.
archeology *n* archéologie *f*.
architect *n* architecte *mf*.
architecture *n* architecture *f*.
archives *npl* archives *fpl*.
arctic *adj* arctique.
ardent *adj* ardent.
ardour *n* ardeur *f*.
area *n* région *f*; domaine *m*.
argue *vi* se disputer.
argument *n* argument *m*; dispute *f*.
argumentative *adj* raisonneur.
arid *adj* aride.
aridity *n* aridité *f*.
arise *vi* se lever; survenir.
aristocracy *n* aristocratie *f*.
aristocrat *n* aristocrate *mf*.

arithmetic *n* arithmétique *f*.
arm *n* bras *m*; arme *f*:—*vt* armer:—*vi* (s')armer.
armament *n* armement *m*.
armchair *n* fauteuil *m*.
armful *n* brassée *f*.
armistice *n* armistice *m*.
armour *n* armure *f*.
armpit *n* aisselle *f*.
army *n* armée *f*.
aroma *n* arôme *m*.
aromatic *adj* aromatique.
around *prep* autour de:—*adv* autour.
arouse *vt* éveiller; exciter.
arrange *vt* arranger, organiser.
arrangement *n* arrangement *m*.
array *n* série *f*.
arrest *n* arrestation *f*:—*vt* arrêter.
arrival *n* arrivée *f*.
arrive *vi* arriver.
arrogance *n* arrogance *f*.
arrogant *adj* arrogant.
arrow *n* flèche *f*.
arsenal *n* (*mil*) arsenal *m*.
art gallery *n* musée d'art *m*.
art *n* art *m*.
artery *n* artère *f*.
artful *adj* malin, astucieux.
article *n* article *m*.
articulate *vt* articuler.
articulation *n* articulation *f*.
artificial *adj* artificiel.
artillery *n* artillerie *f*.
artisan *n* artisan *m*.
artist *n* artiste *mf*.
artistry *n* habileté *f*.
as *conj* comme; pendant que; aussi:
—~ **for, ~ to** quant à.
ascend *vi* monter.
ascension *n* ascension *f*.
ascent *n* montée *f*.
ascertain *vt* établir.

ascetic *adj* ascétique:—*n* ascète *mf*.

ash *n* (*bot*) frêne *m*; cendre *f*.

ashamed *adj* honteux.

ashore *adv* à terre:—**to go ~** débarquer.

ashtray *n* cendrier *m*.

aside *adv* de côté.

ask *vt* demander.

asleep *adj* endormi:—**to fall ~** s'endormir.

aspect *n* aspect *m*.

aspersion *n* calomnie *f*.

asphyxiate *vt* asphyxier.

asphyxiation *n* asphyxie *f*.

aspirant *n* aspirant *m*, -e *f*.

aspiration *n* aspiration *f*.

aspire *vi* aspirer, désirer.

aspirin *n* aspirine *f*.

assail *vt* assaillir, attaquer.

assailant *n* assaillant.

assassin *n* assassin *m*.

assassinate *vt* assassiner.

assault *n* assaut *m*:—*vt* agresser.

assemble *vt* assembler:—*vi* s'assembler.

assembly *n* assemblée *f*.

assent *n* assentiment *m*:—*vi* donner son assentiment.

assert *vt* soutenir; affirmer.

assertion *n* assertion *f*.

assess *vt* évaluer.

assessment *n* évaluation *f*.

assets *npl* biens *mpl*.

assign *vt* assigner.

assignment *n* allocation *f*.

assimilate *vt* assimiler.

assist *vt* assister, aider.

assistance *n* assistance, aide *f*.

assistant *n* aide *mf*.

associate *vt* associer:—*adj* associé: —*n* associé *m*, -e *f*.

association *n* association *f*.

assortment *n* assortiment *m*.

assume *vt* assumer; supposer.

assumption *n* supposition *f*.

assurance *n* assurance *f*.

assure *vt* assurer.

asthma *n* asthme *m*.

asthmatic *adj* asthmatique.

astonish *vt* surprendre.

astonishment *n* surprise.

astound *vt* ébahir.

astrologer *n* astrologue *mf*.

astrology *n* astrologie *f*.

astronomer *n* astronome *mf*.

astronomy *n* astronomie *f*.

astute *adj* malin.

asylum *n* asile, refuge *m*.

at *prep* à; en.

atheist *n* athée *mf*.

athlete *n* athlète *mf*.

athletic *adj* athlétique.

atlas *n* atlas *m*.

atmosphere *n* atmosphère *f*.

atom *n* atome *m*.

atomic *adj* atomique.

atrocious *adj* atroce.

atrocity *n* atrocité, énormité *f*.

attach *vt* joindre.

attachment *n* attachement *m*.

attack *vt* attaquer:—*n* attaque *f*.

attacker *n* attaquant *m*, -e *f*.

attain *vt* atteindre, obtenir.

attempt *vt* essayer:—*n* essai *m*, tentative *f*.

attend *vt* servir; assister à.

attendance *n* service *m*; assistance *f*.

attention *n* attention *f*; soin *m*.

attentive *adj* attentif:—**~ly** *adv* attentivement.

attic *n* grenier *m*.

attitude *n* attitude *f*.

attract *vt* attirer.

attraction *n* attraction *f*; attrait *m*.

attractive *adj* attrayant.

attribute *vt* attribuer:—*n* attribut *m*.

auction *n* vente aux enchères *f*.

audacious *adj* audacieux.

audacity *n* audace, témérité *f*.

audible *adj* audible.

audience *n* audience *f*.

audit *n* audit *m*:—*vt* vérifier.

auditor *n* auditeur *m*, -trice *f*.

augment *vt vi* augmenter.

August *n* août *m*.

aunt *n* tante *f*.

auspicious *adj* favorable, propice.

austere *adj* austère, sévère.

authentic *adj* authentique

authenticity *n* authenticité *f*.

author *n* auteur *m*.

authoritarian *adj* autoritaire.

authority *n* autorité *f*.

authorization *n* autorisation *f*.

authorize *vt* autoriser.

autocrat *n* autocrate *mf*.

autocratic *adj* autocratique.

autograph *n* autographe *m*.

automatic *adj* automatique.

autonomy *n* autonomie *f*.

autopsy *n* autopsie *f*.

autumn *n* automne *m*.

auxiliary *adj* auxiliaire.

available *adj* disponible.

avalanche *n* avalanche *f*.

avarice *n* avarice *f*.

avenge *vt* venger.

avenue *n* avenue *f*.

average *n* moyenne *f*, moyen terme *m*.

aversion *n* aversion *f*, dégoût *m*.

avert *vt* détourner, écarter.

avoid *vt* éviter; échapper à.

await *vt* attendre.

awake *vt* réveiller:—*vi* se réveiller:—*adj* éveillé.

award *vt* attribuer:—*n* prix *m*; décision *f*.

aware *adj* conscient; au courant.

awareness *n* conscience *f*.

away *adv* absent; loin.

awe *n* peur, crainte *f*.

awful *adj* horrible, terrible.

awkward *adj* gauche, maladroit

axe *n* hache *f*.

axis *n* axe *m*.

axle *n* axe *m*.

B

babble *vi* bavarder, babiller.

babe, baby *n* bébé *m*; nourrisson *m*.

babyhood *n* petite enfance *f*.

babyish *adj* enfantin; puéril.

bachelor *n* célibataire *m*.

back *n* dos *m*:—*adv* en arrière, à l'arrière:—*vt* soutenir.

backbone *n* colonne vertébrale.

backdate *vt* antidater.

backer *n* partisan *m*, -e *f*.

background *n* fond *m*.

backpack *n* sac à dos *m*.

back payment *n* rappel de salaire *m*.

backside *n* derrière *m*.

backward *adj* rétrograde:—*adv* en arrière.

bacon *n* lard *m*.

bad *adj* mauvais, de mauvaise qualité; méchant:—**-ly** *adv* mal.

badge *n* insigne *m*, badge *m*.

badness *n* mauvaise qualité *f*; méchanceté *f*.

baffle *vt* déconcerter, confondre.

bag *n* sac *m*; valise *f*.

baggage *n* bagages *mpl*; équipement *m*.

bait *vt* appâter:—*n* appât *m*.

bake *vt* faire cuire au four.

bakery *n* boulangerie *f*.

baker *n* boulanger *m*, -ère *f*.

baking *n* cuisson *f*; fournée *f*.

balance *n* balance *f*; équilibre *m*:—*vt* équilibrer.

balcony *n* balcon *m*.

bald *adj* chauve.

baldness *n* calvitie *f*.

ball *n* balle *f*; boule *f*; ballon *m*.

ballad *n* ballade *f*.

ballerina *n* ballerine *f*.

ballet *n* ballet *m*.

balloon *n* aérostat *m*.

ballot *n* scrutin *m*; vote *m*:—*vi* voter au scrutin secret.

balm, balsam *n* baume *m*.

bamboo *n* bambou *m*.

ban *n* interdiction *f*:—*vt* interdire.

banal *adj* banal.

banana *n* banane *f*.

band *n* bande *f*; orchestre *m*.

bandage *n* bande *f*, bandage *m*:—*vt* bander.

bang *n* claquement *m*, détonation *f*:—*vt* frapper violemment; claquer.

bangle *n* bracelet *m*.

banish *vt* bannir.

banishment *n* bannissement *m*.

bank *n* rive *f*; banque *f*; banc *m*.

banker *n* banquier *m*, -ière *f*.

banknote *n* billet de banque *m*.

bankrupt *adj* failli:—*n* failli *m*.

bankruptcy *n* banqueroute, faillite *f*.

banquet *n* banquet *m*.

baptism *n* baptême *m*.

baptize *vt* baptiser.

bar *n* bar *m*; barre *f*; obstacle *m*:—*vt* interdire; exclure.

barbarian *n* barbare *mf*:—*adj* barbare, cruel.

barbarity *n* barbarie, atrocité *f*.

barbecue *n* barbecue *m*.

barber *n* coiffeur (pour hommes) *m*.

bare *adj* nu; pur:—*vt* dénuder, découvrir.

barefoot(ed) *adj* aux pieds nus.

barely *adv* à peine, tout juste.

bareness *n* nudité *f*.

bargain *n* affaire *f*; contrat:—*vi* conclure un marché.

bark *n* écorce *f*; aboiement *m*:—*vi* aboyer.

barn *n* grange *f*; étable *f*.

barometer *n* baromètre *m*.

barracks *npl* caserne *f*.

barrage *n* barrage *m*.

barrel *n* tonneau, fût *m*.

barren *adj* stérile, infertile.

barricade *n* barricade *f*:—*vt* barricader.

barrier *n* barrière *f*; obstacle *m*.

barring *adv* excepté, sauf.

bartender *n* barman *m*.

barter *vi* faire du troc:—*vt* troquer, échanger.

base *n* base *f*; partie inférieure *f*:—*vt* fonder sur:—*adj* vil, abject.

basement *n* sous-sol *m*.

baseness *n* bassesse, vilenie *f*.

bashful *adj* timide, modeste.

basic *adj* fondamental, de base.

basin *n* cuvette *f*; lavabo *m*.

basis *n* base *f*; fondement *m*.

basket *n* panier *m*, corbeille *f*.

bass *n* (*mus*) contrebasse *f*.

bastard n, adj bâtard m.

baste vt arroser.

bat n chauve-souris f.

batch n fournée f.

bath n bain m.

bathe vt (vi) (se) baigner.

bathing suit n maillot de bain m.

bathroom n salle de bain f.

baths npl piscine f.

bathtub n baignoire f.

batter vt battre:—n pâte à frire f.

battery n pile, batterie f.

battle n bataille f:—vi se battre.

battlefield n champ de bataille m.

bawdy adj paillard.

bawl vi brailler, (fam) gueuler.

bay n baie f; laurier m.

bazaar n bazar m.

be vi être.

beach n plage f.

beacon n phare m.

bead n perle f.

beak n bec m.

beaker n gobelet m.

beam n rayon m; poutre f:—vi rayonner.

bean n haricot m.

bear n ours m.

bear vt porter, supporter.

bearable adj supportable.

beard n barbe f.

bearded adj barbu.

bearer n porteur m, -euse f.

beast n bête f; brute f.

beat vt battre:—vi battre:—n battement m; pulsation f.

beating n raclée f; battement m.

beautiful adj beau m belle f.

beautify vt embellir; décorer.

beauty n beauté f.

because conj parce que:—prép ~ of en raison de.

become vi devenir, se faire.

becoming adj convenable, seyant.

bed n lit m.

bedclothes npl couvertures et draps mpl.

bedroom n chambre f.

bedspread n dessus-de-lit m invar.

bee n abeille f.

beef n bœuf (viande) m.

beefsteak n bifteck m.

beeline n ligne droite f.

beer n bière f.

befit vt convenir à.

before adv prep avant; devant:—conj avant de, avant que.

beforehand adv à l'avance, au préalable.

beg vt mendier.

beggar n mendiant m, -e f.

begin vt vi commencer.

beginner n débutant m, -e f.

beginning n commencement m.

behave vi se comporter, se conduire.

behaviour n conduite f.

behead vt décapiter.

behind prep derrière:—adv derrière, par-derrière, en arrière.

behold vt voir; contempler.

being n existence f; être m.

belated adj tardif.

belch vi éructer:—n éructation f, rot m.

belie vt démentir, tromper.

belief n foi, croyance f.

believable adj croyable.

believe vt croire:—vi penser, croire.

believer n croyant m, -e f.

belittle vt rabaisser.

bell n cloche f.

belligerent adj belligérant.

bellow vi beugler, mugir.

belly n ventre m.

belong vi appartenir à.

beloved adj chéri, bien-aimé.

below adv en dessous, en bas:—prep sous, au-dessous de.

belt n ceinture f.

bench n banc m.

bend vt courber:—vi se courber:—n courbe f.

beneath adv au-dessous:—prep sous, au-dessous de.

benefactor n bienfaiteur m, -trice f.

beneficent adj bienfaisant.

beneficial adj profitable, salutaire, utile.

beneficiary n bénéficiaire mf.

benefit n profit m; bienfait m:—vi bénéficier.

benevolence n bienveillance f.

benevolent adj bienveillant.

benign adj bienveillant, doux.

bequeath vt léguer à.

bequest n legs m.

bereavement n perte f; deuil m.

beret n béret m.

berserk adj fou furieux.

beseech vt supplier, implorer.

beset vt assaillir.

beside(s) prep à côté de; excepté:—adv de plus, en outre.

besiege vt assiéger.

best adj le meilleur, la meilleure:—adv le mieux:—n le meilleur, le mieux m.

bestial adj bestial, brutal.

bestiality n bestialité, brutalité f.

bestow vt accorder, conférer.

bet n pari m:—vt parier.

betray vt trahir.

betrayal n trahison f.

better adj adv meilleur, mieux:—vt améliorer.

between prep entre;* adv au milieu.

beverage n boisson f.

bewilder vt déconcerter.

bewilderment n perplexité f.

beyond prep au-delà de:—adv au-delà, plus loin.

bias n préjugé m; inclination f.

Bible n Bible f.

bibliography n bibliographie f.

bicycle n bicyclette f.

bid vt ordonner; offrir:—n offre, tentative f.

bide vt attendre, supporter.

biennial adj biennal, bisannuel.

big adj grand, gros; important.

bigness n grandeur, grosseur f.

bigot n fanatique mf.

bigoted adj fanatique.

bike n vélo m.

bikini n bikini m.

bilingual adj bilingue.

bill n bec (d'oiseau) m; addition f; billet m.

billet n logement m.

billion n mil milliard m.

bin n coffre m.

bind vt attacher; lier.

biochemistry n biochimie f.

binoculars npl jumelles f pl.

biographer n biographe mf.

biography n biographie f.

biological adj biologique.

biology n biologie f.

bird n oiseau m.

birth n naissance f.

birth certificate n extrait de naissance m.

birth control n limitation des naissances f.

birthday n anniversaire m.

biscuit n biscuit m.

bishop n évêque m.

bit n morceau m; peu m.

bite *vt* mordre:—*n* morsure *f.*

bitter *adj* amer, âpre; acerbe.

bitterness *n* amertume *f.*

bizarre *adj* étrange, bizarre.

black *adj* noir, obscur:—*n* noir *m.*

blackboard *n* tableau (noir) *m.*

blacken *vt* noircir, ternir.

blackleg *n* jaune *m.*

blackmail *n* chantage *m:*—*vt* faire chanter.

blackness *n* noirceur *f.*

blacksmith *n* forgeron *m.*

bladder *n* vessie *f.*

blade *n* lame *f.*

blame *vt* blâmer:—*n* faute *f.*

blameless *adj* irréprochable.

blanch *vt* blanchir.

bland *adj* affable, suave.

blank *adj* blanc; vide:—*n* blanc *m.*

blanket *n* couverture *f.*

blare *vi* retentir.

blaspheme *vt* blasphémer.

blasphemy *n* blasphème *m.*

blast *n* souffle d'air *m;* explosion *f:*—*vt* faire sauter.

blatant *adj* flagrant.

blaze *n* flamme *f:*—*vi* flamber.

bleach *vt* blanchir.

bleak *adj* morne, lugubre.

bleakness *n* froid *m;* austérité *f.*

bleat *n* bêlement *m:*—*vi* bêler.

bleed *vi, vt* saigner.

bleeding *n* saignement *m.*

blemish *vt* gâter:—*n* tache *f.*

blend *vt* mélanger.

bless *vt* bénir.

blessing *n* bénédiction *f;* bienfait *m.*

blight *vt* détruire.

blind *adj* aveugle:—*vt* aveugler; éblouir.

blindly *adv* à l'aveuglette, aveuglément.

blindness *n* cécité *f.*

blink *vi* clignoter.

bliss *n* bonheur extrême *m.*

blissful *adj* heureux; béat.

blister *n* ampoule *f.*

blizzard *n* tempête de neige *f.*

bloated *adj* gonflé.

blob *n* goutte, tache *f.*

bloc *n* bloc *m.*

block *n* bloc *m;* pâté de maisons *m:* —~ **(up)** *vt* bloquer.

blockade *n* blocus *m:*—*vt* bloquer.

blond *adj* blond:—*n* blond *m,* -e *f.*

blood *n* sang *m.*

blood donor *n* donneur(-euse) de sang *m(f).*

blood group *n* groupe sanguin *m.*

bloodiness *n* (*fig*) cruauté *f.*

blood pressure *n* pression artérielle *f.*

bloodstream *n* système sanguin *m.*

bloodthirsty *adj* sanguinaire.

blood transfusion *n* transfusion sanguine *f.*

blood vessel *n* vaisseau sanguin *m.*

bloody *adj* sanglant, ensanglanté.

blossom *n* fleur *f.*

blot *vt* tacher; sécher:—*n* tache *f.*

blouse *n* chemisier *m.*

blow *vi* souffler; sonner:—*vt* souffler:—*n* coup *m.*

blubber *n* blanc de baleine *m:*—*vi* pleurnicher.

blue *adj* bleu.

blueprint *n* (*fig*) projet *m.*

bluff *n* esbroufe *f:*—*vt* faire de l'esbroufe.

bluish *adj* bleuâtre.

blunder *n* gaffe *f:*—*vi* faire une gaffe.

blunt *adj* émoussé:—*vt* émousser.

blur *n* tache *f:*—*vt* tacher.

blush *n* rougeur *f:*—*vi* rougir.

board n planche f; table f; conseil m:
—vt monter à bord de.

boarder n pensionnaire mf.

boarding house n internat m; pension (de famille) f.

boast vi se vanter:—n vantardise f.

boastful adj vantard.

boat n bateau m; canot mf.

boating n canotage m.

bobsleigh n bobsleigh m.

bodily adj adv physique(ment).

body n corps m; cadavre m.

bodywork n (auto) carrosserie f.

bog n marécage m.

bogus adj faux.

boil vi bouillir:—n furoncle m.

boiler n casserole f; chaudière f.

boisterous adj bruyant; turbulent.

bold adj audacieux.

boldness n audace f.

bolt n verrou m:—vt verrouiller.

bomb n bombe f.

bombard vt bombarder.

bombardment n bombardement m.

bond n lien m; engagement m.

bone n os m:—vt désosser.

bonnet n bonnet m.

bonus n prime f.

bony adj osseux.

boo vt huer.

book n livre m.

bookcase n bibliothèque f.

bookkeeper n comptable mf.

bookkeeping n comptabilité f.

bookseller n libraire mf.

bookstore n librairie f.

bookworm n rat de bibliothèque m.

boom n essor m.

boot n botte f; coffre m.

booth n cabine f; baraque f.

border n bord m; frontière f:—vt border, avoisiner.

bore vt forer; ennuyer:—n perceuse f; raseur m.

boredom n ennui m.

boring adj ennuyeux.

born adj né.

borrow vt emprunter.

borrower n emprunteur m, -euse f.

bosom n sein m, poitrine f.

boss n chef m; patron(ne) m(f).

botanic(al) adj botanique.

botany n botanique f.

botch vt cochonner.

both pron tou(te)s les deux, l'un(e) et l'autre:—adj les deux.

bother vt ennuyer.

bottle n bouteille f.

bottleneck n embouteillage m.

bottle-opener n ouvre-bouteille m invar.

bottom n fond m:—adj du bas; dernier.

bough n branche f; rameau m.

bounce vi rebondir; bondir.

bound n limite f; saut m:—vi bondir:—adj à destination de.

boundary n limite f; frontière f.

bourgeois adj bourgeois.

bout n attaque f; combat m.

bow vi se courber:—n salut m.

bow n arc m; nœud m.

bowels npl entrailles fpl.

bowl n bol m; boule f.

bowling n boules fpl.

bow tie n nœud papillon m.

box n boîte, caisse f; loge f:—vt mettre en boîte:—vi boxer.

boxer n boxeur m.

box office n guichet m.

boy n garçon m.

boycott vt boycotter:—n boycottage m.

boyfriend n petit ami m.

bra n soutien-gorge m.

bracelet n bracelet m

bracket n tranche f; parenthèse f; crochet m.

brag n fanfaronnade f:—vi fanfaronner.

braid n tresse f:—vt tresser.

brain n cerveau m; tête f.

brainwave n idée lumineuse f.

brainy adj intelligent.

brake n frein m:—vi freiner.

brake light n feu de stop m.

branch n branche f:—vi se ramifier.

brand n marque f.

brandy n cognac m.

brash adj grossier; impertinent.

brat n môme, gosse mf.

brave adj courageux, brave.

bravery n bravoure f; courage m.

brawl n bagarre, rixe f:—vi se bagarrer.

braze vt souder au laiton.

breach n brèche f; violation f.

bread n pain m:—**brown ~** pain bis m.

breadth n largeur f.

break vt casser; briser:—vi se casser:—n cassure, rupture f; interruption f.

breakdown n panne f; dépression nerveuse f.

breakfast n petit déjeuner m:—vi déjeuner.

breast n poitrine f, sein m.

breaststroke n brasse f.

breath n haleine f; respiration f.

breathe vt vi respirer; exhaler.

breathtaking adj stupéfiant.

breed n race, espèce f:—vt élever:—vi se reproduire.

breeder n éleveur m, -euse f.

breeze n brise f.

brevity n brièveté f; concision f.

brew vt brasser.

brewer n brasseur m.

brewery n brasserie f.

bribe n pot-de-vin m:—vt soudoyer.

brick n brique f.

bricklayer n maçon m.

bride n mariée f.

bridegroom n marié m.

bridge n pont m.

bridle n bride f; frein m.

brief adj bref, concis:—n résumé m.

briefcase n serviette f.

bright adj clair, brillant.

brighten vt faire briller:—vi s'éclairer.

brilliance n éclat m.

brilliant adj éclatant; génial.

bring vt apporter; amener.

brisk adj vif, rapide, frais.

bristle n poil m:—vi se hérisser.

brittle adj cassant, fragile.

broad adj large.

broadcast n émission f:—vt vi diffuser.

broaden vt élargir:—vi s'élargir.

broadness n largeur f.

broccoli n brocoli m.

brochure n brochure f, dépliant m.

broken adj cassé; interrompu.

broker n courtier m.

bronze n bronze m.

brooch n broche f.

brood vi couver; ruminer f.

broom n genêt m; balai m.

brother n frère m.

brother-in-law n beau-frère m.

brow n sourcil m; front m.

brown adj marron; brun:—n marron m:—vt brunir.

browse vt brouter:—vi paître.

bruise n bleu m, ecchymose f.

brush n brosse f; pinceau m.

brutal adj brutal.

brutality n brutalité f.

brute n brute f:—adj bestial.

bubble n bulle f:—vi bouillonner; pétiller.

bucket n seau m.

buckle n boucle f:—vt boucler:—vi se déformer.

budge vi bouger, remuer.

budget n budget m.

buffet n buffet m:—vt gifler.

bug n punaise f.

build vt construire, bâtir.

builder n constructeur m.

building n bâtiment m; immeuble, édifice m.

bulb n bulbe m; oignon m.

bulge vi se renfler:—n renflement m.

bulk n masse f; volume m.

bulky adj volumineux.

bull n taureau m.

bullet n balle f.

bulletproof adj pare-balles, blindé.

bullion n or en barre m.

bully n tyran m:—vt tyraniser.

bump n heurt m; bosse f:—vt heurter.

bumpy adj cahoteux, bosselé.

bun n petit pain m; chignon m.

bunch n botte f; groupe m.

bundle n paquet m, liasse f:—vt empaqueter.

bungle vt bousiller.

bunk n couchette f.

buoy n (mar) bouée f.

buoyancy n flottabilité f.

buoyant adj flottable; gai, enjoué.

burden n charge f:—vt charger.

bureau n commode f; bureau m.

bureaucrat n bureaucrate mf.

burial n enterrement m; obsèques fpl.

burly adj robuste.

burn vt vi brûler:—n brûlure f.

burning adj brûlant.

burst vi éclater:—**to ~ out laughing** éclater de rire.

bury vt enterrer, inhumer.

bus n (auto)bus m.

bush n buisson, taillis m.

business n entreprise f; commerce m.

businessman n homme d'affaires m.

businesswoman n femme d'affaires f.

bus-stop n arrêt d'autobus m.

busy adj occupé; actif.

but conj mais; sauf, excepté, seulement.

butcher n boucher m, -ère f:—vt abattre, massacrer.

butchery n boucherie f, carnage m.

butter n beurre m:—vt beurrer.

butterfly n papillon m.

button n bouton m:—vt boutonner.

buy vt acheter.

buyer n acheteur m, -euse f.

buzz n bourdonnement:—vi bourdonner.

by prep à côté de, près de; par.

bypass n route de contournement f.

by-product n sous-produit m.

by-road n chemin de traverse m.

byte n (comput) octet m.

C

cabbage n chou m.

cabin n cabine f; cabane f.

cabinet n meuble de rangement m; console f.

cable n câble m.

cache n cachette f.

cackle vi caqueter, jacasser.

cafe n café m.

cafeteria n cafétéria f.

caffein(e) n caféine f.

cage n cage f:—vt mettre en cage.

cake n gâteau m.

calamity n calamité f, désastre m.

calculate vt calculer, compter.

calculation n calcul m.

calendar n calendrier m.

calf n veau m.

calibre n calibre m.

call vt appeler; convoquer:—n appel m; cri m.

calligraphy n calligraphie f.

calling n profession, vocation f.

callous adj dur; insensible.

calm n calme m:—adj calme:—vt calmer.

calorie n calorie f.

camera n caméra f.

camouflage n camouflage m.

camp n camp m:—vi camper.

campaign n campagne f.

camper n campeur m, -euse f.

camping n camping m.

campsite n camping m.

campus n campus m.

can v aux pouvoir:—n boîte de conserve f.

canal n conduit m; canal m.

cancel vt annuler.

cancer n cancer m.

candid adj candide, simple.

candidate n candidat(e) m(f).

candle n bougie f; cierge m.

candour n candeur f; sincérité f.

cane n canne f; bâton m.

cannon n canon m.

canoe n canoë m.

canon n canon m; règle f.

can opener n ouvre-boîte m.

canopy n baldaquin m.

cantankerous adj acariâtre.

canteen n cantine f.

canvas n toile f.

canvass vt sonder.

canvasser n prospecteur m, -trice f.

cap n casquette f.

capability n capacité, aptitude.

capable adj capable.

capacity n capacité; potentiel m.

cape n cap, promontoire m.

capital adj capital:—n capital m; capitale f.

capitalist n capitaliste mf.

capitalize vt capitaliser.

capital punishment n peine de mort.

capitulate vi capituler.

capitulation n capitulation f.

capricious adj capricieux.

capsize vt (mar) chavirer.

capsule n capsule f.

captain n capitaine m.

captivate vt captiver.

captivation n fascination f.

captive n captif m, -ive f, prisonnier m, -ière f.

captivity n captivité f.

capture n capture f:—vt capturer.

car n voiture f; wagon m.

caravan n caravane f.

carbohydrates npl hydrates de carbone m pl.

carcass n cadavre m.

card n carte f.

cardboard n carton m.

cardinal adj cardinal, principal:—n cardinal m.

card table n table de jeu f.

care n soin m; souci m:—vi se soucier de.

career n carrière f; cours m.

careful adj soigneux, consciencieux.

careless adj insouciant, négligent.

carelessness n négligence.

caress n caresse f:—vt caresser.

caretaker n concierge mf.

cargo n cargaison f.

caricature n caricature f:—vt caricaturer.

carnage n carnage m.

carnal adj charnel; sensuel.

carnival n carnaval m.

carnivorous adj carnivore.

carpenter n charpentier m.

carpentry n charpenterie f.

carpet n tapis m.

carriage n port m; voiture f.

carrier n porteur, transporteur m.

carrion n charogne f.

carrot n carotte f.

carry vt porter:—vi porter.

cart n charrette f.

cartel n cartel m.

cartilage n cartilage m.

cartoon n dessin animé m.

cartridge n cartouche f.

carve vt tailler, sculpter.

carving n sculpture f.

case n cas m; boîte f; étui m; enveloppe f.

cash n espèces fpl:—vt encaisser.

cashier n caissier m, -ière f.

casing n chambranle m.

casino n casino m.

cask n tonneau, fût m.

casket n cercueil m.

casserole n cocotte f.

cassette n cassette f.

cassette player magnétophone m.

cast vt jeter, lancer:—n moule m.

caste n caste f.

castigate vt punir.

castle n château m.

castrate vt castrer.

castration n castration f.

casual adj accidentel, fortuit.

cat n chat m, chatte f.

catalogue n catalogue m.

catapult n catapulte f.

cataract n cascade f; déluge m.

catastrophe n catastrophe f.

catch vt attraper, saisir:—n prise f.

catchword n slogan m.

catechism n catéchisme m.

categorical adj catégorique.

category n catégorie f.

caterer n fournisseur, traiteur m.

catering n restauration f.

caterpillar n chenille f.

cathedral n cathédrale f.

catholic adj n catholique mf.

cattle n bétail m.

cauliflower n chou-fleur m.

cause n cause f; raison f:—vt causer.

cauterize vt cautériser.

caution n prudence, précaution:—vt avertir.

cautious adj prudent, circonspect.

cavalry n cavalerie f.
cave n grotte f; caverne f.
cavern n caverne f.
cavity n cavité f.
cease vt cesser, arrêter.
ceaseless adj incessant, continuel.
cede vt céder.
ceiling n plafond m.
celebrate vt célébrer, fêter.
celebration n fête f.
celibate adj célibataire.
cell n cellule f.
cellar n cave f; cellier m.
cement n ciment m:—vt cimenter.
cemetery n cimetière m.
censor n censeur m.
censorship n censure f.
censure n censure:—vt censurer.
census n recensement m.
centenary n centenaire m:—adj
centenaire.
centigrade n centigrade m.
centimetre n centimètre m.
central adj central.
centralize vt centraliser.
centre n centre m:—vt centrer.
century n siècle m.
cereal n céréal f.
ceremonial adj n cérémonial m; rituel m.
ceremony n cérémonie f.
certain adj certain, sûr.
certainty n certitude f.
certificate n certificat, acte m.
certification n authentification f.
certify vt certifier, assurer.
cessation n cessation f.
chafe vt irriter; frotter.
chagrin n dépit m.
chain n chaîne f:—vt enchaîner.
chair n chaise f:—vt présider.
chairman n président m.

chalk n craie f.
challenge n défi m:—vt défier.
chamber n pièce f; chambre f.
champagne n champagne m.
champion n champion m, -ionne f:
—vt défendre.
championship n championnat m.
chance n hasard m.
chancellor n chancelier m.
change vt changer:—vi changer, se
transformer:—n modification f;
change m.
changeable adj changeant.
channel n canal m:—vt canaliser.
chant n chant m.
chaotic adj chaotique.
chapel n chapelle f.
chapter n chapitre m.
character n caractère m; personnage m.
characteristic adj caractéristique.
charcoal n charbon de bois m.
charge vt charger; accuser:—n fardeau m; accusation f.
chargeable adj passible.
charitable adj caritatif.
charity n charité, bienfaisance f.
charm n charme m:—vt charmer.
chart n carte (marine) f; diagramme
m.
charter n charte f; privilège m:—vt
affréter.
chase vt poursuivre:—n chasse f.
chaste adj chaste; pur.
chastise vt châtier, punir.
chastisement n châtiment m.
chastity n chasteté, pureté f.
chat vi causer:—n bavardage m.
chatter vi jacasser.
chauffeur n chauffeur m.
chauvinist n chauvin m, -e f.
cheap adj bon marché.

cheapen *vt* baisser le prix de.

cheat *vt* tromper, frauder:—*n* tricheur *m* -euse *f*.

check *vt* vérifier; contrôler; réprimer, enrayer; stopper; enregistrer:—*n* contrôle *m*.

checkup *n* bilan de santé *m*.

cheek *n* joue *f*.

cheer *n* gaieté *f*; applaudissement *m*:—*vt* réconforter.

cheerful *adj* gai, enjoué, joyeux.

cheerfulness *n* gaieté *f*; bonne humeur *f*.

cheese *n* fromage *m*.

chef *n* chef (de cuisine) *m*.

chemist *n* chimiste *mf*; pharmacien *m*, -ienne *f*.

chemistry *n* chimie *f*.

cheque *n* chèque *m*.

cherish *vt* chérir, aimer.

chess *n* échecs *mpl*.

chest *n* poitrine *f*.

chew *vt* mâcher, mastiquer.

chick *n* poussin *m*.

chicken *n* poulet *m*.

chief *adj* principal, en chef:—*n* chef *m*.

chieftain *n* chef *m*.

child *n* enfant *m*.

childbirth *n* accouchement *m*.

childhood *n* enfance *f*.

childish *adj* enfantin.

children *npl* de **child**, enfants *mpl*.

chill *n* froid *m*:—*vt* refroidir.

chilly *adj* froid, très frais.

chimney *n* cheminée *f*.

chin *n* menton *m*.

chip *vt* ébrécher:—*n* fragment, éclat *m*; frite *f*.

chisel *n* ciseau *m*:—*vt* ciseler.

chivalrous *adj* chevaleresque.

chocolate *n* chocolat *m*.

choice *n* choix *m*, préférence.

choir *n* chœur *m*.

choke *vt* étrangler; étouffer.

choose *vt* choisir, élire.

chop *vt* trancher, hacher:—*n* côtelette *f*.

chore *n* corvée *f*; travail routinier *m*.

chorus *n* chœur *m*.

christen *vt* baptiser.

christening *n* baptême *m*.

Christian *adj* *n* chrétien *m*, -ne *f*.

Christmas *n* Noël *f*.

Christmas Eve *n* veille de Noël *f*.

chronic *adj* chronique.

chronicle *n* chronique *f*.

chronicler *n* chroniqueur *m*.

chronological *adj* chronologique

chronology *n* chronologie *f*.

chuckle *vi* rire, glousser.

chum *n* copain *m*, copine *f*.

church *n* église *f*.

cider *n* cidre *m*.

cigar *n* cigare *m*.

cigarette *n* cigarette *f*.

cinder *n* cendre *f*.

cinema *n* cinéma *m*.

circle *n* cercle *m*; groupe *m*:—*vt* encercler.

circuit *n* circuit *m*; tour *m*; tournée *f*.

circular *adj* circulaire:—*n* circulaire *f*.

circulate *vi* circuler.

circulation *n* circulation *f*.

circumference *n* circonférence *f*.

circumnavigation *n* circumnavigation *f*.

circumspect *adj* circonspect.

circumspection *n* circonspection *f*.

circumstance *n* circonstance, situation *f*.

circumvent *vt* circonvenir.

circus *n* cirque *m*.

citation *n* citation *f*.

cite *vt* citer.

citizen *n* citoyen *m*, -enne *f*.

city *n* ville *f*.

civic *adj* civique.

civil *adj* civil, courtois.

civilian *n* civil *m*, -e *f*.

civilization *n* civilisation *f*.

civilize *vt* civiliser.

claim *vt* revendiquer, réclamer:—*n* demande *f*; réclamation *f*.

claimant *n* demandeur *m*.

clamour *n* clameur *f*.

clamp *n* attache *f*:—*vt* serrer.

clandestine *adj* clandestin.

clap *vt vi* applaudir.

clapping *n* applaudissements *mpl*.

clarification *n* clarification *f*.

clarify *vt* clarifier, éclaircir.

clarity *n* clarté *f*.

clash *vi* se heurter.

clasp *n* fermoir *m*; boucle *f*.

class *n* classe *f*; catégorie *f*:—*vt* classer.

classic(al) *adj* classique.

classification *n* classification *f*.

classify *vt* classifier.

classroom *n* salle de classe *f*.

clatter *vi* résonner; cliqueter.

claw *n* griffe *f*; serre *f*.

clean *adj* propre; net:—*vt* nettoyer.

cleaning *n* nettoyage *m*.

cleanliness *n* propreté, pureté *f*.

cleanse *vt* nettoyer.

clear *adj* clair; net:—*vt* clarifier.

cleft *n* fissure, crevasse *f*.

clemency *n* clémence *f*.

clement *adj* clément.

clergy *n* clergé *m*.

clergyman *n* ecclésiastique *m*.

clerical *adj* clérical.

clerk *n* employé *m*.

clever *adj* intelligent; habile.

click *vt* claquer.

client *n* client *m*, -e *f*.

cliff *n* falaise *f*.

climate *n* climat *m*.

climatic *adj* climatique.

climax *n* apogée *m*.

climb *vt vi* grimper, escalader.

climber *n* alpiniste *mf*.

cling *vi* s'accrocher (à).

clinic *n* clinique *f*.

clip *vt* couper:—*n* clip *m*.

cloak *n* cape *f*:—*vt* masquer.

cloakroom *n* vestiaire *m*.

clock *n* horloge *f*.

clog *n* sabot *m*:—*vi* se boucher.

close *vt* fermer:—*n* fin *f*; conclusion *f*:—*adj* proche:—*adv* de près.

closeness *n* proximité *f*.

closure *n* fermeture *f*; clôture *f*.

cloth *n* tissu *m*; toile *f*.

clothe *vt* habiller, vêtir.

clothes *npl* vêtements *mpl*.

cloud *n* nuage *m*; nuée *f*.

cloudiness *n* nébulosité *f*.

cloudy *adj* nuageux.

clover *n* trèfle *m*.

clown *n* clown *m*.

club *n* matraque *f*; club *m*.

clue *n* indice *m*, indication *f*.

clumsiness *n* gaucherie *f*.

clumsy *adj* gauche, maladroit.

cluster *n* grappe *f*:—*vt* grouper.

clutch *n* prise *f*; embrayage *m*:—*vt* empoigner.

coach *n* autocar *m*; wagon *m*; entraîneur *m*:—*vt* entraîner.

coal *n* charbon *m*.

coalesce *vi* s'unir.

coalition *n* coalition *f*.

coarse *adj* rude; grossier.

coast *n* côte *f*.

coastal *adj* côtier.

coastguard *n* gendarmerie maritime *f*.

coastline *n* littoral *m*.

coat *n* manteau *m*; couche *f*:—*vt* enduire.

coating *n* revêtement *m*.

coax *vt* cajôler.

cobweb *n* toile d'araignée *f*.

cock *n* coq *m*.

cockpit *n* cabine de pilotage *f*.

cocoa *n* cacao *m*.

coconut *n* noix de coco *f*.

cocoon *n* cocon *m*.

cod *n* morue *f*.

code *n* code *m*.

coercion *n* coercition.

coexistence *n* coexistence *f*.

coffee *n* café *m*.

coffeepot *n* cafetière *f*.

coffer *n* coffre *m*; caisse *f*.

coffin *n* cercueil *m*.

cog *n* dent d'engrenage *f*.

cogency *n* puissance, force *f*.

cogent *adj* convaincant, puissant.

cognac *n* cognac *m*.

cognizance *n* connaissance *f*; compétence *f*.

cogwheel *n* roue dentée *f*.

cohabit *vi* cohabiter.

cohabitation *n* cohabitation *f*.

cohere *vi* se tenir; être cohérent.

coherent *adj* cohérent; logique.

cohesive *adj* cohésif.

coil *n* rouleau *m*:—*vt* enrouler.

coin *n* pièce de monnaie *f*.

coincide *vi* coïncider.

coincidence *n* coïncidence *f*.

colander *n* passoire *f*.

cold *adj* froid; indifférent:—*n* froid *m*; rhume *m*.

coldness *n* froideur *f*.

collaborate *vi* collaborer.

collaboration *n* collaboration *f*.

collapse *vi* s'écrouler:—*n* écroulement.

collapsible *adj* pliant.

collar *n* col *m*.

collate *vt* collationner.

collateral *adj* concomitant:—*n* nantissement *m*.

collation *n* collation *f*.

colleague *n* collègue *mf*.

collect *vt* rassembler; collectionner.

collection *n* collection *f*.

collective *adj* collectif.

collector *n* collectionneur *m*, -euse *f*.

college *n* collège *m*.

collide *vi* se heurter.

collision *n* collision *f*, heurt *m*.

colloquial *adj* familier.

colloquialism *n* expression familière *f*.

collusion *n* collusion *f*.

colonial *adj* colonial.

colonist *n* colon *m*.

colonize *vt* coloniser.

colony *n* colonie *f*.

colour *n* couleur *f*:—*vt* colorer:—*vi* se colorer.

colourful *adj* coloré.

colouring *n* teint *m*.

column *n* colonne *f*.

columnist *n* chroniqueur *m*.

coma *n* coma *m*.

comatose *adj* comateux.

comb *n* peigne *m*:—*vt* peigner.

combat *n* combat *m*:—*vt* combattre.

combatant *n* combattant *m*, -e *f*.

combination *n* combinaison *f*.

combine *vt* combiner:—*vi* s'unir.

combustion *n* combustion *f*.

come *vi* venir:—**to ~ across, ~ upon** *vt* rencontrer par hasard:—**to ~ round, ~ to** *vi* revenir à soi.

comedian *n* comédien *m*; comique *m*.

comedy *n* comédie *f*.

comet *n* comète *f*.

comfort *n* confort *m*:—*vt* réconforter; soulager.

comfortable *adj* confortable.

comic(al) *adj* comique.

command *vt* ordonner, commander: —*n* ordre *m*.

commander *n* commandant *m*.

commemorate *vt* commémorer.

commemoration *n* commémoration *f*.

commence *vt vi* commencer.

commencement *n* commencement *m*.

commend *vt* recommander.

commendation *n* louange *f*; recommandation *f*.

commensurate *adj* proportionné.

comment *n* commentaire *m*:—*vt* commenter.

commentary *n* commentaire *m*; observation *f*.

commentator *n* commentateur *m*, -trice *f*.

commerce *n* commerce *m*.

commercial *adj* commercial.

commiserate *vt* compatir avec.

commiseration *n* commisération, pitié *f*.

commission *n* commission *f*:—*vt* commissionner.

commit *vt* commettre; confier à; engager.

commitment *n* engagement *m*.

committee *n* comité *m*.

common *adj* commun; ordinaire.

common sense *n* bon sens *m*.

commonly *adv* communément, généralement.

commotion *n* vacarme *m*.

communicable *adj* communicable

communicate *vt* communiquer:—*vi* communiquer.

communication *n* communication *f*.

communion *n* communion *f*.

communist *n* communiste *mf*.

community *n* communauté *f*.

commutable *adj* interchangeable, permutable.

commute *vt* échanger.

compact *adj* compact, serré.

compact disc *n* disque compact *m*.

companion *n* compagnon *m*, compagne *f*.

company *n* compagnie; société *f*.

comparable *adj* comparable.

comparative *adj* comparatif.

compare *vt* comparer.

comparison *n* comparaison *f*.

compartment *n* compartiment *m*.

compass *n* boussole *f*.

compassion *n* compassion *f*.

compassionate *adj* compatissant.

compatibility *n* compatibilité *f*.

compatible *adj* compatible.

compatriot *n* compatriote *mf*.

compel *vt* contraindre, obliger, forcer.

compensate *vt* compenser.

compensation *n* compensation *f*.

compete *vi* rivaliser (avec).

competence *n* compétence *f*; aptitude *f*.

competent *adj* compétent.

competition *n* compétition *f*; concurrence *f*.

competitive *adj* concurrentiel, compétitif.

competitor *n* concurrent *m*, -e *f*.

complacency *n* suffisance *f*.

complacent *adj* suffisant.

complain *vi* se plaindre.

complaint *n* plainte *f*; réclamation *f*.

complement *n* complément *m*.

complementary adj complémentaire.

complete adj complet; achevé:—vt achever.

completion n achèvement m.

complex adj complexe.

complexion n teint m; aspect m.

complexity n complexité f.

compliance n conformité f; soumission f.

complicate vt compliquer.

complication n complication f.

complicity n complicité f.

compliment n compliment m:—vt complimenter.

comply vi se conformer.

component adj composant.

compose vt composer.

composer n compositeur m, -trice f.

composition n composition f.

composure n maîtrise de soi f.

compound vt composer:—adj n composé m.

comprehend vt comprendre.

comprehensible adj compréhensible.

comprehension n compréhension f.

comprehensive adj global; compréhensif.

compress vt comprimer.

comprise vt comprendre, embrasser.

compromise n compromis m:—vt compromettre.

compulsion n compulsion f.

compulsory adj obligatoire.

computer n ordinateur m.

computerize vt traiter par ordinateur, informatiser.

computer science n informatique f.

comrade n camarade mf.

comradeship n camaraderie f.

conceal vt cacher.

concealment n dissimulation f.

concede vt concéder, accorder.

conceit n vanité f.

conceive vt vi concevoir.

concentrate vt concentrer.

concentration n concentration f.

concept n concept m.

conception n conception f.

concern vt concerner:—n affaire f; souci m.

concerning prep en ce qui concerne, concernant.

concert n concert m.

concession n concession f.

conciliate vt concilier.

conciliation n conciliation f.

concise adj concis, succinct.

conclude vt conclure.

conclusion n conclusion.

conclusive adj décisif, concluant.

concoct vt confectionner.

concord n entente, harmonie f.

concordance n accord m.

concrete n béton m:—vt bétonner.

concur vi coïncider; s'entendre.

concurrence n consentement m.

concussion n commotion f.

condemn vt condamner.

condemnation n condamnation f.

condensation n condensation f.

condense vt condenser.

condescend vi condescendre.

condescension n condescendance f.

condition vt conditionner:—n condition, situation f; état m.

conditional adj conditionnel.

condolences npl condoléances fpl.

condom n préservatif m.

conduct n conduite f:—vt conduire.

conduit n conduit m; tuyau m.

cone n cône m.

confectioner n confiseur m, -euse f.

confectionery n confiserie f.

confer vt vi conférer.

conference n conférence f.

confess vt confesser:—vi se confesser.

confession n confession f.

confidant n confident m, -e f.

confide vt confier:—~ in se confier à.

confidence n confiance f; assurance f.

confident adj confiant, sûr (de soi).

confidential adj confidentiel.

confine vt limiter.

confinement n détention f; alitement m.

confirm vt confirmer; ratifier.

confirmation n confirmation f.

confiscate vt confisquer.

confiscation n confiscation f.

conflict n conflit m; lutte f.

conflicting adj contradictoire.

conform vi se conformer (à).

conformity n conformité f.

confront vt confronter.

confrontation n confrontation f.

confuse vt confondre.

confusion n confusion f; désordre m.

congeal vi se congeler.

congenial adj sympathique.

congenital adj congénital.

congestion n congestion f.

congratulate vt complimenter, féliciter.

congratulations npl félicitations fpl.

congregate vt rassembler, réunir.

congregation n assemblée f.

congress n congrès m; conférence f.

congruity n congruence f.

congruous adj congru, approprié.

conifer n conifère m.

conjecture n conjecture.

conjugal adj conjugal.

conjunction n conjonction f.

conjuncture n conjoncture f.

connect vt relier, joindre.

connection n liaison, connexion f.

connoisseur n connaisseur m -euse f.

conquer vt conquérir.

conqueror n conquérant m.

conquest n conquête f.

conscience n conscience f.

conscientious adj consciencieux.

conscious adj conscient.

consciousness n conscience f.

consecrate vt consacrer.

consecration n consécration f.

consecutive adj consécutif.

consensus n consensus m.

consent n consentement:—vi consentir.

consequence n conséquence f; importance f.

consequent adj consécutif.

conservation n conservation f.

conservative adj conservateur.

conserve vt conserver:—n conserve f.

consider vt considérer.

considerable adj considérable.

considerate adj prévenant, attentionné.

consideration n considération f.

consign vt confier, remettre.

consignment n expédition f.

consist vi consister (en).

consistency n consistance f.

consistent adj constant; cohérent.

consolation n consolation f; réconfort m.

console vt consoler.

consolidate vt consolider.

consolidation n consolidation f.

conspicuous adj voyant, manifeste.

conspiracy n conspiration f.

conspire vi conspirer.

constancy n constance.

constant adj constant.

constellation n constellation f.

consternation n consternation f.

constitute *vt* constituer; établir.
constitution *n* constitution *f*.
constitutional *adj* constitutionnel.
constrain *vt* contraindre.
constraint *n* contrainte *f*.
constrict *vt* serrer; gêner.
construct *vt* construire, bâtir.
construction *n* construction *f*.
consulate *n* consulat *m*.
consult *vt* consulter.
consultation *n* consultation.
consume *vt* consommer.
consumer *n* consommateur *m* -trice *f*.
consumerism *n* consumérisme *m*.
consummate *vt* consommer:—*adj* accompli.
consummation *n* consommation *f*.
consumption *n* consommation *f*.
contact *n* contact *m*.
contagious *adj* contagieux.
contain *vt* contenir.
container *n* récipient *m*.
contaminate *vt* contaminer.
contamination *n* contamination *f*.
contemplate *vt* contempler.
contemplation *n* contemplation *f*.
contemporary *adj* contemporain.
contempt *n* mépris, dédain *m*.
contemptible *adj* méprisable.
contemptuous *adj* méprisant.
contend *vi* combattre.
content *adj* content, satisfait:—*vt* contenter, satisfaire:—*n* contentement *m*.
contention *n* querelle, altercation *f*.
contentment *n* contentement *m*, satisfaction *f*.
contest *vt* contester, discuter:—*n* concours *m*.
contestant *n* concurrent *m*, -e *f*.
context *n* contexte *m*.
continent *n* continent *m*.

continental *adj* continental.
contingency *n* contingence *f*.
contingent *n* contingent *m*:—*adj* contingent.
continual *adj* continuel.
continuation *n* continuation.
continue *vt vi* continuer.
continuous *adj* continu.
contort *vt* tordre, déformer.
contortion *n* contorsion *f*.
contour *n* contour *m*.
contraception *n* contraception *f*.
contraceptive *n* contraceptif *m*:—*adj* contraceptif.
contract *vt* contracter:—*n* contrat *m*.
contradict *vt* contredire.
contradiction *n* contradiction *f*.
contradictory *adj* contradictoire.
contraption *n* gadget, bidule (*fam*) *m*.
contrary *adj* contraire:—*n* contraire *m*.
contrast *n* contraste *m*:—*vt* contraster.
contravention *n* infraction *f*.
contribute *vt* contribuer.
contribution *n* contribution *f*.
contrite *adj* contrit, repentant.
contrivance *n* dispositif *m*; invention *f*.
control *n* contrôle *m*; maîtrise *f*:—*vt* maîtriser; contrôler.
controversial *adj* polémique.
controversy *n* polémique *f*.
contusion *n* contusion *f*.
conurbation *n* conurbation *f*.
convalescence *n* convalescence *f*.
convalescent *adj* convalescent.
convene *vt* convoquer.
convenience *n* commodité, convenance *f*.
convenient *adj* commode, pratique.
convention *n* convention *f*.

conventional *adj* conventionnel.

converge *vi* converger.

convergence *n* convergence *f*.

convergent *adj* convergent.

conversant *adj* au courant; compétent.

conversation *n* conversation *f*.

converse *vi* converser.

conversion *n* conversion; transformation *f*.

convert *vt* convertir:—*n* converti *m*, -e *f*.

convey *vt* transporter.

conveyance *n* transport *m*; cession *f*.

convict *n* détenu *m*, -e *f*.

conviction *n* condamnation *f*; conviction *f*.

convince *vt* convaincre, persuader.

convivial *adj* jovial.

conviviality *n* jovialité *f*.

convoke *vt* convoquer.

convoy *n* convoi *m*.

convulse *vt* ébranler.

convulsion *n* convulsion *f*; bouleversement *m*.

convulsive *adj* convulsif.

cook *n* cuisinier *m*, -ière *f*:—*vt* cuire.

cooker *n* cuisinière *f*.

cookery *n* cuisine *f*.

cool *adj* frais:—*n* fraîcheur *f*:—*vt* rafraîchir.

coolness *n* fraîcheur *f*; sang-froid *m*.

cooperate *vi* coopérer.

cooperation *n* coopération *f*.

cooperative *adj* coopératif.

coordinate *vt* coordonner.

coordination *n* coordination *f*.

cope *vi* se débrouiller.

copious *adj* copieux.

copy *n* copie *f*:—*vt* copier.

copyright *n* droit d'auteur *m*.

coral *n* corail *m*.

cord *n* corde *f*, cordon *m*.

cordial *adj* cordial, chaleureux.

core *n* trognon *m*; noyau, centre, cœur *m*.

cork *n* bouchon *m*:—*vt* boucher.

corkscrew *n* tire-bouchon *m*.

corn *n* maïs *m*; grain *m*; blé *m*.

corner *n* coin *m*; angle *m*.

cornerstone *n* pierre angulaire *f*.

corollary *n* corollaire *m*.

coronation *n* couronnement *m*.

coroner *n* coroner *m*.

corporate *adj* en commun; d'entreprise.

corporation *n* corporation *f*; société par actions *f*.

corps *n* corps *m*.

corpse *n* cadavre *m*.

corpulent *adj* corpulent.

correct *vt* corriger; rectifier:—*adj* correct.

correction *n* correction *f*; rectification *f*.

corrective *adj* correcteur, correctif:—*n* correcteur *m*.

correctness *n* correction *f*.

correlation *n* corrélation *f*.

correlative *adj* corrélatif.

correspond *vi* correspondre.

correspondence *n* correspondance *f*.

correspondent *adj* correspondant:—*n* correspondant *m*, -e *f*.

corridor *n* couloir, corridor *m*.

corroborate *vt* corroborer.

corrode *vt* corroder.

corrosion *n* corrosion *f*.

corrosive *adj n* corrosif *m*.

corrupt *vt* corrompre:—*adj* corrompu.

corruption *n* corruption *f*; dépravation *f*.

cosmetic *adj n* cosmétique *m*.

cosmic adj cosmique.

cosmopolitan adj cosmopolite.

cost n prix, coût m:—vi coûter.

costly adj coûteux, cher.

costume n costume m.

cottage n cottage m.

cotton n coton m.

cotton wool n coton hydrophile m.

couch n canapé, divan m.

cough n toux f:—vi tousser.

council n conseil m.

counsel n conseil m; avocat m.

counsellor n conseiller m, -ère f.

count vt compter:—n compte m.

countenance n visage m.

counter n comptoir m; jeton m.

counteract vt contrecarrer.

counterbalance vt contrebalancer.

counterfeit vt contrefaire:—adj faux.

counterpart n contrepartie f.

countersign vt contresigner.

countrified adj rustique; campagnard.

country n pays m; patrie f:—adj rustique; campagnard.

countryman n campagnard m; compatriote m.

county n comté m.

couple n couple m:—vt unir, associer.

coupon n coupon m.

courage n courage m.

courageous adj courageux.

courier n messager m; guide m.

course n cours m; route f; chemin m:
—**of** ~ bien sûr.

court n cour f; tribunal m:—vt courtiser.

courteous adj courtois

courtesy n courtoisie f.

courthouse n palais de justice m.

courtroom n salle de tribunal f.

cousin n cousin m, -e f.

cover n couverture f:—vt (re)couvrir.

covert adj voilé; caché.

cover-up n dissimulation f.

covet vt convoiter.

cow n vache f.

coward n lâche mf.

cowardice n lâcheté f.

cowboy n cowboy m.

coy adj timide; coquet; évasif.

coyness n timidité f; modestie f.

crab n crabe m.

crack n craquement m; fente f:—vt fêler; vi se fêler; craquer.

crackle vi crépiter, pétiller.

cradle n berceau m:—vt bercer.

craft n habileté f; barque f.

craftsman n artisan m.

crafty adj astucieux, rusé.

cram vt bourrer:—vi s'entasser.

cramp n crampe f:—vt entraver.

crane n grue f.

crash vi s'écraser:—n fracas m; collision f.

crate n caisse f; cageot m.

crater n cratère m.

crawl vi ramper.

crayon n crayon m.

craze n manie f, engouement m.

craziness n folie f.

crazy adj fou.

creak vi grincer, craquer.

cream n crème f:—adj crème.

crease n pli m:—vt froisser.

create vt créer; causer.

creation n création f.

creature n créature f.

credence n croyance; créance f.

credibility n crédibilité f.

credible adj crédible.

credit n crédit m; honneur m.

creditable adj estimable, honorable.

credit card n carte de crédit f.

creditor *n* créancier *m*, -ière *f*.

creep *vi* ramper.

cremate *vt* incinérer.

cremation *n* incinération, crémation *f*.

crematorium *n* crématoire *m*.

crest *n* crête *f*.

crevice *n* fissure, lézarde *f*.

crew *n* bande, équipe *f*; équipage *m*.

crib *n* berceau *m*; mangeoire *f*.

crime *n* crime *m*; délit *m*.

criminal *adj* criminel:—*n* criminel *m*, -elle *f*.

cripple *n*, *adj* invalide *mf*:—*vt* paralyser.

crisis *n* crise *f*.

criterion *n* critère *m*.

critic *n* critique *m*.

critic(al) *adj* critique.

criticism *n* critique *f*.

criticize *vt* critiquer.

croak *vi* coasser, croasser.

crockery *n* poterie *f*.

crocodile *n* crocodile *m*.

crook *n* (*fam*) escroc *m*.

crop *n* culture *f*; récolte *f*.

cross *n* croix *f*; croisement *m*:—*adj* fâché:—*vt* traverser, croiser.

crossbreed *n* hybride *m*.

crossing *n* traversée *f*; passage pour piétons *m*.

cross-reference *n* renvoi *m*, référence *f*.

crossroad *n* carrefour *m*.

crouch *vi* s'accroupir, se tapir.

crow *n* corbeau *m*.

crowd *n* foule *f*; monde *m*; *vi* s'entasser.

crown *n* couronne *f*:—*vt* couronner.

crucial *adj* crucial.

crucifix *n* crucifix *m*.

crude *adj* brut, grossier.

cruel *adj* cruel.

cruelty *n* cruauté *f*.

crumb *n* miette *f*.

crumble *vt* émietter; effriter:—*vi* s'émietter.

crunch *vt* croquer.

crush *vt* écraser; opprimer:—*n* cohue *f*.

crust *n* croûte *f*.

crutch *n* béquille *f*.

crux *n* cœur *m*.

cry *vt* *vi* crier; pleurer:—*n* cri *m*; sanglot *m*.

crystal *n* cristal *m*.

crystalline *adj* cristallin; pur.

crystallize *vi* se cristalliser.

cube *n* cube *m*.

cuddle *vt* embrasser.

cuff *n* manchette *f*.

culinary *adj* culinaire.

culminate *vi* culminer.

culpable *adj* coupable.

culprit *n* coupable *mf*.

cult *n* culte *m*.

cultivate *vt* cultiver.

cultivation *n* culture *f*.

culture *n* culture *f*.

cumbersome *adj* encombrant.

cumulative *adj* cumulatif.

cunning *adj* astucieux, rusé.

cup *n* tasse, coupe *f*.

cupboard *n* placard *m*.

curb *n* frein *m*:—*vt* freiner, juguler.

cure *n* remède *m*; cure *f*:—*vt* guérir.

curiosity *n* curiosité *f*.

curious *adj* curieux.

curl *n* boucle de cheveux *f*:—*vt* boucler.

curly *adj* frisé, bouclé.

currency *n* monnaie *f*; cours *m*.

current *adj* courant; actuel:—*n* courant *m*.

current affairs *npl* actualité *f*.

curse *vt* maudire.

curt *adj* succinct; sec.

curtain *n* rideau *m*.

curve *vt* courber:—*n* courbe *f*.

cushion *n* coussin *m*.

custodian *n* gardien *m*, -ienne *f*.

custom *n* coutume *f*, usage *m*.

customary *adj* habituel, coutumier.

customer *n* client *m*, -e *f*.

customs *npl* douane *f*.

customs officer *n* douanier *m*.

cut *vt* découper; couper:—*n* coup *m*; coupure *f*.

cutlery *n* couverts *mpl*.

cutting *n* coupure *f*.

cycle *n* cycle *m*; bicyclette *f*:—*vi* aller à bicyclette.

cycling *n* cyclisme *m*.

cyclist *n* cycliste *mf*.

cylinder *n* cylindre *m*; rouleau *m*.

cynic(al) *adj* cynique:—*n* cynique *mf*.

D

dad(dy) *n* papa *m*.

daily *adj* quotidien:—*adv* quotidiennement.

daintiness *n* élégance *f*; délicatesse *f*.

dainty *adj* délicat; élégant.

dairy *n* laiterie *f*.

dam *n* barrage *m*:—*vt* endiguer.

damage *n* dommage *m*; tort *m*:—*vt* endommager.

damnation *n* damnation *f*.

damp *adj* humide:—*vt* humidifier.

dampen *vt* humidifier.

dance *n* danse *f*; soirée dansante *f*:—*vi*, *vt* danser.

dancer *n* danseur *m*, -euse *f*.

danger *n* danger *m*.

dangerous *adj* dangereux.

dangle *vi* pendre.

dare *vi* oser:—*vt* défier.

daring *n* audace *f*:—*adj* audacieux.

dark *adj* sombre, obscur:—*n* obscurité *f*; ignorance *f*.

darken *vt* assombrir:—*vi* s'assombrir.

darkness *n* obscurité *f*.

darling *n*, *adj* chéri *m*, -e *f*.

dart *n* dard *m*.

dash *vi* se dépêcher.

data *n* données *fpl*.

data processing *n* traitement de données *m*.

date *n* date *f*; rendez-vous *m*.

dated *adj* démodé.

daughter *n* fille *f*:—~ **in-law** belle-fille *f*.

dawn *n* aube *f*.

day *n* jour *m*, journée *f*:—~ **by** ~ de jour en jour.

daylight *n* lumière du jour.

daze *vt* étourdir.

dazzle *vt* éblouir.

dead *adj* mort*l*.

deaden *vt* amortir.

deadline *n* date limite *f*.

deadlock *n* impasse *f*.

deadly *adj* mortel.

deaf *adj* sourd.

deafen *vt* assourdir.

deafness *n* surdité *f*.

deal n accord m; marché m:—a great ~ beaucoup:—vt distribuer.
dealer n commerçant m; trafiquant m.
dear adj ~ly adv cher.
dearness n cherté f.
death n mort f.
death certificate n acte de décès m.
death penalty n peine de mort f.
debar vt exclure.
debase vt dégrader.
debasement n dégradation f.
debatable adj discutable.
debate n débat m:—vt discuter; examiner.
debilitate vt débiliter.
debit n débit m:—vt débiter.
debt n dette f:—get into ~ s'endetter.
debtor n débiteur m, -trice f.
decade n décennie f.
decadence n décadence f.
decaffeinated adj décaféiné.
decay vi décliner; pourrir:—n pourrissement m.
deceased adj décédé.
deceit n tromperie f.
deceive vt tromper.
December n décembre m.
decency n décence f; pudeur f.
decent adj décent; bien, bon.
decide vt decider:—vi se décider.
decided adj décidé.
decimate vt décimer.
decipher vt déchiffrer.
decision n décision, détermination f.
decisive adj décisif.
deck n pont m:—vt orner.
declaration n déclaration f.
declare vt déclarer.
decode vt décoder.
decor n décor m; décoration f.
decorate vt décorer, orner.
decoration n décoration f.

decorative adj décoratif.
decoy n leurre m.
decrease vt diminuer:—n diminution f.
decree n décret m:—vt décréter; ordonner.
decrepit adj décrépit.
dedicate vt dédier; consacrer.
dedication n dédicace f; consacration f.
deduce vt déduire, conclure.
deduct vt déduire, soustraire.
deed n action f; exploit m.
deep adj profond.
deepen vt approfondir.
deepness n profondeur f.
default n défaut m:—vi manquer à ses engagements.
defeat n défaite f:—vt vaincre; frustrer.
defect n défaut m.
defective adj défectueux.
defend vt défendre; protéger.
defendant n accusé m, -e f.
defense n défense f; protection f.
defensive adj défensif.
defer vt déférer.
deference n déférence f.
defiance n défi m.
deficiency n défaut m; manque m.
deficient adj insuffisant.
define vt définir.
definite adj sûr; précis.
definition n définition f.
definitive adj définitif.
deflect vt dévier.
deform vt déformer.
deformity n déformité f.
defraud vt frauder.
deft adj habile.
degenerate vi dégénérer:—adj dégénéré.

degeneration n dégénération f.

degradation n dégradation f.

degrade vt dégrader.

degree n degré m; diplôme m.

dejected adj découragé.

dejection n découragement m.

delay vt retarder:—n retard m.

delegate vt déléguer:—n délégué m, -e f.

delegation n délégation f.

delete vt effacer.

deliberate vt examiner:—adj délibéré.

deliberation n délibération f.

delicacy n délicatesse f.

delicate adj délicat.

delicious adj délicieux.

delight n délice m:—vt enchanter.

delighted adj enchanté.

delightful adj charmant.

delinquency n délinquance f.

delinquent n délinquant m, -e f.

delirious adj délirant.

deliver vt livrer; délivrer.

delivery n livraison f.

delude vt tromper.

delusion n tromperie f; illusion f.

demand n demande f:—vt exiger; réclamer.

demanding adj exigeant.

demean vi s'abaisser.

demeanour n conduite f.

democracy n démocratie f.

democratic adj démocratique.

demolish vt démolir.

demolition n démolition f.

demonstrate vt démontrer, prouver: —vi manifester.

demonstration n démonstration f.

demonstrator n manifestant m, -e f.

demoralization n démoralisation f.

demoralize vt démoraliser.

den n antre m.

denial n dénégation f.

denims npl jean m.

denomination n valeur f; dénomination f.

denote vt dénoter, indiquer.

denounce vt dénoncer.

dense adj dense, épais.

dentist n dentiste mf.

dentistry n dentisterie f.

denture n dentier m.

denunciation n dénonciation f.

deny vt nier.

deodorant n déodorant m.

depart vi partir.

department n département m; service m.

department store n grand magasin m.

departure n départ m.

depend vi dépendre.

dependable adj fiable; sûr.

dependent adj dépendant.

depict vt dépeindre, décrire.

deplorable adj déplorable.

deplore vt déplorer, lamenter.

depopulated adj dépeuplé.

deport vt déporter.

deportation n déportation f.

deportment n comportement m.

deposit vt déposer:—n dépôt m; caution f.

deposition n déposition f.

depot n dépôt m.

depreciate vi se déprécier.

depreciation n dépréciation f.

depress vt déprimer.

depression n dépression f.

deprivation n privation f.

deprive vt priver.

depth n profondeur f.

deputation n députation f.

depute vt députer, déléguer.

deputy *n* député *m*.
deranged *adj* dérangé.
derelict *adj* abandonné.
deride *vt* se moquer de.
derision *n* dérision *f*.
derivative *n* dérivé *m*.
derive *vt vi* dériver.
descend *vi* descendre.
descendant *n* descendant *m*, -e *f*.
descent *n* descente *f*.
describe *vt* décrire.
description *n* description *f*.
descriptive *adj* descriptif.
desert *n* désert *m*:—*adj* désert.
desert *vt* abandonner; déserter:—*n* mérite *m*.
desertion *n* désertion *f*.
deserve *vt* mériter.
design *vt* concevoir; dessiner:—*n* dessein *m*.
designate *vt* désigner.
desirable *adj* désirable.
desire *n* désir *m*:—*vt* désirer.
desist *vi* abandonner.
desk *n* bureau *m*.
desolate *adj* désert, désolé.
despair *n* désespoir *m*:—*vi* se désespérer.
desperate *adj* désespéré.
desperation *n* désespoir *m*.
despicable *adj* méprisable.
despise *vt* mépriser.
despite *prep* malgré.
despondency *n* abattement *m*.
despondent *adj* abattu.
dessert *n* dessert *m*.
destination *n* destination *f*.
destine *vt* destiner.
destiny *n* destin, sort *m*.
destitute *adj* indigent.
destitution *n* indigence *f*.
destroy *vt* détruire.

destruction *n* destruction *f*.
detach *vt* séparer, détacher.
detachable *adj* détachable.
detail *n* détail *m*:—in ~ en détail:—*vt* détailler.
detain *vt* retenir; détenir.
detect *vt* détecter.
detection *n* détection *f*; découverte *f*.
detective *n* détective *m*.
detention *n* détention *f*.
deteriorate *vt* détériorer.
deterioration *n* détérioration *f*.
determination *n* détermination *f*.
determine *vt* déterminer, décider.
detest *vt* détester.
detestable *adj* détestable.
detour *n* déviation *f*.
detriment *n* détriment *m*.
devaluation *n* dévaluation *f*.
devastate *vt* dévaster.
devastation *n* dévastation *f*.
develop *vt* développer.
development *n* développement *m*.
deviate *vi* dévier.
deviation *n* déviation *f*.
device *n* mécanisme *m*.
devil *n* diable, démon *m*.
devise *vt* inventer; concevoir.
devoid *adj* dépourvu.
devote *vt* consacrer.
devoted *adj* dévoué.
devotion *n* dévotion *f*.
devour *vt* dévorer.
dew *n* rosée *f*.
dexterity *n* dextérité *f*.
diagnosis *n* (*med*) diagnostic *m*.
diagram *n* diagramme *m*.
dialect *n* dialecte *m*.
dialogue *n* dialogue *m*.
diamond *n* diamant *m*.
diary *n* journal *m*.
dictate *vt* dicter:—*n* ordre *m*.

dictionary n dictionnaire m.

die vi mourir.

diet n diète f; régime m:—vi être au régime.

differ vi différer.

difference n différence f.

different adj différent.

difficult adj difficile.

difficulty n difficulté f.

dig vt creuser.

digest vt digérer.

digestion n digestion f.

digestive adj digestif.

digit n chiffre m.

digital adj digital.

dignified adj digne.

dignity n dignité f.

digression n digression f.

dilemma n dilemme m.

diligence n assiduité f.

diligent adj assidu.

dilute vt diluer.

dim adj indistinct; faible; sombre.

dimension n dimension f.

diminish vt vi diminuer.

diminutive n diminutif m.

din n vacarme m.

dine vi dîner.

dinner n dîner m.

dint n:—**by ~ of** à force de.

dip vt tremper.

diploma n diplôme m.

diplomat n diplomate m.

diplomatic adj diplomatique.

dire adj atroce, affreux.

direct adj direct:—vt diriger.

direction n direction f; instruction f.

director n directeur m, -trice f.

directory n annuaire m.

dirt n saleté f.

dirty adj sale.

disability n incapacité f; infirmité f.

disabled adj infirme.

disadvantage n désavantage m:—vt désavantager.

disagree vi ne pas être d'accord.

disagreeable adj désagréable.

disagreement n désaccord m.

disallow vt rejeter.

disappear vi disparaître.

disappearance n disparition f.

disappoint vt décevoir.

disappointment n déception f.

disapproval n désapprobation f.

disapprove vt désapprouver.

disarm vt désarmer.

disaster n désastre m.

disastrous adj désastreux.

disbelief n incrédulité f.

discard vt jeter.

discern vt discerner, percevoir.

discerning adj perspicace.

disciple n disciple m.

discipline n discipline f:—vt discipliner.

disclose vt révéler.

disclosure n révélation f.

disco n discothèque f.

discomfort n incommodité f.

disconnect vt débrancher.

disconsolate adj inconsolable.

discontent n mécontentement m:—adj mécontent.

discontented adj mécontent.

discontinue vt interrompre.

discord n discorde f.

discount n escompte m:—vt escompter.

discourage vt décourager.

discouragement n découragement m.

discourse n discours m.

discourteous adj discourtois.

discover vt découvrir.

discovery n découverte f.

discredit vt discréditer.

discreet adj discret.

discrepancy n contradiction f.

discretion n discrétion f.

discretionary adj discrétionnaire.

discriminate vt distinguer; discriminer.

discrimination n discrimination f.

discuss vt discuter.

discussion n discussion f.

disdain vt dédaigner:—n dédain, mépris m.

disdainful adj dédaigneux.

disease n maladie f.

disembark vt vi débarquer.

disenchant vt désenchanter.

disenchanted adj désenchanté.

disengage vt dégager.

disfigure vt défigurer.

disgrace n honte f; scandale m:—vt déshonorer.

disgraceful adj honteux.

disguise vt déguiser:—n déguisement m.

disgust n dégoût m:—vt dégoûter.

dish n plat m; assiette f.

dishearten vt démoraliser.

dishonest adj malhonnête.

dishonesty n malhonnêteté f.

disillusion vt désillusionner.

disillusioned adj désillusionné.

disinfect vt désinfecter.

disinfectant n désinfectant m.

disinherit vt déshériter.

disintegrate vi se désintégrer.

disinterested adj désintéressé.

disk n disque m; disquette f.

dislike n aversion f:—vt ne pas aimer.

dislocate vt disloquer.

dislocation n dislocation f.

dislodge vt déloger.

disloyal adj déloyal.

dismantle vt démonter.

dismay n consternation f.

dismiss vt renvoyer; écarter.

dismissal n renvoi m; rejet m.

disobedience n désobéissance f.

disobedient adj désobéissant.

disobey vt désobéir.

disorder n désordre m.

disorderly adj en désordre, confus.

disorganization n désorganisation f.

disparage vt dénigrer.

disparity n disparité f.

dispatch vt envoyer:—n envoi m; dépêche f.

dispel vt dissiper.

dispensary n dispensaire m.

dispense vt dispenser; distribuer.

disperse vt disperser.

displace vt déplacer.

display vt exposer:—n exposition f.

displeased adj mécontent.

displeasure n mécontentement m.

dispose vt disposer.

disposition n disposition f.

disprove vt réfuter.

dispute n dispute f; controverse f:—vt mettre en cause.

disqualify vt rendre incapable.

dissatisfaction n mécontentement m.

dissatisfied adj mécontent.

disseminate vt disséminer.

dissension n dissension f.

dissent n dissension f.

dissertation n thèse f.

dissident n dissident m, -e f.

dissimilar adj dissemblable.

dissimilarity n dissemblance f.

dissipate vt dissiper.

dissipation n dissipation f.

dissolution n dissolution f.

dissolve vt dissoudre.

dissonance n dissonance f.

dissuade *vt* dissuader.

distance *n* distance *f*.

distant *adj* distant.

distaste *n* dégoût *m*.

distasteful *adj* désagréable.

distil *vt* distiller.

distinct *adj* distinct.

distinction *n* distinction *f*.

distinctive *adj* distinctif.

distinguish *vt* distinguer; discerner.

distort *vt* déformer.

distortion *n* distortion *f*.

distract *vt* distraire.

distracted *adj* distrait.

distraction *n* distraction *f*; confusion *f*.

distress *n* souffrance *f*:—*vt* désoler.

distribute *vt* distribuer, répartir.

distribution *n* distribution *f*.

district *n* district *m*.

disturb *vt* déranger.

disturbance *n* dérangement *m*; trouble *m*.

disturbed *adj* troublé.

disturbing *adj* troublant.

disuse *n* désuétude *f*.

disused *adj* abandonné.

ditch *n* fossé *m*.

dive *vi* plonger.

diver *n* plongeur *m*, -euse *f*.

diverge *vi* diverger.

divergent *adj* divergent.

diverse *adj* divers, différent.

diversion *n* diversion *f*.

diversity *n* diversité *f*.

divert *vt* dévier; divertir.

divide *vt* diviser:—*vi* se diviser.

divine *adj* divin.

divinity *n* divinité *f*.

divisible *adj* divisible.

division *n* division *f*.

divorce *n* divorce *m*:—*vi* divorcer.

divorced *adj* divorcé.

divulge *vt* divulguer.

dizziness *n* vertige *m*.

dizzy *adj* pris de vertige.

do *vt* faire.

docile *adj* docile.

dock *n* dock *m*.

do-it-yourself *n* bricolage *m*.

doctor *n* docteur *m*.

doctrine *n* doctrine *f*.

document *n* document *m*.

documentary *adj* documentaire.

dodge *vt* esquiver.

dog *n* chien *m*.

dogmatic *adj* dogmatique.

doll *n* poupée *f*.

dolphin *n* dauphin *m*.

dome *n* dôme *m*.

domestic *adj* domestique.

domesticate *vt* domestiquer.

domesticity *n* domesticité *f*.

domicile *n* domicile *m*.

dominate *vi* dominer.

domination *n* domination *f*.

donate *vt* donner, faire don de.

donation *n* donation *f*.

donkey *n* âne *m*.

donor *n* donneur *m*; donateur *m*.

door *n* porte *f*.

doorway *n* entrée *f*.

dormant *adj* latent; dormant.

dormitory *n* dortoir *m*.

dosage *n* dose *f*; dosage *m*.

dose *n* dose *f*:—*vt* doser.

dossier *n* dossier *m*.

dot *n* point *m*.

double *adj* double:—*vt* doubler:—*n* double *m*.

double room *n* chambre pour deux *f*.

double-dealing *n* duplicité *f*.

doubt *n* doute *m*:—*vt* douter de.

doubtful *adj* douteux.

douse vt éteindre.

dove n colombe f.

down n duvet m:—prep en bas:— upside ~ à l'envers.

down-to-earth adj pratique; terre à terre.

downfall n ruine f.

downhearted adj découragé.

downhill adv en descendant, dans la descente.

downstairs adv en bas.

dowry n dot f.

doze vi somnoler.

dozen n douzaine f.

drab adj gris; morne.

drag vt tirer:—n drague f; ennui m.

drain vt drainer; vider:—n tuyau d'écoulement m.

drama n drame m.

dramatic adj dramatique.

dramatist n dramaturge mf.

draught n courant d'air m.

draw vt tirer; dessiner.

drawback n désavantage.

drawer n tiroir m.

drawing n dessin m.

drawing room n salon m.

dread n terreur f:—vt redouter

dreadful adj horrible.

dream n rêve m:—vi, vt rêver.

dreary adj triste, morne.

dress vi s'habiller:—n robe f.

dressing n pansement m; sauce f.

dressy adj élégant.

drift vi aller à la dérive.

drill n perceuse f; vt percer.

drink vt vi boire:—n boisson f.

drinker n buveur m, -euse f.

drip vi goutter:—n goutte f.

drive vt vi conduire.

driver n conducteur m, -trice f; chauffeur m.

driving licence n permis m de conduire.

drizzle vi pleuvasser.

drop n goutte f:—vt laisser tomber.

drought n sécheresse f.

drown vt noyer:—vi se noyer.

drowsiness n somnolence f.

drug n drogue f:—vt droguer.

drum n tambour m:—vi jouer du tambour.

drunk adj ivre.

drunken adj ivre.

drunkenness n ivresse f.

dry adj sec:—vt faire sécher:—vi sécher.

dryness n sécheresse f.

dual adj double.

dub adj doubler.

due adj dû, f due n droit m.

duel n duel m.

dull adj terne; insipide.

duly adv dûment.

dumb adj muet.

dump n tas m:—vt jeter.

duplicate vt dupliquer.

duplicity n duplicité f.

durability n durabilité f.

durable adj durable.

duration n durée f.

during prep pendant.

dusk n crépuscule m.

dust n poussière f:—vt épousseter.

dutiful adj obéissant, soumis.

duty n devoir m; obligation f.

dwarf n nain m, naine f:—vt rapetisser.

dwell vi habiter, vivre.

dwelling n habitation f; domicile m.

dye vt teindre:—n teinture f.

dying p, adj mourant.

dynamic adj dynamique.

dynasty n dynastie f.

E

each *pn* chacun:—**~ other** les un(e)s les autres.
eager *adj* enthousiaste.
eagerness *n* enthousiasme *m*.
eagle *n* aigle *m*.
ear *n* oreille *f*; ouïe *f*.
early *adj* premier:—*adv* tôt.
earn *vt* gagner.
earnest *adj* sérieux
earth *n* terre *f*:—*vt* brancher à la terre.
earthquake *n* tremblement de terre *m*.
ease *n* aise *f*; facilité *f*.
easiness *n* facilité *f*.
east *n* est *m*; orient *m*.
Easter *n* Pâques *fpl*.
eastern *adj* de l'est, oriental.
easy *adj* facile.
eat *vt vi* manger.
ebb *n* reflux *m*:—*vi* refluer.
eccentric *adj* excentrique.
eccentricity *n* excentricité *f*.
echo *n* écho *m*:—*vi* résonner.
eclipse *n* éclipse *f*:—*vt* éclipser.
ecology *n* écologie *f*.
economic *adj* économique
economist *n* économiste *mf*.
economize *vt* économiser.
economy *n* économie *f*.
ecstasy *n* extase *f*.
ecstatic *adj* extatique.
edge *n* fil *m*; pointe *f*.
edible *adj* mangeable.
edifice *n* édifice *m*.
edit *vt* diriger; rédiger.
edition *n* édition *f*.

editor *n* rédacteur *m*, -trice *f*.
educate *vt* éduquer; instruire.
education *n* éducation *f*.
efface *vt* effacer.
effect *n* effet *mf*:—**~s** *npl* biens *mpl*: —*vt* effectuer.
effective *adj* efficace; effectif.
effectiveness *n* efficacité *f*.
effectual *adj* efficace.
effeminate *adj* efféminé.
effervescence *n* effervescence *f*.
efficiency *n* efficacité *f*.
efficient *adj* efficace.
effort *n* effort *m*.
egg *n* œuf *m*.
ego(t)ist *n* égoïste *mf*.
ego(t)istical *adj* égoïste.
eight *adj n* huit *m*.
eighteen *adj n* dix-huit *m*.
eighteenth *adj n* dix-huitième *mf*.
eighth *adj n* huitième *mf*.
eightieth *adj n* quatre-vingtième *mf*.
eighty *adj n* quatre-vingt.
either *pn* n'importe lequel/laquelle: —*conj* ou, soit.
eject *vt* éjecter, expulser.
ejection *n* éjection, expulsion *f*.
elaborate *vt* élaborer:—*adj* élaboré.
elapse *vi* passer.
elastic *adj* élastique.
elbow *n* coude *m*.
elder *adj* aîné.
eldest *adj* aîné.
elect *vt* élire; choisir.
election *n* élection *f*; choix *m*.
electoral *adj* électoral.

electorate *n* électorat *m*.
electric(al) *adj* électrique.
electrician *n* électricien *m*.
electricity *n* électricité *f*.
electrify *vt* électriser.
electronic *adj* électronique.
elegance *n* élégance *f*.
elegant *adj* élégant.
element *n* élément *m*.
elementary *adj* élémentaire.
elephant *n* éléphant *m*.
elevate *vt* élever, hausser.
elevation *n* élévation *f*; hauteur *f*.
eleven *adj n* onze *m*.
eleventh *adj n* onzième *mf*.
eligibility *n* éligibilité *f*.
eligible *adj* éligible.
eliminate *vt* éliminer.
elocution *n* élocution *f*.
eloquence *n* éloquence *f*.
eloquent *adj* éloquent.
else *pn* autre.
elsewhere *adv* ailleurs.
elude *vt* éluder; éviter.
emaciated *adj* émacié.
emancipate *vt* émanciper.
emancipation *n* émancipation *f*.
embargo *n* embargo *m*.
embark *vt* embarquer.
embarkation *n* embarcation *f*.
embarrass *vt* embarrasser.
embarrassment *n* embarras *m*.
embassy *n* ambassade *f*.
emblem *n* emblème *m*.
embody *vt* incorporer; incarner.
embrace *vt* étreindre; comprendre.
embryo *n* embryon *m*.
emerald *n* émeraude *f*.
emerge *vi* émerger; apparaître.
emergency *n* urgence *f*.
emergency exit *n* sortie de secours *f*.
emigrate *vi* émigrer.

emigration *n* émigration *f*.
emission *n* émission *f*.
emit *vt* émettre.
emotion *n* émotion *f*.
emotional *adj* émotionnel.
emphasize *vt* souligner, accentuer.
emphatic *adj* emphatique.
empire *n* empire *m*.
employ *vt* employer.
employee *n* employé *m*, -e *f*.
employer *n* employeur *m*.
employment *n* emploi, travail *m*.
emptiness *n* vide *m*.
empty *adj* vide; vain:—*vt* vider.
emulate *vt* imiter.
enable *vt* permettre.
enamour *vt* s'éprendre de.
encamp *vi* camper.
encampment *n* campement *m*.
encase *vt* entourer.
enchant *vt* enchanter.
enchantment *n* enchantement *m*.
encircle *vt* encercler.
enclose *vt* entourer.
enclosure *n* clôture *f*.
encompass *vt* comprendre.
encounter *n* rencontre *f*:—*vt* rencontrer.
encourage *vt* encourager.
encouragement *n* encouragement *m*.
encyclopedia *n* encyclopédie *f*.
end *n* fin *f*; extrémité *f*:—**to the ~ that** afin que:—*vt vi* terminer.
endanger *vt* mettre en danger.
endeavour *vi* s'efforcer:—*n* effort *m*.
endorse *vt* endosser; approuver.
endorsement *n* endos *m*; approbation *f*.
endurable *adj* supportable.
endurance *n* endurance *f*.
endure *vt* supporter:—*vi* durer.
enemy *n* ennemi *mf*.

energetic *adj* énergique.
energy *n* énergie, force *f*.
enfeeble *vt* affaiblir.
enfold *vt* envelopper.
enforce *vt* mettre en vigueur.
engage *vt* aborder.
engaged *adj* fiancé; occupé.
engagement *n* engagement *m*.
engender *vt* engendrer.
engine *n* moteur *m*; locomotive *f*.
engineer *n* ingénieur *m*; mécanicien *m*.
engineering *n* ingénierie *f*.
enigma *n* énigme *f*.
enjoy *vr*:—**to ~ oneself** s'amuser.
enjoyable *adj* agréable; amusant.
enjoyment *n* plaisir *m*; jouissance *f*.
enlarge *vt* agrandir; étendre.
enlargement *n* agrandissement *m*.
enlist *vt* recruter.
enliven *vt* animer; égayer.
enmity *n* inimitié *f*; haine *f*.
enormous *adj* énorme.
enough *adv* suffisamment; assez:— *n* assez *m*.
enrich *vt* enrichir; orner.
enrichment *n* enrichissement *m*.
enrol *vt* enrôler; inscrire.
ensue *vi* s'ensuivre.
ensure *vt* assurer.
entail *vt* impliquer, entraîner.
enter *vt* entrer dans; inscrire.
enterprise *n* entreprise *f*.
enterprising *adj* entreprenant.
entertain *vt* divertir.
entertaining *adj* divertissant, amusant.
enthusiasm *n* enthousiasme *m*.
enthusiast *n* enthousiaste *mf*.
enthusiastic *adj* enthousiaste.
entire *adj* entier, complet.
entitle *vt* intituler.

entity *n* entité *f*.
entrance *n* entrée *f*; admission *f*.
entrant *n* participant *m*, -e *f*.
entreat *vt* implorer.
entrust *vt* confier.
entry *n* entrée *f*.
enumerate *vt* énumérer.
envelop *vt* envelopper.
envelope *n* enveloppe *f*.
envious *adj* envieux.
environment *n* environnement *m*.
environmental *adj* relatif à l'environnement.
envisage *vt* envisager.
envy *n* envie *f*:—*vt* envier.
epidemic *adj* épidémique:—*n* épidémie *f*.
episode *n* épisode *m*.
epitomize *vt* incarner; résumer.
equable *adj* uniforme.
equal *adj* égal; semblable:—*n* égal *m*, -e *f*:—*vt* égaler.
equality *n* égalité *f*.
equalize *vt* égaliser.
equanimity *n* équanimité *f*.
equate *vt* égaliser.
equator *n* équateur *m*.
equilibrium *n* équilibre *m*.
equip *vt* équiper.
equipment *n* équipement *m*.
equivalent *adj n* équivalent *m*.
equivocal *adj* équivoque.
equivocate *vt* équivoquer.
era *n* ère *f*.
eradicate *vt* supprimer.
eradication *n* suppression *f*.
erase *vt* effacer.
eraser *n* gomme *f*.
erect *vt* ériger:—*adj* droit, debout.
erode *vt* éroder; ronger.
erotic *adj* érotique.
err *vi* se tromper.

errand n message m.

erratic adj changeant; irrégulier.

erroneous adj erroné.

error n erreur f.

erudite adj érudit.

eruption n éruption f.

escalate vi monter en flèche.

escape vt éviter:—vi s'évader, s'échapper:—n évasion.

escort n escorte f:—vt escorter.

especial adj spécial.

essay n essai m.

essence n essence f.

essential n essentiel m:—adj essentiel.

establish vt établir.

establishment n établissement m.

estate n état m; biens mpl.

esteem vt estimer:—n estime f.

esthetic adj esthétique f.

estimate vt estimer; évaluer.

estimation n estimation.

estuary n estuaire m.

eternal adj éternel.

eternity n éternité f.

ethical adj éthique.

ethics npl éthique f.

ethnic adj ethnique.

etiquette n étiquette f.

evacuate vt évacuer.

evacuation n évacuation f.

evade vt éviter; échapper à.

evaluate vt évaluer.

evaporate vi s'évaporer.

evaporation n évaporation f.

evasion n dérobade f.

evasive adj évasif.

eve n veille f.

even adj pair:—adv même:—vt égaliser.

evening n soir m, soirée f.

evenness n égalité f; impartialité f.

event n événement m.

eventual adj final:—~ly adv finalement, en fin de comptes.

eventuality n éventualité f.

ever adv toujours; jamais.

everlasting adj éternel.

every adj chacun, chacune:—~where partout:—~thing tout:—~one, ~body tout le monde.

evict vt expulser.

eviction n expulsion f.

evidence n évidence f.

evident adj évident.

evil adj malveillant:—n mal m.

evocative adj évocateur.

evoke vt évoquer.

evolution n évolution f.

evolve vi évoluer.

exacerbate vt exacerber.

exact adj exact:—vt exiger.

exacting adj exigeant.

exaction n exaction f; extorsion f.

exactness n exactitude f.

exaggerate vt exagérer.

exaggeration n exagération f.

exalt vt exalter; élever.

examination n examen m.

examine vt examiner.

example n exemple m.

exasperate vt exaspérer.

exasperation n exaspération f.

excavate vt excaver, creuser.

excavation n excavation f.

exceed vt excéder, dépasser.

excel vt surpasser; vi exceller.

excellence n excellence f.

excellent adj excellent.

except vt excepter:—~(ing) prep excepté, à l'exception de.

exception n exception f.

exceptional adj exceptionnel.

excess n excès m.

excessive *adj* excessif.
exchange *vt* échanger:—*n* échange *m*.
exchange rate *n* taux de change *m*.
excise *n* impôt *m*.
excitable *adj* excitable.
excite *vt* exciter; animer.
excited *adj* animé, enthousiaste.
excitement *n* animation *f*.
exciting *adj* passionnant; stimulant.
exclaim *vi* s'exclamer.
exclamation *n* exclamation *f*.
exclude *vt* exclure.
exclusion *n* exclusion *f*; exception *f*.
exclusive *adj* exclusif.
excommunicate *vt* excommunier.
exculpate *vt* disculper; justifier.
excursion *n* excursion *f*; digression *f*.
excusable *adj* excusable.
excuse *vt* excuser:—*n* excuse *f*.
execute *vt* exécuter.
execution *n* exécution *f*.
executive *adj* exécutif.
exemplary *adj* exemplaire.
exemplify *vt* exemplifier.
exempt *adj* exempt.
exemption *n* exemption *f*.
exercise *n* exercice *m*:—*vt* exercer.
exert *vt* employer, exercer.
exertion *n* effort *m*.
exhale *vt* exhaler.
exhaust *n* *vt* épuiser.
exhaustion *n* épuisement *m*.
exhaustive *adj* exhaustif.
exhibit *vt* exhiber.
exhibition *n* exposition, présentation *f*.
exhilarating *adj* stimulant.
exhilaration *n* joie *f*; stimulation *f*.
exhume *vt* exhumer, déterrer.
exile *n* exil *m*:—*vt* exiler, déporter.
exist *vi* exister.
existence *n* existence *f*.

existent *adj* existant.
exit *n* sortie *f*:—*vi* sortir.
exonerate *vt* disculper.
exoneration *n* disculpation *f*.
exorbitant *adj* exorbitant, excessif.
exotic *adj* exotique.
expand *vt* étendre.
expanse *n* étendue *f*.
expansion *n* expansion *f*.
expect *vt* attendre; espérer.
expectancy *n* attente *f*; espoir *m*.
expectation *n* expectative *f*; attente *f*.
expediency *n* convenance *f*; opportunité *f*.
expedient *adj* opportun.
expedite *vt* accélérer; expédier.
expedition *n* expédition *f*.
expel *vt* expulser.
expend *vt* dépenser; utiliser.
expense *n* dépense *f*; coût *m*.
expensive *adj* cher; coûteux.
experience *n* expérience *f*; pratique *f*:—*vt* ressentir; connaître.
experienced *adj* expérimenté.
experiment *n* expérience *f*:—*vi* expérimenter.
experimental *adj* expérimental.
expert *adj* expert.
expertise *n* habileté *f*.
explain *vt* expliquer.
explanation *n* explication *f*.
explanatory *adj* explicatif.
explicit *adj* explicite.
explode *vt* faire exploser:—*vi* exploser.
exploit *vt* exploiter:—*n* exploit *m*.
exploitation *n* exploitation *f*.
exploration *n* exploration *f*.
explore *vt* explorer; sonder.
explorer *n* explorateur *m*, -trice *f*.
explosion *n* explosion *f*.
explosive *adj* *n* explosif *m*.

export *vt* exporter.

exportation *n* exportation *f*.

exporter *n* exportateur *m*, -trice *f*.

expose *vt* exposer; dévoiler.

exposition *n* exposition *f*.

exposure *n* exposition *f*; temps de pose *m*.

expound *vt* exposer; interpréter.

express *vt* exprimer:—*adj* exprès:—*n* exprès *m*; (*rail*) rapide *m*.

expression *n* expression *f*.

expressive *adj* expressif.

expropriate *vt* exproprier.

expulsion *n* expulsion *f*.

exquisite *adj* exquis.

extemporize *vi* improviser.

extend *vt* étendre:—*vi* s'étendre.

extension *n* extension *f*.

extensive *adj* étendu.

extent *n* extension *f*.

extenuate *vt* atténuer.

exterior *adj n* extérieur *m*.

exterminate *vt* exterminer.

external *adj* externe.

extinct *adj* disparu; éteint.

extinction *n* extinction *f*.

extinguish *vt* éteindre.

extinguisher *n* extincteur *m*.

extort *vt* extorquer.

extortion *n* extorsion *f*.

extra *adv* particulièrement; *n* supplément *m*.

extract *vt* extraire:—*n* extrait *m*.

extraction *n* extraction *f*; origine *f*.

extraneous *adj* superflu; sans rapport.

extraordinary *adj* extraordinaire.

extravagance *n* extravagance *f*.

extravagant *adj* extravagant.

extreme *adj* extrême.

extremist *adj n* extrémiste *mf*.

extricate *vt* extirper, démêler.

extrovert *adj n* extraverti *m*, -e *f*.

exuberance *n* exubérance *f*.

exuberant *adj* exubérant.

eye *n* œil *m*:—*vt* regarder; lorgner.

eyebrow *n* sourcil *m*.

eyelash *n* cil *m*.

eyelid *n* paupière *f*.

eyesight *n* vue *f*.

F

fabric *n* tissu *m*.

fabricate *vt* fabriquer; inventer.

fabrication *n* fabrication *f*.

fabulous *adj* fabuleux.

face *n* visage *m*; mine *f*; apparence *f*:—*vt* faire face à.

facet *n* facette *f*.

facile *adj* facile.

facilitate *vt* faciliter.

facility *n* facilité *f*; équipement *m*.

facing *n* revers *m*:—*prep* en face de.

fact *n* fait *m*; réalité *f*:—**in ~** en fait.

factory *n* usine *f*.

factual *adj* factuel.

faculty *n* faculté *f*.

fail *vt* échouer à; omettre:—*vi* échouer; faiblir; manquer.

failure *n* faillite *f*; manquement *m*.

faint vi s'évanouir, défaillir:—n évanouissement m:—adj faible.

fair adj beau; blond; équitable; considérable:—n foire f.

fairness n beauté f; justice f.

fair play n fair-play.

faith n foi f; croyance f; fidélité f.

faithful adj fidèle, loyal.

fake n falsification f:—adj faux:—vt falsifier.

fall vi tomber; baisser:—n chute f; automne m.

fallacy n erreur f; tromperie f.

fallibility n faillibilité f.

fallible adj faillible.

false adj faux.

false alarm n fausse alerte f.

falsify vt falsifier.

falter vi vaciller.

fame n réputation f; renommée.

familiar adj familier.

familiarity n familiarité f.

familiarize vt familiariser.

family n famille f.

famine n famine f.

famous adj célèbre, fameux.

fan n éventail m; ventilateur m:—vt éventer.

fancy n caprice m:—vt avoir envie de; s'imaginer.

fantastic adj fantastique; excentrique.

fantasy n fantaisie f.

far adv loin:—adj lointain, éloigné.

fare n prix (du voyage) m; tarif m; régime alimentaire m.

farewell n adieu m.

farm n ferme f:—vt cultiver.

farmer n fermier m; agriculteur m.

farming n agriculture f.

fascinate vt fasciner, captiver.

fascination n fascination f; charme m.

fashion n manière, façon f; mode f: —vt façonner.

fashionable adj à la mode; chic.

fast vi jeûner:—n jeûne m:—adj rapide:—adv rapidement.

fasten vt attacher; fixer.

fast food n restauration rapide f.

fat adj gros, gras:—n graisse f.

fatal adj mortel.

fatality n fatalité f.

fate n destin, sort m.

father n père m.

fatherhood n paternité f.

fatigue n fatigue f:—vt fatiguer.

fatuous adj imbécile.

fault n défaut m, faute f; délit m.

faulty adj défectueux.

favour n faveur f:—vt favoriser.

favourable adj favorable.

favourite n favori m:—adj favori.

fax n fax m:—vt envoyer par fax.

fear vt craindre:—n crainte f.

fearful adj effrayant; craintif.

fearless adj intrépide, courageux.

feasibility n faisabilité f.

feasible adj faisable.

feast n banquet m; fête f.

feat n exploit m; prouesse f.

feather n plume f.

feature n trait m:—vi figurer.

February n février m.

fed-up adj:—**to be ~** en avoir marre.

fee n honoraires mpl.

feeble adj faible, frêle.

feebleness n faiblesse f.

feed vt nourrir:—vi manger; se nourrir.

feel vt sentir; toucher:—n sensation f.

feeling n sensation f; sentiment m.

feign vt feindre, simuler.

fellow n homme, type m.

female n femelle f:—adj femelle.

feminine *adj* féminin.

feminist *n* féministe *mf*.

fence *n* barrière *f*; clôture *f*.

ferment *n* agitation *f*:—*vi* fermenter.

ferocious *adj* féroce.

ferocity *n* férocité *f*.

ferry *n* bac *m*; ferry *m*:—*vt* transporter.

fertile *adj* fertile, fécond.

fertility *n* fertilité, fécondité *f*.

fervent *adj* fervent; ardent.

fervour *n* ferveur *f*.

festival *n* fête *f*; festival *m*.

festive *adj* de fête.

fetch *vt* aller chercher.

fetching *adj* charmant, séduisant.

feud *n* rivalité *f*.

fever *n* fièvre *f*.

feverish *adj* fiévreux.

few *adj* peu:—**a ~** quelques.

fibre *n* fibre *f*.

fickle *adj* volage, inconstant.

fiction *n* fiction *f*; invention *f*.

fictional *adj* fictif.

fictitious *adj* fictif, imaginaire.

fidelity *n* fidélité, loyauté *f*.

fidget *vi* s'agiter, remuer.

fidgety *adj* agité, remuant.

field *n* champ *m*; domaine *m*.

fiend *n* démon *m*.

fiendish *adj* diabolique.

fierce *adj* féroce; acharné.

fierceness *n* férocité, fureur *f*.

fifteen *adj n* quinze *m*.

fifteenth *adj n* quinzième *mf*.

fifth *adj n* cinquième *mf*.

fiftieth *adj n* cinquantième *mf*.

fifty *adj n* cinquante *m*.

fight *vt vi* combattre; lutter:—*n* combat *m*.

fighter *n* combattant *m*.

figure *n* figure *f*; image *f*; chiffre *m*.

file *n* file *f*; liste *f*; dossier *m*; fichier *m*:—*vt* enregistrer; classer.

fill *vt* remplir.

fillet *n* filet *m*.

film *n* pellicule *f*; film *f*:—*vt* filmer:—*vi* s'embuer.

filter *n* filtre *m*:—*vt* filtrer.

filth *n* immondice, ordure *f*.

filthy *adj* crasseux, dégoûtant.

fin *n* nageoire *f*.

final *adj* dernier; définitif.

finalize *vt* parachever.

finance *n* finance *f*.

financial *adj* financier.

financier *n* financier *m*.

find *vt* trouver:—*n* trouvaille *f*.

findings *npl* résultats *mpl*.

fine *adj* fin; pur; délicat:—*n* amende *f*.

finesse *n* finesse, subtilité *f*.

finger *n* doigt *m*:—*vt* manier.

fingernail *n* ongle *m*.

finish *vt* finir, terminer.

fir (tree) *n* sapin *m*

fire engine *n* voiture de pompiers *f*.

fire extinguisher *n* extincteur *m*.

fire *n* feu *m*; incendie *m*:—*vt* incendier:—*vi* s'enflammer.

fire station *n* caserne de pompiers *f*.

firearm *n* arme à feu *f*.

fireman *n* pompier *m*.

fireplace *n* cheminée *f*, foyer *m*.

fireproof *adj* ignifugé.

fireworks *npl* feu d'artifice *m*.

firm *adj* ferme:—*n* (*com*) compagnie *f*.

firmness *n* fermeté *f*; résolution *f*.

first *adj* premier:—*adv* premièrement.

first aid *n* premiers secours *mpl*.

first name *n* prénom *m*.

first-class *adj* de première classe.

first-hand *adj* de première main.

first-rate *adj* de première qualité.
fish *n* poisson *m*:—*vi* pêcher.
fisherman *n* pêcheur *m*.
fishing *n* pêche *f*.
fissure *n* fissure, crevasse *f*.
fist *n* poing *m*.
fit *n* accès *m*:—*adj* en forme; capable:—*vt* adapter:—*vi* (bien) aller.
fitness *n* forme physique *f*.
fitting *adj* qui convient, approprié:
—*n* accessoire *ml*.
five *adj n* cinq *m*.
fix *vt* fixer, établir.
fixation *n* obsession *f*.
fixed *adj* fixe.
fizz(le) *vi* pétiller.
fizzy *adj* gazeux.
flabby *adj* mou, *f* molle, flasque.
flag *n* drapeau *m*:—*vi* s'affaiblir.
flagrant *adj* flagrant.
flair *n* flair *m*; talent *m*.
flake *n* flocon *m*:—*vi* s'effriter.
flamboyant *adj* flamboyant.
flame *n* flamme *f*; ardeur *f*.
flammable *adj* inflammable.
flank *n* flanc *m*.
flap *n* battement *m*; rabat *m*.
flare *vi* luire, briller:—*n* flamme *f*.
flash *n* éclat *m*:—*vt* allumer.
flask *n* flasque *f*; flacon *m*.
flat *adj* plat; insipide.
flatten *vt* aplanir; aplatir.
flatter *vt* flatter.
flattery *n* flatterie *f*.
flaunt *vt* étaler, afficher.
flavour *n* saveur *m*:—*vt* assaisonner.
flaw *n* défaut *m*; imperfection *f*.
fleck *n* petite tache *f*; particule *f*.
flee *vt* fuir de:—*vi* s'enfuir.
fleece *n* toison *f*.
fleet *n* flotte *f*; parc *m*.
fleeting *adj* fugace, fugitif.

flesh *n* chair *f*.
flex *n* cordon *m*:—*vt* fléchir.
flexibility *n* flexibilité *f*.
flexible *adj* flexible, souple.
flicker *vt* vaciller; trembloter.
flier *n* aviateur *m*, -trice *f*.
flight *n* vol *m*; fuite *f*; volée *f*.
flight attendant *n* steward *m*, hôtesse de l'air *f*.
flimsy *adj* léger; fragile.
flinch *vi* sourciller.
fling *vt* lancer, jeter.
flip *vt* lancer.
flippant *adj* désinvolte, cavalier.
flipper *n* nageoire *f*.
flirt *vi* flirter:—*n* charmeur *m*, -euse *f*.
flirtation *n* flirt *f*.
float *vt* faire flotter:—*vi* flotter:—*n* flotteur *m*; char (de carnaval) *m*.
flock *n* troupeau *m*; foule *f*:—*vi* affluer.
flood *n* inondation *f*; déluge *m*:—*vt* inonder.
floodlight *n* projecteur *m*.
floor *n* sol *m*; plancher *m*; étage *m*:
—*vt* parqueter.
flop *n* four, fiasco *m*.
floppy *adj* lâche:—*n* disquette *f*.
flora *n* flore *f*.
floral *adj* floral.
florid *adj* fleuri.
florist *n* fleuriste *mf*.
flounder *n* flet *m*:—*vi* patauger.
flour *n* farine *f*.
flourish *vi* fleurir; prospérer.
flourishing *adj* florissant.
flout *vt* mépriser.
flow *vi* couler; circuler:—*n* flux *m*; écoulement *m*; flot *m*.
flower *n* fleur *f*:—*vi* fleurir.
flowery *adj* fleuri.
fluctuate *vi* fluctuer.

fluctuation n fluctuation f.

fluency n aisance f.

fluent adj coulant; facile.

fluff n peluche f.

fluid adj n fluide m.

fluke n veine f.

flurry n rafale f; agitation f.

flush vi rougir:—n rougeur f; éclat m.

flushed adj rouge.

fluster vt énerver.

flute n flûte f.

flutter vi voleter; s'agiter.

fly vt piloter:—vi voler; fuir:—n mouche f; braguette f.

flying n aviation f.

foam n écume f:—vi écumer.

foamy adj écumeux.

focus n foyer m; centre m.

foe n ennemi m, -e f.

fog n brouillard m.

foggy adj brumeux.

fold n pli m:—vt plier.

folder n chemise f; dépliant m.

folding adj pliant.

foliage n feuillage m.

folio n folio m.

folk n gens mpl.

folklore n folklore m.

follow vt suivre:—vi suivre, s'ensuivre.

follower n partisan m, -e f; adhérent m, -e f.

folly n folie, extravagance f.

fond adj affectueux:—**to be ~ of** aimer.

fondle vt caresser.

fondness n prédilection f; affection f.

food n nourriture f.

food processor n robot m.

foodstuffs npl denrées alimentaires fpl.

fool n imbécile mf:—vt duper.

foolhardy adj téméraire.

foolish adj idiot, insensé.

foolproof adj infaillible.

foolscap n papier ministre m.

foot n pied m.

football n football m; ballon de football m.

footballer n footballeur m, -euse f.

footbridge n passerelle f.

footnote n note (de bas de page) f.

footpath n sentier m.

footprint n empreinte (de pas) f.

footstep n pas m.

for prep pour; en raison de; pendant: —conj car:—**as ~ me** quant à moi.

foray n incursion f.

forbid vt interdire, défendre.

forbidding adj menaçant; sévère.

force n force f; puissance:—vt forcer, contraindre.

forceful adj énergique.

forceps n forceps m.

forcible adj énergique, vigoureux.

forearm n avant-bras m.

foreboding n pressentiment m.

forecast vt prévoir:—n prévision f.

forefinger n index m.

foregone adj passé; anticipé.

foreground n premier plan m.

forehead n front m.

foreign adj étranger.

foreigner n étranger m, -ère f.

foreman n contremaître m.

foremost adj principal.

forensic adj judiciaire.

forerunner n précurseur m.

foresee vt prévoir.

foresight n prévoyance f; prescience f.

forest n forêt f.

foretaste n avant-goût m.

foretell vt prédire.

forever adv toujours; un temps infini.

forewarn vt prévenir à l'avance.

foreword n préface f.

forfeit n amende f:—vt perdre.

forge n forge f:—vt forger.

forger n faussaire mf.

forgery n contrefaçon f.

forget vt vi oublier.

forgetful adj étourdi; négligent.

forgive vt pardonner.

forgiveness n pardon m.

fork n fourchette f; fourche f:—vi bifurquer.

forked adj fourchu.

form n forme f; formalité f; moule m:—vt former.

formal adj formel.

formality n formalité f.

format n format m:—vt formater.

formation n formation f.

formative adj formateur m, -trice f.

former adj précédent, ancien:—~ly adv autrefois, jadis.

formula n formule f.

forsake vt abandonner, renoncer à.

fort n fort m.

forthcoming adj prochain; sociable.

forthwith adv immédiatement, tout de suite.

fortieth adj n quarantième mf.

fortification n fortification f.

fortify vt fortifier, renforcer.

fortnight n quinze jours mpl:—adj ~ly bimensuel:—adv ~ly tous les quinze jours.

fortuitous adj fortuit; imprévu.

fortunate adj chanceux.

fortune n chance f, sort m; fortune f.

forty adj n quarante m.

forward adj avancé; précoce; présomptueux:—~(s) adv en avant:— vt transmettre.

forwardness n précocité f.

fossil n fossile m.

foster vt élever.

foster child n enfant adoptif m.

foul adj infect:—vt polluer.

found vt fonder, créer; établir.

foundation n foundation f; fondement m.

foundry n fonderie f.

fountain n fontaine f.

four adj n quatre m.

fourfold adj quadruple.

fourteen adj n quatorze m.

fourteenth adj n quatorzième mf.

fourth adj n quatrième mf:—n quart m.

fowl n volaille f.

fox n renard f.

foyer n vestibule m.

fracas n rixe f.

fraction n fraction f.

fracture n fracture f:—vt fracturer.

fragile adj fragile.

fragility n fragilité f.

fragment n fragment m.

fragmentary adj fragmentaire.

fragrance n parfum m.

fragrant adj parfumé, odorant.

frail adj frêle, fragile.

frailty n fragilité f; faiblesse f.

frame n charpente f; cadre m:—vt encadrer.

franchise n droit de vote m; franchise f.

frank adj franc, direct.

frankness n franchise f.

frantic adj frénétique.

fraternal adv fraternel.

fraternize vi fraterniser.

fratricide n fratricide mf.

fraud n fraude, tromperie f.

fraudulent adj frauduleux.

free *adj* libre; autonome; gratuit; dégagé:—*vt* affranchir; libérer; débarrasser.

freedom *n* liberté *f*.

freelance *adj* indépendant:—*adv* en indépendant.

freely *adv* librement; libéralement.

freewheel *vi* rouler au point mort.

free will *n* libre arbitre *m*.

freeze *vi* geler:—*vt* congeler; geler.

freezer *n* congélateur *m*.

freezing *adj* gelé.

freight *n* cargaison *f*; fret *m*.

freighter *n* affréteur *m*.

French fries *npl* frites *fpl*.

French window *n* porte-fenêtre *f*.

frenzied *adj* fou, frénétique.

frenzy *n* frénésie *f*; folie *f*.

frequency *n* fréquence *f*.

frequent *adj* fréquent:—*vt* fréquenter.

fresco *n* fresque *f*.

fresh *adj* frais; nouveau, récent.

freshen *vt* rafraîchir:—*vi* se rafraîchir.

freshly *adv* récemment.

freshness *n* fraîcheur *f*.

freshwater *adj* d'eau douce.

fret *vi* s'agiter, se tracasser.

friction *n* friction *f*.

Friday *n* vendredi *m*:—**Good ~** Vendredi Saint *m*.

friend *n* ami *m*, -e *f*.

friendliness *n* amitié, bienveillance *f*.

friendly *adj* amical.

friendship *n* amitié *f*.

fright *n* peur, frayeur *f*.

frighten *vt* effrayer.

frightened *adj* effrayé, apeuré.

frightful *adj* épouvantable.

frigid *adj* glacé; frigide.

fringe *n* frange *f*.

frisk *vt* fouiller.

frivolity *n* frivolité *f*.

frivolous *adj* frivole.

fro *adv*:—**to go to and ~** aller et venir.

frock *n* robe *f*.

frog *n* grenouille *f*.

frolic *vi* folâtrer.

from *prep* de; depuis; à partir de.

front *n* avant, devant *m*; front *m*:— *adj* de devant; premier.

front door *n* porte d'entrée *f*.

frontier *n* frontière *f*.

front-wheel drive *n* (*auto*) traction avant *f*.

frost *n* gel *m*; gelée *f*:—*vt* geler.

frostbite *n* engelure *f*.

frostbitten *adj* gelé.

frosty *adj* glacial; givré.

froth *n* écume *f*:—*vi* écumer.

frothy *adj* mousseux, écumeux.

frown *vt* froncer les sourcils.

frozen *adj* gelé.

frugal *adj* frugal; économique.

fruit *n* fruit *m*.

fruiterer *n* fruitier *m*, -ière *f*.

fruitful *adj* fécond, fertile; fructueux.

fruition *n* réalisation *f*.

fruitless *adj* stérile.

frustrate *vt* contrecarrer; annuler.

frustrated *adj* frustré.

frustration *n* frustration *f*.

fry *vt* frire.

frying pan *n* poêle *f*.

fudge *n* caramel *m*.

fuel *n* combustible, carburant *m*.

fuel tank *n* réservoir à carburant *m*.

fugitive *adj* *n* fugitif *m*, -ive *f*.

fulfil *vt* accomplir; réaliser.

fulfilment *n* accomplissement *m*.

full *adj* plein, rempli; complet:— *adv* pleinement, entièrement.

full moon *n* pleine lune *f*.

fullness *n* plénitude *f*; abondance *f*.
full-time *adj* à plein temps.
fully *adv* pleinement, entièrement.
fumble *vi* farfouiller.
fume *vi* rager, fumer.
fumigate *vt* fumiger.
fun *n* amusement *m*:—**to have ~** (bien) s'amuser.
function *n* fonction *f*.
functional *adj* fonctionnel.
fund *n* fonds *m*:—*vt* financer.
fundamental *adj* fondamental.
funeral service *n* office des morts *m*.
funeral *n* enterrement *m*.
funnel *n* entonnoir *m*; cheminée *f*.
funny *adj* amusant; curieux.
fur *n* fourrure *f*.
furious *adj* furieux; déchaîné.
furnace *n* fourneau *m*; chaudière *f*.
furnish *vt* meubler; fournir.
furniture *n* meubles *mpl*.

furrow *n* sillon *m*:—*vt* sillonner.
furry *adj* à poil.
further *adj* supplémentaire; plus lointain:—*adv* plus loin; en outre; de plus:—*vt* favoriser; promouvoir.
further education *n* formation continue *f*.
furthermore *adv* de plus.
furtive *adj* furtif; secret.
fury *n* fureur *f*; colère *f*.
fuse *vi* fondre, sauter:—*n* fusible *m*; amorce *f*.
fuse box *n* boîte à fusibles *f*.
fusion *n* fusion *f*.
fuss *n* tapage *m*.
fussy *adj* tatillon, chipoteur.
futile *adj* futile, vain.
futility *n* futilité *f*.
future *adj* futur:—*n* futur *m*; avenir *m*.
fuzzy *adj* flou, confus.

G

gabble *vi* baragouiner:—*n* charabia *m*.
gadget *n* gadget *m*.
gaiety *n* gaieté *f*.
gain *n* gain *m*; bénéfice *m*:—*vt* gagner.
gait *n* démarche *f*; maintien *m*.
galaxy *n* galaxie *f*.
gale *n* grand vent *m*.
gallant *adj* galant.
gallery *n* galerie *f*.
gallop *n* galop *m*:—*vi* galoper.
galore *adv* en abondance.

galvanize *vt* galvaniser.
gamble *vi* jouer; spéculer:—*n* risque *m*; pari *m*.
gambler *n* joueur *m*, -euse *f*.
gambling *n* jeu *m*.
game *n* jeu *m*; divertissement *m*:—*vi* jouer.
gang *n* gang *m*, bande *f*.
gangway *n* passerelle *f*.
gap *n* vide *m*; écart *m*.
garage *n* garage *m*.
garbage *n* ordures *fpl*.
garbage can *n* poubelle *f*.

garden *n* jardin *m*.

gardener *n* jardinier *m*, -ière *f*.

gardening *n* jardinage *m*.

garlic *n* ail *m*.

garment *n* vêtement *m*.

garnish *vt* garnir:—*n* garniture *f*.

garret *n* mansarde *f*.

garrulous *adj* locace, bavard.

garter *n* jarretelle *f*.

gas *n* gaz *m*; essence *f*.

gas cylinder *n* bouteille de gaz *f*.

gaseous *adj* gazeux.

gash *n* entaille *f*:—*vt* entailler.

gasoline *n* essence *f*.

gasp *vi* haleter.

gas station *n* poste d'essence *m*.

gassy *adj* gazeux.

gastronomic *adj* gastronomique.

gate *n* porte *f*; portail *m*.

gather *vt* rassembler; ramasser:—*vi* se rassembler.

gaudy *adj* criard.

gauge *n* calibre *m*:—*vt* calibrer.

gaunt *adj n* maigre *mf*.

gay *adj* gai; vif.

gaze *vi* contempler:—*n* regard *m*.

gear *n* équipement *m*, matériel *m*; vitesse *f*.

gearbox *n* boîte de vitesses *f*.

gem *n* pierre précieuse *f*; perle *f*.

gender *n* genre *m*.

gene *n* gène *m*.

genealogical *adj* généalogique.

genealogy *n* généalogie *f*.

general *adj* général:—**in ~** en général:—*n* général *m*.

generalization *n* généralisation *f*.

generalize *vt* généraliser.

generation *n* génération *f*.

generator *n* générateur *m*.

generosity *n* générosité, libéralité *f*.

generous *adj* généreux.

genial *adj* bienveillant; doux.

genitals *npl* organes génitaux *mpl*.

genius *n* génie *m*.

gentle *adj* doux, *f* douce, modéré.

gentleman *n* gentleman *m*.

gentleness *n* douceur *f*.

genuine *adj* authentique; sincère.

genus *n* genre *m*.

geographer *n* géographe *mf*.

geography *n* géographie *f*.

geologist *n* géologue *mf*.

geology *n* géologie *f*.

geometry *n* géométrie *f*.

germinate *vi* germer.

gesticulate *vi* gesticuler.

gesture *n* geste *m*.

get *vt* avoir; obtenir:—*vi* devenir.

geyser *n* geyser *m*; chauffe-eau *m invar*.

ghost *n* fantôme, spectre *m*.

giant *n* géant *m*, -e *f*.

gibe *vi* se moquer:—*n* moquerie *f*.

giddiness *n* vertige *m*.

giddy *adj* vertigineux.

gift *n* cadeau *m*.

gifted *adj* talentueux; doué.

gigantic *adj* gigantesque.

gild *vt* dorer.

gills *pl* branchies *fpl*.

ginger *n* gingembre *m*.

ginger-haired *adj* roux, *f* rousse.

girl *n* fille *f*.

girlfriend *n* amie *f*; petite amie *f*.

gist *n* essence *f*.

give *vt* donner; remettre.

gizzard *n* gésier *m*.

glacial *adj* glacial.

glacier *n* glacier *m*.

glad *adj* joyeux, content.

gladden *vt* réjouir.

glamour *n* attrait *m*, séduction *f*.

glamorous *adj* attrayant, séduisant.

glance *vi* jeter un coup d'œil.

glare *n* éclat *m*:—*vi* éblouir.

glass *n* verre *m*:—**~es** *pl* lunettes *fpl*.

glaze *vt* vitrer.

gleam *n* rayon *m*.

glee *n* joie *f*; exultation *f*.

glide *vi* glisser; planer.

glimmer *n* lueur *f*:—*vi* luire.

glimpse *n* aperçu *m*:—*vt* entrevoir.

glint *vi* briller, scintiller.

glitter *vi* luire, briller.

global *adj* global; mondial.

globe *n* globe *m*; sphère *f*.

gloom *n* obscurité *f*; mélancolie.

gloomy *adj* sombre, mélancolique.

glorious *adj* glorieux, illustre.

glory *n* gloire, célébrité *f*.

glove *n* gant *m*.

glow *vi* rougeoyer:—*n* rougeoiment *m*.

glue *n* colle *f*:—*vt* coller.

glum *adj* abattu, triste.

glutton *n* glouton *m*, -onne *f*.

gnome *n* gnome *m*.

go *vi* aller:—**~ away** s'en aller.

goal *n* but, objectif *m*.

gobble *vt* engloutir.

God *n* Dieu *m*.

godfather *n* parrain *m*.

godlike *adj* divin.

godmother *n* marraine *f*.

gold *n* or *m*.

golden *adj* doré; d'or.

goldsmith *n* orfèvre *m*.

golf *n* golf *m*.

golfer *n* golfeur *m*, -euse *f*.

gong *n* gong *m*.

good *adj* bon; valable:—*n* bien *m*:—**~s** *pl* biens *mpl*.

goodbye! *excl* au revoir!

good-looking *adj* beau.

goodness *n* bonté *f*; qualité *f*.

goodwill *n* bienveillance *f*.

goose *n* oie *f*.

gorge *n* gorge *f*:—*vt* engloutir, avaler.

gorgeous *adj* merveilleux.

gory *adj* sanglant.

gossip *n* potins *mpl*:—*vi* potiner.

govern *vt* gouverner, diriger.

government *n* gouvernement *m*.

governor *n* gouverneur *m*.

gown *n* toge *f*; robe *f*.

grab *vt* saisir.

grace *n* grâce *f*:—*vt* honorer.

graceful *adj* gracieux.

gradation *n* gradation *f*.

grade *n* grade *m*.

gradual *adj* graduel.

graduate *vi* obtenir son diplôme.

graft *n* greffe *f*:—*vt* greffer.

grain *n* grain *m*.

grammar *n* grammaire *f*.

grammatical *adj* grammatical.

grand *adj* grandiose; magnifique.

grandchild *n* petit-fils *m*; petite-fille *f*:—**grandchildren** *pl* petits-enfants *m pl*.

grandad *n* pépé *m*.

granddaughter *n* petite-fille *f*.

grandeur *n* grandeur *f*; pompe *f*.

grandfather *n* grand-père *m*.

grandma *n* mémé *f*.

grandmother *n* grand-mère *f*.

grandparents *npl* grands-parents *mpl*.

grandson *n* petit-fils *m*.

grandstand *n* tribune *f*.

granny *n* mémé *f*.

grant *vt* accorder:—*n* bourse *f*.

granulate *vt* granuler.

granule *n* granule *m*.

grape *n* raisin *m*.

grapefruit *n* pamplemousse *m*.

graph *n* graphe, graphique *m*.

graphic(al) *adj* graphique.

grasp *vt* saisir, empoigner; comprendre.

grass *n* herbe *f.*

grasshopper *n* sauterelle *f.*

grassy *adj* herbeux.

grate *n* grille *f.*:—*vt* râper:—*vi* grincer.

grateful *adj* reconnaissant.

gratification *n* satisfaction *f.*

gratify *vt* satisfaire.

gratifying *adj* réjouissant.

gratis *adv* gratis, gratuitement.

gratitude *n* gratitude, reconnaissance *f.*

gratuitous *adj* gratuit; volontaire.

gratuity *n* gratification *f.*

grave *n* tombe *f.*:—*adj* grave.

graveyard *n* cimetière *m.*

gravity *n* gravité *f.*

gravy *n* jus de viande *m*; sauce *f.*

graze *vt* paître:—*vi* paître.

grease *n* graisse *f.*:—*vt* graisser.

great *adj* grand; important.

greatness *n* grandeur *f*; importance *f.*

greed *n* avidité *f*; gloutonnerie *f.*

greedy *adj* avide; glouton.

green *adj* vert:—*n* vert *m*; verdure *f.*

greenery *n* verdure *f.*

greenhouse *n* serre *f.*

greenish *adj* verdâtre.

greet *vt* saluer; accueillir.

greeting *n* salutation *f*; accueil *m.*

grey *adj* gris:—*n* gris *m.*

greyish *adj* grisâtre; grisonnant.

grid *n* grille *f*; réseau *m.*

grief *n* chagrin *m*, douleur.

grievance *n* grief *m*; doléance *f.*

grieve *vt* peiner:—*vi* se chagriner.

grievous *adj* douloureux; grave.

grill *n* gril *m*:—*vt* faire griller.

grim *adj* peu engageant.

grimace *n* grimace *f*; moue *f.*

grime *n* saleté *f.*

grind *vt* moudre.

grip *n* prise *f*; poignée *f.*:—*vt* saisir, agripper.

groan *vi* gémir; grogner:—*n* gémissement *m.*

grocer *n* épicier *m*, -ière *f.*

groom *n* valet *m*; marié *m*:—*vt* panser; préparer.

groove *n* rainure *f.*

grope *vt* chercher à tâtons:—*vi* tâtonner.

gross *adj* gros; grossier.

grotesque *adj* grotesque.

ground *n* terre *f*, sol *m*; terrain:—*vt* fonder.

ground floor *n* rez-de-chaussée *m.*

groundless *adj* sans fondement.

group *n* groupe *m*:—*vt* regrouper.

grove *n* bosquet *m.*

grovel *vi* se traîner; ramper.

grow *vt* cultiver:—*vi* pousser.

grower *n* cultivateur *m*, -trice *f.*

growl *vi* grogner.

growth *n* croissance *f.*

grudge *n* rancune *f.*

gruelling *adj* difficile, pénible.

gruesome *adj* horrible.

grumble *vi* grogner; grommeler.

guarantee *n* garantie *f.*:—*vt* garantir.

guard *n* garde *f.*:—*vt* garder.

guardian *n* tuteur *m*, -trice *f.*

guardianship *n* tutelle *f.*

guess *vt* deviner:—*vi* deviner:—*n* conjecture *f.*

guest *n* invité *m*, invitée *f.*

guidance *n* guidage *m*; direction *f.*

guide *vt* guider, diriger:—*n* guide *m.*

guidebook *n* guide *m.*

guild *n* association *f*; corporation *f.*

guile *n* astuce *f.*

guilt *n* culpabilité *f.*

guilty *adj* coupable.
guise *n* apparence *f*.
guitar *n* guitare *f*.
gull *n* mouette *f*.
gullibility *n* crédulité *f*.
gullible *adj* crédule.
gulp *n* gorgée *f*:—*vi*, *vt* avaler.
gum *n* gomme *f*:—*vt* coller.
gun *n* pistolet *m*; fusil *m*.
gunpowder *n* poudre à canon *f*.
gunshot *n* coup de feu *m*.
gurgle *vi* gargouiller.
gush *vi* jaillir; bouillonner:—*n* jaillissement *m*.

gust *n* rafale *f*; bouffée *f*.
gusto *n* plaisir *m*, délectation *f*.
gusty *adj* venteux.
gut *n* intestin *m*:—*vt* vider.
gutter *n* gouttière *f*; caniveau *m*.
guy *n* mec, type *m*.
guzzle *vt* bouffer, engloutir.
gymnasium *n* gymnase *m*.
gymnast *n* gymnaste *mf*.
gymnastic *adj* gymnastique:—**~s** *npl* gymnastique *f*.
gynecologist *n* gynécologue *mf*.
gypsy *n* gitan *m*, -e *f*.

H

habit *n* habitude *f*.
habitable *adj* habitable.
habitat *n* habitat *m*.
habitual *adj* habituel.
haemorrhage *n* hémorragie *f*.
haggard *adj* décharné hagard.
haggle *vi* marchander.
hail *n* grêle *f*:—*vt* saluer:—*vi* grêler.
hair *n* cheveu *m*; poil *m*.
haircut *n* coupe de cheveux *f*.
hairless *adj* chauve; sans poils.
hairstyle *n* coiffure *f*.
hairy *adj* chevelu; poilu.
hale *adj* vigoureux.
half *n* moitié *f*:—*adj* demi:—*adv* à moitié.
half-hearted *adj* peu enthousiaste.
half-hour *n* demi-heure *f*.
half-moon *n* demi-lune *f*.
halfway *adv* à mi-chemin.

hall *n* vestibule *m*.
hallow *vt* consacrer, sanctifier.
hallucination *n* hallucination *f*.
halt *vi* s'arrêter:—*n* arrêt *m*; halte *f*.
ham *n* jambon *m*.
hammer *n* marteau *m*:—*vt* marteler.
hammock *n* hamac *m*.
hamper *n* panier *m*:—*vt* entraver.
hand *n* main *f*:—*vt* donner, passer.
handbag *n* sac à main *m*.
handbrake *n* frein à main *m*.
handful *n* poignée *f*.
handicap *n* handicap *m*.
handicapped *adj* handicapé.
handkerchief *n* mouchoir *m*.
handle *n* manche *m*:—*vt* manier.
handlebars *npl* guidon *m*.
handrail *n* garde-fou *m*.
handsome *adj* beau.
handwriting *n* écriture *f*.

hang *vt* accrocher; pendre:—*vi* pendre.

hangover *n* gueule de bois *f*.

haphazard *adj* fortuit.

hapless *adj* malheureux.

happen *vi* se passer.

happening *n* événement *m*.

happily *adv* heureusement.

happiness *n* bonheur *m*.

happy *adj* heureux.

harass *vt* harceler.

harbour *n* port *m*:—*vt* héberger.

hard *adj* dur; pénible; sévère.

harden *vt vi* durcir.

hardiness *n* robustesse *f*.

hardly *adv* à peine:—~ **ever** presque jamais.

hardness *n* dureté *f*; difficulté *f*.

hard-up *adj* fauché.

hardy *adj* fort, robuste.

hare *n* lièvre *m*.

harm *n* mal *m*; tort *m*:—*vt* nuire à.

harmful *adj* nuisible.

harmonious *adj* harmonieux.

harmony *n* harmonie *f*.

harp *n* harpe *f*.

harsh *adj* dur; austère; rude.

harshness *n* aspérité, dureté *f*; austérité *f*.

harvest *n* moisson *f*:—*vt* moissonner.

harvester *n* moissonneur *m*, -euse *f*.

haste *n* hâte *f*.

hasten *vt* accélérer:—*vi* se dépêcher.

hasty *adj* hâtif; irréfléchi.

hat *n* chapeau *m*.

hatch *vt* couver; faire éclore:—*n* écoutille *f*.

hatchet *n* hachette *f*.

hate *n* haine *f*:—*vt* haïr, détester.

hatred *n* haine *f*.

haughtiness *n* orgueil *m*.

haughty *adj* orgueilleux.

haul *vt* tirer:—*n* prise *f*.

haunt *vt* hanter:—*n* repaire *m*.

have *vt* avoir; posséder.

haversack *n* sac à dos *m*.

havoc *n* ravages *mpl*.

hay *n* foin *m*.

hay fever *n* rhume des foins *m*.

hazard *n* risque, danger *m*:—*vt* risquer.

hazardous *adj* risqué, dangereux.

haze *n* brume *f*.

hazelnut *n* noisette *f*.

hazy *adj* brumeux.

he *pn* il.

head *n* tête *f*; chef *m*:—*vt* conduire.

headache *n* mal de tête *m*.

headland *n* promontoire *m*.

headlight *n* phare *m*.

headline *n* titre *m*.

headlong *adv* à toute allure.

headstrong *adj* têtu.

headwaiter *n* maître d'hôtel *m*.

heady *adj* capiteux.

heal *vt vi* guérir.

health *n* santé *f*.

healthiness *n* bonne santé *f*.

healthy *adj* en bonne santé; sain.

heap *n* tas *m*:—*vt* entasser.

hear *vt* entendre; écouter:—*vi* entendre.

hearing *n* ouïe *f*.

heart *n* cœur *m*.

heart failure *n* arrêt cardiaque *m*.

hearth *n* foyer *m*.

heartless *adj* cruel.

hearty *adj* cordial.

heat *n* chaleur *f*:—*vt* chauffer.

heater *n* radiateur *m*.

heathen *n* païen *m*, païenne *f*.

heating *n* chauffage *m*.

heatwave *n* onde de chaleur *f*.

heave vt lever; tirer.

heaven n ciel m.

heaviness n lourdeur f.

heavy adj lourd, pesant.

hectic adj agité.

hedge n haie f.

hedgehog n hérisson m.

heed vt tenir compte de:—n attention f.

heedless adj inattentif, étourdi.

heel n talon m.

hefty adj fort; gros.

height n hauteur f; altitude f.

heighten vt rehausser.

heinous adj atroce.

heir n héritier m.

helicopter n hélicoptère m.

hell n enfer m.

helmet n casque m.

help vt aider, secourir:—n aide f; secours m.

helper n aide mf.

helpful adj utile.

helpless adj impuissant.

hemisphere n hémisphère m.

hen n poule f.

henceforward adv dorénavant.

hen-house n poulailler m.

hepatitis n hépatite f.

her pn son, sa, ses; elle; la; lui.

herb n herbe f.

herbalist n herboriste mf.

herd n troupeau m.

here adv ici.

hereby adv par la présente.

hereditary adj héréditaire.

heredity n hérédité f.

heritage n patrimoine, héritage m.

hermit n ermite m.

hernia n hernie f.

hero n héros m.

heroic adj héroïque.

hers pn le sien, la sienne, le(s) sien(ne)s, à elle.

herself pn elle-même.

hesitate vi hésiter.

hesitation n hésitation f.

heterogeneous adj hétérogène.

heterosexual adj n hétérosexuel m, -elle f.

hiatus n (gr) hiatus m.

hiccup n hoquet m:—vi avoir le hoquet.

hide vt cacher:—n cuir m; peau f.

hideaway n cachette f.

hideous adj hideux; horrible.

hierarchy n hiérarchie f.

hi-fi n hi-fi f invar.

high adj haut; élevé.

highlight n point fort m.

highness n hauteur f; altesse f.

hike vi faire une randonnée.

hilarious adj hilarant; hilare.

hill n colline f.

hillside n coteau m.

hilly adj montagneux.

him pn lui; le.

himself pn lui-même; soi.

hinder vt gêner, entraver.

hindrance n gêne f, obstacle m.

hindsight n:—**with ~** rétrospectivement.

hint n allusion f:—vt insinuer; suggérer.

hip n hanche f.

hire vt louer:—n location f.

his poss adj son, sa, ses; poss pn le sien, la sienne, les sien(ne)s; à lui.

hiss vt vi siffler.

historian n historien m, -ienne f.

historic(al) adj historique.

history n histoire f.

hit vt frapper; atteindre.

hitch-hike vi faire du stop.

hoard n stock m; trésor caché m:—
vt accumuler.

hoarse adj rauque.

hoarseness n voix rauque f.

hobby n passe-temps m invar.

hoist vt hisser:—n grue f.

hold vt tenir; détenir:—n prise f;
pouvoir m.

holder n détenteur m, -trice f.

holdup n hold-up m.

hole n trou m.

holiday n jour de congé m:—~s pl
vacances fpl.

hollow adj creux:—n creux m:—vt
creuser.

holocaust n holocauste m.

holy adj saint; bénit.

homage n hommage m.

home n maison f; domicile m.

homeless adj sans abri.

homely adj simple.

homesick adj nostalgique.

homesickness n nostalgie f.

homework n devoirs mpl.

homicide n homicide m; homicide
mf.

homogeneous adj homogène.

homosexual adj n homosexuel m, -
elle f.

honest adj honnête.

honesty n honnêteté f.

honey n miel m.

honor n honneur m:—vt honorer.

honorable adj honorable.

honorary adj honoraire.

hood n capot m; capuche f.

hoof n sabot m.

hook n crochet m; hameçon m:—vt
accrocher.

hoop n cerceau m.

hooter n sirène f.

hop n saut m:—vi sauter.

hope n espoir m, espérance f:—vi
espérer.

hopeful adj plein d'espoir; prometteur.

horizon n horizon m.

horizontal adj horizontal.

hormone n hormone f.

horn n corne f.

horoscope n horoscope m.

horrible adj horrible.

horrific adj horrible, affreux.

horrify vt horrifier.

horror n horreur f.

hors d'œuvre n hors-d'œuvre m
invar.

horse n cheval m.

horseback adv:—on ~ à cheval.

horseman n cavalier m.

horsepower n cheval-vapeur m;
puissance en chevaux f.

horseshoe n fer à cheval m.

horticulture n horticulture f.

horticulturist n horticulteur m, -trice
f.

hospitable adj hospitalier.

hospital n hôpital m.

hospitality n hospitalité f.

host n hôte m; hostie f.

hostage n otage m.

hostess n hôtesse f.

hostile adj hostile.

hostility n hostilité f.

hot adj chaud; épicé.

hotel n hôtel m.

hotelier n hôtelier m, -ière f.

hotheaded adj exalté.

hotplate n plaque chauffante f.

hour n heure f.

hour-glass n sablier m.

hourly adv toutes les heures.

house n maison f; maisonnée f:—vt
loger.

houseboat n péniche f.
household n famille f, ménage m.
householder n propriétaire mf; chef de famille m.
housekeeper n gouvernante f.
housewife n ménagère f.
housework n travaux ménagers mpl.
housing n logement m.
hovel n taudis m.
hover vi planer.
how adv comme; comment:—~ do you do! enchanté.
however adv de quelque manière que; cependant, néanmoins.
howl vi hurler:—n hurlement m.
hub n centre m; moyeu m.
hue n teinte f; nuance f.
hug vt étreindre:—n étreinte f.
huge adj énorme.
hull n (mar) coque f.
hum vi chantonner.
human adj humain.
humane adj humain.
humanist n humaniste mf.
humanity n humanité f.
humanize vt humaniser.
humble adj humble:—vt humilier.
humdrum adj monotone.
humid adj humide.
humiliate vt humilier.
humiliation n humiliation f.
humility n humilité f.

humorous adj humoristique.
humour n sens de l'humour m, humour m.
hump n bosse f.
hundred adj cent:—n centaine f.
hundredth adj centième.
hunger n faim f:—vi avoir faim.
hungry adj affamé.
hunt vt chasser:—n chasse f.
hunter n chasseur m.
hurdle n haie f.
hurl vt jeter.
hurricane n ouragan m.
hurry vt presser:—vi se presser:—n hâte f.
hurt vt faire mal à; blesser:—n mal m.
hurtful adj blessant.
husband n mari m.
hut n cabane, hutte f.
hydrant n bouche d'incendie f.
hydraulic adj hydraulique.
hydroelectric adj hydroélectrique.
hygiene n hygiène f.
hygienic adj hygiénique.
hypochondriac adj n hypocondriaque mf.
hypocrisy n hypocrisie f.
hypocritical adj hypocrite.
hypothesis n hypothèse f.
hypothetical adj hypothétique.
hysterical adj hystérique.
hysterics npl hystérie f.

I

I pn je, j'; moi
ice n glace f:—vt glacer.
ice cream n glace f.

ice rink n patinoire f.
ice skating n patinage sur glace m.
icy adj glacé.

idea *n* idée *f*.
ideal *adj* idéal.
identical *adj* identique.
identification *n* identification *f*.
identify *vt* identifier.
identity *n* identité *f*.
idiot *n* imbécile *mf*.
idiotic *adj* idiot, bête.
idle *adj* désœuvré; au repos.
idleness *n* paresse *f*.
idler *n* paresseux *m*, -euse *f*.
idol *n* idole *f*.
idolize *vt* idôlatrer.
idyllic *adj* idyllique.
if *conj* si:—~ **not** sinon.
ignite *vt* allumer, enflammer.
ignoble *adj* ignoble; bas.
ignominious *adj* ignominieux.
ignorance *n* ignorance *f*.
ignorant *adj* ignorant.
ignore *vt* ne pas tenir compte de.
ill *adj* malade:—*n* mal *m*.
illegal *adj* illégal.
illegality *n* illégalité *f*.
illegible *adj* illisible.
illegitimacy *n* illégitimité *f*.
illegitimate *adj* illégitime.
illicit *adj* illicite.
illiterate *adj* analphabète.
illness *n* maladie *f*.
illogical *adj* illogique.
illuminate *vt* illuminer.
illusion *n* illusion *f*.
illusory *adj* illusoire.
illustrate *vt* illustrer.
illustration *n* illustration *f*.
illustrious *adj* illustre.
image *n* image *f*.
imaginary *adj* imaginaire.
imagination *n* imagination *f*.
imagine *vt* imaginer.
imbecile *adj* imbécile, idiot.

imitate *vt* imiter.
imitation *n* imitation *f*.
immaterial *adj* insignifiant.
immeasurable *adj* incommensurable.
immediate *adj* immédiat.
immense *adj* immense.
immigrant *n* immigrant *m*, -e *f*.
immigration *n* immigration *f*.
imminent *adj* imminent.
immobile *adj* immobile.
immobility *n* immobilité *f*.
immoderate *adj* immodéré.
immoral *adj* immoral.
immorality *n* immoralité *f*.
immortal *adj* immortel.
immune *adj* immunisé.
immunize *vt* immuniser.
immutable *adj* immuable.
impact *n* impact *m*.
impalpable *adj* impalpable.
impart *vt* communiquer.
impartial *adj* impartial.
impartiality *n* impartialité *f*.
impassive *adj* impassible.
impatience *n* impatience *f*.
impatient *adj* impatient.
impeccable *adj* impeccable.
impede *vt* empêcher; entraver.
impending *adj* imminent.
impenetrable *adj* impénétrable.
imperceptible *adj* imperceptible.
imperfect *adj* imparfait.
imperfection *n* imperfection *f*; défaut *m*.
impermeable *adj* imperméable.
impersonal *adj* impersonel.
impertinence *n* impertinence *f*.
impertinent *adj* impertinent.
impetuosity *n* impétuosité *f*.
impetuous *adj* impétueux.
implant *vt* implanter.
implement *n* outil *m*; ustensile *m*.

implicate *vt* impliquer.
implication *n* implication *f*.
implicit *adj* implicite.
implore *vt* supplier.
imply *vt* supposer.
impolite *adj* impoli.
import *vt* importer:—*n* importation *f*.
importance *n* importance *f*.
important *adj* important.
impose *vt* imposer.
imposition *n* imposition *f*.
impossibility *n* impossibilité *f*.
impossible *adj* impossible.
impostor *n* imposteur *m*.
impotence *n* impotence *f*.
impotent *adj* impotent.
impoverish *vt* appauvrir.
impoverishment *n* appauvrissement *m*.
impracticable *adj* impraticable.
imprecise *adj* imprécis.
impress *vt* impressionner.
impression *n* impression *f*; édition *f*.
impressionable *adj* impressionnable.
impressive *adj* impressionnant.
imprint *n* empreinte *f*:—*vt* imprimer.
imprison *vt* emprisonner.
imprisonment *n* emprisonnement *m*.
improbability *n* improbabilité *f*.
improbable *adj* improbable.
improper *adj* indécent; impropre.
improve *vt* améliorer:—*vi* s'améliorer.
improvement *n* amélioration *f*.
improvise *vt* improviser.
imprudent *adj* imprudent.
impudent *adj* impudent.
impulse *n* impulsion *f*.
impulsive *adj* impulsif.
impunity *n* impunité *f*.
in *prep* dans; en.
inability *n* incapacité *f*.

inaccurate *adj* inexact.
inactive *adj* inactif.
inadequate *adj* inadéquat.
inadmissible *adj* inadmissible.
inane *adj* inepte.
inanimate *adj* inanimé.
inapplicable *adj* inapplicable.
inaudible *adj* inaudible.
incalculable *adj* incalculable.
incapable *adj* incapable.
incapacitate *vt* mettre dans l'incapacité.
incapacity *n* incapacité *f*.
incarcerate *vt* incarcérer.
incautious *adj* imprudent.
incentive *n* prime, aide *f*.
inception *n* commencement *m*.
incessant *adj* incessant, continuel.
incidence *n* fréquence *f*.
incident *n* incident *m*.
incidental *adj* fortuit.
incisive *adj* incisif.
incite *vt* inciter, encourager.
inclination *n* inclination, propension *f*.
incline *vt* incliner:—*vi* s'incliner.
include *vt* inclure, comprendre.
including *prep* inclus, y compris.
incognito *adv* incognito.
incoherence *n* incohérence *f*.
incoherent *adj* incohérent.
income *n* revenu *m*; recettes *fpl*.
incomparable *adj* incomparable.
incompetence *n* incompétence *f*.
incompetent *adj* incompétent.
incomplete *adj* incomplet.
incomprehensible *adj* incompréhensible.
inconceivable *adj* inconcevable.
incongruity *n* incongruité *f*.
incongruous *adj* incongru.
inconsiderate *adj* inconsidéré.

inconsistent *adj* inconsistant.

inconspicuous *adj* discret.

incontrovertible *adj* incontestable.

inconvenience *n* inconvénient:—*vt* incommoder.

inconvenient *adj* incommode.

incorporate *vt* incorporer:—*vi* s'incorporer.

incorporation *n* incorporation *f*.

incorrect *adj* incorrect.

increase *vt vi* augmenter:—*n* augmentation *f*.

increasing *adj* croissant.

incredible *adj* incroyable.

incredulous *adj* incrédule.

incriminate *vt* incriminer.

incur *vt* encourir.

incurable *adj* incurable.

incursion *n* incursion *f*.

indebted *adj* endetté; redevable.

indecent *adj* indécent.

indecision *n* indécision, irrésolution *f*.

indecisive *adj* indécis, irrésolu.

indefatigable *adj* infatigable.

indefinite *adj* indéfini.

indemnify *vt* indemniser.

indemnity *n* indemnité *f*.

independence *n* indépendance *f*.

independent *adj* indépendant.

indeterminate *adj* indéterminé.

index *n* indice *m*.

indicate *vt* indiquer.

indication *n* indication *f*; indice *m*.

indifference *n* indifférence *f*.

indifferent *adj* indifférent.

indigenous *adj* indigène.

indigent *adj* indigent.

indigestion *n* indigestion *f*.

indignant *adj* indigné.

indignation *n* indignation *f*.

indirect *adj* indirect.

indiscreet *adj* indiscret.

indiscretion *n* indiscrétion *f*.

indispensable *adj* indispensable.

indisputable *adj* indiscutable.

indistinct *adj* indistinct.

indistinguishable *adj* indistinctible.

individual *adj* individuel:—*n* individu *m*.

individuality *n* individualité *f*.

indolence *n* indolence *f*.

indolent *adj* indolent.

indoors *adv* à l'intérieur.

induce *vt* persuader; provoquer.

inducement *n* encouragement *m*; incitation *f*.

indulge *vt* céder à; *vi* se permettre.

indulgent *adj* indulgent.

industrial *adj* industriel.

industrialize *vt* industrialiser.

industrious *adj* travailleur.

industry *n* industrie *f*.

inebriated *vt* ivre.

inedible *adj* non comestible.

inefficiency *n* inefficacité *f*.

inefficient *adj* inefficace.

ineligible *adj* inéligible.

inept *adj* inepte; déplacé.

inequality *n* inégalité *f*.

inertia *n* inertie *f*.

inestimable *adj* inestimable.

inevitable *adj* inévitable.

inexhaustible *adj* inépuisable.

inexpedient *adj* imprudent, inopportun.

inexpensive *adj* bon marché.

inexplicable *adj* inexplicable.

infallible *adj* infaillible.

infamous *adj* vil, infâme.

infancy *n* enfance *f*.

infant *n* bébé *m*; enfant *mf*.

infantile *adj* infantile.

infatuated *adj* fou.

infatuation *n* folie *f*; obsession *f*.

infect vt infecter.
infectious adj infectieux.
infer vt inférer.
inference n inférence f.
inferior adj inférieur.
inferiority n infériorité f.
infernal adj infernal.
infest vt infester.
infidelity n infidélité f.
infiltrate vi s'infiltrer.
infinite adj infini.
infinity n infini m; infinité f.
infirm adj infirme.
infirmity n infirmité f.
inflame vt enflammer:—vi s'enflammer.
inflammation n inflammation f.
inflatable adj gonflable.
inflate vt gonfler.
inflation n inflation f.
inflict vt infliger.
influence n influence f:—vt influencer.
influential adj influent.
influenza n grippe f.
inform vt informer.
informal adj informel.
informality n simplicité f.
information n information f.
infrequent adj rare.
infringe vt enfreindre.
infringement n infraction f.
infuriate vt rendre furieux.
ingenious adj ingénieux.
ingenuity n ingéniosité f.
ingenuous adj ingénu.
inglorious adj honteux.
ingot n lingot m.
ingratitude n ingratitude f.
ingredient n ingrédient m.
inhabit vt vi habiter.
inhabitable adj habitable.

inhabitant n habitant m, -e f.
inhale vt inhaler.
inherit vt hériter.
inheritance n héritage m.
inhibit vt inhiber.
inhibition n inhibition f.
inhospitable adj inhospitalier.
inhuman adj inhumain.
inhumanity n inhumanité.
inimical adj hostile, ennemi.
inimitable adj inimitable.
initial adj initial:—n initiale f.
initiate vt commencer; initier.
initiation n initiation f.
initiative n initiative f.
inject vt injecter.
injection n injection f.
injunction n injonction f.
injure vt blesser.
injury n blessure f; tort m.
injustice n injustice f.
ink n encre f.
inlet n entrée f; bras de mer m.
inn n auberge f; hôtel m.
innate adj inné.
inner adj intérieur.
innkeeper n aubergiste mf.
innocence n innocence f.
innocent adj innocent.
innocuous adj inoffensif.
innovate vt innover.
innuendo n allusion f; insinuation f.
innumerable adj innombrable.
inoculate vt inoculer.
inoffensive adj inoffensif.
inopportune adj inopportun.
inquest n enquête f.
inquire vt vi demander.
inquiry n enquête f.
inquisition n investigation f.
inquisitive adj curieux.
insane adj fou, f folle.

insanity *n* folie *f*.
insatiable *adj* insatiable.
inscribe *vt* inscrire.
inscription *n* inscription *f*.
inscrutable *adj* impénétrable.
insect *n* insecte *m*.
insecure *adj* peu assuré.
insecurity *n* insécurité *f*.
insemination *n* insémination *f*.
insensible *adj* inconscient.
insensitive *adj* insensible.
inseparable *adj* inséparable.
insert *vt* introduire, insérer.
insertion *n* insertion *f*.
inside *n* intérieur *m*:—*adv* à l'intérieur.
inside out *adv* à l'envers.
insidious *adj* insidieux.
insight *n* perspicacité *f*.
insignificant *adj* insignifiant.
insinuate *vt* insinuer.
insinuation *n* insinuation *f*.
insipid *adj* insipide.
insist *vi* insister.
insistence *n* insistance *f*.
insistent *adj* insistant.
insolence *n* insolence *f*.
insolent *adj* insolent.
inspect *vt* examiner, inspecter.
inspection *n* inspection *f*.
inspector *n* inspecteur *m*, -trice *f*.
instability *n* instabilité *f*.
instal *vt* installer.
installation *n* installation *f*.
instalment *n* installation *f*.
instance *n* exemple *m*.
instant *adj* instantané:—*n* instant.
instead (of) *pr* au lieu.
instigate *vt* inciter; susciter.
instinct *n* instinct *m*.
instinctive *adj* instinctif.
institute *vt* instituer.

institution *n* institution *f*.
instruct *vt* instruire.
instrument *n* instrument *m*.
insufficiency *n* insuffisance *f*.
insufficient *adj* insuffisant.
insular *adj* insulaire.
insulate *vt* isoler.
insulation *n* isolation *f*.
insult *vt* insulter:—*n* insulte *f*.
insurance *n* (*com*) assurance *f*.
insure *vt* assurer.
intact *adj* intact.
integrate *vt* intégrer.
integration *n* intégration *f*.
integrity *n* intégrité *f*.
intellect *n* intellect *m*.
intellectual *adj* intellectuel.
intelligence *n* intelligence *f*.
intelligent *adj* intelligent.
intelligible *adj* intelligible.
intend *vt* avoir l'intention de.
intense *adj* intense.
intensify *vt* intensifier.
intensity *n* intensité *f*.
intensive *adj* intensif.
intention *n* intention *f*, dessein *m*.
intentional *adj* intentionnel:—-ly *adv* à dessein, intentionnellement.
intercede *vi* intercéder.
intercept *vt* intercepter.
interest *vt* intéresser:—*n* intérêt *m*.
interesting *adj* intéressant.
interfere *vi* s'ingérer.
interior *adj* intérieur.
interlock *vi* s'entremêler.
interlude *n* intermède *m*.
intermediary *n* intermédiaire *mf*.
intermediate *adj* intermédiaire.
interminable *adj* interminable.
intermingle *vt* entremêler:—*vi* s'entremêler.
intermittent *adj* intermittent.

intern n interne mf.
internal adj intérieur; interne.
international adj international.
interpret vt interpréter.
interpretation n interprétation f.
interpreter n interprète mf.
interrogate vt interroger.
interrogation n interrogatoire m.
interrupt vt interrompre.
interruption n interruption f.
intersect vi se croiser.
intersection n croisement m.
intertwine vt entrelacer.
interval n intervalle m; mi-temps f.
intervene vi intervenir.
intervention n intervention f.
interview n entrevue f; interview f.
interviewer n interviewer m.
intestine n intestin m.
intimacy n intimité f.
intimate adj intime vt insinuer.
intimidate vt intimider.
into prep dans, en.
intolerable adj intolérable.
intolerant adj intolérant.
intonation n intonation f.
intoxicate vt enivrer.
intoxication n ivresse f.
intricacy n complexité f.
intricate adj complexe.
intrigue n intrigue f:—vi intriguer.
intriguing adj intrigant.
intrinsic adj intrinsèque.
introduce vt introduire.
introduction n introduction f.
introvert n introverti m, -ie f.
intruder n intrus m, -e f.
intuition n intuition f.
intuitive adj intuitif.
inundate vt inonder.
invade vt envahir.
invader n envahisseur m, -euse f.

invalid n invalide mf.
invalidate vt invalider.
invaluable adj inappréciable.
invasion n invasion f.
invent vt inventer.
invention n invention f.
inventor n inventeur m, -trice f.
investigation n investigation f.
investigator n investigateur m, -trice f.
invincible adj invincible.
inviolable adj inviolable.
invisible adj invisible.
invitation n invitation f.
invite vt inviter.
invoice n facture f.
invoke vt invoquer.
involuntary adj involontaire.
involve vt impliquer, entraîner.
involvement n implication f.
irascible adj irascible.
irate adj irrité.
iron n fer m:—adj de fer.
ironic adj ironique.
irony n ironie f.
irrational adj irrationnel.
irreconcilable adj irréconciliable.
irregular adj irrégulier.
irregularity n irrégularité f.
irreparable adj irréparable.
irreplaceable adj irremplaçable.
irresistible adj irrésistible.
irresponsible adj irresponsable.
irreverence n irrévérence f.
irrigate vt irriguer.
irrigation n irrigation f.
irritability n irritabilité f.
irritable adj irritable.
irritate vt irriter.
irritation n irritation f.
island n île f.
isle n île f.

isolate *vt* isoler.
isolation *n* isolement *m*.
issue *n* sujet *m*, question *f*:—*vt* publier.
it *pn* il, elle; le, la; cela, ça, ce, c'.
itch *n* démangeaison *f*:—*vi* avoir des démangeaisons.

item *n* article *m*.
itinerant *adj* itinérant.
itinerary *n* itinéraire *m*.
its *pn* son, sa, ses.
itself *pn* lui-même, elle-même.
ivory *n* ivoire *m*.
ivy *n* lierre *m*.

J

jabber *vi* bafouiller.
jack *n* cric *m*; valet *m*.
jacket *n* veste *f*; couverture *f*.
jackpot *n* gros lot *m*.
jagged *adj* dentelé.
jail *n* prison *f*.
jailer *n* geôlier *m*, -ière *f*.
jam *n* confiture *f*; embouteillage *m*.
January *n* janvier *m*.
jar *vi* (*mus*) détonner:—*n* pot *m*.
jargon *n* jargon *m*.
jaw *n* mâchoire *f*.
jazz *n* jazz *m*.
jealous *adj* jaloux.
jealousy *n* jalousie *f*.
jeans *npl* jean *m*.
jeer *vi* railler:—*n* raillerie.
jelly *n* gelée *f*.
jeopardize *vt* mettre en péril.
jerk *n* secousse *f*.
jersey *n* jersey *m*.
jest *n* blague.
jester *n* bouffon *m*.
jet *n* avion à réaction *m*; jet *m*.
jettison *vt* se défaire de.
jewel *n* bijou *m*.
jewellery *n* bijouterie *f*.

Jewish *adj* juif.
jibe *n* raillerie, moquerie *f*.
jigsaw *n* puzzle *m*.
jinx *n* porte-malheur *m invar*.
job *n* travail *m*.
jockey *n* jockey *m*.
jocular *adj* joyeux; facétieux.
jog *vi* faire du jogging.
join *vt* joindre, unir.
joint *n* articulation *f*:—*adj* commun.
joke *n* blague:—*vi* blaguer.
joker *n* blagueur *m*, -euse *f*.
jolly *adj* gai, joyeux.
jostle *vt* bousculer.
journal *n* revue *f*.
journalism *n* journalisme *m*.
journalist *n* journaliste *mf*.
journey *n* voyage *m*:—*vi* voyager.
joy *n* joie *f*.
joyful *adj* joyeux.
jubilation *n* jubilation *f*.
jubilee *n* jubilé *m*.
Judaism *n* judaïsme *m*.
judge *n* juge *m*:—*vt* juger.
judgment *n* jugement *m*.
judicious *adj* judicieux.
judo *n* judo *m*.

jug *n* cruche *f.*

juggle *vi* jongler.

juice *n* jus *m;* suc *m.*

juicy *adj* juteux.

July *n* juillet *m.*

jumble *vt* mélanger:—*n* mélange *m.*

jump *vi* sauter:—*n* saut *m.*

June *n* juin *m.*

jungle *n* jungle *f.*

junior *adj* plus jeune.

jurisdiction *n* juridiction *f.*

juror *n* juré *m.*

jury *n* jury *m.*

just *adj* juste:—*adv* justement, exactement.

justice *n* justice *f.*

justification *n* justification *f.*

justify *vt* justifier.

juvenile *adj* juvénile.

juxtaposition *n* juxtaposition *f.*

K

kaleidoscope *n* kaléidoscope *m.*

kangaroo *n* kangourou *m.*

keen *adj* enthousiaste; vif.

keenness *n* enthousiasme *m.*

keep *vt* garder, conserver.

kernel *n* amande *f;* noyau *m.*

kettle *n* bouilloire *f.*

key *n* clé, clef *f; (mus)* ton *m;* touche *f.*

keyboard *n* clavier *m.*

key ring *n* porte-clefs *m invar.*

keystone *n* clef de voûte *f.*

kick *vi (vt)* donner un coup de pied (à).

kidnap *vt* kidnapper.

kidney *n* rein *m;* rognon *m.*

killer *n* assassin *m.*

killing *n* assassinat *m.*

kiln *n* four *m.*

kilo *n* kilo *m.*

kilogram *n* kilogramme *m.*

kilometre *n* kilomètre *m.*

kin *n* parents *mpl.*

kind *adj* gentil:—*n* genre *m.*

kindle *vt* allumer:—*vi* s'allumer.

kindliness *n* gentillesse, bonté *f.*

kindly *adj* bon, bienveillant.

kindness *n* bonté *f.*

king *n* roi *m.*

kingdom *n* royaume *m.*

kiss *n* baiser *m:—vt* embrasser.

kit *n* équipement *m.*

kitchen *n* cuisine *f.*

kitten *n* chaton *m.*

knack *n* don, chic *m.*

knead *vt* pétrir.

knee *n* genou *m.*

kneel *vi* s'agenouiller.

knife *n* couteau *m.*

knight *n* chevalier *m.*

knit *vt vi* tricoter.

knob *n* bouton *m.*

knock *vt vi* cogner, frapper:—*n* coup *m.*

knot *n* nœud *m:—vt* nouer.

know *vt vi* savoir; connaître.

know-how *n* savoir-faire *m.*

knowledge *n* connaissances *fpl.*

knowledgeable *adj* bien informé.

knuckle *n* articulation *f.*

L

label *n* étiquette *f*.

laboratory *n* laboratoire *m*.

labour *n* travail *m*:—*vi* travailler.

labourer *n* ouvrier *m*.

labourious *adj* laborieux.

lace *vt* lacer.

lacerate *vt* lacérer.

lack *vt* manquer de:—*vi* manquer:— *n* manque *m*.

lad *n* garçon *m*.

ladder *n* échelle *f*.

lady *n* dame *f*.

lag *vi* se laisser distancer.

lagoon *n* lagune *f*.

lair *n* repaire *m*.

lake *n* lac *m*.

lame *adj* boiteux.

lament *vt* se lamenter sur:—*n* lamentation *f*.

lamentable *adj* lamentable.

lamentation *n* lamentation *f*.

lamp *n* lampe *f*.

lance *n* lance *f*:—*vt* inciser.

lancet *n* bistouri *m*.

land *n* pays *m*; terre *f*:—*vi* atterrir.

landlord *n* propriétaire *m*.

landmark *n* point de repère *m*.

landscape *n* paysage *m*.

landslide *n* glissement de terrain *m*.

lane *n* allée, ruelle *f*; file *f*.

language *n* langue *f*; langage *m*.

languish *vi* languir.

lantern *n* lanterne *f*.

lapel *n* revers *m*.

lapse *n* laps *m*; défaillance *f*:—*vi* expirer.

larder *n* garde-manger *m invar*.

large *adj* grand:—**at ~** en liberté.

larva *n* larve *f*.

lascivious *adj* lascif.

lash *n* coup de fouet *m*:—*vt* fouetter

last *adj* dernier:—*vi* durer.

last-minute *adj* de dernière minute.

late *adj* en retard; défunt:—*adv* tard: —**~ly** *adv* récemment.

latent *adj* latent.

lateral *ad* latérale.

lather *n* mousse *f*.

latitude *n* latitude *f*.

laudable *adj* louable.

laugh *vi* rire:—**to ~ at** *vt* rire de:—*n* rire *m*.

laughter *n* rires *mpl*.

launch *vt* lancer:—*vi* se lancer.

laundry *n* lessive *f*.

lava *n* lave *f*.

lavatory *n* toilettes *fpl*.

lavish *adj* prodigue:—*vt* prodiguer.

law *n* loi *f*; droit *m*.

lawful *adj* légal; légitime.

lawmaker *n* législateur *m*, -trice *f*.

lawn *n* pelouse *f*, gazon *m*.

lawyer *n* avocat *m*; notaire *m*.

lax *adj* relâché.

laxative *n* laxatif *m*.

lay *vt* mettre; pondre.

layer *n* couche *f*.

laziness *n* paresse *f*.

lazy *adj* paresseux.

lead *n* plomb *m*:—*vt vi* conduire, mener.

leader *n* chef *m*.

leadership n direction f.

leading adj principal; premier.

leaf n feuille f.

leaflet n feuillet m.

league n ligue f; lieue f.

leak n fuite f:—vi (mar) faire eau.

lean vi s'appuyer:—adj maigre.

leap vi sauter:—n saut m.

learn vt vi apprendre.

learning n érudition f.

lease n bail m:—vt louer.

leash n laisse f.

least adj moindre:—at ~ au moins.

leather n cuir m.

leave n permission f; congé m:—vt laisser.

lecture n conférence f:—vi faire une conférence.

lecturer n conférencier m, -ière f.

leeway n liberté d'action f.

left adj gauche.

left-handed adj gaucher.

left-luggage office n consigne f.

leftovers npl restes mpl.

leg n jambe f; patte f.

legal adj légal, légitime.

legality n légalité, légitimité f.

legalize vt légaliser.

legend n légende f.

legendary adj légendaire.

legible adj lisible.

legion n légion f.

legislate vi, vt légiférer.

legislation n législation f.

legislative adj législatif.

legislature n corps législatif m.

legitimacy n légitimité f.

legitimate adj légitime:—vt légitimer.

leisure n loisir m:—-ly adj tranquille.

lemon n citron m.

lemonade n limonade f.

lend vt prêter.

length n longueur f; durée f:—at ~ longuement.

lengthen vt allonger:—vi s'allonger.

lengthy adj long.

lenient adj indulgent.

lens n lentille f.

leotard n justaucorps m.

lesbian n lesbienne f.

less adj moins:—adv moins.

lessen vt vi diminuer.

lesser adj moindre.

lesson n leçon f.

let vt laisser, permettre.

lethal adj mortel.

lethargic adj léthargique.

lethargy n léthargie f.

letter n lettre f.

lettering n inscription f.

lettuce n salade f.

level adj plat, égal:—n niveau m:—vt niveler.

lever n levier m.

levity n légèreté f.

liability n responsabilité f.

liable adj sujet (à); responsable.

liaise vi effectuer une liaison.

liaison n liaison f.

liar n menteur m, -euse f.

liberal adj libéral; généreux.

liberate vt libérer.

liberation n libération f.

liberty n liberté f.

librarian n bibliothécaire mf.

library n bibliothèque f.

licence n licence f; permis m.

lick vt lécher.

lid n couvercle m.

lie n mensonge m:—vi mentir; être allongé.

lieu n:—in ~ of au lieu de.

life n vie f.

life jacket *n* gilet de sauvetage *m*.

lifeless *adj* mort; sans vie.

life sentence *n* condamnation à perpétuité *f*.

life-sized *adj* grandeur nature.

lift *vt* lever.

ligament *n* ligament *m*.

light *n* lumière *f*:—*adj* léger; clair:—*vt* allumer.

lighten *vi* s'éclaircir:—*vt* éclairer; éclaircir.

lighthouse *n* (*mar*) phare *m*.

lighting *n* éclairage *m*.

lightning *n* éclair *m*.

light year *n* année-lumière *f*.

like *adj* pareil:—*adv* comme:—*vt vi* aimer.

likelihood *n* probabilité *f*.

likely *adj* probable, vraisemblable.

liken *vt* comparer.

likeness *n* ressemblance *f*.

likewise *adv* pareillement.

liking *n* goût *m*.

limb *n* membre *m*.

limit *n* limite *f*:—*vt* limiter.

limitation *n* limitation *f*; restriction *f*.

limp *vi* boiter:—*n* boitement *m*:—*adj* mou.

line *n* ligne *f*; ride *f*:—*vt* rayer; rider.

linear *adj* linéaire.

liner *n* transatlantique *m*.

linger *vi* traîner.

linguist *n* linguiste *mf*.

linguistic *adj* linguistique.

link *n* chaînon *m*:—*vt* relier.

lion *n* lion *m*.

lip *n* lèvre *f*; bord *m*.

lip-read *vi* lire sur les lèvres.

lipstick *n* rouge à lèvres *m*.

liqueur *n* liqueur *f*.

liquid *adj* liquide:—*n* liquide *m*.

liquidize *vt* liquéfier.

liquor *n* spiritueux *m*.

lisp *vi* zézayer:—*n* zézaiement *m*.

list *n* liste *f*:—*vt* faire une liste de.

listen *vi* écouter.

literal *adj* littéral.

literary *adj* littéraire.

literature *n* littérature *f*.

litigation *n* litige *m*.

litigious *adj* litigieux.

litre *n* litre *m*.

litter *n* litière *f*; ordures *fpl*:—*vt* recouvrir.

little *adj* petit:—*n* peu *m*.

live *vi* vivre; habiter:—*adj* vivant.

livelihood *n* moyens de subsistance *mpl*.

liveliness *n* vivacité *f*.

lively *adj* vif.

liver *n* foie *m*.

livid *adj* livide; furieux.

living *n* vie *f*:—*adj* vivant.

living room *n* salle de séjour *f*.

load *vt* charger:—*n* charge *f*.

loaf *n* pain *m*.

loan *n* prêt *m*.

loathe *vt* détester.

loathing *n* aversion *f*.

lobster *n* langouste *f*.

local *adj* local.

locate *vt* localiser.

location *n* situation *f*.

lock *n* serrure *f*:—*vt* fermer à clé.

locker *n* casier *m*.

lockout *n* grève patronale *f*.

locomotive *n* locomotive *f*.

lodge *vi* se loger.

lodger *n* locataire *mf*.

log *n* bûche *f*.

logic *n* logique *f*.

logical *adj* logique.

loiter *vi* s'attarder.

lollipop *n* sucette *f*.

lonely *adj* seul, solitaire.
loneliness *n* solitude *f*.
long *adj* long, *f* longue:—*vi* désirer.
longevity *n* longévité *f*.
longing *n* désir *m*.
long-range *adj* à longue portée.
long-term *adj* à long terme.
look *vi* regarder; sembler:—*n* aspect *m*; regard *m*.
loop *n* boucle *f*.
loose *adj* lâché; desserré
loosen *vt* lâcher; desserrer.
loot *vt* piller:—*n* butin *m*.
loquacious *adj* loquace.
loquacity *n* loquacité *f*.
lose *vt vi* perdre.
loss *n* perte *f*.
lot *n* sort *f*; lot *m*:—**a ~** beaucoup.
lotion *n* lotion *f*.
loud *adj* fort, bruyant.
loudspeaker *n* haut-parleur *m*.
lounge *n* salon *m*.
lovable *adj* sympathique.
love *n* amour *m*:—*vt* aimer.
loveliness *n* beauté *f*.
lovely *adj* beau.
lover *n* amant *m*.
loving *adj* affectueux.
low *adj* bas:—*vi* meugler.

lower *vt* baisser.
lowly *adj* humble.
loyal *adj* loyal, fidèle.
loyalty *n* loyauté *f*; fidélité *f*.
lucid *adj* lucide.
luck *n* chance *f*.
luckless *adj* malchanceux.
lucky *adj* chanceux.
lucrative *adj* lucratif.
ludicrous *adj* absurde.
luggage *n* bagages *mpl*.
lukewarm *adj* tiède.
lull *vt* bercer:—*n* répit *m*.
luminous *adj* lumineux.
lump *n* bosse *f*; grosseur *f*.
lunch *n* déjeuner *m*.
lungs *npl* poumons *mpl*.
lure *n* leurre *m*; attrait *m*:—*vt* séduire, attirer.
lurk *vi* se cacher.
lush *adj* luxuriant.
lust *n* luxure *f*:—*vi* désirer.
lustre *n* lustre *m*.
luxuriance *n* luxuriance *f*.
luxuriant *adj* luxuriant.
luxurious *adj* luxueux.
luxury *n* luxe *m*.
lyrical *adj* lyrique.
lyrics *npl* paroles *fpl*.

M

macerate *vt* macérer.
machination *n* machination *f*.
machine *n* machine *f*.
machinery *n* machinerie *f*; mécanisme *m*.

mad *adj* fou, *f* folle; insensé.
madam *n* madame *f*.
madden *vt* rendre fou; rendre furieux.
madman *n* fou *m*.

madness n folie f.

magazine n magazine m, revue f; magasin m.

magic n magie f:—adj magique.

magnanimous adj magnanime.

magnet n aimant m.

magnetic adj magnétique.

magnetism n magnétisme m.

magnificence n magnificence f.

magnificent ad magnifique.

magnify vt grossir; exagérer.

magnitude n magnitude f.

maid n bonne f.

mail n courrier m.

mail train n (rail) train-poste m.

maim vt mutiler.

main adj principal; essentiel:—in the ~ en général.

mainland n continent m.

main line n (rail) grande ligne f.

main street n rue principale f.

maintain vt maintenir; soutenir.

maintenance n entretien m.

majestic adj majestueux.

majesty n majesté f.

major adj majeur.

majority n majorité f.

make vt faire n marque f.

makeshift adj improvisé, de fortune.

make-up n maquillage m.

malady n maladie f.

malaise n malaise m.

malaria n malaria f.

malcontent adj n mécontent m, -e f.

male adj mâle; masculin:—n mâle m.

malevolence n malveillance f.

malevolent adj malveillant.

malice n malice f.

malicious adj méchant.

malign adj nocif:—vt calomnier.

malleable adj malléable.

malnutrition n malnutrition f.

malpractice n négligence f.

maltreat vt maltraiter.

mammal n mammifère m.

man n homme m.

manage vt diriger; réussir:—vi réussir.

management n direction f.

manager n directeur m.

managing director n directeur général m.

mandate n mandat m.

mandatory n obligatoire.

manhandle vt maltraiter; manutentionner.

maniac n maniaque mf.

manic adj maniaque.

manifest adj manifeste:—vt manifester.

manifestation n manifestation f.

manipulate vt manipuler.

manipulation n manipulation f.

mankind n humanité f.

manliness n virilité f.

manly adj viril.

man-made n artificiel.

manner n manière f.

manoeuvre n manœuvre f.

manual adj n manuel m.

manufacture n fabrication f.

manufacturer n fabricant m.

manuscript n manuscrit m.

many adj beaucoup de:—how ~? combien?

map n carte f; plan m.

mar vt gâter, gâcher.

marble n marbre m:—adj marbré.

March n mars m.

march n marche f:—vi marcher.

margarine n margarine f.

margin n marge f; bord m.

marginal *adj* marginal.

marine *adj* marin.

maritime *adj* maritime.

mark *n* marque *f*; signe *m*:—*vt* marquer.

marker *n* marque *f*; marqueur *m*.

market *n* marché *m*.

marketable *adj* vendable.

marmalade *n* confiture d'oranges *f*.

marriage *n* mariage *m*.

marriageable *adj* mariable.

married *adj* marié; conjugal.

marry *vi* se marier.

marsh *n* marécage *m*.

marshy *adj* marécageux.

martial *adj* martial.

martyr *n* martyr *m*, -e *f*.

marvel *n* merveille *f*:—*vi* s'émerveiller.

marvellous *adj* merveilleux.

masculine *adj* masculin, viril.

mask *n* masque *m*:—*vt* masquer.

mason *n* maçon *m*.

mass *n* masse *f*; messe *f*; multitude *f*.

massacre *n* massacre *m*:—*vt* massacrer.

massage *n* massage *m*.

massive *adj* énorme.

mast *n* mât *m*.

master *n* maître *m*:—*vt* maîtriser.

mastermind *vt* diriger.

mastery *n* maîtrise *f*.

match *n* allumette *f*:—*vt* égaler.

matchless *adj* incomparable, sans pareil.

mate *n* camarade *mf*:—*vt* accoupler.

material *adj* matériel.

maternal *adj* maternel.

maternity hospital *n* maternité *f*.

mathematical *adj* mathématique.

mathematics *npl* mathématiques *fpl*.

matrimonial *adj* matrimonial.

matted *adj* emmêlé.

matter *n* matière, substance *f*:—*vi* importer.

mattress *n* matelas *m*.

mature *adj* mûr:—*vi* mûrir.

maturity *n* maturité *f*.

maximum *n* maximum *m*.

may *v aux* pouvoir:—**be** peut-être.

May *n* mai *m*.

mayor *n* maire *m*.

maze *n* labyrinthe *m*.

me *pn* moi; me.

meadow *n* prairie *f*, pré *m*.

meagre *adj* pauvre.

meal *n* repas *m*.

mean *adj* avare, mesquin; moyen:— ~s *npl* moyens *mpl*:—*vt vi* signifier.

meander *vi* serpenter.

meaning *n* sens *m*.

meanness *n* avarice, mesquinerie *f*.

meantime *adv* pendant ce temps-là.

measure *n* mesure *f*:—*vt* mesurer.

measurement *n* mesure *f*.

meat *n* viande *f*.

mechanic *n* mécanicien *m*.

mechanical *adj* mécanique.

mechanism *n* mécanisme *m*.

medal *n* médaille *f*.

media *npl* média *mpl*.

mediate *vi* agir en tant que médiateur.

mediator *n* médiateur *m*, -trice *f*.

medical *adj* médical.

medicinal *adj* médicinal.

medicine *n* médecine *f*.

mediocre *adj* médiocre.

meditate *vi* méditer.

meditation *n* méditation *f*.

meditative *adj* méditatif.

Mediterranean *adj* méditerranéen.

medium *n* milieu *m*; médium *m*:— *adj* moyen.

medium wave *n* ondes moyennes *fpl*.

meek *adj* doux.

meekness *n* douceur *f*.

meet *vt* rencontrer:—*vi* se rencontrer.

meeting *n* réunion *f*; congrès *m*.

melancholy *n* mélancolie *f*:—*adj* mélancolique.

mellow *adj* mûr; doux:—*vi* mûrir.

melody *n* mélodie *f*.

melon *n* melon *m*.

melt *vt* faire fondre:—*vi* fondre.

member *n* membre *m*.

memorable *adj* mémorable.

memorandum *n* mémorandum *m*.

memorize *vt* mémoriser.

memory *n* mémoire *f*; souvenir *m*.

menace *n* menace *f*.

mend *vt* réparer; raccommoder.

menial *adj* vil.

menstruation *n* menstruation *f*.

mental *adj* mental.

mentality *n* mentalité *f*.

mention *n* mention *f*:—*vt* mentionner.

menu *n* menu *m*.

mercantile *adj* commercial.

mercenary *adj n* mercenaire *f*.

merchandise *n* marchandise *f*.

merchant *n* négociant *m*, -e *f*.

merciful *adj* miséricordieux.

mercy *n* pitié *f*.

mere *adj* simple.

merge *vt vi* fusionner.

merger *n* fusion *f*.

merit *n* mérite *m*:—*vt* mériter.

merry *adj* joyeux.

mesh *n* maille *f*.

mesmerize *vt* hypnotiser.

mess *n* désordre *m*; confusion *f*.

message *n* message *m*.

messenger *n* messager *m*, -ère *f*.

metal *n* métal *m*.

metallic *adj* métallique.

meteorological *adj* météorologique.

meteorology *n* météorologie *f*.

meter *n* compteur *m*; mètre *m*.

method *n* méthode *f*.

methodical *adj*, **~ly** *adv* méthodique(ment).

metropolitan *adj* métropolitain.

mew *vi* miauler.

microphone *n* microphone *m*.

microscope *n* microscope *m*.

mid *adj* demi; mi-.

midday *n* midi *m*.

middle *adj* moyen; du milieu:—*n* milieu *m*.

middling *adj* moyen.

midnight *n* minuit *m*.

midway *adv* à mi-chemin.

midwife *n* sage-femme *f*.

might *n* force *f*.

mighty *adj* fort, puissant.

migrate *vi* émigrer.

migration *n* émigration *f*.

mild *adj* doux; modéré.

mildness *n* douceur *f*.

mile *n* mille *m*.

militant *adj* militant.

militate *vi* militer.

milk *n* lait *m*:—*vt* traire.

milky *adj* laiteux.

mill *n* moulin *m*:—*vt* moudre.

millimetre *n* millimètre *m*.

million *n* million *m*.

millionaire *n* millionaire *mf*.

millionth *adj n* millionième *mf*.

mime *n* mime *m*.

mimic *vt* mimer.

mimicry *n* mimique *f*.

mince *vt* hacher.

mind *n* esprit *m*:—*vt* prendre soin de.

minded *adj* disposé.

mindful *adj* conscient; attentif.

mine *pn* le mien, la mienne, les mien(ne)s; à moi:—*n* mine *f*.

miner n mineur m.
mineral adj n minéral m.
mingle vt mêler.
miniature n miniature f.
minimize vt minimiser.
minimum n minimum m.
minister n ministre m:—vt servir.
ministry n ministère m.
minor adj mineur:—n mineur m, -e f.
minority n minorité f.
minus adv moins.
minute adj minuscule.
minute n minute f.
miracle n miracle m.
miraculous adj miraculeux.
mirage n mirage m.
mirror n miroir m.
misadventure n mésaventure f.
misbehave vi se conduire mal.
misbehaviour n mauvaise conduite f.
miscarriage n fausse couche f.
miscellaneous adj divers, varié.
miscellany n mélange, assortiment m.
mischief n mal, tort m.
mischievous adj mauvais; espiègle.
misconception n méprise f.
misconduct n mauvaise conduite f.
misdeed n méfait m.
misdemeanour n délit m.
miser n avare mf.
miserable adj malheureux.
misery n malheur m; misère f.
misfortune n infortune f.
misgovern vt mal gouverner.
mishap n mésaventure f.
misjudge vt méjuger.
mislead vt induire en erreur.
misogynist n misogyne mf.
misprint n coquille f.
Miss n Mlle, Mademoiselle f.
miss vt rater; s'ennuyer de.
missing adj perdu; absent.

mission n mission f.
mist n brouillard m.
mistake vt confondre:—vi se tromper:—n erreur f.
Mister n Monsieur m.
mistress n maîtresse f.
mistrust vt se méfier de:—n méfiance f.
misty adj brumeux.
misunderstanding n malentendu m.
misuse vt faire un mauvais usage de.
mitigate vt atténuer.
mitigation n atténuation f.
mix vt mélanger.
mixed adj mélangé; mixte.
mixture n mélange m.
moan n gémissement m:—vi gémir.
moat n fossé m.
mob n foule f; masse f.
mobile adj mobile.
mobility n mobilité f.
mobilize vt mobiliser.
mock vt se moquer de.
mockery n moquerie f.
mode n mode m.
model n modèle m:—vt modeler.
moderate adj modéré:—vt modérer.
moderation n modération f.
modern adj moderne.
modernize vt moderniser.
modest adj modeste.
modesty n modestie f.
modification n modification f.
modify vt modifier.
moist adj humide.
moisten vt humidifier.
moisture n humidité f.
molest vt importuner.
molten adj fondu.
moment n moment m.
momentary adj momentané.
monastery n monastère m.

monastic *adj* monastique.
Monday *n* lundi *m*.
monetary *adj* monétaire.
money *n* argent *m*; pièce de monnaie *f*.
monk *n* moine *m*.
monkey *n* singe *m*.
monopolize *vt* monopoliser.
monopoly *n* monopole *m*.
monotonous *adj* monotone.
monotony *n* monotonie *f*.
monster *n* monstre *m*.
monstrous *adj* monstrueux.
month *n* mois *m*.
monthly *adj* mensuel; *adv* mensuellement.
mood *n* humeur *f*.
moon *n* lune *f*.
moonlight *n* clair de lune *m*.
moped *n* vélomoteur *m*.
moral *adj* moral:—**s** *npl* moralité *f*.
morale *n* moral *m*.
morality *n* moralité *f*.
morbid *adj* morbide.
more *adj adv* plus:—**~ and ~** de plus en plus.
moreover *adv* de plus, en outre.
morning *n* matin *m*:—**good ~** bonjour.
morsel *n* bouchée *f*; morceau *m*.
mortal *adj* mortel:—*n* mortel *m*, -elle *f*.
mortality *n* mortalité *f*.
mortgage *n* hypothèque *f*:—*vt* hypothéquer.
mortuary *n* morgue *f*.
mosque *n* mosquée *f*.
most *adj pn* la plupart de:—**ly** *adv* surtout, essentiellement.
mother *n* mère *f*.
motherhood *n* maternité *f*.
mother-in-law *n* belle-mère *f*.
motherly *adj* maternel.

mother tongue *n* langue maternelle *f*.
motif *n* motif *m*.
motion *n* mouvement *m*.
motionless *adj* immobile.
motivated *adj* motivé.
motive *n* motif *m*.
motor *n* moteur *m*.
motorbike *n* moto *f*.
motor vehicle *n* automobile *f*.
motto *n* devise *f*.
mould *n* moule *m*:—*vt* mouler.
mound *n* monticule *m*.
mount *n* mont *m*:—*vt* gravir.
mountain *n* montagne *f*.
mountaineer *n* alpiniste *mf*.
mountainous *adj* montagneux.
mourn *vt* pleurer.
mourning *n* deuil *m*.
mouse *n* (*pl* mice) souris *f*.
moustache *n* moustache *f*.
mouth *n* bouche *f*; embouchure *f*.
mouthful *n* bouchée *f*.
movable *adj* mobile.
move *vt* déplacer:—*vi* bouger:—*n* mouvement *m*.
movement *n* mouvement *m*.
moving *adj* touchant, émouvant.
mow *vt* tondre.
Mrs *n* Mme, Madame *f*.
much *adj pn* beaucoup:—*adv* beaucoup, très.
mud *n* boue *f*.
muddy *adj* boueux.
multiple *adj* multiple.
multiplication *n* multiplication *f*.
multiply *vt* multiplier.
multitude *n* multitude *f*.
mumble *vt vi* grommeler.
munch *vt* mâcher.
mundane *adj* banal.
municipal *adj* municipal.
mural *n* mural *m*.

murder *n* meurtre *m*:—*vt* assassiner.
murderer *n* assassin, meurtrier *m*.
murky *adj* obscur.
murmur *n* murmure *m*:—*vt vi* murmurer.
muscle *n* muscle *m*.
muscular *adj* musculaire.
museum *n* musée *m*.
music *n* musique *f*.
musical *adj* musical; mélodieux.
musician *n* musicien *m*, -ienne *f*.
must *v aux* devoir.
musty *adj* moisi.

mute *adj* muet, silencieux.
mutilate *vt* mutiler.
mutilation *n* mutilation *f*.
mutter *vt vi* grommeler:—*n* grom-
mellement *m*.
mutual *adj* mutuel, réciproque.
my *pn* mon, ma, mes.
myriad *n* myriade *f*.
myself *pn* moi-même.
mysterious *adj* mystérieux.
mystery *n* mystère *m*.
myth *n* mythe *m*.
mythology *n* mythologie *f*.

N

nag *vt* harceler.
nail *n* ongle *m*; clou *m*:—*vt* clouer.
naive *adj* naïf.
naked *adj* nu; dénudé; pur.
name *n* nom *m*:—*vt* nommer.
nap *n* sieste *f*, somme *m*.
nape *n* nuque *f*.
napkin *n* serviette *f*.
narrate *vt* narrer, raconter.
narrative *adj* narratif:—*n* narration *f*.
narrow *adj* étroit.
nasty *adj* méchant; mauvais.
nation *n* nation *f*.
national *adj* national.
nationalist *adj n* nationaliste *mf*.
nationality *n* nationalité *f*.
native *adj* natal:—*n* autochtone *mf*.
natural *adj* naturel.
naturalist *n* naturaliste *mf*.
nature *n* nature *f*; sorte *f*.

naughty *adj* méchant.
nausea *n* nausée.
nauseous *adj* écœurant.
navel *n* nombril *m*.
navigate *vi* naviguer.
navigation *n* navigation *f*.
navy *n* marine *f*.
near *prep* près de:—*adv* près; à
côté:—*adj* proche.
nearly *adv* presque.
neat *adj* soigné; net.
necessary *adj* nécessaire.
necessitate *vt* nécessiter.
necessity *n* nécessité *f*.
neck *n* cou *m*.
necklace *n* collier *m*.
need *n* besoin *m*:—*vt* avoir besoin de.
needle *n* aiguille *f*.
needy *adj* nécessiteux.
negation *n* négation *f*.

negative *adj* négatif:—*n* négative *f.*

neglect *vt* négliger:—*n* négligence *f.*

negligence *n* négligence *f.*

negligent *adj* négligent.

negotiate *vt vi* négocier.

negotiation *n* négociation *f.*

Negro *adj* noir:—*n* Noire *m.*

neighbour *n* voisin *m*, -e *f.*

neighbouring *adj* voisin.

neither *conj* ni:—*pn* aucun(e), ni l'un(e) ni l'autre.

nephew *n* neveu *m.*

nerve *n* nerf *m*; courage *m.*

nervous *adj* nerveux.

nest *n* nid *m*; nichée *f.*

net *n* filet *m.*

net curtain *n* voile *m.*

nettle *n* ortie *f.*

network *n* réseau *f.*

neutral *adj* neutre.

neutrality *n* neutralité *f.*

never *adv* jamais.

nevertheless *adv* cependant, néanmoins.

new *adj* neuf; nouveau.

newborn *adj* nouveau-né, *f* nouveau-née.

news *npl* nouvelles, informations *fpl.*

newspaper *n* journal *m.*

New Year *n* Nouvel An *m*:—~'s Day *n* Jour du Nouvel An *m*:—~'s Eve Saint-Sylvestre *f.*

next *adj* prochain:—*adv* ensuite, après.

nibble *vt* mordiller.

nice *adj* gentil, *f* gentille; agréable.

niche *n* niche *f.*

nickname *n* surnom *m*:—*vt* surnommer.

niece *n* nièce *f.*

night *n* nuit *f*:—**good ~** bonne nuit.

nightly *adv* toutes les nuits:—*adj* nocturne.

nightmare *n* cauchemar *m.*

nimble *adj* léger; agile.

nine *adj n* neuf *m.*

nineteen *adj n* dix-neuf *m.*

nineteenth *adj n* dix-neuvième *mf.*

ninetieth *adj n* quatre-vingt-dixième *mf.*

ninety *adj n* quatre-vingt-dix *m.*

ninth *adj n* neuvième *mf.*

no *adv* non:—*adj* aucun; pas de.

noble *adj* noble:—*n* noble *mf.*

nobody *pn* personne.

nocturnal *adj* nocturne.

nod *n* signe de tête *m*:—*vi* faire un signe de la tête.

noise *n* bruit *m.*

noisiness *n* bruit, tapage *m.*

nominal *adj* nominal.

nominate *vt* nommer.

nomination *n* nomination *f.*

nonchalant *adj* nonchalant.

none *pn* aucun; personne.

nonentity *n* nullité *f.*

nonetheless *adv* cependant.

nonplussed *adj* perplexe.

nonsense *n* absurdité *f.*

nonsensical *adj* absurde.

nonstop *adj* direct.

noon *n* midi *m.*

nor *conj* ni.

normal *adj* normal.

north *n* nord *m*:—*adj* du nord.

northeast *n* nord-est *m.*

northern *adj* du nord.

northwest *n* nord-ouest *m.*

nose *n* nez *m.*

nostalgia *n* nostalgie *f.*

nostril *n* narine *f.*

not *adv* pas; non.

notable *adj* notable.

note *n* note *f*; billet *m*:—*vt* noter, marquer.

notebook *n* carnet *m*.

nothing *n* rien *m*.

notice *n* notice *f*; avis *m*:—*vt* remarquer.

noticeable *adj* visible.

notify *vt* notifier.

notion *n* notion *f*; idée *f*.

notoriety *n* notoriété *f*.

notorious *adj* notoire.

nourish *vt* nourrir, alimenter.

nourishment *n* nourriture *f*, aliments *mpl*.

novel *n* roman *m*.

novelty *n* nouveauté *f*.

November *n* novembre *m*.

novice *n* novice *mf*.

now *adv* maintenant.

nowadays *adv* de nos jours.

nowhere *adv* nulle part.

nuance *n* nuance *f*.

nuclear *adj* nucléaire.

nude *adj* nu.

nudity *n* nudité *f*.

nuisance *n* ennui *m*; gêne *f*.

null *adj* nul.

numb *adj* engourdi:—*vt* engourdir.

number *n* numéro, nombre *m*:—*vt* numéroter.

numbness *n* engourdissement *m*.

numeral *n* chiffre *m*.

numerical *adj* numérique.

nurse *n* infirmière *f*:—*vt* soigner.

nursery *n* crèche *f*.

nurture *vt* élever.

nut *n* noix *f*.

nutritious *adj* nutritif.

nylon *n* nylon *m*.

O

oak *n* chêne *m*.

oar *n* rame *f*.

oath *n* serment *m*.

obedience *n* obéissance *f*.

obedient *adj* obéissant.

obese *adj* obèse.

obesity *n* obésité *f*.

obey *vt* obéir à.

object *n* objet *m*:—*vt* objecter.

objection *n* objection *f*.

objective *adj n* objectif *m*.

obligation *n* obligation *f*.

obligatory *adj* obligatoire.

oblige *vt* obliger.

obliging *adj* obligeant.

oblique *adj* oblique.

oblivious *adj* oublieux.

obnoxious *adj* odieux.

obscene *adj* obscène.

obscure *adj* obscur:—*vt* obscurcir.

obscurity *n* obscurité *f*.

observant *adj* observateur.

observation *n* observation *f*.

observatory *n* observatoire *m*.

observe *vt* observer.

obsess *vt* obséder.

obsessive *adj* obsédant.

obsolete *adj* désuet.

obstacle *n* obstacle *m*.

obstinate *adj* obstiné.

obstruct *vt* obstruer; entraver.

obstruction *n* obstruction *f*; encombrement *m*.

obtain *vt* obtenir.

obtainable *adj* disponible.

obvious *adj* évident.

occasion *n* occasion *f*:—*vt* occasionner.

occasional *adj* occasionnel.

occupant *n* occupant *m*, -e *f*.

occupation *n* occupation *f*; emploi *m*.

occupy *vt* occuper.

occur *vi* se produire, arriver.

occurrence *n* incident *m*.

ocean *n* océan *m*.

oceanic *adj* océanique.

October *n* octobre *m*.

odd *adj* impair; étrange.

odious *adj* odieux.

odour *n* odeur *f*; parfum *m*.

of *prep* de; à.

off *adj* éteint; fermé; annulé.

offend *vt* offenser, blesser.

offense *n* offense *f*; injure *f*.

offensive *adj* offensant.

offer *vt* offrir:—*n* offre *f*.

office *n* bureau *m*; poste *m*.

officer *n* officier *m*; fonctionnaire *mf*.

official *adj* officiel:—*n* employé *m*, -e *f*.

officiate *vi* officier.

offset *vt* compenser; décaler.

offshore *adj* côtier.

offspring *n* progéniture *f*.

oil *n* huile *f*:—*vt* huiler.

oil painting *n* peinture à l'huile *f*.

oil tanker *n* pétrolier *m*.

ointment *n* onguent *m*.

O.K., okay *excl* O.K., d'accord.

old *adj* vieux, *f* vieille.

old age *n* vieillesse *f*.

olive *n* olivier *m*; olive *f*.

olive oil *n* huile d'olive *f*.

omelette *n* omelette *f*.

omission *n* omission *f*; négligence *f*.

omit *vt* omettre.

on *prep* sur, dessus; en; pour:—*adj* allumé, branché.

once *adv* une fois:—~ **more** encore une fois.

one *adj* un, une.

onerous *adj* lourd; onéreux.

oneself *pn* soi-même.

one-sided *adj* partial.

onion *n* oignon *m*.

onlooker *n* spectateur *m*, -trice *f*.

only *adj* seul, unique:—*adv* seulement.

onus *n* responsabilité *f*.

opaque *adj* opaque.

open *adj* ouvert; sincère, franc:—*vt* ouvrir; *vi* s'ouvrir.

opening *n* ouverture *f*.

openness *n* clareté *f*.

opera *n* opéra *m*.

operate *vi* fonctionner; opérer.

operation *n* fonctionnement *m*; opération *f*.

operator *n* opérateur *m*, -trice *f*.

opine *vt* être d'avis (que).

opinion *n* opinion *f*; jugement *m*.

opinion poll *n* sondage *m*.

opponent *n* opposant *m*, -e *f*.

opportune *adj* opportun.

opportunity *n* occasion *f*.

oppose *vt* s'opposer à.

opposing *adj* opposé.

opposite *adj* opposé:—*adv* en face:—*prep* en face de:—*n* contraire *m*.

opposition *n* opposition *f*.

oppress *vt* opprimer.

oppressive *adj* oppressif.

optimist *n* optimiste *mf*.
optimistic *adj* optimiste.
optimum *adj* optimum.
option *n* option *f*.
optional *adj* optionnel.
opulent *adj* opulent.
or *conj* ou.
oral *adj* oral, verbal.
orange *n* orange *f*.
orbit *n* orbite *f*.
orchestra *n* orchestre *m*.
ordain *vt* ordonner.
order *n* ordre *m*; commande *f*:—*vt* ordonner.
orderly *adj* ordonné; réglé.
ordinary *adj* ordinaire.
ore *n* minerai *m*.
organ *n* organe *m*.
organic *adj* organique.
organism *n* organisme *m*.
organization *n* organisation *f*.
organize *vt* organiser.
oriental *adj* oriental.
orifice *n* orifice *m*.
origin *n* origine *f*.
original *adj* original.
originality *n* originalité *f*.
ornament *n* ornement *m*:—*vt* ornementer.
ornate *adj* ornementé.
orphan *adj n* orphelin *m*, -e *f*.
orthodox *adj* orthodoxe.
oscillate *vi* osciller.
other *pn* autre.
otherwise *adv* autrement.
ought *v aux* devoir; falloir.
our *pn* notre, *pl* nos.
ours *pn* le nôtre, la nôtre, les nôtres; à nous.
ourselves *pn pl* nous-mêmes.
out *adv* dehors; éteint.
outburst *n* explosion *f*.

outcome *n* résultat *m*.
outdo *vt* surpasser.
outdoor *adj* de plein air:—*s adv* à l'extérieur.
outer *adj* extérieur.
outfit *n* tenue *f*; équipement *m*.
outgoing *adj* extroverti; sortant.
outlay *n* dépenses *fpl*, frais *mpl*.
outline *n* contour *m*; grandes lignes *fpl*.
outlook *n* perspective *f*.
output *n* rendement *m*; sortie *f*.
outrage *n* outrage *m*:—*vt* outrager.
outright *adv* absolument:—*adj* absolu.
outset *n* commencement *m*.
outside *n* surface *f*; extérieur *m*:—*adv* dehors:—*prep* en dehors de.
outstrip *vt* devancer; surpasser.
oval *n, adj* ovale *m*.
ovary *n* ovaire *m*.
oven *n* four *m*.
over *prep* sur, dessus; plus de; pendant:—*adj* fini.
overall *adj* total:—*s npl* salopette *f*.
overbalance *vi* perdre l'équilibre.
overcast *adj* couvert.
overcharge *vt* surcharger.
overcoat *n* pardessus *m*.
overcome *vt* vaincre.
overdo *vi* exagérer.
overdraft *n* découvert *m*.
overdue *adj* en retard; arriéré.
overestimate *vt* surestimer.
overflow *vi* déborder:—*n* surplus *m*.
overhaul *vt* réviser:—*n* révision *f*.
overland *adj adv* par voie de terre.
overlap *vi* se chevaucher.
overlook *vt* donner sur; oublier; tolérer; négliger.
overnight *adv* pendant la nuit:—*adj* de nuit.

overpower *vt* dominer, écraser.

overrate *vt* surévaluer.

overrun *vt* envahir; infester; dépasser.

overseas *adv* à l'étranger; outre-mer:—*adj* étranger.

oversee *vt* inspecter, surveiller.

oversight *n* oubli *m*; erreur *f.*

oversleep *vi* se réveiller en retard.

overtake *vt* doubler.

overthrow *vt* renverser:—*n* renversement *m.*

overtime *n* heures supplémentaires *fpl.*

overturn *vt* renverser.

overwhelm *vt* écraser.

overwhelming *adj* écrasant.

overwork *vi* se surmener.

owe *vt* devoir.

owing *adj* dû:—~ **to** en raison de.

owl *n* chouette *f.*

own *adj* propre:—*vt* posséder.

owner *n* propriétaire *mf.*

ox *n* bœuf *m.*

oxygen *n* oxygène *m.*

oyster *n* huître *f.*

ozone *n* ozone *m.*

P

pace *n* pas *m*; allure *f*:—*vi* marcher.

pacific *adj* pacifique.

pacification *n* pacification *f.*

pacify *vt* pacifier.

pack *n* paquet *m*; bande *f*:—*vt* empaqueter:—*vi* faire ses valises.

package *n* paquet *m.*

packet *n* paquet *m.*

pact *n* pacte *m.*

pad *n* bloc *m*; tampon *m*; (*sl*) piaule *f*:—*vt* rembourrer.

paddle *vi* ramer:—*n* pagaie *f.*

pagan *adj n* païen *m*, païenne *f.*

page *n* page *f*; page *m.*

pail *n* seau *m.*

pain *n* douleur *f*; peine *f*:—*vt* peiner.

pained *adj* peiné.

painful *adj* douloureux; pénible.

painstaking *adj* soigneux.

paint *vt* peindre.

painter *n* peintre *m.*

painting *n* peinture *f*; tableau *m.*

pair *n* pair *m.*

palatable *adj* savoureux.

palate *n* palais *m.*

pale *adj* pâle; clair.

palette *n* palette *f.*

pallet *n* palette *f.*

pallid *adj* pâle.

palpable *adj* palpable; évident.

palpitation *n* palpitation *f.*

pamper *vt* gâter, dorloter.

pamphlet *n* pamphlet *m*; brochure *f.*

pan *n* casserole *f*; poêle *f.*

panache *n* panache *m.*

pane *n* vitre *f.*

panel *n* panneau *m*; comité *m.*

pang *n* angoisse *f*; tourment *m.*

panic *adj n* (de) panique *f.*

pant *vi* haleter.

panther *n* panthère *f.*

pantry *n* placard *m.*

pants *npl* slip *m*; pantalon *m*.

paper *n* papier *m*; journal *m*:—*adj* en papier:—*vt* tapisser.

paperweight *n* presse-papiers *m*.

par *n* équivalence *f*; pair *m*.

parachute *n* parachute *m*.

parade *n* parade *f*.

paradise *n* paradis *m*.

paradox *n* paradoxe *m*.

paragraph *n* paragraphe *m*.

parallel *adj* parallèle:—*n* parallèle *f*.

paralyse *vt* paralyser.

paralysis *n* paralysie *f*.

paramount *adj* suprême, supérieur.

paranoid *adj* paranoïaque.

parasite *n* parasite *m*.

parcel *n* paquet *m*; parcelle *f*:—*vt* empaqueter.

parch *vt* dessécher.

pardon *n* pardon *m*:—*vt* pardonner.

parent *n* père *m*; mère *f*:—~s parents *mpl*.

park *n* parc *m*:—*vt* garer; *vi* se garer.

parking *n* stationnement *m*.

parking lot *n* parking *m*.

parliament *n* parlement *m*.

parody *n* parodie *f*:—*vt* parodier.

parry *vt* parer.

part *n* partie *f*; part *f*; rôle (d'acteur) *m*:—*vt* séparer; diviser:—*vi* se séparer; se diviser:—~ly *adv* en partie.

partial *adj* partial.

participate *vi* participer (à).

participation *n* participation *f*.

particle *n* particule *f*.

particular *adj* particulier:—*n* particulier *m*; particularité *f*.

partition *n* partition, séparation *f*:—*vt* partager,

partner *n* associé *m*, -e *f*.

party *n* parti *m*; fête *f*.

pass *vt* passer; dépasser:—*vi* passer:—*n* permis *m*; passage *m*.

passage *n* passage *m*.

passenger *n* passager *m*, -ère *f*.

passer-by *n* passant *m*, -e *f*.

passion *n* passion *f*; amour *m*.

passionate *adj* passionné.

passive *adj* passif.

passport *n* passeport *m*.

past *adj* passé:—*n* passé *m*:—*prep* au-delà de; après.

paste *n* pâte *f*; colle *f*:—*vt* coller.

pastime *n* passe-temps *m invar*.

pastry *n* pâtisserie *f*.

pasture *n* pâture *f*.

patch *n* pièce *f*; terrain *m*:—*vt* rapiécer.

patent *adj* évident:—*n* brevet *m*:—*vt* faire breveter.

patentee *n* détenteur d'un brevet *m*.

paternal *adj* paternel.

paternity *n* paternité *f*.

path *n* chemin, sentier *m*.

pathetic *adj* pathétique.

patience *n* patience *f*.

patient *adj* patient:—~ly *adv* patiemment:—*n* patient *m*, -e *f*.

patrol *n* patrouille *f*:—*vi* patrouiller.

patron *n* protecteur *m*; client *m*, -e *f*.

patronize *vt* patronner, protéger.

pattern *n* motif *m*; modèle *m*.

pause *n* pause *f*:—*vi* faire une pause; hésiter.

pave *vt* paver; carreler.

pavement *n* trottoir *m*.

paw *n* patte *f*:—*vt* tripoter.

pay *vt* payer:—**to ~ back** *vt* rembourser:—*n* paie *f*; salaire *m*.

payable *adj* payable.

payment *n* paiement *m*.

pea *n* pois *m*.

peace *n* paix *f*.

peaceful *adj* paisible; pacifique.

peak *n* pic *m*; maximum *m*.

pear *n* poire *f*.

pearl *n* perle *f*.

peasant *n* paysan *m*, -anne *f*.

pebble *n* caillou *m*; galet *m*.

peculiar *adj* étrange, singulier.

peculiarity *n* particularité, singularité *f*.

pedal *n* pédale *f*:—*vi* pédaler.

pedestrian *n* piéton *m*, -onne *f*:—*adj* pédestre.

peel *vt* peler:—*n* peau *f*; pelure *f*.

peer *n* pair *m*.

peerless *adj* incomparable.

pelt *n* fourrure *f*.

pen *n* stylo *m*; plume *f*.

penalty *n* peine *f*; sanction *f*; amende *f*.

pencil *n* crayon *m*.

pendulum *n* pendule *m*.

penetrate *vt* pénétrer dans.

peninsula *n* péninsule *f*.

penitentiary *n* pénitencier *m*.

penknife *n* canif *m*.

penpal *n* correspondant *m*, -e *f*.

pension *n* pension *f*:—*vt* pensionner.

pensive *adj* pensif.

penultimate *adj* pénultième.

people *n* peuple *m*; nation *f*; gens *mpl*:—*vt* peupler.

pepper *n* poivre *m*:—*vt* poivrer.

per *prep* par.

per annum *adv* par an.

perceive *vt* percevoir.

percentage *n* pourcentage *m*.

perception *n* perception *f*; notion *f*.

perch *n* perche *f*.

percussion *n* percussion *f*.

perdition *n* perte, ruine *f*.

perennial *adj* perpétuel.

perfect *adj* parfait; idéal:—*vt* parfaire, perfectionner.

perfection *n* perfection *f*.

perform *vt* exécuter:—*vi* donner une représentation.

performance *n* exécution *f*; accomplissement *m*.

performer *n* exécutant *m*, -e *f*; acteur *m*, -trice *f*.

perfume *n* parfum *m*:—*vt* parfumer.

perhaps *adv* peut-être.

peril *n* péril, danger *m*.

perilous *adj* dangereux.

perimeter *n* périmètre *m*.

period *n* période *f*; époque *f*.

periodic *adj* périodique.

perish *vi* périr.

perishable *adj* périssable.

permanent *adj* permanent.

permissible *adj* permis.

permission *n* permission *f*.

permissive *adj* permissif.

permit *vt* permettre:—*n* permis *m*.

perpetrate *vt* perpétrer, commettre.

perpetual *adj* perpétuel.

perplex *vt* confondre, laisser perplexe.

persecute *vt* persécuter; importuner.

persecution *n* persécution *f*.

persevere *vi* persévérer.

persist *vi* persister.

persistence *adj* persistance *f*.

persistent *adj* persistant.

person *n* personne *f*.

personage *n* personnage *m*.

personal *adv* personnel.

personal computer *n* ordinateur individuel *m*.

personality *n* personnalité *f*.

personnel *n* personnel *m*.

perspective *n* perspective *f*.

perspiration *n* transpiration *f*.

perspire vi transpirer.
persuade vt persuader.
persuasion n persuasion f.
persuasive adj persuasif.
pertaining:—— to prep relatif à.
pertinent adj pertinent.
perturb vt perturber.
peruse vt lire; examiner attentivement.
perverse adj pervers, dépravé.
pessimist n pessimiste mf.
pest n insecte nuisible m; casse-pieds (fam) mf invar.
pester vt importuner, fatiguer.
pestilence n peste f.
pet n animal domestique m:—vt gâter.
petal n (bot) pétale m.
petition n pétition f.
petticoat n jupon m.
pettiness n insignifiance f.
petty adj mesquin; insignifiant.
phantom n fantôme m.
pharmacist n pharmacien m, -ienne f.
pharmacy n pharmacie f.
phase n phase f.
phenomenal adj phénoménal.
phenomenon n phénomène m.
philosopher n philosophe mf.
philosophical adj philosophique.
philosophize vi philosopher.
philosophy n philosophie f.
phobia n phobie f.
phone n téléphone m:—vt téléphoner à.
phone book n annuaire m.
phone call n coup de téléphone m.
photograph n photo(graphie) f:—vt photographier.
photographer n photographe mf.
photography n photographie f.
phrase n phrase f:—vt exprimer.

phrase book n guide de conversation m.
physical adv physique.
physician n médecin m.
physicist n physicien m, -ienne f.
physiotherapy n physiothérapie f.
physique n physique m.
pianist n pianiste mf.
piano n piano m.
pick vt choisir; cueillir:—n pic m; choix m.
picnic n pique-nique m.
pictorial adj pictural; illustré.
picture n image f; peinture f:—vt dépeindre.
pie n gâteau m; tarte f; pâté en croûte m.
piece n morceau m; pièce f.
pierce vt percer, transpercer.
piercing adj perçant.
pig n cochon m.
pigeon n pigeon m.
pile n tas m; pile f; amas m:—vt entasser.
pilgrim n pèlerin m.
pill n pilule f.
pillar n pilier m.
pillow n oreiller m.
pilot n pilote m:—vt piloter; (fig) mener.
pin n épingle f:—vt épingler.
pincers n pinces, tenailles fpl.
pine n (bot) pin m:—vi languir.
pineapple n ananas m.
pink n, adj rose m.
pint n pinte f.
pioneer n pionnier m.
pious adj pieux, dévot.
pipe n tube, tuyau m; pipe f.
pipeline n canalisation f.
piracy n piraterie f.
pirate n pirate m.

pistol n pistolet m.

pitch n lancement m:—vt lancer, jeter.

pitcher n cruche f.

pitiable adj pitoyable.

pitiful adj pitoyable.

pity n pitié f:—vt avoir pitié de.

placard n affiche f.

placate vt apaiser.

place n endroit, lieu m:—vt placer.

placid adj placide, calme.

plague n peste f:—vt tourmenter.

plain adj uni; simple; évident:—n plaine f.

plait n pli m; tresse f:—vt plier.

plan n plan m:—vt projeter.

plane n avion m; plan m:—vt aplanir.

planet n planète f.

plank n planche f.

planner n planificateur m, -trice f.

plant n plante f; usine f:—vt planter.

plantation n plantation f.

plaster n plâtre m; emplâtre m:—vt plâtrer.

plastic adj plastique.

plate n assiette f; plaque f; lame f.

platform n plateforme f.

platter n écuelle f; plat m.

plausible adj plausible.

play n jeu m; pièce f de théâtre:—vt vi jouer.

player n joueur m, -euse f; acteur m, -trice f.

playful adj enjoué, amusé.

playwright n dramaturge mf.

plea n appel m; excuse f, prétexte m.

plead vt plaider; prétexter.

pleasant adj agréable; plaisant.

please vt faire plaisir à.

pleased adj content.

pleasure n plaisir m; gré m.

pledge n promesse f; gage m:—vt engager.

plentiful adj copieux; abondant.

plenty n abondance f.

pliable adj pliant; souple.

pliers npl tenailles fpl.

plot n complot m; intrigue f:—vt tracer.

plough n charrue f:—vt labourer.

pluck vt tirer; arracher:—n courage m.

plug n bougie f; prise f:—vt boucher.

plumber n plombier m.

plump adj rondouillet, dodu.

plunge vi plonger; s'élancer.

plural adj n pluriel m.

plus prep plus.

pneumonia n pneumonie f.

poach vt pocher; braconner.

poacher n braconnier m.

pocket n poche f:—vt empocher.

poem n poème m.

poet n poète m.

poetry n poésie f.

poignant adj poignant.

point n pointe f; point m:—vt pointer.

pointed adj pointu; acéré.

poise n attitude f; équilibre m.

poison n poison m:—vt empoisonner.

poisonous adj vénéneux.

poke vt attiser.

poker-faced adj au visage impassible.

pole n pôle m; mât m; perche f.

police n police f.

policeman n agent de police m.

police station n commissariat m.

policy n politique f.

polish vt polir; cirer:—n poli m.

polished adj poli; ciré; élégant.

polite adj poli.

politeness n politesse f.

political adj politique.

politician n homme (femme) politique m(f).

politics npl politique f.

pollute vt polluer.

pollution n pollution.

polytechnic n école d'enseignement technique f.

pompous adj pompeux.

pond n mare f; étang m.

ponder vt considérer.

pony n poney m.

pool n piscine f.

poor adj pauvre; mauvais

populace n populace f.

popular adj populaire.

popularity n popularité f.

populate vi peupler.

population n population f.

porch n porche m.

pork n porc m.

port n port m.

portable adj portable, portatif.

portion n portion, part f.

portrait n portrait m.

portray vt faire le portrait de; dépeindre.

pose n posture f; pose f:—vi, vt poser.

position n position f:—vt mettre en position.

positive adj positif; réel.

possess vt posséder.

possession n possession f.

possibility n possibilité f.

possible adj possible:—~ly adv peut-être.

post n courrier m; poste f; emploi m.

postage stamp n timbre m.

postcard n carte postale f.

poster n poster m.

posterior n postérieur m.

posthumous adj posthume.

postman n facteur m.

post office n poste f, bureau de poste m.

postpone vt remettre; différer.

posture n posture f.

pot n pot m; marmite f:—vt empoter.

potato n pomme de terre.

potent adj puissant.

potential adj potentiel.

potion n potion f.

pouch n sac m.

poultry n volaille f.

pound n livre f; livre sterling f:—vt concasser.

pour vt verser; servir:—vi couler; pleuvoir à verse.

poverty n pauvreté f.

powder n poudre f:—vt poudrer.

powdery adj poudreux.

power n pouvoir m; puissance f; force f:—vt propulser.

powerful adj puissant.

powerless adj impotent.

practicable adj praticable; faisable.

practical adj pratique.

practicality n faisabilité f.

practice n pratique f; usage m; entraînement m.

practise vt pratiquer:—vi s'exercer.

pragmatic adj pragmatique.

praise n louange f:—vt louer.

prance vi cabrioler.

prattle vi jacasser:—n jacasserie f.

prawn n crevette f.

pray vi prier.

prayer n prière f.

preach vt prêcher.

preacher n prédicateur m.

precarious adj précaire, incertain.

precaution n précaution f.

precede vt précéder.

precedent adj n précédent m.

precinct n limite f; enceinte f.

precious adj précieux.

precipitate vt précipiter:—adj précipité.

precise *n* précis, exact.

precision *n* précision, exactitude *f*.

precocious *adj* précoce, prématuré.

preconceive *vt* préconcevoir.

preconception *n* préjugé *m*; idée préconçue *f*.

predator *n* prédateur *m*.

predecessor *n* prédécesseur *m*.

predict *vt* prédire.

predictable *adj* prévisible.

prediction *n* prédiction *f*.

predominant *adj* prédominant.

predominate *vt* prédominer.

preface *n* préface *f*.

prefer *vt* préférer.

preferable *adj* préférable.

preference *n* préférence *f*.

preferential *adj* préférentiel.

prefix *vt* préfixer.

pregnancy *n* grossesse *f*.

pregnant *adj* enceinte.

prehistoric *adj* préhistorique.

prejudice *n* préjudice *m*; préjugé *m*: —*vt* préjudicier à.

prejudiced *adj* qui a des préjugés; partial.

prejudicial *adj* préjudiciable.

preliminary *adj* préliminaire.

premature *adj* prématuré.

premeditation *n* préméditation *f*.

premises *npl* locaux *mpl*.

premium *n* prix *m*; prime *f*.

premonition *n* prémonition *f*.

preparation *n* préparation *f*.

preparatory *adj* préparatoire.

prepare *vt* préparer:—*vi* se préparer.

preposterous *adj* ridicule, absurde.

prerogative *n* prérogative *f*.

prescribe *vt* prescrire.

prescription *n* prescription *f*.

presence *n* présence *f*.

present *n* cadeau *m*:—*adj* présent; actuel:—**ly** *adv* actuellement:— *vt* présenter.

presentable *adj* présentable.

presenter *n* présentateur *m*, -trice *f*.

preservation *n* préservation *f*.

preserve *vt* préserver:—*n* conserve *f*; confiture *f*.

preside *vi* présider; diriger.

president *n* président *m*.

press *vt* appuyer sur:—*vi* se presser: —*n* presse *f*; pressoir *m*.

pressing *adj* pressant; urgent.

pressure *n* pression *f*.

prestige *n* prestige *m*.

presumable *adj* vraisemblable.

presume *vt* présumer, supposer.

presumption *n* présomption *f*.

pretence *n* prétexte *m*; simulation *f*.

pretend *vi* prétendre; faire semblant.

pretext *n* prétexte *m*.

pretty *adj* joli, mignon.

prevail *vi* prévaloir; prédominer.

prevalent *adj* prédominant.

prevent *vt* prévenir; empêcher.

prevention *n* prévention *f*.

previous *adj* précédent; antérieur:— **ly** *adv* auparavant.

prey *n* proie *f*.

price *n* prix *m*.

prick *vt* piquer:—*n* piqûre *f*; pointe *f*.

pride *n* orgueil *m*; vanité *f*; fierté *f*.

priest *n* prêtre *m*.

priesthood *n* sacerdoce *m*, prêtrise *f*.

primacy *n* primauté *f*.

primarily *adv* principalement, surtout.

primary *adj* primaire; principal, premier.

primate *n* primate *m*.

prime *n* (*fig*) fleur *f*; commencement *m*:—*adj* premier; principal.

prime minister *n* premier ministre *m*.

primitive *adj* primitif.

prince *n* prince *m*.

princess *n* princesse *f*.

principal *adj* principal:—*n* principal *m*.

principle *n* principe *m*.

print *vt* imprimer:—*n* impression *f*; estampe *f*.

printer *n* imprimeur *m*; imprimante *f*.

prior *adj* antérieur, précédent.

priority *n* priorité *f*.

prison *n* prison *f*.

prisoner *n* prisonnier *m*, -ière *f*.

privacy *n* intimité *f*.

private *adj* privé; secret; particulier:—**~ly** *adv* en privé.

privilege *n* privilège *m*.

prize *n* prix *m*:—*vt* apprécier, évaluer.

pro *prep* pour.

probability *n* probabilité *f*; vraisemblance *f*.

probable *adj* probable, vraisemblable.

probation *n* essai *m*; probation *f*.

probationary *adj* d'essai.

probe *n* sonde *f*:—*vt* sonder.

problem *n* problème *m*.

problematical *adj* problématique.

procedure *n* procédure *f*.

proceed *vi* procéder; provenir.

process *n* processus *m*; procédé *m*.

procession *n* procession *f*.

proclaim *vt* proclamer; promulguer.

proclamation *n* proclamation *f*; décret *m*.

procure *vt* procurer.

procurement *n* obtention *f*.

prod *vt* pousser.

prodigious *adj* prodigieux.

prodigy *n* prodige *m*.

produce *vt* produire; créer.

producer *n* producteur *m*, -trice *f*.

product *n* produit *m*; œuvre *f*; fruit *m*.

production *n* production *f*; produit *m*.

productive *adj* productif.

profess *vt* professer; déclarer.

profession *n* profession *f*.

professional *adj* professionnel.

professor *n* professeur *m*.

proficiency *n* capacité *f*.

proficient *adj* compétent.

profile *n* profil *m*.

profit *n* bénéfice, profit *m*:—*vi* profiter (de).

profitability *n* rentabilité *f*.

profitable *adj* profitable, avantageux.

profound *adj* profond.

program(me) *n* programme *m*.

programmer *n* programmeur *m*, -euse *f*.

progress *n* progrès *m*; cours *m*:—*vi* progresser.

progression *n* progression *f*; avance *f*.

progressive *adj* progressif.

prohibit *vt* prohiber; défendre.

project *vt* projeter:—*n* projet *m*.

projection *n* projection *f*.

prolific *adj* prolifique, fécond.

prolong *vt* prolonger.

promenade *n* promenade *f*.

prominence *n* proéminence *f*.

prominent *adj* proéminent.

promise *n* promesse *f*:—*vt* promettre.

promising *adj* prometteur.

promote *vt* promouvoir.

promoter *n* promoteur *m*.

promotion *n* promotion *f*.

prompt *adj* prompt:—*vt* suggérer.

prone *adj* enclin (à).

pronounce *vt* prononcer; déclarer.

pronounced *adj* marqué, prononcé.

pronouncement *n* déclaration *f*.

pronunciation n prononciation f.

proof n preuve f:—adj imperméable; résistant.

prop vt soutenir:—n appui, soutien m.

propaganda n propagande f.

propel vt propulser.

propeller n hélice f.

propensity n propension, tendance f.

proper adj propre; convenable.

property n propriété f.

prophecy n prophétie f.

prophet n prophète m.

proportion n proportion f.

proportional adj proportionnel.

proposal n proposition f; offre f.

propose vt proposer.

proposition n proposition f.

proprietor n propriétaire mf.

prosecute vt poursuivre en justice.

prosecution n poursuites fpl; accusation f.

prospect n perspective f:—vt vi prospecter.

prospective adj probable; futur.

prosper vi prospérer.

prosperity n prospérité f.

prosperous adj prospère.

prostitute n prostituée f.

protagonist n protagoniste mf.

protect vt protéger; abriter.

protection n protection f.

protective adj protecteur.

protein n protéine f.

protest vi protester:—n protestation f.

Protestant n protestant m, -e f.

protester n protestataire mf.

prototype n prototype m.

proud adj fier, orgueilleux.

prove vt prouver; justifier:—vi s'avérer; se révéler.

proverb n proverbe m.

provide vt fournir.

provided conj:—~ that pourvu que.

providence n providence f.

province n province f.

provincial adj n provincial m, -e f.

provision n provision f; disposition f.

provisional adj provisoire.

provocation n provocation f.

provocative adj provocateur.

provoke vt provoquer.

prowess n prouesse f.

prowl vi rôder.

prowler n rôdeur m, -euse f.

proximity n proximité f.

prudence n prudence f.

prudent adj prudent.

pry vi espionner.

pseudonym n pseudonyme m.

psychiatric adj psychiatrique.

psychiatrist n psychiatre mf.

psychic adj psychique.

psychoanalyst n psychanaliste mf.

psychologist n psychologue mf.

psychology n psychologie f.

puberty n puberté f.

public adj public; commun:—n public m.

publication n publication f; édition f.

publicity n publicité f.

publish vt publier.

publisher n éditeur m, -trice f.

publishing n édition f.

pudding n pudding m; dessert m.

puddle n flaque d'eau f.

puff n souple m; bouffée f:—vt souffler; dégager.

pull vt tirer; arracher:—n tirage m; secousse f.

pulley n poulie f.

pulsate vi battre.

pulse n pouls m.

pulverize vt pulvériser.

pump n pompe f:—vt pomper; puiser.

punch *n* coup de poing *m*:—*vt* cogner.

punctual *adj* ponctuel, exact.

punctuate *vt* ponctuer.

punctuation *n* ponctuation *f*.

punish *vt* punir.

punishment *n* châtiment *m*, punition *f*; peine *f*.

puny *adj* chétif, maigrelet.

pupil *n* élève *mf*; pupille *mf*.

puppet *n* marionnette *f*.

puppy *n* chiot *m*.

purchase *vt* acheter:—*n* achat *m*; acquisition *f*.

purchaser *n* acheteur *m*, -euse *f*.

pure *adj* pur.

purification *n* purification *f*.

purify *vt* purifier.

purity *n* pureté *f*.

purple *adj n* pourpre, violet *m*.

purpose *n* intention *f*; but, dessein *m*:—**on ~** exprès, à dessein.

purse *n* sac à main *m*; porte-monnaie *m invar*.

pursue *vi* poursuivre; suivre.

pursuit *n* poursuite *f*; occupation *f*.

push *vt* pousser; presser:—*n* poussée *f*; impulsion *f*.

put *vt* mettre, poser.

putrid *adj* putride.

putty *n* mastic *m*.

puzzle *n* énigme *f*; casse-tête *m invar*.

puzzling *adj* curieux; inexplicable.

pyjamas *npl* pyjama *m*.

pylon *n* pylône *m*.

pyramid *n* pyramide *f*.

python *n* python *m*.

Q

quack *vi* cancaner:—*n* (*sl*) charlatan *m*.

quagmire *n* marécage *m*.

quaint *adj* désuet; bizarre.

quake *vi* trembler.

qualification *n* qualification *f*.

qualified *adj* qualifié.

qualify *vt* qualifier:—*vi* se qualifier.

quality *n* qualité *f*.

qualm *n* scrupule *m*.

quantity *n* quantité *f*.

quarantine *n* quarantaine *f*.

quarrel *n* querelle *f*:—*vi* se quereller.

quarrelsome *adj* querelleur.

quarry *n* carrière *f*.

quarter *n* quart *m*:—*vt* diviser en quatre.

quarterly *adj* trimestriel:—*adv* tous les trimestres.

quash *vt* écraser; annuler.

quay *n* quai *m*.

queen *n* reine *f*; femme *f*.

queer *adj* extrange:—*n* (*sl*) pédale *f*.

quell *vt* étouffer.

quench *vt* assouvir.

query *n* question *f*:—*vt* demander.

quest *n* recherche *f*.

question *n* question *f*:—*vt* questionner.

questionable *adj* discutable; douteux.

questioner n interrogateur m.

questionnaire n questionnaire m.

quibble vi chicaner.

quick adj rapide; vif.

quicken vt accélérer:—vi s'accélérer.

quiet adj calme; silencieux.

quietness n calme m, tranquillité f; silence m.

quip n sarcasme m:—vt railler.

quit vt arrêter de:—vi abandonner.

quite adv assez; complètement, absolument.

quiver vi trembler.

quiz n concours m; examen m:—vt interroger.

quota n quota m.

quotation n citation f.

quote vt citer.

R

rabbit n lapin m.

rabble n cohue f.

rabies n rage f.

race n course f; race f:—vi courir; foncer.

racial adj racial:—~ist adj n raciste mf.

rack n casier m; étagère f.

racket n vacarme m; raquette f.

radiant adj rayonnant, radieux.

radiate vt vi rayonner, irradier.

radiation n irradiation f.

radiator n radiateur m.

radical adj radical.

radio n radio f.

radioactive adj radioactif.

raft n radeau.

rag n lambeau m, loque f.

rage n rage f; fureur f:—vi faire rage.

ragged adj déguenillé.

raging adj furieux, enragé.

raid n raid m:—vt faire un raid sur.

rail n rambarde f; (rail) rail, chemin de fer m.

railway n chemin de fer m.

rain n pluie f:—vi pleuvoir.

rainbow n arc-en-ciel m.

rainy adj pluvieux.

raise vt lever, soulever.

raisin n raisin sec m.

rally vt (mil) rallier:—vi se rallier.

ramble vi errer; faire une randonnée.

ramp n rampe f.

ramshackle adj délabré.

rancid adj rance.

rancour n rancœur f.

random adj fortuit, fait au hasard.

range vt ranger:—vi s'étendre:—n rangée f; chaîne f; fourneau de cuisine m.

rank n rang m, classe f, grade m.

ransack vt saccager, piller.

ransom n rançon f.

rape n viol m:—vt violer.

rapid adj rapide.

rapidity n rapidité f.

rapist n violeur m.

rapt adj extasié; absorbé.

rapture n ravissement m; extase f.

rare adj rare.

rarity n rareté f.

rash adj imprudent:—n éruption (cutanée) f.

rashness n imprudence f.

rat n rat m.

rate n taux, prix m; vitesse f:—vt estimer, évaluer.

rather adv plutôt.

ratification n ratification f.

ratify vt ratifier.

ration n ration f.

rational adj rationnel.

rattle vi s'entrechoquer:—n hochet m; cliquetis m.

ravage vt ravager:—n ravage m.

rave vi délirer.

ravenous adj vorace.

ravine n ravin m.

raw adj cru; brut.

rawness n crudité f; inexpérience f.

ray n rayon m.

raze vt raser.

razor n rasoir m.

reach vt atteindre:—vi porter:—n portée f.

react vi réagir.

reaction n réaction f.

read vt vi lire.

reader n lecteur m, -trice f.

readily adv volontiers.

readiness n bonne volonté f.

reading n lecture f.

readjust vt réajuster.

ready adj prêt; enclin.

real adj réel, vrai.

reality n réalité f.

realization n réalisation f.

realize vt se rendre compte de; réaliser.

reappear vi réapparaître.

rear n arrière m; derrière m:—vt élever.

reason n raison f; cause f:—vt vi raisonner.

reasonable adj raisonnable.

reasoning n raisonnement m.

reassure vt rassurer.

rebel n rebelle mf:—vi se rebeller.

rebellion n rébellion f.

rebound vi rebondir.

rebuild vt reconstruire.

rebuke vt réprimander:—n réprimande f.

recall vt (se) rappeler.

recapture n reprise f.

recede vi reculer.

receipt n reçu m; réception f.

receivable adj recevable.

receive vt recevoir; accueillir.

recent adj récent, neuf.

receptacle n récipient m.

reception n réception f.

recession n récession f.

recipe n recette f.

recipient n destinataire mf.

reciprocal adj ~ly adv réciproque(ment).

recital n récit m.

recite vt réciter.

reckless adj téméraire.

reckon vt compter:—vi calculer.

reclaim vt assainir; récupérer.

recline vt reposer:—vi être allongé.

recognition n reconnaissance f.

recognize vt reconnaître.

recoil vi reculer.

recollect vt se rappeler.

recollection n souvenir m.

recommend vt recommander.

recompense n récompense f:—vt récompenser.

reconcile vt réconcilier.

reconciliation n réconciliation f.

reconsider vt reconsidérer.

record *vt* enregistrer:—*n* rapport *m*, registre *m*; disque *m*; record *m*.

recount *vt* raconter.

recourse *n* recours *m*.

recover *vt* retrouver:—*vi* se remettre.

recovery *n* guérison *f*; reprise *f*.

recreation *n* détente *f*; récréation *f*.

recriminate *vi* récriminer.

recrimination *n* récrimination *f*.

recruit *vt* recruter:—*n* (*mil*) recrue *f*.

rectangle *n* rectangle *m*.

rectification *n* rectification *f*.

rectify *vt* rectifier.

recumbent *adj* couché, étendu.

recur *vi* se reproduire.

recurrence *n* répétition *f*.

recurrent *adj* répétitif.

red *adj* rouge:—*n* rouge *m*.

redden *vt vi* rougir.

redeem *vt* racheter, rembourser.

redemption *n* rachat *m*.

redness *n* rougeur, rousseur *f*.

redouble *vt vi* redoubler.

redress *vt* réparer; redresser.

reduce *vt* réduire; diminuer.

reduction *n* réduction *f*; baisse *f*.

redundancy *n* licenciement *m*.

redundant *adj* superflu.

reel *n* bobine *f*; dévidoir *m*:—*vi* chanceler.

re-enter *vt* rentrer.

re-establish *vt* rétablir; réhabiliter.

refer *vt* se référer à:—*vi* se référer.

referee *n* arbitre *m*.

reference *n* référence *f*.

refine *vt* raffiner, affiner.

refinement *n* raffinement *m*.

reflect *vt* réfléchir, refléter:—*vi* réfléchir.

reflection *n* réflexion, pensée *f*.

reform *vt* réformer:—*vi* se réformer.

reform *n* réforme *f*.

reformer *n* réformateur *m*, -trice *f*.

refrain *vi*:—~ **from** s'abstenir de.

refresh *vt* rafraîchir.

refrigerator *n* glacière *f*; réfrigérateur *m*.

refuge *n* refuge, asile *m*.

refugee *n* réfugié *m*, -e *f*.

refund *vt* rembourser:—*n* remboursement *m*.

refusal *n* refus *m*.

refuse *vt* refuser:—*n* déchets *mpl*.

regain *vt* recouvrer.

regal *adj* royal.

regard *vt* regarder:—*n* considération *f*.

regardless *adv* quand même.

regenerate *vt* régénérer.

regeneration *n* régénération *f*.

regime *n* régime *m*.

region *n* région *f*.

register *n* registre *m*:—*vt* enregistrer.

registration *n* enregistrement *m*.

regressive *adj* régressif.

regret *n* regret *m*:—*vt* regretter.

regular *adj* régulier:—*n* habitué *m*, -e *f*.

regularity *n* régularité *f*.

regulate *vt* régler.

regulation *n* règlement *m*.

rehabilitate *vt* réhabiliter.

rehabilitation *n* réhabilitation *f*.

reimburse *vt* rembourser.

reimbursement *n* remboursement *m*.

reinforce *vt* renforcer.

reiterate *vt* réitérer.

reiteration *n* réitération *f*.

reject *vt* rejeter.

rejection *n* refus *m*.

rejoice *vt* réjouir:—*vi* se réjouir.

relapse *vi* retomber:—*n* rechute *f*.

relate *vt* relater:—*vi* se rapporter.

relation *n* rapport *m*; parent *m*.

relationship *n* lien de parenté *m*; relation *f*; rapport *m*.

relative *adj* relatif:—*n* parent *m*, -e *f*.

relax *vt* relâcher:—*vi* se relâcher.

relaxation *n* relâchement *m*; détente *f*.

relay *n* relais *m*:—*vt* retransmettre.

release *vt* libérer:—*n* libération *f*.

relevant *adj* pertinent.

reliable *adj* fiable.

reliance *n* confiance *f*.

relief *n* soulagement *m*; secours *m*.

relieve *vt* soulager, alléger.

religion *n* religion *f*.

religious *adj* religieux.

relinquish *vt* abandonner.

reluctant *adj* peu disposé.

rely *vi* compter sur.

remain *vi* rester, demeurer.

remainder *n* reste, restant *m*.

remark *n* remarque:—*vt* (faire) remarquer.

remarkable *adj* remarquable, notable.

remedy *n* remède *m*:—*vt* remédier à.

remember *vt* se souvenir de.

remind *vt* rappeler.

reminiscence *n* réminiscence *f*.

remit *vt* remettre, pardonner.

remnant *n* reste, restant *m*.

remonstrate *vi* protester.

remote *adj* lointain, éloigné.

remoteness *n* éloignement *m*; isolement *m*.

removable *adj* amovible.

removal *n* suppression *f*.

remove *vt* enlever.

remunerate *vt* rémunérer.

render *vt* rendre, remettre.

renew *vt* renouveler.

renewal *n* renouvellement *m*.

renounce *vt* renoncer à.

renovate *vt* rénover.

renown *n* renommée *f*; célébrité *f*.

rent *n* loyer *m*:—*vt* louer.

renunciation *n* renonciation *f*.

reorganization *n* réorganisation *f*.

reorganize *vt* réorganiser.

repair *vt* réparer:—*n* réparation *f*.

repatriate *vt* rapatrier.

repay *vt* rembourser.

repayment *n* remboursement *m*.

repeal *vt* abroger:—*n* abrogation *f*.

repeat *vt* répéter.

repel *vt* repousser, rebuter.

repent *vi* se repentir.

repetition *n* répétition *f*.

replace *vt* replacer.

replenish *vt* remplir de nouveau.

replete *adj* rempli.

reply *n* réponse *f*:—*vi* répondre.

report *vt* rapporter:—*n* rapport *m*; compte rendu *m*.

reporter *n* journaliste *mf*.

reprehend *vt* condamner.

reprehensible *adj* répréhensible.

represent *vt* représenter.

representation *n* représentation *f*.

representative *adj* représentatif:—*n* représentant(e) *m(f)*.

repress *vt* réprimer, contenir.

repression *n* répression *f*.

reprieve *n* sursis *m*.

reprimand *vt* réprimander.

reprisal *n* représailles *fpl*.

reproach *n* reproche:—*vt* reprocher.

reproduce *vt* reproduire.

reproduction *n* reproduction *f*.

republic *n* république *f*.

republican *adj n* républicain *m*, -e *f*.

repudiate *vt* renier.

repulse *vt* repousser.

repulsion *n* répulsion *f*.

repulsive *adj* répulsif.

reputation *n* réputation *f*.

request *n* requête *f:*—*vt* demander.

require *vt* demander, nécessiter.

requirement *n* besoin *m;* exigence *f.*

requisite *adj* nécessaire, indispensable.

rescue *vt* sauver, secourir:—*n* secours *m.*

research *vt* faire de la recherche:—*n* recherche *f.*

resemblance *n* ressemblance *f.*

resemble *vt* ressembler à.

resent *vt* être contrarié.

resentment *n* ressentiment *m.*

reservation *n* réservation *f.*

reserve *vt* réserver:—*n* réserve *f.*

reside *vi* résider.

residence *n* résidence *f.*

resident *n* résident *m,* -e *f.*

resign *vt* démissionner de:—*vi* démissionner.

resignation *n* démission *f.*

resist *vt* résister, s'opposer.

resistance *n* résistance *f.*

resolute *adj* résolu.

resolution *n* résolution *f.*

resolve *vt* resoudre:—*vi* (se) résoudre.

resort *vi* recourir:—*n* lieu de vacances *m.*

resource *n* ressource *f.*

respect *n* respect *m;* égard *m:*—*vt* respecter.

respectability *n* respectabilité *f.*

respectable *adj* respectable.

respectful *adj* respectueux.

respecting *prep* en ce qui concerne.

respective *adj* respectif.

respite *n* répit *m.*

respond *vi* répondre.

response *n* réponse.

responsibility *n* responsabilité *f.*

responsible *adj* responsable.

rest *n* repos *m;* reste, restant *m:*—*vi* se reposer.

restitution *n* restitution *f.*

restive *adj* rétif, récalcitrant.

restoration *n* restauration *f.*

restore *vt* restaurer.

restrain *vt* retenir.

restrict *vt* restreindre.

restriction *n* restriction *f.*

restrictive *adj* restrictif.

result *vi* résulter:—*n* résultat *m.*

resume *vt* reprendre; résumer.

resuscitate *vt* réanimer.

retail *vt* détailler:—*n* vente au détail *f.*

retain *vt* retenir, conserver.

retaliate *vi* se venger.

reticence *n* réticence *f.*

retire *vt* retirer:—*vi* se retirer.

retired *adj* retraité.

retirement *n* isolement *m.*

retort *vt* rétorquer:—*n* réplique *f.*

retrace *vt* retracer.

retreat *vi* se retirer.

retribution *n* récompense *f.*

retrieve *vt* récupérer, recouvrer.

return *vt* rendre:—*n* retour *m.*

reunion *n* réunion *f.*

reunite *vt* réunir:—*vi* se réunir.

reveal *vt* révéler.

revelation *n* révélation *f.*

revenge *vt* venger:—*n* vengeance *f.*

revengeful *adj* vindicatif.

revenue *n* revenu *m;* rente *f.*

reverberate *vt* réverbérer:—*vi* résonner.

reverberation *n* réverbération *f.*

reversal *n* renversement *m.*

reverse *vt* renverser:—*vi* faire marche arrière:—*n* inverse *m.*

reversible *adj* réversible.

reversion *n* retour *m;* réversion *f.*

revert *vi* revenir; retourner.

review vt revoir:—n revue f; examen m.

revise vt réviser.

revision n révision f.

revival n reprise f; renouveau m.

revive vt ranimer.

revoke vt révoquer.

revolt vi se révolter:—n révolte f.

revolution n révolution f.

revolutionary adj n révolutionnaire mf.

revolve vt (re)tourner:—vi tourner.

revue n revue f.

reward n récompense f:—vt récompenser.

rhetorical adj rhétorique.

rheumatic adj rhumatisant.

rheumatism n rhumatisme m.

rhyme n rime f:—vi rimer.

rhythm n rythme m.

rhythmical adj rythmique.

rib n côte f.

ribbon n ruban m.

rice n riz m.

rich adj riche; somptueux.

richness n richesse f; abondance f.

rid vt débarrasser.

riddle n crible m:—vt cribler.

ride vi monter (à cheval); aller (en voiture).

ridge n arête, crête f.

ridicule n ridicule m:—vt ridiculiser.

ridiculous adj **~ly** adv ridicule.

rife adj répandu, abondant.

rifle n fusil m.

rig vt équiper; truquer:—n plateforme de forage f.

right adj droit, bien:—~! bien!, bon!; à juste titre:—n droit m; droite f.

righteous adj droit, vertueux.

rigid adj rigide; sévère.

rigorous adj rigoureux.

rigour n rigueur f; sévérité f.

rim n bord m, monture f.

ring n anneau, cercle, rond m:—vt sonner:—vi sonner, retentir.

rink n (also **ice** ~) patinoire f.

rinse vt rincer.

riot n émeute f.

riotous adj séditieux; dissolu.

rip vt déchirer.

ripe adj mûr.

ripen vt vi mûrir.

ripple n ondulation f, ride f.

rise vi se lever; monter:—n hausse f; augmentation f.

rising n insurrection f.

risk n risque:—vt risquer.

risky adj risqué.

rite n rite m.

ritual adj n rituel m.

rival adj rival:—n rival m, -e f:—vt rivaliser avec.

rivalry n rivalité f.

river n rivière f.

road n route f.

roam vt errer dans:—vi errer.

roar vi rugir:—n rugissement m.

roast vt rôtir; griller.

rob vt voler.

robber n voleur m, -euse f.

robbery n vol m.

robust adj robuste.

robustness n robustesse f.

rock n roche f:—vt bercer; balancer.

rocket n fusée f.

rocking chair n fauteuil à bascule m.

rocky adj rocheux.

rodent n rongeur m.

rogue n coquin, polisson m; gredin m.

roll vt rouler:—vi (se) rouler:—n roulement m; rouleau m.

roller n rouleau, cylindre m.

romance n romance f; roman m.

romantic *adj* romantique.

roof *n* toit *m*; voûte *f*:—*vt* couvrir.

room *n* pièce, salle *f*; espace *m*.

root *n* racine *f*; origine *f*.

rope *n* corde *f*; cordage *m*.

rose *n* rose *f*.

rosemary *n* (*bot*) romarin *m*.

rot *vi* pourrir:—*n* pourriture *f*.

rotate *vt* faire tourner:—*vi* tourner.

rotation *n* rotation *f*.

rotund *adj* rond, replet.

rouge *n* rouge (à joues) *m*.

rough *adj* accidenté, rugueux; rude.

roughness *n* rugosité *f*; rudesse *f*.

round *adj* rond, circulaire:—*n* cercle *m*; rond *m*; tour *m*; tournée *f*:—*adv* autour de; environ:—*vt* arrondir.

roundness *n* rondeur *f*.

rouse *vt* réveiller; exciter.

rout *n* déroute.

route *n* itinéraire *m*; route *f*.

routine *adj* habituel:—*n* routine *f*.

rove *vi* vagabonder.

row *n* querelle *f*.

row *n* rangée, file *f*.

royal *adj* royal; princier.

royalty *n* royauté *f*; droits d'auteur *mpl*.

rub *vt* frotter; irriter:—*n* frottement *m*.

rubber *n* caoutchouc *m*.

rubbish *n* détritus *mpl*; ordures *fpl*.

rudder *n* gouvernail *m*.

ruddiness *n* teint vif *m*, rougeur *f*.

rude *adj* impoli, rude.

rudeness *n* impolitesse *f*; rudesse *f*.

ruffle *vt* ébouriffer, déranger.

rug *n* tapis *m*.

rugged *adj* accidenté, déchiqueté.

ruin *n* ruine *f*:—*vt* ruiner.

ruinous *adj* ruineux.

rule *n* règle *f*; règlement *m*:—*vt* gouverner, dominer.

rumble *vi* gronder, tonner.

ruminate *vt* ruminer.

rummage *vi* fouiller.

rumour *n* rumeur *f*.

run *vt* diriger:—*vi* courir.

rung *n* barreau, échelon *m*.

runner *n* coureur *m*.

runway *n* piste de décollage *f*.

rupture *n* rupture *f*:—*vt* rompre:— *vi* se rompre.

ruse *n* ruse *f*, stratagème *m*.

rush *n* ruée *f*; hâte *f*:—*vi* se précipiter.

rust *n* rouille *f*:—*vi* se rouiller.

rustic *adj* rustique:—*n* paysan, rustaud *m*.

rustle *vi* bruire:—*vt* faire bruire; froisser.

rusty *adj* rouillé; roux.

ruthless *adj* cruel, impitoyable.

rye *n* seigle *m*.

S

sabotage *n* sabotage *m*.

sachet *n* sachet *m*.

sack *n* sac *m*

sacrement *n* sacrement *m*.

sacred *adj* saint, sacré.

sacrifice *n* sacrifice *m*:—*vt* sacrifier.

sacrilege *n* sacrilège *m*.

sad *adj* triste, déprimé.

sadden vt attrister.

saddle n selle f; col m:—vt seller.

sadness n tristesse f.

safe adj sûr; en sécurité:—n coffre-fort m.

safeguard n sauvegarde f:—vt sauvegarder.

safety n sécurité f; sûreté f.

sage n sage m:—adj sage.

sail n voile f:—vt piloter:—vi aller à la voile.

sailing n navigation f.

sailor n marin m.

saint n saint m, -e f.

sake n bien m, égard m.

salad n salade f.

salary n salaire m.

sale n vente f; solde m.

salesman n vendeur m.

saliva n salive f.

salmon n saumon m.

saloon n bar m.

salt n sel m:—vt saler.

salt cellar n salière f.

salubrious adj salubre, sain.

salubrity n salubrité f.

salutary adj salutaire.

salute vt saluer:—n salut m.

salvation n salut m.

same adj même, identique.

sameness n identité f.

sample n échantillon m:—vt goûter.

sanatorium n sanatorium m.

sanctify vt sanctifier.

sanction n sanction f:—vt sanctionner.

sanctuary n sanctuaire m; asile m.

sand n sable m:—vt sabler.

sandal n sandale f.

sandwich n sandwich m.

sandy adj sablonneux, sableux.

sane adj sain.

sanguine adj sanguin.

sanity n santé mentale, raison f.

sapling n jeune arbre m.

sarcasm n sarcasme m.

sarcastic adj sarcastique.

sardine n sardine f.

satchel n cartable m.

satellite n satellite m.

sate vt rassasier, assouvir.

satin n satin m:—adj en ou de satin.

satire n satire f.

satirical adj satirique.

satisfaction n satisfaction f.

satisfactory adj satisfaisant.

satisfy vt satisfaire.

saturate vt saturer.

Saturday n samedi m.

sauce n sauce f; assaisonnement m.

saucepan n casserole f.

saucer n soucoupe f.

saunter vi flâner, se balader.

sausage n saucisse f.

savage adj sauvage:—n sauvage mf.

savagery n sauvagerie, barbarie f.

save vt sauver; économiser:—adv sauf, à l'exception de.

saving prep sauf, à l'exception de: —n sauvetage m.

savings bank n caisse d'épargne f.

savour n saveur f:—vt savourer.

saw n scie f:—vt scier.

say vt dire.

saying n dicton, proverbe m.

scaffolding n échafaudage m.

scald vt échauder:—n brûlure f.

scale n balance f; échelle f:—vt escalader.

scan vt scruter; explorer; scander.

scandal n scandale m; infamie f.

scandalize vt scandaliser.

scandalous adj scandaleux.

scant adj rare, insuffisant.

scantiness *n* insuffisance, pauvreté *f*.

scapegoat *n* bouc émissaire *m*.

scar *n* cicatrice *f*.

scarce *adj* rare.

scare *vt* effrayer:—*n* peur; panique *f*.

scarf *n* écharpe *f*.

scarlet *n* écarlate *f*:—*adj* écarlate.

scatter *vt* éparpiller; disperser.

scene *n* scène *f*; lieu *m*.

scenery *n* vue *f*; décor (de théâtre) *m*.

scenic *adj* scénique.

scent *n* parfum *m*, odeur *f*:—*vt* parfumer.

sceptic *n* sceptique *mf*.

sceptic(al) *adj* sceptique.

schedule *n* horaire *m*; programme *m*.

scheme *n* projet, plan *m*; schéma *m*: —*vt* machiner:—*vi* intriguer.

scholar *n* élève *mf*; érudit *m*, -e *f*.

school *n* école *f*:—*vt* instruire.

schoolboy *n* écolier, élève *m*.

schoolgirl *n* écolière, élève *f*.

schoolteacher *n* instituteur/trice *mf*; professeur *mf*.

science *n* science *f*.

scientific *adj* scientifique.

scientist *n* scientifique *mf*.

scintillate *vi* scintiller, étinceler.

scissors *npl* ciseaux *mpl*.

scoff *vi* se moquer.

scold *vt* réprimander:—*vi* grogner.

scope *n* portée, envergure.

scorch *vt* brûler:—*vi* se brûler.

score *n* score *m*; marque *f*; entaille *f*: —*vt* marquer.

scorn *vt* mépriser:—*n* mépris *m*.

scornful *adj* dédaigneux.

scoundrel *n* vaurien *m*.

scour *vt* récurer, frotter.

scout *n* (*mil*) éclaireur *m*, -euse *f*; guetteur *m*.

scowl *vi* se renfrogner.

scramble *vi* grimper; se battre, se disputer:—*n* bousculade *f*.

scrap *n* bout *m*; bagarre *f*; ferraille *f*.

scrape *vt vi* racler, gratter:—*vt* érafler.

scratch *vt* griffer, égratigner:—*n* égratignure *f*.

scream *vi* hurler:—*n* hurlement *m*.

screen *n* écran *m*; paravent *m*:—*vt* abriter; sélectionner.

screw *n* vis *f*:—*vt* visser.

screwdriver *n* tournevis *m*.

scribble *vt* gribouiller:—*n* gribouillage *m*.

script *n* scénario *m*; script *m*.

Scripture *n* Ecriture sainte *f*.

scrub *vt* récurer; annuler:—*n* broussailles *fpl*.

scruple *n* scrupule *m*.

scrupulous *adj* scrupuleux.

scuffle *n* rixe *f*:—*vi* se bagarrer.

sculptor *n* sculpteur *m*, -trice *f*.

sculpture *n* sculpture *f*.

scum *n* écume *f*; crasse *f*.

sea *n* mer *f*:—*adj* marin.

seafood *n* fruits de mer *mpl*.

seagull *n* mouette *f*.

seal *n* sceau *m*; phoque *m*:—*vt* sceller.

seamy *adj* sordide.

search *vt* fouiller; inspecter:—*n* fouille *f*; recherche *f*.

seashore *n* bord de mer *m*.

seasickness *n* mal de mer *m*.

season *n* saison *f*.

seasonable *adj* opportun, à propos.

seasoning *n* assaisonnement *m*.

seat *n* siège *m*; place *f*:—*vt* (faire) asseoir.

seaweed *n* algue *f*.

seclude *vt* éloigner, isoler.

seclusion *n* solitude *f*; isolement *m*.

second *adj* deuxième:—*n* second *m*; seconde *f*.

secondary *adj* secondaire.

secrecy *n* secret *m*; discrétion *f*.

secret *adj n* secret *m*.

secretary *n* secrétaire *mf*.

secretive *adj* secret, dissimulé.

section *n* section *f*.

sector *n* secteur *m*.

secular *adj* séculaire.

secure *adj* sûr; en sûreté:—*vt* assurer.

security *n* sécurité *f*; sûreté *f*.

sedative *n* sédatif *m*.

sediment *n* sédiment *m*; lie *f*.

sedition *n* sédition *f*.

seduce *vt* séduire.

seduction *n* séduction *f*.

seductive *adj* séduisant.

see *vt* voir, remarquer.

seed *n* graine *f*:—*vi* monter en graine.

seek *vt* chercher; demander.

seem *vi* paraître, sembler.

seemliness *n* bienséance *f*.

seemly *adj* convenable, bienséant.

seesaw *n* bascule *f*:—*vi* osciller.

segment *n* segment *m*.

seize *vt* saisir.

seizure *n* saisie *f*.

seldom *adv* rarement, peu souvent.

select *vt* sélectionner.

selection *n* sélection *f*.

self *n* soi-même:—**the ~** le moi:— *pref* auto-.

self-confident *adj* sûr de soi.

self-defence *n* autodéfense *f*.

self-employed *adj* indépendant.

self-interest *n* intérêt personnel *m*.

selfish *adj* égoïste.

selfishness *n* égoïsme *m*.

self-portrait *n* autoportrait *m*.

self-respect *n* respect de soi *m*.

self-service *adj* libre-service.

self-styled *adj* soi-disant.

self-sufficient *adj* autosuffisant.

self-taught *adj* autodidacte.

sell *vt* vendre:—*vi* se vendre.

seller *n* vendeur *m*, -euse *f*.

semblance *n* semblant *m*.

semicircle *n* demi-cercle *m*.

senate *n* sénat *m*.

senator *n* sénateur *m*, -trice *f*.

send *vt* envoyer.

senile *adj* sénile.

senility *n* sénilité *f*.

senior *n* aîné *m*, -e *f*:—*adj* aîné.

seniority *n* ancienneté *f*.

sensation *n* sensation *f*.

sense *n* sens *m*; sensation *f*.

senseless *adj* insensé.

sensible *adj* sensé; sensible.

sensibly *adj* raisonnablement.

sensitive *adj* sensible.

sensual *adj* sensuel.

sensuality *n* sensualité *f*.

sentence *n* phrase *f*; condamnation *f*.

sentiment *n* sentiment *m*.

sentimental *adj* sentimental.

sentinel *n* sentinelle *f*.

separable *adj* séparable.

separate *vt* séparer:—*vi* se séparer: —*adj* séparé.

separation *n* séparation *f*.

September *n* septembre *m*.

sepulchre *n* sépulcre *m*.

sequel *n* conséquence *f*; suite *f*.

sequence *n* ordre *m*, série *f*.

serenade *n* sérénade *f*:—*vt* jouer une sérénade pour.

serene *adj* serein.

serenity *n* sérénité *f*.

sergeant *n* sergent *m*.

serial *adj* de/en série:—*n* feuilleton *m*.

series *n* série *f*.

serious *adj* sérieux, grave.

sermon *n* sermon *m*.

serpent *n* serpent *m*.

servant n domestique mf.

serve vt servir; desservir:—vi servir; être utile.

service n service m; entretien m:—vt entretenir.

serviceable adj utilisable; pratique.

servile adj servile.

servitude n servitude f.

session n séance, session f.

set vt mettre, poser:—n jeu m; ensemble m:—adj fixe, figé.

setting n disposition f; cadre m; monture f:—~ **of the sun** coucher du soleil m.

settle vt poser, installer:—vi se poser; s'installer.

settlement n règlement m; établissement m.

seven adj n sept m.

seventeen adj n dix-sept m.

seventeenth adj n dix-septième mf.

seventh adj n septième mf.

seventieth adj n soixante-dixième mf.

seventy adj n soixante-dix m.

several adj pn plusieurs.

severe adj sévère, rigoureux.

severity n sévérité f.

sew vt vi coudre.

sewer n égout m.

sex n sexe m.

sexist adj n sexiste mf.

sexual adj sexuel.

shabby adj miteux.

shackle vt enchaîner.

shade n ombre f; nuance f:—vt ombrager.

shadow n ombre f.

shady adj ombreux, ombragé.

shaft n fût m; (tech) arbre m; rayon m.

shake vt secouer:—vi trembler:—n secousse f.

shallow adj peu profond, superficiel.

sham vt feindre:—n imposture f.

shame n honte f:—vt déshonorer.

shamefaced adj honteux, confus.

shameful adj honteux; scandaleux.

shampoo n shampooing m.

shape vt former; façonner:—vi prendre forme:—n forme f.

shapely adj bien proportionné.

share n part, portion f:—vt partager.

shark n requin m.

sharp adj aigu, acéré.

sharpen vt aiguiser, affûter.

sharpness n acuité f; aigreur f.

shatter vt fracasser.

shave vi se raser.

shaver n rasoir électrique m.

shaving n rasage m.

shawl n châle m.

she pn elle.

sheaf n gerbe f; liasse f.

shear vt tondre.

shed n hangar m; cabane f.

sheep n mouton m.

sheer adj pur; abrupt:—adv abruptement.

sheet n drap m; plaque f.

shelf n étagère f.

shell n coquille f; écorce f:—vt écosser, décortiquer; bombarder.

shelter n abri m:—vt abriter:—vi s'abriter.

shepherd n berger m.

sheriff n shérif m.

shield n bouclier m:—vt protéger.

shift vi changer; se déplacer:—vt changer, bouger:—n changement m.

shine vi briller.

shining adj resplendissant.

ship n bateau m; navire m:—vt embarquer.

shipment n cargaison f.

shipwreck n naufrage m.

shirt n chemise f.

shiver vi frissonner.

shock n choc m; coup m:—vt bouleverser; choquer.

shoe n chaussure f.

shoemaker n cordonnier m.

shoot vt tirer:—vi pousser:—n pousse f.

shooting n fusillade f; tir m.

shop n magasin m; atelier m.

shopper n acheteur m, -euse f.

shore n rivage, bord m.

short adj court, bref.

shortcoming n insuffisance f.

shorten vt raccourcir; abréger.

short-sighted adj myope.

shortwave n ondes courtes fpl.

shot n coup m; décharge f.

shotgun n fusil de chasse m.

shoulder n épaule f; accotement m.

shout vt vi crier:—n cri m.

shove vt vi pousser:—n poussée f.

shovel n pelle f:—vt pelleter.

show vt montrer:—vi se voir:—n exposition f.

shower n averse f; douche f.

showy adj voyant, ostentatoire.

shred n lambeau m:—vt mettre en lambeaux.

shrewd adj astucieux; perspicace.

shriek vt vi hurler:—n hurlement m.

shrill adj aigu, strident.

shrimp n crevette f.

shrink vi rétrécir.

shrivel vi se ratatiner.

shroud n voile m; linceul m.

shrub n arbuste m.

shudder vi frissonner:—n frisson m.

shun vt fuir, éviter.

shut vt fermer; vi (se) fermer.

shutter n volet m.

shy adj timide; réservé.

shyness n timidité f.

sick adj malade; écœuré.

sicken vt rendre malade.

sickly adj maladif.

sickness n maladie f.

side n côté m; parti m:—adj latéral.

sideboard n buffet m.

sidelong adj oblique.

siege n (mil) siège m.

sieve n tamis m:—vt tamiser.

sift vt tamiser.

sigh vi soupirer:—n soupir m.

sight n vue f; spectacle m.

sightseeing n tourisme m.

sign n signe m, indication f:—vt signer.

signal n signal m.

signature n signature f.

significance n importance f.

significant adj considérable.

signify vt signifier.

silence n silence m.

silent adj silencieux.

silicon chip n puce de silicium f.

silk n soie f.

silken adj soyeux.

sill n rebord m; seuil m.

silliness n bêtise, niaiserie f.

silly adj bête, stupide.

silver n argent m:—adj en argent.

silvery adj argenté.

similar adj semblable; similaire.

similarity n ressemblance f.

simile n comparaison f.

simmer vi cuire à feux doux, mijoter.

simper vi minauder:—n sourire affecté m.

simple adj simple; naïf.

simplicity n simplicité f.

simplification n simplification f.

simplify vt simplifier.

simulate vt simuler, feindre.

simultaneous *adj* simultané.

sin *n* péché *m*:—*vi* pécher.

since *adv prep* depuis:—*conj* depuis que; puisque.

sincere *adj* sincère; réel, vrai:—*-ly adv* sincère(ment).

sincerity *n* sincérité *f*.

sinew *n* tendon *m*; nerf *m*.

sing *vt vi* chanter.

singe *vt* roussir.

singer *n* chanteur *m*, -euse *f*.

single *adj* seul, unique; célibataire.

singly *adv* séparément.

singular *adj* singulier.

singularity *n* singularité *f*.

sinister *adj* sinistre.

sink *vi* couler:—*n* évier *m*.

sinner *n* pécheur *m*, pécheresse *f*.

sinuous *adj* sinueux.

siphon *n* siphon *m*.

sir *n* monsieur *m*.

sister *n* sœur *f*.

sister-in-law *n* belle-sœur *f*.

sit *vi* s'asseoir.

site *n* emplacement *m*; site *m*.

sitting *n* séance, réunion *f*.

sitting room *n* salle de séjour *f*.

situation *n* situation *f*.

six *adj n* six *m*.

sixteen *adj n* seize *m*.

sixteenth *adj n* seizième *mf*.

sixth *adj n* sixième *mf*.

sixtieth *adj n* soixantième *mf*.

sixty *adj n* soixante *m*.

size *n* taille, grandeur *f*.

sizeable *adj* assez grand.

skate *n* patin *m*:—*vi* patiner.

skating rink *n* patinoire *f*.

skeleton *n* squelette *m*.

sketch *n* croquis *m*.

skewer *n* broche *f*; brochette *f*:—*vt* embrocher.

ski *n* ski *m*:—*vi* skier.

skid *n* dérapage *m*:—*vi* déraper.

skier *n* skieur *m*, -euse *f*.

skiing *n* ski *m*.

skill *n* habileté, adresse *f*.

skilful *adj* adroit, habile.

skim *vt* écrémer; effleurer.

skin *n* peau *f*:—*vt* écorcher.

skinny *adj* maigre, efflanqué.

skip *vi* sautiller.

skirmish *n* escarmouche *f*.

skirt *n* jupe *f*; bordure *f*:—*vt* contourner.

skulk *vi* rôder furtivement.

skull *n* crâne *m*.

sky *n* ciel *m*.

skylight *n* lucarne *f*.

skyscraper *n* gratte-ciel *m invar*.

slab *n* dalle *f*.

slack *adj* lâche, négligent.

slack(en) *vt* relâcher:—*vi* se relâcher.

slackness *n* ralentissement *m*.

slam *vt* claquer violemment.

slander *vt* calomnier:—*n* calomnie *f*.

slanderous *adj* calomnieux.

slang *n* argot *m*.

slant *vi* pencher:—*n* inclinaison *f*.

slap *n* gifle *f*:—*vt* gifler.

slaughter *n* carnage, massacre *m*:—*vt* abattre.

slave *n* esclave *mf*.

slavery *n* esclavage *m*.

slay *vt* tuer.

sleazy *adj* louche.

sledge *n* traîneau *m*.

sleep *vi* dormir:—*n* sommeil *m*.

sleeper *n* dormeur *m*, -euse *f*.

sleepiness *n* envie de dormir *f*.

sleepwalking *n* somnambulisme *m*.

sleepy *adj* qui a envie de dormir; endormi.

sleet *n* neige fondue *f*.

sleeve n manche f.

slender adj svelte, mince.

slenderness n sveltesse f, minceur f.

slice n tranche f; spatule f:—vt couper.

slide vi glisser:—n glissade f; diapositive f.

slight adj léger, mince:—n affront m.

slightness n fragilité f; insignifiance f.

slim adj mince:—vi maigrir.

slimming n amaigrissement m.

sling n écharpe f:—vt lancer.

slip vi (se) glisser:—vt glisser:—n glissade f; faux pas m.

slipper n pantoufle f.

slippery adj glissant.

slit vt fendre, inciser.

slogan n slogan m.

slope n inclinaison f; pente f:—vt incliner.

sloth n paresse f.

slovenliness n manque de soin m.

slovenly adj négligé, débraillé.

slow adj lent; lourd.

slowness n lenteur, lourdeur f.

sluggish adj paresseux; léthargique.

sluice n écluse f.

slum n taudis m.

slump n récession f.

slur vt dénigrer; mal articuler:—n calomnie f.

slush n neige fondante f.

sly adj rusé.

slyness n ruse, finesse f.

smack n claque f:—vt donner une claque à.

small adj petit, menu.

smallness n petitesse f.

smart adj élégant; astucieux:—vi brûler.

smartness n astuce, vivacité, finesse f.

smash vt casser, briser, se fracasser:—n fracas m.

smear vt enduire; salir.

smell vt vi sentir:—n odorat m; odeur f.

smelt vt fondre.

smile vi sourire:—n sourire m.

smite vt frapper.

smith n forgeron m.

smoke n fumée f:—vt vi fumer.

smoker n fumeur m, -euse f.

smoky adj enfumé; qui fume.

smooth adj lisse, uni:—vt lisser; adoucir.

smoothness n douceur f; aspect lisse m.

smother vt étouffer.

smudge vt salir:—n tache f.

smuggle vt passer en contrebande.

smuggler n contrebandier m, -ière f.

snack n collation f.

snail n escargot m.

snake n serpent m.

snap vt casser net:—claquer:—n claquement m.

snare n piège m; collet m.

snatch vt saisir.

sneer vi ricaner.

sneeze vi éternuer.

sniff vt renifler.

snivel n pleurnicherie f:—vi pleurnicher.

snob n snob mf.

snobbish adj snob.

snooze n petit somme m.

snore vi ronfler.

snow n neige f:—vi neiger.

snowman n bonhomme de neige m.

snowplough n chasse-neige m invar.

snowy adj neigeux; enneigé.

snub vt repousser, rejeter.

snug adj confortable, douillet.

so adv si, tellement, aussi; ainsi.

soak vi tremper:—vt faire tremper.

soap *n* savon *m*:—*vt* savonner.

soar *vi* monter en flèche.

sob *n* sanglot *m*:—*vi* sangloter.

sober *adj* sobre; sérieux.

sobriety *n* sobriété *f*.

sociability *n* sociabilité *f*.

sociable *adj* sociable.

social *adj* social, sociable.

socialist *n* socialiste *mf*.

social worker *n* assistant(e) social(e) *m(f)*.

society *n* société *f*; compagnie *f*.

sociologist *n* sociologue *mf*.

sock *n* chaussette *f*.

socket *n* prise de courant *f*.

sofa *n* sofa *m*.

soft *adj* doux, moelleux.

soften *vt* (r)amollir, adoucir.

softness *n* douceur, mollesse *f*.

software *n* logiciel *m*.

soil *vt* salir:—*n* sol *m*; terre *f*.

solace *vt* consoler:—*n* consolation *f*.

solar *adj* solaire.

solder *vt* souder:—*n* soudure *f*.

soldier *n* soldat *m*.

sole *n* plante du pied *f*:—*adj* seul, unique.

solemn *adj* solennel.

solemnity *n* solennité *f*.

solicit *vt* solliciter.

solicitor *n* notaire *m*.

solicitude *n* sollicitude *f*.

solid *adj* solide, compact:—*n* solide *m*.

solidify *vt* solidifier.

solidity *n* solidité *f*.

solitary *adj* solitaire, retiré.

solitude *n* solitude *f*.

solstice *n* solstice *m*.

soluble *adj* soluble.

solution *n* solution *f*.

solve *vt* résoudre.

solvency *n* solvabilité *f*.

solvent *adj* solvable.

some *adj* du, de la, de l', des; quelques; quelconque; certain(e)s; quelque.

somebody *pn* quelqu'un.

somehow *adv* d'une façon ou d'une autre.

something *pn* quelque chose.

sometimes *adv* quelquefois, parfois.

somewhat *adv* quelque peu.

somewhere *adv* quelque part.

somnolence *n* somnolence *f*.

somnolent *adj* somnolent.

son *n* fils *m*.

song *n* chanson *f*.

son-in-law *n* gendre *m*.

sonorous *adj* sonore.

soon *adv* bientôt.

sooner *adv* plus tôt; plutôt.

soot *n* suie *f*.

soothe *vt* calmer.

sophisticate *vt* sophistiquer.

sophisticated *adj* sophistiqué.

soporific *adj* soporifique.

sordid *adj* sordide, sale.

sore *n* plaie *f*:—*adj* douloureux, sensible.

sorrow *n* peine *f*:—*vi* se lamenter.

sorrowful *adj* triste, affligé.

sorry *adj* désolé; déplorable.

sort *n* sorte *f*; genre *m*:—*vt* classer; trier.

soul *n* âme *f*.

sound *adj* sain; valide:—*n* son *m*; bruit *m*:—*vt* sonner (de).

soundness *n* santé *f*; solidité *f*.

soup *n* soupe *f*.

sour *adj* aigre, acide.

source *n* source *f*; origine *f*.

souvenir *n* souvenir *m*.

south *n* sud *m*.

southern *adj* du sud, sud, méridional.

southward(s) *adv* vers le sud.

sovereign *adj n* souverain *m*, -e *f*.

sovereignty *n* souveraineté *f*.

sow *vt* semer.

space *n* espace *m*; intervalle *m*:—*vt* espacer.

spacious *adj* spacieux.

spade *n* bêche *f*.

span *n* envergure *f*:—*vt* enjamber.

spare *vt vi* épargner; ménager:—*adj* de trop; de réserve.

sparing *adj* limité, modéré.

spark *n* étincelle *f*.

sparkle *n* scintillement *m*:—*vi* étinceler.

sparse *adj* clairsemé.

spasm *n* spasme *m*.

spatter *vt* éclabousser.

speak *vt* parler; dire.

speaker *n* interlocuteur *m*, -trice *f*; orateur *m*.

spear *n* lance *f*.

special *adj* spécial.

speciality *n* spécialité *f*.

species *n* espèce *f*.

specific *adj* spécifique.

specification *n* spécification *f*.

specify *vt* spécifier.

specimen *n* spécimen *m*.

spectacle *n* spectacle *m*.

spectator *n* spectateur *m*, -trice *f*.

spectre *n* spectre *m*.

speculate *vi* spéculer.

speculation *n* spéculation *f*.

speculative *adj* spéculatif, méditatif.

speech *n* parole *f*; discours *m*.

speed *n* vitesse *f*; rapidité *f*.

speediness *n* promptitude, célérité *f*.

speed limit *n* limitation de vitesse *f*.

speedy *adj* rapide, prompt.

spell *n* charme *m*; période *f*:—*vt* écrire.

spelling *n* ortographe *f*.

spend *vt* dépenser; passer.

sphere *n* sphère *f*.

spherical *adj* sphérique.

spice *n* épice *f*:—*vt* épicer.

spicy *adj* épicé.

spider *n* araignée *f*.

spike *n* clou *m*:—*vt* clouter.

spill *vt* répandre:—*vi* se répandre.

spin *vt* filer:—*vi* tourner:—*n* tournoiement *m*.

spinal *adj* spinal.

spine *n* colonne vertébrale.

spire *n* flèche *f*; aiguille *f*.

spirit *n* esprit *m*; âme *f*; caractère *m*.

spirited *adj* vif, fougueux.

spiritless *adj* sans entrain, abattu.

spiritual *adj* spirituel.

spirituality *n* spiritualité *f*.

spit *n* crachat *m*:—*vt vi* cracher.

spite *n* dépit *m*:—**in ~ of** malgré.

spiteful *adj* rancunier.

splash *vt* éclabousser:—*n* éclaboussure *f*.

splendid *adj* splendide.

splendour *n* splendeur *f*.

splinter *n* éclat *m*:—*vt* (*vi*) (se) fendre en éclats.

split *n* fente *f*:—*vt* fendre.

spoil *vt* abîmer.

spokesman *n* porte-parole *m invar*.

sponge *n* éponge *f*.

sponsor *n* parrain *m*.

sponsorship *n* parrainage *m*.

spontaneity *n* spontanéité *f*.

spontaneous *adj* spontané.

spoon *n* cuiller *f*.

sporadic(al) *adj* sporadique.

sport *n* sport *m*; jeu *m*.

sportsman *n* sportif *m*.

sportswoman *n* sportive *f*.

spot *n* tache *f*; endroit *m*:—*vt* apercevoir.

spotless *adj* impeccable.

spouse *n* époux *m*; épouse *f*.

spout *vi* jaillir:—*vt* faire jaillir:—*n* bec *m*.

sprain *n* entorse *f*.

spray *n* spray *m*; pulvérisation *f*.

spread *vt* étendre:—*vi* s'étendre:—*n* diffusion *f*.

spring *vi* bondir:—*n* printemps *m*; saut *m*.

sprinkle *vt* arroser.

sprout *n* pousse *f*.

spruce *adj* net, impeccable.

spur *n* éperon *m*; stimulant *m*:—*vt* éperonner; stimuler.

spurn *vt* repousser avec mépris.

sputter *vi* bafouiller.

spy *n* espion *m*, -onne *f*:—*vt* espionner.

squabble *vi* se quereller:—*n* querelle *f*.

squad *n* équipe *f*.

squadron *n* escadron *m*.

squalid *adj* misérable, sordide.

squall *n* rafale *f*.

squalor *n* saleté *f*; misère *f*.

square *adj* carré:—*n* carré *m*; place *f*.

squash *vt* écraser.

squat *vi* s'accroupir.

squeak *vi* grincer, crier.

squeal *vi* couiner.

squeeze *vt* presser, tordre.

squint *vi* loucher:—*n* strabisme.

squirt *vt* faire gicler:—*n* giclée *f*.

stab *vt* poignarder.

stability *n* stabilité.

stable *n* écurie *f*:—*adj* stable.

stack *n* pile *f*:—*vt* empiler.

staff *n* personnel *m*; bâton *m*.

stage *n* étape *f*; scène *f*.

stagger *vi* vaciller.

stagnation *n* stagnation *f*.

stagnate *vi* stagner.

stain *vt* tacher:—*n* tache *f*.

stair *n* marche *f*.

stairs *n* escalier *m*.

stake *n* pieu *m*:—*vt* marquer.

stale *adj* rance.

stalk *n* tige *f*.

stall *n* stalle *f*; étalage *m*:—*vt* caler.

stamina *n* résistance *f*.

stammer *vi* bégayer:—*n* bégaiement *m*.

stamp *vt* trépigner; timbrer:—*n* timbre *m*; estampille *f*.

stand *vi* être debout:—*vt* supporter:—*n* position, prise de position *f*; étalage *m*.

standard *n* étendard *m*; norme *f*:—*adj* normal.

standing *n* importance *f*; rang *m*.

standstill *n* arrêt *m*.

staple *n* agrafe *f*:—*adj* principal, de base.

star *n* étoile *f*.

starch *n* amidon *m*.

stare *vi*:—**to ~ at** regarder fixement.

starry *adj* étoilé.

start *vi,vt* commencer:—*n* début *m*.

starter *n* starter, démarreur *m*.

startle *vt* faire sursauter.

starvation *n* inanition, faim *f*.

starve *vi* mourir de faim.

state *n* état *m*; condition *f*:—*vt* déclarer.

stately *adj* majestueux, imposant.

statement *n* déclaration *f*.

statesman *n* homme d'Etat *m*.

static *adj* statique.

station *n* station *f*; (*rail*) gare *f*:—*vt* placer.

stationary *adj* stationnaire.

stationery *n* papeterie *f*.

statistical *adj* statistique.

statue *n* statue *f*.

stature *n* stature, taille *f*.

statute *n* statut *m*; loi *f*.

stay *n* séjour *m*:—*vi* rester.

steadfast *adj* ferme, résolu.

steadiness *n* fermeté *f*.

steady *adj* stable:—*vt* affermir.

steak *n* bifteck *m*; steak *m*.

steal *vt vi* voler.

stealthy *adj* furtif.

steam *n* vapeur *f*:—*vt* cuire à la vapeur.

steam engine *n* locomotive à vapeur *f*.

steel *n* acier *m*:—*adj* d'acier.

steep *adj* abrupt:—*vt* tremper.

steepness *n* raideur *f*.

steer *vt* diriger.

steering wheel *n* volant *m*.

stem *n* tige *f*.

stenographer *n* sténographe *mf*.

stenography *n* sténographie *f*.

step *n* pas *m*, marche *f*:—*vi* faire un pas.

stepbrother *n* demi-frère *m*.

stepsister *n* demi-sœur *f*.

stereotype *vt* stéréotyper.

sterile *adj* stérile.

sterility *n* stérilité *f*.

sterling *adj* de bon aloi, veritable.

stern *adj* sévère, rigide.

stew *n* ragoût *m*.

steward *n* intendant *m*.

stewardess *n* hôtesse de l'air *f*.

stick *n* bâton *m*:—*vt* coller.

sticky *adj* collant, poisseux.

stiff *adj* raide, rigide.

stiffen *vt* raidir:—*vi* se raidir.

stiffness *n* raideur.

stifle *vt* étouffer.

stifling *adj* suffocant.

stigmatize *vt* stigmatiser.

still *vt* calmer:—*adj* calme:—*adv* encore; toujours.

stillness *n* calme *m*.

stimulate *vt* stimuler.

stimulus *n* stimulant *m*.

sting *vt* piquer; piqûre *f*.

stinginess *n* mesquinerie *f*.

stingy *adj* mesquin.

stink *vi* puer:—*n* puanteur *f*.

stipulate *vt* stipuler.

stipulation *n* stipulation *f*.

stir *vt* remuer; agiter.

stitch *vt* coudre:—*n* point *m*.

stock *n* réserve *f*, provision *f*:—*vt* approvisionner.

stockbroker *n* agent de change *m*.

stock exchange *n* Bourse *f*.

stocking *n* bas *m*.

stoical *adj* stoïque.

stomach *n* estomac *m*.

stone *n* pierre *f*:—*adj* de pierre:—*vt* empierrer.

stony *adj* pierreux.

stool *n* tabouret *m*.

stoop *vi* se pencher.

stop *vt* arrêter:—*vi* s'arrêter:—*n* arrêt *m*.

stoppage *n* obstruction *f*.

storage *n* emmagasinage *m*.

store *n* provision *f*:—*vt* emmagasiner.

stork *n* cigogne *f*.

storm *n* tempête *f*, orage *m*.

stormy *adj* orageux.

story *n* histoire *f*; récit *m*.

stout *adj* corpulent, robuste.

stoutness *n* corpulence *f*.

stove *n* cuisinière *f*.

stow *vt* arrimer.

straight *adj* droit; direct:—*adv* droit; directement.

straightaway *adv* immédiatement.

straighten *vt* redresser.

strain *vt* tendre:—*n* tension *f*; effort *m*.

strait *n* détroit *m*.

strand *n* rive *f*.

strange *adj* inconnu; étrange.

strangeness *n* étrangeté *f*.

stranger *n* inconnu(e) *m(f)*, étranger *m*, -ère *f*.

strangle *vt* étrangler.

strap *n* lanière.

stratagem *n* stratagème *m*.

strategic *adj* stratégique *m*.

strategy *n* stratégie *f*.

straw *n* paille *f*.

strawberry *n* fraise *f*.

stray *vi* s'égarer:—*adj* perdu; errant.

streak *n* raie *f*.

stream *n* ruisseau *m*:—*vi* ruisseler.

street *n* rue *f*.

strength *n* force, puissance *f*.

strengthen *vt* fortifier.

stress *n* pression *f*; stress *m*:—*vt* souligner.

stretch *vt* étendre:—*vi* s'étendre:— *n* extension *f*; étendue *f*.

stretcher *n* brancard *m*.

strew *vt* éparpiller.

strict *adj* strict, rigoureux.

strictness *n* sévérité *f*.

stride *n* grand pas *m*.

strife *n* conflit *m*, lutte *f*.

strike *vt* frapper:—*n* coup *m*; grève *f*.

striker *n* gréviste *mf*.

striking *adj* frappant; saisissant.

string *n* ficelle *f*; corde *f*.

stringent *adj* rigoureux.

strip *vi* se déshabiller:—*n* bande *f*; langue *f*.

stripe *n* raie *f*:—*vt* rayer.

strive *vi* s'efforcer.

stroke *n* coup *m*; caresse *f*:—*vt* caresser.

stroll *vi* flâner.

strong *adj* fort, vigoureux.

strongbox *n* coffre-fort *m*.

structure *n* structure *f*; construction *f*.

struggle *vi* lutter:—*n* lutte *f*.

strut *vi* se pavaner.

stubborn *adj* entêté, obstiné.

stubbornness *n* entêtement *m*.

stud *n* clou *m*; crampon *m*.

student *n*, *adj* étudiant *m*, -e *f*.

studio *n* studio, atelier *m*.

studious *adj* studieux.

study *n* étude *f*:—*vt* étudier.

stuff *n* matière *f*; étoffe *f*:—*vt* (rem)bourrer.

stuffing *n* rembourrage *m*.

stumble *vi* trébucher:—*n* trébuchement *m*.

stump *n* souche *f*; moignon *m*.

stun *vt* étourdir.

stunt *n* cascade *f*:—*vt* empêcher de croître.

stupefy *vt* stupéfier.

stupendous *adj* prodigieux.

stupid *adj* stupide.

stupidity *n* stupidité *f*.

stupor *n* stupeur *f*.

sturdiness *n* force, robustesse *f*.

sturdy *adj* robuste; hardi.

stutter *vi* bégayer.

style *n* style *m*:—*vt* appeler; dessiner.

stylish *adj* élégant.

suave *adj* suave.

subdivide *vt* subdiviser.

subdue *vt* assujettir.

subject *adj* soumis; sujet à:—*n* sujet *m*; thème *m*:—*vt* soumettre.

subjection *n* sujétion *f*.

subjugate *vt* subjuguer.

subjugation *n* subjugation *f*.

sublimate vt sublimer.

sublime adj sublime.

sublimity n sublimité f.

submarine adj n sous-marin m.

submerge vt submerger.

submersion n submersion f.

submission n soumission f.

submissive adj soumis.

submit vt soumettre:—vi se soumettre.

subordinate adj subalterne:—vt subordonner.

subscribe vi souscrire:—vt signer.

subscriber n souscripteur m, -trice f.

subscription n souscription f.

subsequent adj ~ly adv ultérieur(-ement).

subside vi s'affaisser.

subsidence n affaissement m.

subsidiary adj subsidiaire.

subsidize vt subventionner.

subsidy n subvention f.

subsist vi subsister; exister.

subsistence n subsistance f.

substance n substance f; fond m.

substantial adj substantiel.

substantiate vt justifier.

substitute vt substituer.

substitution n substitution f.

subterranean adj souterrain.

subtitle n sous-titre m.

subtle adj subtile.

subtlety n subtilité f.

subtract vt soustraire.

suburb n banlieue f.

suburban adj de banlieue.

subversive adj subversif.

subvert vt subvertir.

succeed vi réussir:—vt succéder à, suivre.

success n succès m.

successful adj couronné de succès.

succession n succession f.

successive adj successif.

successor n successeur m.

succinct adj succinct.

succumb vi succomber.

such adj tel, pareil.

suck vt vi sucer.

suckle vt allaiter.

sudden adj soudain.

suddenness n soudaineté f.

sue vt poursuivre en justice.

suffer vi souffrir.

suffering n souffrance f; douleur f.

suffice vi suffire, être suffisant.

sufficient adj suffisant.

suffocate vt vi étouffer.

suffocation n suffocation f.

sugar n sucre m:—vt sucrer.

sugary adj sucré.

suggest vt suggérer.

suggestion n suggestion f.

suicidal adj suicidaire.

suicide n suicide m; suicidé m, -e f.

suit n pétition f; costume m:—vt convenir à.

suitable adj approprié.

suitcase n valise f.

sulky adj boudeur, maussade.

sullen adj maussade; sombre.

sultry adj étouffant; chaud.

sum n somme f; total m:—**to ~ up** vt résumer.

summary adj n résumé m.

summer n été m.

summit n sommet m; cime f.

summon vt convoquer.

summons n convocation f.

sumptuous adj somptueux.

sun n soleil m.

sunbathe vi se faire bronzer.

sunburnt adj bronzé.

Sunday n dimanche m.

sundry adj divers, différent.
sunflower n tournesol m.
sunny adj ensoleillé.
sunrise n lever du soleil m.
sunset n coucher du soleil m.
sunshade n parasol m.
sunshine n ensoleillement m.
sunstroke n insolation f.
suntan n bronzage m.
super adj (fam) sensationnel.
superb adj superbe.
supercilious adj hautain.
superficial adj superficiel.
superfluity n superfluité f.
superfluous adj superflu.
superior adj n supérieur m, -e f.
superiority n supériorité f.
superlative adj n superlatif m.
supermarket n supermarché m.
supernatural n surnaturel.
supersede vt remplacer.
supersonic adj supersonique.
superstition n superstition f.
superstitious adj superstitieux.
supervene vi survenir.
supervise vt superviser.
supervision n surveillance f.
supervisor n surveillant m, -e f.
supper n dîner m.
supplant vt supplanter.
supple adj souple.
supplement n supplément m.
supplementary adj supplémentaire.
suppleness n souplesse f.
supplicate vt supplier.
supplication n supplication f.
supplier n fournisseur m.
supply vt fournir:—n approvision-
nement m; provision f.
support vt soutenir:—n appui m.
supporter n partisan m.
suppose vt vi supposer.

supposition n supposition f.
suppress vt supprimer.
suppression n suppression f.
supremacy n suprématie f.
supreme adj suprême.
surcharge vt surcharger:—n surtaxe f.
sure adj sûr, certain:—~ly adv sûre-
ment.
sureness n certitude, sûreté f.
surf n (mar) ressac m.
surface n surface f:—vi remonter à
la surface.
surfboard n planche (de surf) f.
surge n vague, montée f.
surgeon n chirurgien m.
surgery n chirurgie m.
surgical adj chirurgical.
surly adj revêche, bourru.
surmise vt conjecturer:—n conjecture f.
surmount vt surmonter.
surname n nom de famille m.
surpass vt surpasser.
surplus n excédent m:—adj en surplus.
surprise vt surprendre:—n surprise f.
surrender vi se rendre:—n reddi-
tion f.
surreptitious adj subreptice.
surrogate n substitut m.
surround vt entourer.
survey vt examiner:—n enquête f.
survive vi survivre:—vt survivre à.
survivor n survivant m, -e f.
susceptibility n sensibilité f.
susceptible adj sensible.
suspect vt soupçonner:—n suspect
m, -e f.
suspend vt suspendre.
suspense n incertitude f; suspense m.
suspicion n soupçon m.
suspicious adj soupçonneux.

sustain *vt* soutenir.

sustenance *n* (moyens de) subsistance *f*.

swagger *vi* plastronner.

swallow *vt* avaler.

swamp *n* marais *m*.

swap *vt* échanger:—*n* échange *m*.

swarm *n* essaim *m*:—*vi* fourmiller.

swathe *vt* emmailloter:—*n* bande *f*.

sway *vi* se balancer, osciller:—*n* balancement *m*; emprise.

swear *vt* jurer:—*vi* jurer.

sweat *n* sueur *f*:—*vi* suer.

sweep *vt* balayer.

sweet *adj* doux, agréable; suave:—*n* bonbon *m*.

sweeten *vt* sucrer; adoucir.

sweetener *n* édulcorant *m*.

sweetness *n* goût sucré *m*, douceur *f*.

swell *vi* gonfler:—*n* houle *f*.

swelling *n* gonflement *m*.

swerve *vt* dévier.

swift *adj* rapide.

swiftness *n* rapidité, promptitude *f*.

swim *vi* nager:—*n* baignade *f*.

swimming *n* natation *f*.

swimming pool *n* piscine *f*.

swimsuit *n* maillot de bain *m*.

swindle *vt* escroquer.

swing *vi* se balancer:—*vt* balancer:
—*n* balancement *m*.

swirl *n* tourbillon.

switch *n* interrupteur *m*:—*vt* changer de:—**to ~ off** éteindre:—**to ~ on** allumer.

swivel *vt* faire pivoter.

swoon *vi* s'évanouir:—*n* évanouissement *m*.

swoop *vi* fondre sur.

sword *n* épée *f*.

sycophant *n* sycophante *mf*.

syllabic *adj* syllabique.

syllable *n* syllabe *f*.

syllabus *n* programme d'un cours *m*.

symbol *n* symbole *m*.

symbolic(al) *adj* symbolique.

symbolize *vt* symboliser.

symmetrical *adj* symétrique.

symmetry *n* symétrie *f*.

sympathetic *adj* compatissant.

sympathize *vi* compatir.

sympathy *n* compassion *f*.

symphony *n* symphonie *f*.

symptom *n* symptôme *m*.

synagogue *n* synagogue *f*.

syndrome *n* syndrome *m*.

synonym *n* synonyme *m*.

synonymous *adj* synonyme.

synopsis *n* synopsis *f*; résumé *m*.

syntax *n* syntaxe *f*.

synthesis *n* synthèse *f*.

syringe *n* seringue *f*.

system *n* système *m*.

systematic *adj* systématique.

T

table *n* table *f*:—*vt* mettre en forme de tableau.

tablecloth *n* nappe *f*.

tablet *n* tablette *f*; comprimé *m*.

tacit *adj* tacite.

taciturn *adj* taciturne.

tack n broquette f:—vt clouer.

tackle n attirail, équipement.

tact n tact m.

tactics npl tactique f.

tag n ferret m:—vt ferrer.

tail n queue f.

tailor n tailleur m.

tailoring n métier de tailleur m.

taint vt infecter.

tainted adj infecté.

take vt prendre.

takeoff n décollage m.

takeover n prise de possession f.

takings npl recette f.

talc n talc m.

talent n talent m.

talented adj talentueux.

talk vi parler; causer:—n conversation f.

talkative adj loquace.

tall adj grand, élevé.

tally vi correspondre.

tame adj apprivoisé:—vt apprivoiser.

tamper vi toucher à.

tan vt vi bronzer:—n bronzage m.

tangible adj tangible.

tangle vt enchevêtrer.

tank n réservoir m.

tanker n pétrolier m.

tantrum n accès de colère m.

tap vt taper doucement:—n petite tape f; robinet m.

tape n ruban m:—vt enregistrer.

tape recorder n magnétophone m.

target n cible f.

tariff n tarif m.

tarnish vt ternir.

tart n tarte, tartelette f.

task n tâche f.

taste n goût m; saveur f:—vt déguster.

tasteful adj de bon goût.

tasty adj savoureux.

tattoo n tatouage m:—vt tatouer.

taunt vt railler:—n raillerie f.

taut adj tendu.

tawdry adj tapageur.

tax n impôt m:—vt imposer.

taxable adj imposable.

taxation n imposition f.

taxi n taxi m.

tax payer n contribuable mf.

tea n thé m.

teach vt enseigner.

teacher n professeur m.

teaching n enseignement m.

team n équipe f.

teapot n théière f.

tear vt déchirer.

tear n larme f.

tearful adj larmoyant.

tease vt taquiner.

teaspoon n petite cuiller f.

technical adj technique.

technician n technicien m, -ienne f.

technique n technique f.

technological adj technologique.

technology n technologie f.

tedious adj ennuyeux.

tedium n ennui, manque d'intérêt m.

teenage adj adolescent:—~r n adolescent(e) m(f).

teethe vi faire ses premières dents.

telegram n télégramme m.

telegraph n télégraphe m.

telepathy n télépathie f.

telephone n téléphone m.

telephone directory n annuaire m.

telephone number n numéro de téléphone m.

telescope n télescope m.

telescopic adj télescopique.

televise vt téléviser.

television n télévision f.

television set n téléviseur.

tell vt dire; raconter.
temper vt tempérer:—n colère f.
temperament n tempérament m.
temperate adj tempéré.
temperature n température f.
tempest n tempête f.
temple n temple m; tempe f.
temporary adj temporaire.
tempt vt tenter.
temptation n tentation f.
ten adj n dix m.
tenacious adj tenance.
tenacity n ténacité f.
tenant n locataire mf.
tend vt garder.
tendency n tendance f.
tender adj tendre:—n offre f:—vt
offrir.
tendon n tendon m.
tennis n tennis m.
tenor n (mus) ténor m; sens m.
tense adj tendu:—n (gr) temps m.
tension n tension f.
tent n tente f.
tentative adj timide, hésitant.
tenth adj n dixième mf.
tenuous adj ténu.
tepid adj tiède.
term n terme m:—vt appeler.
terminal adj terminal:—n aérogare
f; terminal m.
terminate vt terminer.
termination n fin, conclusion f.
terrace n terrace f.
terrain n terrain m.
terrestrial adj terrestre.
terrible adj terrible.
terrific adj terrifiant.
terrify vt terrifier.
territorial adj territorial.
territory n territoire m.
terror n terreur f.

terrorist n terroriste mf.
terrorize vt terroriser.
terse adj concis, net.
test n essai m:—vt essayer.
testify vt témoigner.
testimony n témoignage m.
test tube n éprouvette f.
tether vt attacher.
text n texte m.
textual adj textuel.
texture n texture f.
than adv que; de.
thank vt remercier.
thankful adj reconnaissant.
thanks npl remerciement(s) m(pl).
that pn cela, ça, ce; qui, que; celui-
là:—conj que.
thatch n chaume m.
thaw n dégel m:—vi dégeler.
the art le, la, l', les.
theatre n théâtre m.
theatrical adj théâtral.
theft n vol m.
their poss adj leur(s).
theirs poss pn le leur; la leur; les leurs.
them pn les; leur.
theme n thème m.
themselves pn pl eux-mêmes mpl,
elles-mêmes fpl; se.
then adv alors; ensuite:—conj donc;
en ce cas.
theological adj théologique.
theology n théologie f.
theorem n théorème m.
theoretic(al) adj théorique.
theory n théorie f.
therapist n thérapeute mf.
therapy n thérapie f.
there adv y, là.
thereafter adv par la suite; après.
therefore adv donc, par conséquent.
thermal adj thermal.

thermometer *n* thermomètre *m*.

these *pn pl* ceux-ci, celles-ci.

thesis *n* thèse *f*.

they *pn pl* ils, elles.

thick *adj* épais, gros.

thicken *vi* (s')épaissir.

thickness *n* épaisseur *f*.

thickset *adj* trapu.

thief *n* voleur *m*, -euse *f*.

thigh *n* cuisse *f*.

thin *adj* mince, fin.

thing *n* chose *f*; objet *m*; truc *m*.

think *vi vt* penser:—~ **over** *vt* réfléchir à.

thinker *n* penseur *m*, -euse *f*.

thinking *n* pensée *f*; réflexion *f*.

third *adj* troisième:—*n* troisième *mf*; tiers *m*.

thirst *n* soif *f*.

thirsty *adj* assoiffé.

thirteen *adj n* treize *m*.

thirteenth *adj n* treizième *mf*.

thirtieth *adj n* trentième *mf*.

thirty *adj n* trente *m*.

this *adj* ce, cet, cette, ces:—*pn* ceci, ce.

thistle *n* chardon *m*.

thorn *n* épine *f*.

thorough *adj* consciencieux, approfondi:—~**ly** *adv* minutieusement, à fond.

thoroughfare *n* rue, artère *f*.

those *pn pl* ceux-là, celles-la:—*adj* ces, ces... là.

though *conj* bien que:—*adv* pourtant.

thought *n* pensée, réflexion *f*.

thoughtful *adj* pensif.

thoughtless *adj* étourdi; irréfléchi.

thousand *adj n* mille *m*.

thousandth *adj n* millième *mf*.

thrash *vt* battre.

thread *n* fil *m*.

threat *n* menace *f*.

threaten *vt* menacer.

three *adj n* trois *m*.

threshold *n* seuil *m*.

thrifty *adj* économe.

thrill *vt* faire frissonner:—*n* frisson *m*.

thrive *vi* prospérer.

throat *n* gorge *f*.

throb *vi* palpiter.

throne *n* trône *m*.

throng *n* foule *f*.

throttle *n* accélérateur *m*:—*vt* étrangler.

through *prep* à travers; pendant; par:—*adj* direct.

throughout *prep* partout dans:—*adv* partout.

throw *vt* jeter:—*n* jet *m*; lancement *m*.

throwaway *adj* à jeter.

thrust *vt* enfoncer:—*n* poussée *f*.

thug *n* voyou *m*.

thumb *n* pouce *m*.

thump *n* coup de poing *m*:—*vt* cogner à.

thunder *n* tonnerre *m*:—*vi* tonner.

thunderclap *n* coup de tonnerre *m*.

thunderstorm *n* orage *m*.

Thursday *n* jeudi *m*.

thus *adv* ainsi.

thwart *vt* contrecarrer.

tic *n* tic *m*.

tick *vt* tic-tac *m*; instant *m*.

ticket *n* billet, ticket *m*.

ticket office *n* guichet *m*.

tickle *vt* chatouiller.

tidal wave *n* raz-de-marée *m*.

tide *n* marée *f*.

tidy *adj* rangé, en ordre.

tie *vt* attacher:—*n* attache *f*; lacet *m*.

tier *n* gradin *m*; étage *m*.

tiger *n* tigre *m*.

tight adj raide, tendu.

tighten vt (re)serrer, tendre.

tile n tuile f; carreau m.

till n caisse f:—vt labourer.

tilt vt pencher:—vi s'incliner.

timber n bois de construction m.

time n temps m; période f; heure f:— vt fixer; chronométrer.

time lag n décalage m.

timeless adj éternel.

timely adj opportun.

time zone n fuseau horaire m.

timid adj timide.

timidity n timidité f.

tin n étain m; boîte (de conserve) f.

tinge n teinte f.

tingle vi picoter.

tinkle vi tinter.

tint n teinte f:—vt teinter.

tinted adj teinté; fumé.

tiny adj minuscule.

tip n pointe f, bout m; pourboire m: —vt donner un pourboire à.

tirade n diatribe f.

tire vt fatiguer:—vi se fatiguer.

tireless adj infatigable.

tiresome adj ennuyeux, fatigant.

tissue n tissu m.

titbit n friandise f.

titillate vt titiller.

title n titre m.

titular adj titulaire.

to prep à; vers; en.

toast vt (faire) griller:—n toast m.

toaster n grille-pain m invar.

tobacco n tabac m.

toboggan n toboggan m.

today adv aujourd'hui.

toe n orteil m; pointe f.

together adv ensemble.

toil vi travailler dur:—n labeur m; peine f.

toilet n toilette f; toilettes fpl:—adj de toilette.

toilet paper n papier hygiénique m.

toiletries npl articles de toilette mpl.

token n signe m; marque f; jeton m.

tolerable adj tolérable.

tolerant adj tolérant.

tolerate vt tolérer.

toll n péage m:—vi sonner.

tomato n tomate f.

tomb n tombeau m; tombe f.

tombstone n pierre tombale f.

tomorrow adv n demain m.

ton n tonne f.

tone n ton m; tonalité f:—vi s'harmoniser.

tongs npl pinces fpl.

tongue n langue f.

tonight adv n ce soir (m).

too adv aussi; trop.

tool n outil m; ustensile m.

tooth n dent f.

toothache n rage de dents f.

toothbrush n brosse à dents f.

toothpaste n dentifrice m.

top n sommet m; haut m; tête f; dessus m:—adj du haut:—vt dépasser.

topic n sujet m.

topical adj d'actualité.

topmost adj le plus haut.

topographic(al) adj topographique.

topography n topographie f.

topple vt renverser:—vi basculer.

torch n torche f.

torment vt tourmenter:—n tourment m.

tornado n tornade f.

torrent n torrent m.

tortuous adj tortueux, sinueux.

torture n torture f:—vt torturer.

toss vt lancer, secouer.

total adj total, global.

totality n totalité f.

totter vi chanceler.

touch vt toucher; contact m; touche f.

touchdown n atterrissage m; but m.

touching adj touchant.

tough adj dur; pénible.

toughen vt durcir.

tour n voyage m; visite f.

tourism n tourisme m.

tourist n touriste mf.

tournament n tournoi m.

tow n remorquage m:—vt remorquer.

toward(s) prep vers.

towel n serviette f.

tower n tour f.

town n ville f.

town hall n mairie f.

towrope n câble de remorquage m.

toy n jouet m.

trace n trace, piste f:—vt tracer.

track n trace f; empreinte f.

tract n étendue; brochure f.

traction n traction f.

trade n commerce m; métier m:—vi commercer.

trademark n marque de fabrique f.

trader n négociant m, -e f.

trade(s) union n syndicat m.

trade unionist n syndicaliste mf.

trading n commerce m:—adj commercial.

tradition n tradition f

traditional adj traditionnel.

traffic n circulation f; négoce m.

traffic jam n embouteillage m.

tragedy n tragédie f.

tragic adj tragique.

trail vt traîner:—n traînée f.

train vt entraîner:—n train m.

trainer n entraîneur m.

training n entraînement m.

trait n trait m.

traitor n traître m.

tramp n clochard m, -e f:—vt piétiner.

trance n transe f; extase f.

tranquil adj tranquille.

transact vt traiter.

transaction n transaction f.

transcend vt transcender.

transcription n transcription f.

transfer vt transférer:—n transfert m.

transform vt transformer.

transfusion n transfusion f.

transition n transition f.

transitional adj de transition.

translate vt traduire.

translation n traduction f.

translator n traducteur m, -trice f.

transmission n transmision f.

transmit vt transmettre.

transparency n transparence f.

transparent adj transparent.

transplant vt transplanter.

transport vt transporter:—n transport m.

trap n piège m:—vt prendre au piège.

travel vi voyager:—n voyage m.

traveller n voyageur m, -euse f.

traveller's cheque n chèque de voyage m.

travesty n parodie f.

tray n plateau m.

treacherous adj traître.

treachery n traîtrise f.

tread vi marcher:—n pas m.

treason n trahison f.

treasure n trésor m.

treasurer n trésorier m, -ière f.

treat vt traiter:—n cadeau m.

treatment n traitement m.

treaty n traité m.

treble adj triple:—vt vi tripler.

tree n arbre m.

trek n randonnée f; étape f.

tremble *vi* trembler.
tremendous *adj* terrible; formidable.
trend *n* tendance *f*; mode *f*.
trespass *vt* transgresser.
trial *n* procès *m*; essai *m*.
triangle *n* triangle *m*.
tribal *adj* tribal.
tribe *n* tribu *f*.
tribunal *n* tribunal *m*.
tributary *adj n* tributaire *m*.
trick *n* ruse, astuce *f*:—*vt* attraper.
tricky *adj* délicat; difficile.
trifle *n* bagatelle, vétille *f*.
trifling *adj* futile, insignifiant.
trigger *n* détente *f*.
trim *adj* net, soigné:—*vt* arranger.
trip *vi* trébucher:—*n* faux pas *m*; voyage *m*.
triple *adj* triple:—*vt vi* tripler.
trite *adj* banal; usé.
triumph *n* triomphe *m*:—*vi* triompher.
triumphant *adj* triomphant.
trivia *npl* futilités *fpl*.
trivial *adj* insignifiant.
triviality *n* banalité *f*.
troop *n* bande *f*.
tropical *adj* tropical.
trouble *vt* affliger:—*n* problème *m*; ennui *m*.
troublesome *adj* pénible.
trousers *npl* pantalon *m*.
trout *n* truite *f*.
truck *n* camion *m*; wagon *m*.
truck driver *n* routier *m*.
truculent *adj* brutal, agressif.
true *adj* vrai, véritable.
trump *n* atout *m*.
trumpet *n* trompette *f*.
trunk *n* malle *f*.
trust *n* confiance *f*:—*vt* confier à.
trustworthy *adj* digne de confiance.

trusty *adj* fidèle, loyal.
truth *n* vérité *f*.
truthful *adj* véridique.
truthfulness *n* véracité *f*.
try *vt* essayer:—*n* tentative *f*; essai *m*.
tub *n* cuve *f*, bac *m*.
tube *n* tube *m*.
tuck *n* pli *m*:—*vt* mettre.
Tuesday *n* mardi *m*.
tug *vt* remorquer:—*n* remorqueur *m*.
tuition *n* cours, enseignement *m*.
tulip *n* tulipe *f*.
tumble *vi* tomber:—*n* chute *f*.
tumbler *n* verre *m*.
tumultuous *adj* tumultueux.
tune *n* air *m*; accord *m*.
tuneful *adj* mélodieux, harmonieux.
tunnel *n* tunnel *m*.
turbulence *n* turbulence.
turbulent *adj* turbulent.
turf *n* gazon *m*.
turkey *n* dinde *f*.
turmoil *n* agitation *f*; trouble *m*.
turn *vtr* (se) tourner; *vt* monter:—*n* tour *m*; tournure.
turning *n* embranchement *m*.
turnover *n* chiffre d'affaires *m*.
turnstile *n* tourniquet *m*.
turquoise *n* turquoise *f*.
turtle *n* tortue marine *f*.
tusk *n* défense *f*.
tutor *n* professeur particulier *m*.
tweezers *npl* pince à épiler *f*.
twelfth *adj n* douzième *mf*.
twelve *adj n* douze *m*.
twentieth *adj n* vingtième *mf*.
twenty *adj n* vingt *m*.
twice *adv* deux fois.
twilight *n* crépuscule *m*.
twin *n* jumeau *m*, -elle *f*.
twine *vi* s'enrouler.
twinkle *vi* scintiller.

twirl *vi* tournoyer.

twist *vt* tordre, tortiller.

twitch *n* tic *m*.

two *adj n* deux *m*.

twofold *adj* double:—*adv* au double.

tycoon *n* magnat *m*.

type *n* type *m*:—*vi* taper à la machine.

typeface *n* œil de caractère *m*.

typewriter *n* machine à écrire *f*.

typical *adj* typique.

tyrannical *adj* tyrannique.

tyrant *n* tyran *m*.

tyre *n* pneu *m*.

U

ugliness *n* laideur *f*.

ugly *adj* laid.

ulcer *n* ulcère *m*.

ulterior *adj* ultérieur.

ultimate *adj* final:—**~ly** *adv* finalement; à la fin.

ultimatum *n* ultimatum *m*.

umbrella *n* parapluie *m*.

umpire *n* arbitre *m*.

unable *adj* incapable.

unaccomplished *adj* inaccompli.

unaccountable *adj* inexplicable.

unaccustomed *adj* inaccoutumé.

unacknowledged *adj* non reconnu.

unadulterated *adj* pur; sans mélange.

unaltered *adj* inchangé.

unanimity *n* unanimité *f*.

unanimous *adj* unanime.

unanswerable *adj* incontestable.

unapproachable *adj* inaccessible.

unarmed *adj* désarmé.

unattached *adj* indépendant; libre.

unattainable *adj* inaccessible.

unavoidable *adj* inévitable.

unaware *adj* ignorant; inconscient.

unbalanced *adj* déséquilibré.

unbearable *adj* insupportable.

unbelievable *adj* incroyable.

unbiased *adj* impartial.

unbreakable *adj* incassable.

unbroken *adj* intact; ininterrompu.

unbutton *vt* déboutonner.

unceasing *adj* incessant.

unceremonious *adj* brusque.

uncertain *adj* incertain.

uncertainty *n* incertitude *f*.

unchangeable *adj* immuable.

uncharitable *adj* peu charitable.

uncivil *adj* impoli, grossier.

uncivilized *adj* non civilisé.

uncle *n* oncle *m*.

uncomfortable *adj* inconfortable.

uncommon *adj* rare, extraordinaire.

uncompromising *adj* intransigeant.

unconcerned *adj* indifférent.

unconditional *adj* inconditionnel, absolu.

unconscious *adj* inconscient.

uncork *vt* déboucher.

uncouth *adj* grossier.

uncover *vt* découvrir.

uncultivated *adj* inculte.

undecided *adj* indécis.

undeniable *adj* indéniable.

under *prep* sous; dessous:—*adv* au-dessous.

underclothing n sous-vêtements mpl.

undercover adj secret, clandestin.

underdeveloped adj sous-développé.

underestimate vt sous-estimer.

undergo vt subir.

undergraduate n étudiant(e) en licence m(f).

undergrowth n brouissailles fpl.

underhand adj secret, clandestin.

underline vt souligner.

underneath adv (en) dessous:— prep sous, au-dessous de.

underpaid adj sous-payé.

underprivileged adj défavorisé.

underside n dessous m.

understand vt comprendre.

understandable adj compréhensible.

understanding n compréhension:— adj compréhensif.

undertake vt entreprendre.

undertaking n entreprise f.

undervalue vt sous-estimer.

underwater adj sous-marin:—adv sous l'eau.

underwear n sous-vêtements mpl.

underwrite vt souscrire à.

undeserved adj immérité.

undetermined adj indéterminé.

undisciplined adj indiscipliné.

undisputed adj incontesté.

undivided adj indivisé, entier.

undo vt défaire; détruire.

undoing n ruine f.

undoubted adj ~ly adv indubitable(ment).

undress vi se déshabiller.

undue adj excessif.

unduly adv trop, excessivement.

uneasy adj inquiet; gêné.

uneducated adj sans instruction.

unemployed adj au chômage.

unemployment n chômage m.

unending adj interminable.

unequal adj inégal.

unequalled adj inégalé.

uneven adj inégal; impair.

unexpected adj inattendu.

unfailing adj infaillible, certain.

unfair adj injuste.

unfaithful adj infidèle.

unfashionable adj démodé.

unfasten vt détacher, défaire.

unfavourable adj défavorable.

unfeeling adj insensible.

unfinished adj inachevé.

unfit adj inapte; impropre.

unfold vt déplier.

unforeseen adj imprévu.

unforgettable adj inoubliable.

unfortunate adj malheureux.

unfounded adj sans fondement.

unfriendly adj inamical.

ungrateful adj ingrat.

unhappiness n tristesse f.

unhappy adj malheureux.

unhealthy adj malsain.

unheeding adj insouciant.

unhook vt décrocher.

unhurt adj indemne.

uniform adj uniforme.

uniformity adj uniformité f.

unify vt unifier.

unimaginable adj inimaginable.

uninhabitable adj inhabitable.

uninhabited adj inhabité, désert.

uninjured adj indemne.

unintelligible adj inintelligible.

unintentional adj involontaire.

uninterested adj indifférent.

uninterrupted adj ininterrompu.

union n union f; syndicat m.

unique adj unique, exceptionnel.

unison n unisson m.

unit n unité f.

unite *vt* unir:—*vi* s'unir.

unity *n* unité, harmonie *f*, accord *m*.

universal *adv* universel.

universe *n* univers *m*.

university *n* université *f*.

unjust *adj* injuste.

unknown *adj* inconnu.

unlawful *adj* illégal.

unlawfulness *n* illégalité *f*.

unleash *vt* lâcher.

unless *conj* à moins que/de, sauf.

unlicensed *adj* illicite.

unlikely *adj* improbable.

unlikelihood *n* improbabilité *f*.

unlimited *adj* illimité.

unload *vt* décharger.

unlucky *adj* malchanceux.

unmask *vt* démasquer.

unmerited *adj* immérité.

unmistakable *adj* indubitableun-moved** *adj* insensible, impassible.

unnecessary *adj* inutile, superflu.

unnoticed *adj* inaperçu.

unobserved *adj* inaperçu.

unoccupied *adj* inoccupé.

unoffending *adj* inoffensif.

unpack *vt* défaire.

unparalleled *adj* incomparable; sans pareil.

unpleasant *adj* désagréable.

unpopular *adj* impopulaire.

unprecedented *adj* sans précédent.

unpredictable *adj* imprévisible.

unprejudiced *adj* impartial.

unprofitable *adj* inutile; peu rentable.

unpublished *adj* inédit.

unqualified *adj* non qualifié; sans réserve.

unquestionable *adj* incontestable, indiscutable.

unreal *adj* irréel.

unreasonable *adv* déraisonnable.

unrelated *adj* sans rapport.

unrelenting *adj* implacable.

unreserved *adj* sans réserve; franc.

unrest *n* agitation *f*; troubles *mpl*.

unripe *adj* vert, pas mûr.

unroll *vt* dérouler.

unsafe *adj* dangereux, peu sûr.

unsatisfactory *adj* peu satisfaisant.

unscrew *vt* dévisser.

unseasonable *adj* hors de saison, inopportun.

unseemly *adj* inconvenant.

unsettle *vt* perturber.

unsociable *adj* insociable.

unspeakable *adj* ineffable.

unstable *adj* instable.

unsteady *adj* instable.

untamed *adj* sauvage.

untapped *adj* non exploité.

untenable *adj* insoutenable.

unthinkable *adj* inconcevable.

untidiness *n* désordre *m*.

untidy *adj* en désordre.

untie *vt* dénouer, défaire.

until *prep* jusqu'à:—*conj* jusqu'à ce que.

untimely *adj* intempestif.

untold *adj* jamais révélé; indicible.

untouched *adj* intact.

untroubled *adj* tranquille, paisible.

untrue *adj* faux.

untrustworthy *adj* indigne de confiance.

unused *adj* neuf, inutilisé.

unusual *adj* inhabituel, exceptionnel:—**~ly** *adv* exceptionnellement.

unveil *vt* dévoiler.

unwelcome *adj* importun.

unwell *adj* indisposé.

unwilling *adj* peu disposé:—**~ly** *adv* de mauvaise grâce.

unwind *vt* dérouler:—*vi* se détendre.

unwise *adj* imprudent.
unwitting *adj* involontaire.
unworkable *adj* impraticable.
unworthy *adj* indigne.
up *adv* en haut, en l'air; levé:—*prep* au haut de; vers.
upbringing *n* éducation *f*.
update *vt* mettre à jour.
upheaval *n* bouleversement *m*.
uphold *vt* soutenir.
upholstery *n* tapisserie *f*.
upkeep *n* entretien *m*.
upon *prep* sur.
upper *adj* supérieur; (plus) élevé.
uppermost *adj* le plus haut, le plus élevé:—**to be ~** prédominer.
upright *adj* droit; honnête.
uprising *n* soulèvement *m*.
uproar *n* tumulte, vacarme *m*.
uproot *vt* déraciner.
upset *vt* renverser; déranger, bouleverser:—*n* désordre *m*; bouleversement *m*:—*adj* vexé; bouleversé.
upshot *n* résultat *m*; aboutissement *m*.
upside-down *adv* sens dessus dessous.
upstairs *adv* en haut (d'un escalier).
up-to-date *adj* à jour.

upturn *n* amélioration *f*.
urban *adj* urbain.
urbane *adj* courtois.
urchin *n* oursin *m*.
urge *vt* pousser:—*n* impulsion *f*.
urgency *n* urgence *f*.
urgent *adj* urgent.
urinate *vi* uriner.
urn *n* urne *f*.
us *pn* nous.
usage *n* traitement *m*; usage *m*.
use *n* usage *m*; emploi *m*:—*vt* utiliser.
used *adj* usagé.
useful *adj* utile.
usefulness *n* utilité *f*.
useless *adj* inutile.
uselessness *n* inutilité *f*.
usher *n* huissier *m*; placeur *m*.
usual *adj* habituel, courant.
usurp *vt* usurper.
utensil *n* ustensile *m*.
uterus *n* utérus *m*.
utility *n* utilité *f*.
utmost *adj* extrême.
utter *adj* complet; total:—*vt* prononcer.
utterly *adv* complètement.

V

vacancy *n* chambre libre *f*.
vacant *adj* vacant.
vacate *vt* quitter.
vacation *n* vacances *fpl*.
vaccinate *vt* vacciner.
vacuum *n* vide *m*.
vague *adj* vague.

vain *adj* vain.
valiant *adj* courageux.
valid *adj* valide.
valley *n* vallée *f*.
valuable *adj* précieux, de valeur.
value *n* valeur *f*:—*vt* évaluer.
valve *n* soupape *f*.

van n camionnette f.
vandalize vt saccager.
vanish vi disparaître.
vanity n vanité f.
vanquish vt vaincre.
vantage point n position avantageuse f.
vapour n vapeur f.
variable adj variable; changeant.
variation n variation f.
variety n variété f.
various adj divers, différent.
vary vt vi varier:—vi changer.
vase n vase m.
vast adj vaste; immense.
vault n voûte f:—vi sauter.
vegetable adj végétal:—n légume m.
vegetarian n végétarien m, -ienne f.
vegetate vi végéter.
vegetation n végétation f.
vehemence n véhémence.
vehement adj véhément.
vehicle n véhicule m.
veil n voile m.
vein n veine f; nervure f.
velocity n vitesse f.
velvet n velours m.
vendor n vendeur m.
venerate vt vénérer.
veneration n vénération f.
vengeance n vengeance f.
venom n venin m.
venomous adj vénéneux.
ventilate vt aérer.
ventilation n ventilation, aération f.
venture n entreprise f:—vi s'aventurer.
verb n (gr) verbe m.
verbal adj verbal, oral.
verification n vérification f.
verify vt vérifier.
versatile adj versatile.

verse n vers m.
version n version f.
versus prep contre.
vertical adj vertical.
vertigo n vertige m.
very adv très, fort, bien.
vessel n récipient m; navire m.
veteran adj n vétéran m.
veterinarian n vétérinaire mf.
veterinary adj vétérinaire.
veto n véto m.
vex vt contrarier.
vexed adj contrarié.
via prep via, par.
viaduct n viaduc m.
vibrate vi vibrer.
vibration n vibration f.
vice n vice m; défaut m.
vicinity n voisinage m.
vicious adj méchant.
victim n victime f.
victor n vainqueur m.
victory n victoire f.
video n vidéo f; vidéocassette f.
viewer n téléspectateur m, -trice f.
vie vi rivaliser.
view n vue f:—vt voir; examiner.
vigil n veille f; vigile f.
vigilance n vigilance f.
vigilant adj vigilant.
vigour n vigueur f.
vigorous adj vigoureux.
vile adj vil.
village n village m.
vindicate vt venger.
vindication n défense f.
vindictive adj vindicatif.
vine n vigne f.
vinegar n vinaigre m.
vineyard n vignoble m.
violate vt violer.
violation n violation f.

violence n violence f.
violent adj violent.
violin n (mus) violon m.
virgin n, adj vierge f.
virile adj viril.
virility n virilité f.
virtual adj vrai, virtuel.
virtue n vertu f.
virtuous adj virtueux.
virulent adj virulent.
visa n visa m.
vis-a-vis prep vis-à-vis.
visibility n visibilité f.
visible adj visible.
vision n vision f; vue f.
visit vt visiter:—n visite f.
visitor n visiteur m, -euse f.
visual adj visuel.
visualize vt s'imaginer.
vital adj vital; essentiel.
vitality n vitalité f.
vitamin n vitamine f.
vivacious adj vif.
vivid adj vif; vivant.

vocabulary n vocabulaire m.
vocal adj oral.
vocation n vocation f.
voice n voix f:—vt exprimer.
void adj vide:—n vide m.
volatile adj volatile.
volcano n volcan m.
volition n volonté f.
voltage n voltage m.
voluble adj volubile.
volume n volume m.
voluntary adj volontaire.
volunteer n volontaire mf.
voluptuous adj voluptueux.
vomit vt vi vomir.
voracious adj vorace.
vote n vote m; voix f:—vt voter.
voter n électeur m, -trice f.
voucher n bon m.
vow n vœu m:—vt jurer.
voyage n traversée f.
vulgar adj vulgaire; grossier.
vulnerable adj vulnérable.

W

wade vi patauger.
wafer n gaufrette f; plaque f.
wag vt vi remuer.
wage n salaire m.
wager n pari m:—vt parier.
wages npl salaire m.
waggon n chariot m; (rail) wagon m.
wail n gémissement m:—vi gémir.
waist n taille f.
wait vi attendre:—n attente f.

waiter n garçon m; serveur m.
waive vt renoncer à.
wake vi se réveiller:—vt réveiller.
walk vi marcher:—vt parcourir:—n promenade f.
walker n marcheur m, -euse f.
walking stick n canne f.
wall n mur m; paroi f.
wallet n portefeuille m.
wallow vi se vautrer.

wallpaper n papier peint m.
walnut n noix f; noyer m.
wander vi errer.
wane vi décroître.
want vt vouloir:—vi manquer:—n besoin m.
wanton adj lascif.
war n guerre f.
wardrobe n garde-robe f.
warehouse n entrepôt m.
wariness n circonspection f.
warm adj chaud; chaleureux:—vt réchauffer.
warm-hearted adj affectueux.
warmth n chaleur f.
warn vt prévenir.
warning n avertissement m.
warp vi se voiler:—vt voiler.
warrant n garantie f; mandat m.
warrior n guerrier m, -ière f.
wary adj prudent, circonspect.
wash vt laver:—vi se laver.
washbowl n lavabo m.
washing n lessive f.
washing machine n machine à laver f.
washing-up n vaisselle f.
wasp n abeille f.
wastage n gaspillage m.
waste vt gaspiller:—n gaspillage m.
wasteful adj gaspilleur.
watch n montre f:—vt regarder.
watchful adj vigilant.
water n eau f:—vt arroser.
water closet n W.C. mpl.
watercolour n aquarelle f.
waterfall n cascade f.
watering-can n arrosoir m.
watermark n filigrane m.
watershed n moment critique m.
watertight adj étanche.
wave n vague:—vi faire signe de la main.

waver vi vaciller, osciller.
wavy adj ondulé.
wax n cire f.
way n chemin m; voie.
wayward adj capricieux.
we pn nous.
weak adj faible.
weaken vt affaiblir.
weakness n faiblesse f.
wealth n richesse f.
wealthy adj riche.
weapon n arme f.
wear vt porter; user:—vi s'user:—n usage m.
weariness n lassitude f.
weary adj las.
weather n temps m:—~ **forecast** n prévisions météorologiques fpl.
weave vt tisser.
web n toile f.
wed vi se marier.
wedding n mariage m; noces fpl.
wedding ring n alliance f.
wedge n cale f:—vt caler.
Wednesday n mercredi m.
weed n mauvaise herbe f:—vt désherber.
week n semaine f.
weekday n jour de semaine m.
weekend n week-end m, fin de semaine f.
weekly adj de la semaine, hebdomadaire.
weep vt vi pleurer.
weigh vt vi peser.
weight n poids m.
weighty adj lourd; important.
welcome adj opportun:—~! bienvenue !:—n accueil m:—vt accueillir.
welfare n bien-être m.
well n puits m:—adj bien, bon:—adv bien.

well-being n bien-être m.

well-bred adj bien élevé.

well-deserved adj bien mérité.

well-known adj connu, célèbre.

well-off adj aisé, dans l'aisance.

west n ouest, Occident m:—adj ouest, de/à l'ouest:—adv vers/à l'ouest.

westerly, western adj (d')ouest.

wet adj humide:—n humidité f:—vt mouiller.

whale n baleine f.

wharf n quai m.

what pn qu'est-ce qui,(qu'est-ce) que, quoi; que, qui; ce qui, ce que; quel(le), que:—adj quel(s), quelle(s):—excl quoi! comment!.

whatever pn quoi que; n'importe quoi.

wheat n blé m.

wheel n roue f:—rouler.

wheelbarrow n brouette f.

wheelchair n fauteuil roulant m.

when adv conj quand.

whenever adv quand; chaque fois que.

where adv où:—conj où.

whereas conj tandis que; attendu que.

whereby pn par lequel (laquelle).

wherever adv où que.

whereupon conj sur quoi.

whet vt aiguiser.

whether conj si.

which pn lequel; celui que, celui qui; ce qui, ce que; quoi; ce dont: —adj quel(s), quelle(s).

while n moment m:—conj pendant que; alors que; quoique.

whim n caprice m.

whimsical adj capricieux.

whip n fouet m:—vt fouetter.

whirl vi tourbillonner.

whirlpool n tourbillon m.

whirlwind n tornade f.

whisper vi chuchoter:—n chuchotement m.

whistle vi siffler:—n sifflement m.

white adj blanc:—n blanc m.

whiten vt vi blanchir.

whiteness n blancheur f.

who pn qui.

whoever pn quiconque, quel(le) que soit.

whole adj tout, entier:—n tout m; ensemble m.

wholesale n vente en gros f.

wholesome adj sain, salubre.

wholly adv complètement.

whom pn qui; que.

why n pourquoi m:—conj pourquoi.

wicked adj méchant, mauvais.

wickedness n méchanceté.

wide adj large, ample.

widen vt élargir, agrandir.

widow n veuve f.

widower n veuf m.

width n largeur f.

wield vt manier, brandir.

wife n femme f; épouse f.

wild adj sauvage, féroce.

wild life n faune f.

wilful adj délibéré.

wilfulness n obstination f.

will n volonté f; testament m.

willing adj prêt, disposé:—**ly** adv volontiers.

willpower n volonté f.

wily adj astucieux.

win vt gagner.

wind n vent m; souffle m.

wind vt enrouler:—vi serpenter.

windmill n moulin à vent m.

window n fenêtre f.

window pane n carreau m.

windpipe n tranchée f.

windscreen n pare-brise m invar.

windy adj venteux.

wine n vin m.

wine cellar n cave (à vin) f.

wing n aile f.

wink n clin d'œil m.

winner n gagnant m, -e f.

winter n hiver m:—vi hiverner.

wintry adj d'hiver, hivernal.

wipe vt essuyer.

wire n fil m.

wisdom n sagesse, prudence f.

wise adj sage, avisé.

wish vt souhaiter, désirer:—n souhait, désir m.

wit n esprit m, intelligence f.

witch n sorcière f.

with prep avec; à; de; contre.

withdraw vt retirer:—vi se retirer.

withdrawal n retrait m.

wither vi se flétrir.

withhold vt retenir.

within prep à l'intérieur de:—adv dedans.

without prep sans.

withstand vt résister à.

witness n témoin m:—vt attester.

wittingly adv sciemment, à dessein.

witty adj spirituel, plein d'esprit.

woe n malheur m; affliction f.

woeful adj triste, malheureux.

wolf n loup m.

woman n femme f.

womanly adj féminin, de femme.

womb n utérus m.

wonder n merveille f:—vi s'émerveiller.

wonderful adj merveilleux.

woo vt faire la cour à.

wood n bois m.

woodcut n gravure sur bois f.

wooden adj de bois, en bois.

woodwork n menuiserie f.

wool n laine f.

woollen adj de laine.

word n mot m; parole f:—vt exprimer

wording n rédaction f.

word processing n traitement de texte m.

work vi travailler:—vt faire fonctionner; façonner:—n travail m; œuvre f; emploi m.

worker n travailleur m, -euse f.

workforce n main-d'œuvre f.

workshop n atelier m.

world n monde m.

worldly adj mondain.

worldwide adj mondial.

worn-out adj épuisé; usé.

worry vt inquiéter; n souci m.

worrying adj inquiétant.

worse adj adv pire.

worship n culte m; adoration f:—vt adorer.

worst adj le pire:—adv le plus mal: —n le pire m.

worth n valeur f; mérite m.

worthily adv dignement.

worthless adj sans valeur.

worthy adj digne; louable.

wound n blessure f:—vt blesser.

wrap vt envelopper.

wreath n couronne, guirlande f.

wreck n naufrage m; ruines fpl:—vt démolir.

wrench vt tordre:—n clé f; torsion violente f.

wrestle vi lutter.

wretched adj misérable.

wrinkle n ride f:—vt rider:—vi se rider.

wrist n poignet m.

wristwatch n montre-bracelet f.

write vt écrire; composer.

writer *n* écrivain *m*; auteur *m*.

writing *n* écriture *f*.

wrong *n* mal *m*; tort *m*:—*adj* mauvais; injuste:—*adv* mal, inexactement:—*vt* faire du tort à, léser.

wrongful *adj* injuste.

wrongly *adv* injustement.

wry *adj* ironique.

XYZ

xenophobe *n* xénophobe *mf*.

xenophobic *adj* xénophobique.

X-ray *n* rayon X *m*.

xylophone *n* xylophone *m*.

yacht *n* yacht *m*.

yawn *vi* bâiller:—*n* bâillement *m*.

year *n* année *f*.

yearbook *n* annuaire *m*.

yearly *adj adv* annuel(lement).

yearn *vi* languir.

yeast *n* levure *f*.

yell *vi* hurler:—*n* hurlement *m*.

yellow *adj n* jaune *m*.

yes *adv* oui.

yesterday *adv n* hier *m*.

yet *conj* pourtant:—*adv* encore.

yield *vt* produire:—*vi* se rendre:—*n* production *f*.

yog(h)urt *n* yaourt *m*.

you *pn* vous; tu; te; toi.

young *adj* jeune.

youngster *n* jeune *mf*.

your *poss adj* ton, ta, tes; votre, vos.

yours *poss pn* le tien; le vôtre.

yourself *pn* toi-même; vous-même(s).

youth *n* jeunesse *f*; jeune homme *m*.

zeal *n* zèle *m*; ardeur *f*.

zealous *adj* zélé.

zenith *n* zénith *m*.

zero *n* zéro *m*.

zest *n* enthousiasme *m*.

zigzag *n* zigzag *m*.

zip *n* fermeture éclair *f*.

zodiac *n* zodiaque *m*.

zone *n* zone *f*; secteur *m*.

zoo *n* zoo *m*.

zoologist *n* zoologiste *mf*.

zoology *n* zoologie *f*.